FOURTH EDITION

AN OBJECT-ORIENTED APPROACH TO PROGRAMMING LOGIC AND DESIGN

JOYCE FARRELL

COURSE TECHNOLOGY
CENGAGE Learning®

Australia • Brazil • Japan • Korea • Mexico • Singapore • Spain • United Kingdom • United States

COURSE TECHNOLOGY
CENGAGE Learning®

An Object-Oriented Approach to Programming Logic and Design
Joyce Farrell

Executive Editor: Marie Lee

Acquisitions Editor: Brandi Shailer

Senior Product Manager: Alyssa Pratt

Developmental Editor: Dan Seiter

Content Project Manager:
  Matthew Hutchinson

Associate Product Manager:
  Stephanie Lorenz

Associate Art Director: Faith Brosnan

Text Designer: Shawn Girsberger

Cover Designer: Lisa Kuhn/Curio Press,
  LLC, *www.curiopress.com*

Image credit: © Leigh Prather/Veer

Print Buyer: Julio Esperas

Copyeditor: Foxxe Editorial

Proofreader: Camille Kiolbasa

Indexer: Liz Cunningham

Compositor: Integra

For product information and technology assistance, contact us at
Cengage Learning Customer & Sales Support, www.cengage.com/support.

For permission to use material from this text or product,
submit all requests online at **cengage.com/permissions.**
Further permissions questions can be e-mailed to
permissionrequest@cengage.com.

Library of Congress Control Number: 2011944411

ISBN-13: 978-1-133-18822-3

ISBN-10: 1-133-18822-2

Course Technology
20 Channel Center Street
Boston, MA 02210
USA

Some of the product names and company names used in this book have been used for identification purposes only and may be trademarks or registered trademarks of their respective manufacturers and sellers.

Course Technology, a part of Cengage Learning, reserves the right to revise this publication and make changes from time to time in its content without notice.

Cengage Learning is a leading provider of customized learning solutions with office locations around the globe, including Singapore, the United Kingdom, Australia, Mexico, Brazil, and Japan. Locate your local office at:
www.cengage.com/global

Cengage Learning products are represented in Canada by
Nelson Education, Ltd.

To learn more about Course Technology, visit **www.cengage.com/coursetechnology**

Purchase any of our products at your local college store or at our preferred online store: **www.ichapters.com**

Printed in the United States of America
2 3 4 5 6 7 16 15 14 13

Brief Contents

Contents

vi

CHAPTER 7   Object-Oriented Programming Concepts . . . 252

CHAPTER 8   More Object Concepts 300

CHAPTER 9   **Event-Driven Programming with Graphical
User Interfaces** **339**

x

CHAPTER 12 Manipulating Larger Quantities of Data . . . **435**

xii

Preface

An Object-Oriented Approach to Programming Logic and Design, Fourth Edition provides the beginning programmer with a guide to developing object-oriented program logic. This textbook assumes no programming language experience. The writing is nontechnical and emphasizes good programming practices. The examples are business examples; they do not assume a mathematical background beyond high school business math. Additionally, the examples illustrate one or two major points; they do not contain so many features that students become lost following irrelevant and extraneous details.

The examples in this book have been created to provide students with a sound background in logic no matter what programming languages they eventually use to write programs. This book can be used in a stand-alone logic course that students take as a prerequisite to a programming course, or as a companion book to a text that teaches Java, Visual Basic, C++, C#, or another object-oriented programming language.

Organization and Coverage

An Object-Oriented Approach to Programming Logic and Design, 4e introduces students to programming concepts, good style, and logical thinking. General programming concepts are introduced in Chapter 1. In Chapter 2, students are introduced to classes, a concept central to object-oriented programming. In Chapter 2, students develop classes with a `main()` method that contains variables, constants, and arithmetic operations. Good program design is emphasized from the start.

Chapters 3, 4, and 5 provide a solid background in programming universals—decision making, looping, and handling arrays. Chapter 6 delves into methods that a `main()` method calls; the student becomes familiar with parameter passing, overloading methods, and the concept of ambiguity. With the background acquired in the first six chapters, the student is well prepared to start thinking in an object-oriented manner.

In Chapter 7, the student is presented with a thorough foundation of object-oriented programming techniques. Topics include class design, private and public access of class members, instance and static class members, and composition. Chapter 8 continues the exploration of object-oriented concepts, including constructors, destructors, and inheritance. Chapter 9 describes event-driven programs that operate in a GUI environment, and Chapter 10 thoroughly explains the object-oriented technique known as exception handling. Chapter 11 teaches the basics of system design and introduces the Unified Modeling Language. Finally, Chapter 12 explains advanced applications such as sorting data and using multidimensional arrays, indexed files, and linked lists.

In addition to the 12 chapters, four appendices provide quick access to conventions used in the book, flowchart symbols, numbering systems, and the foundations of structured programming.

This book combines text explanation with flowcharts and pseudocode examples to provide students with alternative means of expressing structured logic. Numerous detailed, full-program exercises at the end of each chapter reinforce understanding and retention of the material presented.

An Object-Oriented Approach to Programming Logic and Design, 4e is a language-independent introduction to programming logic beginning with object-oriented principles. It distinguishes itself from other programming logic texts in the following ways:

- An object-oriented focus is used from the start. Classes are used immediately, although in early examples they might have only a `main()` method.

- Object-oriented programming terminology is explained in language that is easy to understand, using everyday examples as well as programming examples. Traditional programming concepts such as variables, data types, decisions, loops, and arrays, as well as object-oriented concepts such as classes, objects, inheritance, and polymorphism, are learned before the student is burdened with the syntax of a specific programming language.

- Object-oriented terminology is explained as it refers to GUI objects used in visual languages and to business objects.

- No programming experience is assumed.

- Examples are language-independent; this text can be used in a logic course, or as a companion text in courses for object-oriented programming languages such as Java, Visual Basic, C++, or C#.

- Examples are everyday business examples; no mathematics beyond high school algebra is required. This is not a computer science text; it is an introduction to logic for CIS students who want to get up to speed quickly and develop useful programs.

- Examples are simple; the point under discussion is not lost in examples with too much detail.

- The student will understand data types and gain a solid foundation in the declaration, definition, and use of variables, arithmetic operations, and other basic programming concepts. Within methods, structure is emphasized; students will become proficient in recognizing and using sequences, selections, loops, and arrays.

- Many more types of exercises are provided than in most other texts. In addition to programming problems, this book provides objective review questions, essay-type discussion questions, and three running case projects that continue in every chapter throughout the text. These case projects require much more analysis than the simpler programming problems, and are suited for group or individual student work. Because multiple cases are available, the instructor can choose to assign different cases to different groups in a class, or to assign different cases in subsequent semesters.

- This book is written for students who will go on to study an object-oriented language such as C++, Java, C#, or Visual Basic. The book uses conventions that are appropriate for object-oriented languages, including modern identifier naming conventions, teaching arrays as zero-based, and using parentheses with method names; these features are not included in competing texts. Also, this book does not address topics covered by other texts that do not apply as readily to object-oriented applications, such as stacks, queues, and control break processing.

New in this edition:

- All chapters have been carefully reviewed and edited to provide the clearest possible explanations for what can be challenging programming concepts.

- Most of the programming exercises at the end of each chapter are new.

- All the replaced programming exercises from previous editions are available for instructor use, including solutions.

- Each chapter is accompanied by three or more short videos, written and narrated by the author, that provide helpful instruction for important concepts.

Other Features of the Text

An Object-Oriented Approach to Programming Logic and Design is a superior textbook because it includes the following features:

- **Objectives**. Each chapter begins with a list of objectives so the student knows which topics will be presented in the chapter. In addition to providing a quick reference to topics covered, this feature provides a useful study aid.

- **Chapter summaries**. A summary recaps the programming concepts and techniques covered in the chapter. This feature provides a concise means for students to review and check their understanding of the main points in each chapter.

- **Key terms**. A collection of key terms used in the chapter text appears near the end of each chapter. Definitions are included in the order in which the key terms appear in the chapter.

- **Case projects**. Each chapter concludes with three running case projects for hypothetical businesses. By applying the current chapter's concepts to the continuing business examples, the student discovers that the topics from each chapter contribute to the development of a complete business system.

- **Up for Discussion questions**. Each chapter provides thought-provoking questions that can be used to spark classroom or online discussion.

- **Glossary**. All the key terms are listed alphabetically and defined in a glossary at the back of the book.

Features

This text focuses on helping students become better programmers and understand the big picture in program development through a variety of key features. In addition to chapter Objectives, Summaries, and Key Terms, these useful features will help students regardless of their learning style.

FLOWCHARTS, figures, and illustrations provide the reader with a visual learning experience.

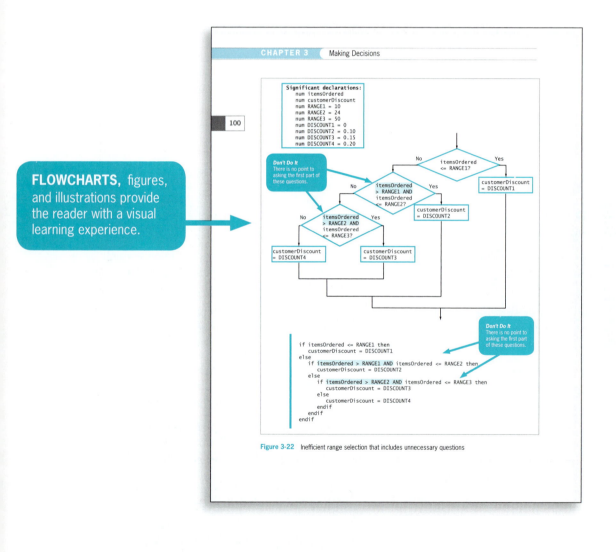

100

Figure 3-22 Inefficient range selection that includes unnecessary questions

VIDEO LESSONS help explain important chapter concepts.

Watch the video *Making Range Selections*.

Understanding Precedence When Combining AND and OR Operators

Most programming languages allow you to combine as many AND and OR operators in an expression as you need. For example, assume that you need to achieve a score of at least 75 on each of three tests to pass a course. You can declare a constant MIN_SCORE equal to 75 and test the multiple conditions with a statement like the following:

```
if score1 >= MIN_SCORE AND score2 >= MIN_SCORE AND score3 >= MIN_SCORE then
    classGrade = "Pass"
else
    classGrade = "Fail"
endif
```

On the other hand, if you need to pass only one of three tests to pass a course, then the logic is as follows:

```
if score1 >= MIN_SCORE OR score2 >= MIN_SCORE OR score3 >= MIN_SCORE then
    classGrade = "Pass"
else
    classGrade = "Fail"
endif
```

The logic becomes more complicated when you combine AND and OR operators within the same statement. When you do, the AND operators take **precedence**, meaning their Boolean values are evaluated first.

NOTES provide additional information— for example, another location in the book that expands on a topic, or a common error to watch out for.

In Chapter 2 you learned that in every programming language, multiplication has precedence over addition in an arithmetic statement. That is, the value of 2 + 3 * 4 is 14 because the multiplication occurs before the addition. Similarly, in every programming language, AND has precedence over OR because computer circuitry treats the AND operator as multiplication and the OR operator as addition.

For example, consider a program that determines whether a movie theater patron can purchase a discounted ticket. Assume that discounts are allowed for children and senior citizens who attend G-rated movies. The following code looks reasonable, but it produces incorrect results because the expression that contains the AND operator (see shading) evaluates before the one that contains the OR operator.

```
if age <= 12 OR age >= 65 AND rating = "G" then
 output "Discount applies"
endif
```

Don't Do It
The AND evaluates first, which is not the intention.

For example, assume that a movie patron is 10 years old and the movie rating is R. The patron should not receive a discount (or be allowed to see the movie!). However, within the if statement, the part of the expression that contains the AND operator, age >= 65 AND rating = "G", is

THE DON'T DO IT ICON illustrates how NOT to do something—for example, having a dead code path in a program. This icon provides a visual jolt to the student, emphasizing that particular figures are NOT to be emulated and making students more careful to recognize problems in existing code.

Assessment

Review Questions

Review Questions

1. Compared to using a command line, an advantage to using an operating system that employs a GUI is _____.

   a. you can interact directly with the operating system
   b. you do not have to deal with confusing icons
   c. you do not have to memorize complicated commands
   d. all of the above

2. When users can initiate actions by _____ is _____ -driven.

   a. event
   b. prompt

3. A component from which an event _____

   a. base
   b. icon

4. An object that responds to an even _____

   a. source
   b. listener

5. All of the following are user-initiate _____

   a. key press
   b. key drag

6. All of the following are typical GU _____

   a. label
   b. text box

7. GUI components operate like _____

   a. black boxes
   b. procedural functions

8. Which of the following is *not* a pri _____

   a. The interface should be predict:
   b. The fancier the screen design, t
   c. The program should be forgivin
   d. The user should be able to cust

365

Exercises

16. The flow of execution of one set of program statements is a _____.

   a. thread
   b. string
   c. path
   d. route

17. When a computer contains a single CPU, it can execute _____ computer instruction(s) at a time.

   a. one
   b. several
   c. an unlimited number of
   d. from several to thousands of

367

18. Each component on a screen has a horizontal, or _____, position as well as a vertical position.

   a. x-axis
   b. y-axis
   c. v-axis
   d. h-axis

19. You create computer animation by _____.

   a. drawing an image and setting its animation property to true
   b. drawing a single image and executing it on a multiprocessor system
   c. drawing a sequence of frames that is shown in rapid succession
   d. Animation is not used in computer applications.

20. You can use sophisticated, predrawn animated images to achieve graphic effects within your programs _____

   a. by loading them in a separate thread of execution
   b. only by subscribing to expensive imaging services
   c. with multiprocessing systems, but not on a computer with a single processor
   d. two of the above

Exercises

1. Take a critical look at three GUI applications you have used—for example, a spreadsheet, a word-processing program, and a game. Describe how well each conforms to the GUI design guidelines listed in this chapter.

2. Select one element of poor GUI design in a program you have used. Describe how you would improve the design.

3. Select a GUI program that you have never used before. Describe how well it conforms to the GUI design guidelines listed in this chapter.

Supplementary Material

This book can be enhanced by the following materials:

- **Videos**. The author has created and narrated 39 short videos that explain and clarify key chapter topics. These videos are available for complimentary download at *www.cengagebrain.com*.

- **Visual Logic™, version 2.0**. Visual Logic is a simple but powerful tool for teaching programming logic and design without traditional high-level programming language syntax. Visual Logic uses flowcharts to explain the essential programming concepts discussed in this book, including variables, input, assignment, output, conditions, loops, procedures, arrays, and files. Visual Logic also interprets and executes flowcharts, providing students with immediate and accurate feedback. Visual Logic combines the power of a high-level language with the ease and simplicity of flowcharts. Visual Logic is available for purchase along with your text. Contact your instructor or your Cengage Learning sales representative for more information.

Instructor Resources

The following teaching tools are available to the instructor on a single CD-ROM. Many are also available for download at our Instructor Companion Site. Simply search for this text at *login.cengage.com*. An instructor login is required.

- **Electronic Instructor's Manual**. The Instructor's Manual follows the text chapter by chapter and includes material to assist in planning and organizing an effective, engaging course. The manual includes Overviews, Chapter Objectives, Teaching Tips, Quick Quizzes, Class Discussion Topics, Additional Projects, Additional Resources, and Key Terms. A sample syllabus is also available.

- **PowerPoint Presentations**. This text provides PowerPoint slides to accompany each chapter. Slides may be used to guide classroom presentations, to make available to students for chapter review, or to print as classroom handouts. Files are provided for every figure in the text. Instructors may use the files to customize PowerPoint slides, illustrate quizzes, or create handouts.

- **Solutions**. Suggested solutions to review questions and exercises are available. Contact your Cengage Learning sales representative for more information.

- **ExamView®**. This textbook is accompanied by ExamView, a powerful testing software package that allows instructors to create and administer printed, LAN-based, and Internet exams. ExamView includes hundreds of questions that correspond to the text, enabling students to generate detailed study guides that include page references for further review. The computer-based and Internet testing components allow students to take exams at their computers, and save the instructor time by grading each exam automatically. These test banks are also available in Blackboard and Angel compatible formats.

Acknowledgments

I would like to thank all of the people who helped to make this book a reality, especially Dan Seiter, Development Editor, who continues to ensure that we produce a superior textbook. Thanks also to Alyssa Pratt, Senior Product Manager; Brandi Shailer, Acquisitions Editor; Stephanie Lorenz, Associate Product Manager; and Green Pen QA, Technical Editors. It is a pleasure to work with so many people who are dedicated to producing high-quality textbooks.

I am grateful to the many reviewers who provided helpful and insightful comments during the development of this book, including John Gerstenberg, Cuyamaca College; John Maxfield, Blue Ridge Community College; and Gene Robeen, Lewis and Clark Community College.

Thanks, too, to my husband, Geoff, whose constant support makes my writing career possible. Finally, this book is dedicated to Leo Geoffrey Edward Farrell, who is loved.

Joyce Farrell

CHAPTER 1

An Overview of Computer Programming

In this chapter, you will learn about:

- ◎ Computer components and operations
- ◎ Simple program logic
- ◎ The evolution of programming models
- ◎ The steps in the programming process
- ◎ Pseudocode and flowcharts
- ◎ Program comments
- ◎ Programming and user environments

Understanding Computer Components and Operations

A **computer system** is a combination of all the components required to process and store data using a computer. Every computer system is composed of multiple pieces of hardware and software.

- **Hardware** is the equipment, or the physical devices, associated with a computer. For example, keyboards, mice, speakers, and printers are all hardware. The devices are manufactured differently for large mainframe computers, smaller laptops, and even smaller computers that are embedded into products such as cars and thermostats. However, the types of operations performed by different-sized computers are very similar. When you think of a computer, you often think of its physical components first, but for a computer to be useful, it needs more than devices; a computer needs to be given instructions. Just as your stereo equipment does not do much until you provide music, computer hardware needs instructions that control how and when data items are input, how they are processed, and the form in which they are output or stored.

- **Software** describes computer instructions that tell the hardware what to do. Software is **programs**, which are instruction sets written by programmers. You can buy programs written by others that are stored on a disk or that you download from the Web. For example, businesses use word-processing and accounting programs, and casual computer users enjoy programs that play music and games. Alternatively, you can write your own programs. Writing software instructions is **programming**. This book focuses on the programming process.

Software can be classified into two broad types:

- **Application software** comprises all the programs you apply to a task—word-processing programs, spreadsheets, payroll and inventory programs, and even games.

- **System software** comprises the programs that you use to manage your computer, including operating systems such as Windows, Linux, or UNIX.

This book focuses on the logic used to write application software, although many of the concepts apply to both types of software.

Together, computer hardware and software accomplish three major operations in most programs:

- **Input**—Data items enter the computer system and are placed in **computer memory**, which is a computer's temporary, internal storage. Hardware devices that perform input operations include keyboards and mice. **Data items** include all the text, numbers, and other raw material that are entered into and processed by a computer. In business, many of the data items used are facts and figures about such entities as products, customers, and personnel. However, data can also include items such as images, sounds, and a user's mouse movements.

- **Processing**—Processing data items may involve organizing or sorting them, checking them for accuracy, or performing calculations with them. Processing converts input data that has been stored in memory into information suitable for output. The hardware component that performs these types of tasks is the **central processing unit**, or **CPU**.

- **Output**—After data items have been processed, the resulting information usually is sent to a printer, monitor, or some other output device so people can view, interpret, and use the results. Programming professionals often use the term *data* for input items but use the term **information** for data that has been processed and output. Sometimes you place output on **storage devices**, such as disks or flash media. People cannot read data directly from these storage devices, but the devices hold information for later retrieval. When you send output to a storage device, sometimes it is used later as input for another program.

You write computer instructions in a computer programming language, such as Visual Basic, C#, C++, or Java. Just as some people speak English and others speak Japanese, programmers also write programs in different languages. Some programmers work exclusively in one language, whereas others know several and use the one that seems most appropriate for the task at hand. The instructions you write in a programming language are **program code**; when you write these instructions, you are **coding the program**.

Each programming language has rules governing its word usage and punctuation. These rules are called the language's **syntax**. Mistakes in a language's usage are **syntax errors**. If you ask, "How the geet too store do I?" in English, most people can figure out what you probably mean, even though you have not used proper English syntax—you have mixed up the word order, misspelled a word, and used an incorrect word. However, computers are not nearly as smart as most people; with a computer, you might as well have asked, "Xpu mxv ort dod nmcad bf B?" Unless the syntax is perfect, the computer cannot interpret the programming language instruction at all.

When you write a program, you usually type its instructions using a keyboard. When you type program instructions, they are stored in computer memory, which is temporary, internal storage. Memory is sometimes called **RAM**, which is an acronym for *random access memory*. Usually, you want to use the temporarily stored instructions multiple times, so you also save them on a permanent storage device, such as a disk, where they can be reloaded into memory again later without retyping.

When a computer carries out program instructions stored in memory, the program **runs**, or **executes**. The statements that carry out a program's actions are **executable statements**. Before any computer program can execute, it must be translated from your **high-level** (English-like) programming language statements to **low-level** programming statements in **machine language** form. Machine language represents the billions of on/off circuits within the computer. Each programming language uses a piece of software, called a **compiler** or an **interpreter**, to translate your program code into machine language. Machine language is also called **binary language** and is represented as a series of 0s and 1s. The compiler or interpreter that translates your code indicates if you have used any programming language component incorrectly. Therefore, syntax errors are relatively easy to locate and correct—your compiler or interpreter lists or points out every syntax error. If you write a computer program using a language such as C++ but spell one of its words incorrectly or reverse the proper order of two words, the translator lets you know that it found a mistake by displaying an error message as soon as you try to translate the program. The program statements you write in a programming language are known as **source code**. The translated machine language statements are known as **object code**.

Although there are differences in how compilers and interpreters work, their basic function is the same—to translate your programming statements into code the computer can use. When you use a compiler, an entire program is translated before it executes; when you use an interpreter, each instruction is translated just prior to execution. Usually, you do not choose which type of translation to use—it depends on the programming language. However, there are some languages for which both compilers and interpreters are available.

4

Watch the video *Understanding Computer Hardware and Software*.

Understanding Simple Program Logic

A program whose source code contains syntax errors cannot be fully translated nor can it execute. A program with no syntax errors can execute, but it still might contain **logical errors** and produce incorrect results. For a program to work properly, you must develop correct **logic**; that is, you must write program instructions in a specific sequence, you must not leave any instructions out, and you must not add extraneous instructions.

Suppose that you instruct someone to make a cake as follows:

```
Stir
Add two eggs
Add a gallon of gasoline
Bake at 350 degrees for 45 minutes
Add three cups of flour
```

Don't Do It
These cake-baking instructions are dangerous and not recommended!

The dangerous cake-baking instructions are shown with a Don't Do It icon. You will see this icon in the book when an unrecommended programming practice is shown as an example of what *not* to do.

Even though you have used the English language syntax correctly, the cake-baking instructions are out of sequence, some instructions are missing, and some instructions belong to procedures other than baking a cake. If you follow these instructions, you will not make an edible cake, and you may end up with a disaster. Logical errors are much more difficult to locate than syntax errors; it is easier for you to determine whether *eggs* is misspelled in a recipe than it is for you to tell if there are too many eggs or they are added too soon.

Programmers often call logical errors **semantic errors**. For example, if you misspell a programming-language word, you commit a syntax error, but if you use a correct word that does not make sense in the current context, you commit a semantic error.

Just as baking directions can be given correctly in Mandarin, Urdu, or Spanish, the same logic of a program can be expressed in any number of programming languages. This book is almost exclusively concerned with the logic development process instead of a specific language, so the programming examples could have been written in Japanese, C++, or Java. The logic is the same in any language. For convenience, the book uses English!

After you learn French, you automatically know, or can easily figure out, the meaning of many Spanish words. Similarly, after you learn one programming language, such as Java, it is much easier to understand several other languages, such as C++ and C#.

Many simple computer programs include steps that perform input, processing, and output. Suppose that you want to write a computer program to double any number you provide. You can write the program in a programming language such as Java or C++, but if you were to write it using English-like statements, it would look like this:

```
input myNumber
myAnswer = myNumber * 2
output myAnswer
```

The number-doubling process includes three instructions:

- The instruction to `input myNumber` is an example of an input operation. When the computer interprets this instruction, it knows to look to an input device to obtain a number. When you learn a specific programming language, you learn how to tell the computer which input device to access for input. Logically, however, it doesn't really matter which hardware device is used, as long as the computer knows to look for a number. When you input a value, the hardware device is irrelevant. For example, when a user enters a number as data for a program, the user might click on the number with a mouse, type it from a keyboard, or speak it into a microphone. The same is true in your daily life. If you follow the instruction "Get eggs for the cake," it does not really matter if you purchase them from a store or harvest them from your own chickens—you get the eggs either way. When the number is retrieved from an input device, it is placed in the computer's memory at the location named `myNumber`. You can substitute many other names for the location number, depending on the rules of the programming language you are using. For example, you could use `number`, `someValue`, `originalInput`, or `x`.

- The instruction `myAnswer = myNumber * 2` is an example of a processing operation. The operation is a mathematical operation; programmers frequently use an asterisk to indicate multiplication. Mathematical operations are not the only kind of processing operations, but they are very typical. As with input operations, the type of hardware used for processing is irrelevant. Again, the same is true in real life. If a recipe instruction requires you to boil water, you could use a gas stove, charcoal grill, or wood campfire. Similarly, a program that doubles a number can be used on computers of different brand names, sizes, and speeds. The instruction takes the value stored in memory at the `myNumber` location, multiplies it by 2, and stores the result in another memory location named `myAnswer`. Again, you could choose any number of names for the answer location. You might prefer `finalAnswer`, `result`, or `y`.

- In the number-doubling program, the `output myAnswer` instruction is an example of an output operation. Within a particular program, this statement could cause the output to appear on a monitor (which might be a flat-panel plasma screen or a cathode-ray tube), go to a printer (which could be laser or ink-jet), be broadcast through a speaker, or be written to a disk or CD. The logic of the output process is the same no matter what hardware device you use. When this instruction executes, the value stored in memory at the location named `myAnswer` is sent to an output device.

Understanding the Evolution of Programming Models

People have been writing modern computer programs since the 1940s. The oldest programming languages required programmers to work with memory addresses and to memorize awkward codes associated with machine languages. Newer programming languages are easier to use for multiple reasons:

- Newer language statements look much more like natural language; for example, to produce output, they typically use a verb such as *output*, *write*, or *print*.

- Newer languages allow programmers to give meaningful names to memory locations instead of using memory addresses. For example, your salary might be stored at a location you can refer to as `salary` instead of using the location's address. Computer programmers often refer to memory addresses using hexadecimal notation, or base 16. Using this system, they might use a value like 482FF01A to refer to a memory address. Despite the use of letters, such an address is still a number. Appendix C describes numbering systems in detail.

- Newer programming languages allow the creation of self-contained modules or program segments that can be pieced together in a variety of ways. The oldest computer programs were written in one piece, from start to finish, but modern programs are rarely written that way—they are created by teams of programmers, each developing reusable and connectable program components. Writing several small modules is easier than writing one large program, just as most large tasks are easier when you break the work into units and get other workers to help with the units.

 Ada Byron Lovelace predicted the development of software in 1843; she is often regarded as the first programmer. However, no modern computers existed then; homes and businesses did not even have electricity. The basis for most modern software was proposed by Alan Turing in 1935.

Currently, programmers use one of two major techniques for developing programs:

- **Procedural programming** focuses on the procedures that programmers create to manipulate data. That is, procedural programmers focus on the actions that are carried out—for example, getting input data for an employee and writing the calculations needed to produce a paycheck from the data. Procedural programmers would approach the job of producing a paycheck by breaking down the process into manageable subtasks. Examples of procedural programming languages include C and Logo.

- **Object-oriented programming** focuses on objects. **Objects** are the "things" or entities used in a program; for example, you might write a program that issues employee paychecks. (Chapter 7 provides a more thorough explanation of objects.) Programmers use the term *OO*, pronounced *oh oh*, as an abbreviation for *object-oriented*. When discussing object-oriented programming, they use *OOP*, which rhymes with *soup*. OOP describes objects' attributes and their behaviors. The **attributes of an object** are the features it "has"; the values of an object's attributes constitute the **state of the object**. For example, an attribute of a paycheck is the monetary value of the check, and the state of one paycheck's monetary value might be $400. The **behaviors of an object** are the things it "does";

for example, a paycheck object can be written and cashed, and it has access to calculations that result in the check amount. Object-oriented programmers might start to design a payroll application by thinking about all the objects needed, such as employees, time cards, and paychecks, and describing their attributes and behaviors. Examples of OO languages include Java, Visual Basic, C++, and C#. You can write procedural programs in OO languages, but you cannot write OO programs in procedural languages.

With either approach, procedural or object-oriented, you can produce a correct paycheck, and both techniques employ reusable program modules. The major difference lies in the focus the programmer takes during the earliest planning stages of a project. Taking an **object-oriented approach** to a problem means defining the objects needed to accomplish a task and developing the objects so that each maintains its own data and carries out tasks when another object requests them. The object-oriented approach is said to be "natural"—it is more natural to think of a world of objects and the ways they interact than a world of systems, data items, and the logic required to manipulate them.

Object-oriented programming employs a large vocabulary; you can learn much of this terminology in Chapter 7.

Originally, object-oriented programming was used most frequently for two major types of applications:

- **Computer simulations**, which attempt to mimic real-world activities so that their processes can be improved or so that users can better understand how the real-world processes operate. **Users** are those who apply programs to tasks after the programs are written; they are also called **end users**.

- **Graphical user interfaces**, or **GUIs** (pronounced *gooeys*), which allow users to interact with a program in a graphical environment.

Thinking about objects in these two types of applications makes sense. For example, a city might want to develop a program that simulates traffic patterns to better prevent traffic tie-ups. By creating a model with objects such as cars and pedestrians that contain their own data and rules for behavior, the simulation can be set in motion. For example, each car object has a specific current speed and a procedure for changing that speed. By creating a model of city traffic using objects, a computer can create a simulation of a real city at rush hour.

Creating a GUI environment for users also is a natural use for object orientation. It is easy to think of the components a user manipulates on a computer screen, such as buttons and scroll bars, as similar to real-world objects. Each GUI object contains data—for example, a button on a screen has a specific size and color. Each object also contains behaviors—for example, each button can be clicked and reacts in a specific way when clicked. Some people consider the term *object-oriented programming* to be synonymous with GUI programming, but object-oriented programming means more. Although many GUI programs are object-oriented, one does not imply the other. Modern businesses use object-oriented design techniques when developing all sorts of business applications, whether they are GUI applications or not.

Understanding the Steps in the Programming Process

Professional programmers develop both systems and individual programs. A system might consist of a group of many programs, such as those needed for payroll, inventory, or billing. For example, payroll systems typically include programs for modifying personnel files, producing paychecks, and completing tax forms. Whether you are creating a system or just one program, you can use an object-oriented approach, which involves the following tasks:

- Analyzing the program or system

- Designing the program or system

- Writing and testing the program or programs that make up the system

Often a programmer performs all of these tasks; sometimes a systems analyst studies the requirements of the system and designs it, and programmers simply write the programs. Sometimes programmers test their own programs; in other situations, **software testers** perform much more thorough evaluations. Sometimes all these tasks are intertwined.

 Software testers run programs using a variety of input data. Some testers run only **black box tests**, in which they provide input and determine whether the output is valid without looking at how the program works internally. More complicated programs often also require **white box tests**, in which the tester looks at how the program works to make sure every possible logical path is tested.

Analyzing the Program or System

Professional computer programmers write programs to satisfy the needs of users. Examples of users include a human resources director who needs to manage insurance premiums and payments for employees, a billing department that needs to handle clients who are overdue on their payments, and an order department that needs an interactive Web site to store buyers' purchases in an online shopping cart and collect credit card data when they are ready to make purchases. Because programmers are providing a service to these users, programmers must first understand what the users want. In object-oriented environments, the process of analyzing users' needs is called **object-oriented analysis**, or **OOA**.

If a program or system has been well thought out, this step might involve only a short meeting with the users. If not, this step might take many hours of meetings. Thoroughly understanding and analyzing a problem may be one of the most difficult aspects of programming. On any job, the description of what the user needs may be vague—worse yet, users may not even really know what they want, and users who think they know what they want frequently change their minds after seeing sample output. A programmer often must revise a program many times before a user is satisfied with the outcome.

Designing the Program or System

When object-oriented designers develop a system or program, they use an approach called **object-oriented design**, or **OOD**. Designers envision the objects they need, consider the objects' attributes and behaviors, and decide how the objects relate to each other.

In the simplest programs, objects and their data types are very basic. Many programs are written using only numeric and text items; the attributes and behaviors of these types are built into every programming language. (For example, numeric types can be added and subtracted.) These simple types often are used as building blocks when you create more complex types. For example, necessary objects for an ordering system might include the product, the customer, the order, and the means of delivery, such as a truck, and those types might be constructed from simpler types. As examples, each product might have attributes that include a stock number, description, size, and price, and each customer might have an ID number, name, and address. A product's behaviors might include stocking and delivering, and a customer's behaviors might include ordering.

Once you have thought about objects, their attributes, and their behaviors, you can decide on relationships between them. **Relationships** describe how objects communicate with and react to each other. Relationships are frequently expressed as verb phrases such as *has a*, *is a*, and *creates a*. For example, a customer creates an order, and an order has a customer and has a product.

When you use object-oriented design techniques, you create general categories that describe objects. Each category is a **class**. Very often, you do not have to build a class from scratch because someone has already created it—for example, your company might already have created a Customer class used in marketing programs, and you might reuse that class in your product ordering program. On the other hand, perhaps the marketing program Customer class does not contain all the attributes your program requires, so you might have to modify the original class before you can use it in your system. Similarly, many object-oriented languages already contain a class you can use to create a form on the screen. However, your form might have a particular size, contain specific words, or require a color that is different from any existing form, so you have to write those instructions. Whether you use prewritten classes or need to create some from scratch, when you design a program you establish the ways you will communicate with the objects, and how they will communicate with each other. You will gain a more thorough understanding of classes in Chapter 7. The first programs you study in this book are simple classes—applications that contain only simple data types and use a few instructions.

Writing and Testing Programs

The act of writing a program consists of several subtasks, including the following:

- Developing the logic of the program
- Coding the program
- Using software to translate the program code into machine language
- Testing the program

Developing Program Logic

The heart of the programming process is developing the program's logic. You may hear programmers refer to planning a program as *developing an algorithm*. An **algorithm** is the sequence of steps necessary to solve any problem. The focus of this book is on developing algorithms with commonly used design tools.

While planning a program's logic, the programmer determines the steps of the program and decides how to order them. You can plan the solution to a problem in many ways, including just thinking about the solution, drawing pictures of it, and writing about it. The two most common planning tools used by professional programmers are pseudocode and flowcharts. Both tools involve writing the steps of the program in English, much as you would plan a trip on paper before getting into the car, or plan a party theme before shopping for food and favors.

The programmer doesn't worry about the syntax of any particular language when planning the logic, but wants to assemble the sequence of events that will lead from the available input to the desired output. Planning the logic includes thinking carefully about all the possible data values a program might encounter and how you want the program to handle each scenario. The process of walking through a program's logic on paper before you actually write the program or enter it into a computer is called **desk-checking**. You will learn more about planning the logic later; in fact, the book focuses on this crucial step almost exclusively.

Coding the Program

When you write program statements in a programming language, you are writing source code, or coding. Well-known object-oriented programming languages include C++, C#, Java, Visual Basic, SmallTalk, OO COBOL, and Simula. Despite their differences, these programming languages are quite alike—each can handle creating objects and establishing communication between them. The objects a program requires and the logic needed to work with the objects can be executed using any number of languages. Only after a language is chosen must the programmer worry about correct spelling and punctuation—in other words, using the correct *syntax*.

Some experienced programmers can successfully combine the planning and coding of the program in one step. This may work for planning and writing a simple program, just as you can plan and write a postcard to a friend using one step. A good term paper or a Hollywood screenplay, however, needs planning before writing, and so do most programs.

Which step is harder: planning the objects and classes or coding them? Right now, it may seem to you that writing in a programming language is a very difficult task, considering all the spelling and grammar rules you must learn. However, the planning step is actually more difficult. Which is more difficult: thinking up memorable characters and how they navigate the tangled plot of a bestselling mystery novel, or translating an already written novel from English to Spanish? And who do you think gets paid more, the writer who creates the characters and plot or the translator? (Try asking friends to name any famous translator!)

Using Software to Translate the Program into Machine Language

Programmers use many different programming languages, but at the lowest level, each computer operates using only one language: its machine language, which consists of 1s and 0s. Computers understand machine language because they are made up of thousands of tiny electrical switches, each of which can be set in either the on or off state, which is represented by a 1 or 0, respectively.

Languages like Java or Visual Basic are usable because of a compiler or interpreter that translates the programmers' English-like, high-level source code into the low-level machine language that the computer understands. If you write a programming language statement incorrectly (for example, by misspelling a word, using a word that doesn't exist in the language, or using "illegal" grammar), the translator program doesn't know what to do and issues an error message identifying a syntax error, or misuse of a language's grammar rules. You receive the same response when you speak nonsense to a human-language translator. Although making errors is never desirable, syntax errors are not a major concern because the compiler or translator catches them all.

A computer program must be free of syntax errors before you can execute it. Typically, a programmer develops objects, writes the code the objects need, compiles the program, and then receives a list of syntax errors. The programmer corrects the syntax errors and compiles the program again. Correcting the first set of errors frequently reveals a new set of errors that originally were not apparent to the compiler. For example, if you could use an English compiler and submit the sentence The dg chase the cat, the compiler at first might point out only one syntax error. The second word, dg, is illegal because it is not part of the English language. Only after you corrected the word dog would the compiler find another syntax error on the third word, chase, because it is the wrong verb form for the subject dog. This doesn't mean chase is necessarily the wrong word. Maybe dog is wrong; perhaps the subject should be dogs, in which case chase is right. Compilers don't always know exactly what you mean, nor do they know what the proper correction should be, but they do know when something is wrong with your syntax.

When writing a program, a programmer might need to recompile the code several times. An executable program is created only when the code is free of syntax errors. Figure 1-1 shows a diagram of this entire process.

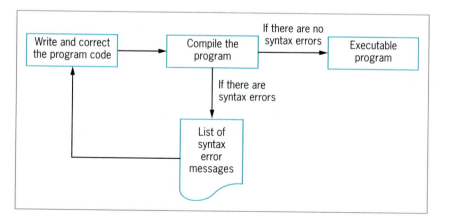

Figure 1-1   Creating an executable program

Testing the Program

A program that is free of syntax errors is not necessarily free of logical errors. A logical error results when you use a syntactically correct statement but use the wrong one for the current context. For example, the sentence The dog chases the cat, although syntactically perfect, is not logically correct if the subject turns out to be a fox or if the cat is the aggressor.

Once a program is free of syntax errors, the programmer can **test the program**—that is, execute it to determine whether the output is correct or whether logical errors exist. If the program does not require any input but simply displays some output, you can read the output and determine whether it shows what you wanted and expected. Many programs, however, require that you enter some data, so you must enter sample data and see whether the results are logically correct.

Recall the number-doubling program:

```
input myNumber
myAnswer = myNumber * 2
output myAnswer
```

If you execute this code, provide the value 2 as input to the program, and the answer 4 is output, you have executed one successful test run of the program.

However, if the answer 40 is output, maybe the program contains a logical error. Maybe the second line of code was mistyped with an extra zero, so that the program reads:

```
input myNumber
myAnswer = myNumber * 20
output myAnswer
```

The programmer typed "20" instead of "2".

Placing 20 instead of 2 in the multiplication statement caused a logical error. Notice that nothing is syntactically wrong with this version of the program—it is just as reasonable to multiply a number by 20 as by 2—but if the programmer intends only to double myNumber, then a logical error has occurred.

Programs should be tested with many sets of data. For example, if you write the program to double a number, then enter 2 and get an output value of 4, that doesn't mean you have a correct program. Perhaps you have typed the following program by mistake:

```
input myNumber
myAnswer = myNumber + 2
output myAnswer
```

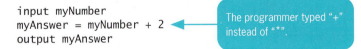

The programmer typed "+" instead of "*".

An input of 2 results in an answer of 4, but that doesn't mean your program doubles a number—it actually only adds 2 to it. If you test your program with additional data and get the wrong answer—for example, if you input 3 and get an answer of 5—you know there is a logical problem with your code.

Selecting test data is somewhat of an art in itself, and it should be done carefully. If the Human Resources Department wants a list of the names of five-year employees, it would be a mistake to test the program with a small sample file of only long-term employees. If no newer employees are part of the data being used for testing, you don't really know if the program would have eliminated them from the five-year list. Many companies don't know that their software has a problem until an unusual circumstance occurs—for example, the first time an employee has more than nine dependents, or the first time a customer orders more than 999 items at a time. A program that does not work correctly can cause a company to lose millions of dollars in business, so programs must be tested very thoroughly.

After the Program is Written and Tested

Once the program is tested adequately, it is ready to use. If you are writing a program for your own use, you might be done with the process at this point. If you are writing the program for an organization, you might have to arrange for some or all of the following:

- Preparing manuals
- Training users
- Converting existing data to a format that is usable by the new system

Conversion, the entire set of actions an organization must take to switch over to using a new program or set of programs, can sometimes take months or years to accomplish.

You also might modify a program months or years after you finish it. **Maintenance** is the act of making required changes to programs after they are put into production. Maintenance can be necessary for many reasons, including the following:

- A previously undiscovered mistake is found in a program—for example, the first time an employee's salary is more than $99,999, it might be discovered that withholding taxes are not calculated correctly.
- Some instructions in the program require alteration—for example, when a new tax rate is legislated for purchased items.
- The format of some input data changes—for example, telephone area codes might universally change from three to four digits, or the post office might start to require nine-digit zip codes on all packages.
- Some input data that was previously available is no longer available—for example, a law might be passed that prevents an institution from collecting and storing customer financial data.
- The user wants additional information not included in the original output specifications—for example, a client who previously wanted a weekly list of his business's sale amounts now might want to include clients' names, the total number of items sold, or the total gross received.

Watch the video *Understanding the Programming Process*.

Using Pseudocode and Flowcharts

When programmers plan the logic for a solution to a programming problem, they often use one of two tools: pseudocode (pronounced *sue-doe-code*) or a flowchart. **Pseudocode** is an English-like representation of the logical steps it takes to solve a problem. A **flowchart** is a pictorial representation of the same thing.

Writing Pseudocode

You have already seen examples of statements that represent pseudocode earlier in this chapter, and there is nothing mysterious about them. The following five statements constitute a pseudocode representation of a number-doubling problem:

```
start
   input myNumber
   myAnswer = myNumber * 2
   output myAnswer
stop
```

Using pseudocode involves writing down all the steps you will use in a program. Usually, programmers preface their pseudocode with a beginning statement like start and end it with a terminating statement like stop. The statements between start and stop look like English and are indented slightly so that start and stop stand out. Most programmers do not bother with punctuation such as periods at the end of pseudocode statements, although it would not be wrong to use them if you prefer that style. Similarly, there is no need to capitalize the first word in a sentence, although you might choose to do so. This book follows the conventions of using lowercase letters for verbs that begin pseudocode statements and omitting periods at the end of statements.

 Appendix A contains a summary of all conventions used in this book. **Conventions** are standards of format and style that are selected for consistency while acknowledging that others might prefer different customs that are equally correct.

Pseudocode is fairly flexible because it is a planning tool, and not the final product. Therefore, for example, you might prefer any of the following language alternatives:

- Instead of start and stop, some pseudocode developers would use the terms begin and end.

- Instead of writing input myNumber, some developers would write get myNumber or read myNumber. The verb must convey that data values are entered into the program.

- Instead of writing myAnswer = myNumber * 2, some developers would write myAnswer = myNumber times 2 or compute myAnswer as myNumber doubled. The statement must convey that the number entered is multiplied by two.

- Instead of writing output myAnswer, many pseudocode developers would write display myAnswer, print myAnswer, or write myAnswer. The verb must express that information is output from the program.

The point is, the pseudocode statements are instructions to retrieve an original number from an input device and store it in memory where it can be used in a calculation, and then to get the calculated answer from memory and send it to an output device so a person can see it. When you eventually convert your pseudocode to a specific programming language, you do not have such flexibility because specific syntax will be required. For example, if you use the C# programming language and write the statement to output the answer, you will code the following:

```
Console.Write(myAnswer);
```

The exact use of words, capitalization, and punctuation are important in the C# statement, but not in the pseudocode statement.

Drawing Flowcharts

Some professional programmers prefer writing pseudocode to drawing flowcharts because using pseudocode is more similar to writing the final statements in the programming language. Others prefer drawing flowcharts to represent the logical flow, because flowcharts allow programmers to visualize more easily how the program statements will connect. Especially for beginning programmers, flowcharts are an excellent tool to help visualize how the statements in a program are interrelated.

Procedural programmers probably use flowcharts more frequently than object-oriented programmers for several reasons. First, procedural programmers focus more on the steps of a task, and that approach fits flowcharting. Also, object-oriented modules are typically short, making flowcharting less necessary. This book uses many flowcharts in the early chapters while you are learning fundamental programming logic, but favors pseudocode in later chapters where the focus is purely object oriented.

When you create a flowchart, you draw geometric shapes that contain the individual statements and that are connected with arrows. Common flowchart symbols include:

- **Input symbols**, represented by parallelograms, indicating input operations.

- **Processing symbols**, represented by rectangles, indicating processing steps, such as arithmetic statements.

- **Output symbols**, represented by parallelograms just as input symbols are, and indicating output operations. Because the parallelogram is used for both input and output, it is often called the **input/output symbol** or **I/O symbol**.

All the flowchart symbols used in this book are summarized in Appendix B.

Some programs that use flowcharts (such as Visual Logic) use a left-slanting parallelogram to represent output. As long as the flowchart creator and the flowchart reader are communicating, the actual shape used is irrelevant. This book will follow the most standard convention of always using the right-slanting parallelogram for both input and output.

- **Terminal symbols**, represented by lozenges (ovals with flattened tops) that mark the beginning and end of a sequence of steps.

- **Decision symbols** represented by diamonds. Decision symbols hold questions that allow program logic to follow divergent paths.

To show the correct sequence of these symbols for the logic you are developing, you use arrows, or **flowlines**, to connect the steps. Whenever possible, most of a flowchart should read from top to bottom or from left to right on a page. That's the way we read English, so when flowcharts follow this convention, they are easier for us to understand.

Figure 1-2 shows a complete flowchart for the program that doubles a number, and the pseudocode for the same problem. You can see from the figure that the flowchart and pseudocode statements are the same—only the presentation format differs.

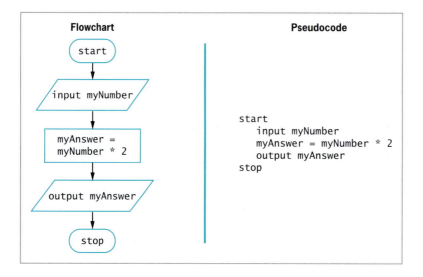

Figure 1-2   Flowchart and pseudocode of program that doubles a number

Figure 1-3 shows a flowchart that contains a decision symbol and the pseudocode that corresponds to it. You will learn much more about decision making in Chapter 3, but for now, you can see that decisions are questions that split the path of the logical flow in a program. In this example, the number-doubling program has been modified to only double numbers that are less than 10; otherwise, an error message is output.

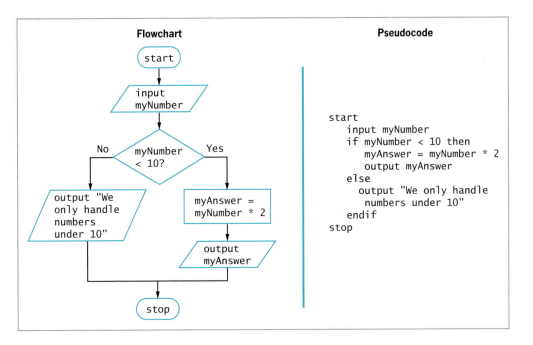

Flowchart

Pseudocode

```
start
    input myNumber
    if myNumber < 10 then
        myAnswer = myNumber * 2
        output myAnswer
    else
        output "We only handle
            numbers under 10"
    endif
stop
```

Figure 1-3   Flowchart and pseudocode of program that doubles a number if it is less than 10

When you draw a flowchart for your own use, you can draw it by hand or you can use software that contains flowcharting tools such as Microsoft Word and Microsoft PowerPoint. You also can use several other programs, such as Visio and Visual Logic, which are specifically designed to create flowcharts. Programmers seldom create both pseudocode and a flowchart for the same problem. They usually use one or the other. In a large program, you might even prefer to use pseudocode for some parts and draw a flowchart for others.

 When you tell a friend how to get to your house, you might write a series of instructions or you might draw a map, or you might use a combination of the two. Pseudocode is similar to written, step-by-step instructions; a flowchart, like a map, is a visual representation of the same thing.

 You will learn to use several other graphic tools when programming. In Chapter 6, you will create class diagrams, and in Chapter 11 you will learn the details of the Unified Modeling Language (UML).

 Watch the video *Flowcharts and Pseudocode*.

Understanding Program Comments

The flowchart and pseudocode examples in Figures 1-2 and 1-3 are brief. Many programs contain hundreds or even thousands of statements. When you write larger applications, perhaps over a period of weeks or months, it becomes increasingly difficult to remember why you included specific steps. Documenting your program code helps you remember why you wrote statements the way you did. **Program comments** are nonexecuting statements that you add to a program for the purpose of documentation. Programmers use comments to leave notes for themselves and for others who might read their programs in the future. At the very least, most programs include comments indicating the program's author, the date the program was written, and the purpose of the program.

When you learn a programming language, you will learn the syntax for creating comments within that language. Many languages have several specific types of comments. At least three popular object-oriented programming languages (C++, Java, and C#) support a line comment that starts with two forward slashes. If you see a statement like the following in a C++, Java, or C# program, it is a nonexecuting program comment included for documentation:

```
// This is a comment
```

Because this comment style is popular, this book will use line comments that start with two forward slashes in pseudocode when an explanation is needed for a programming statement. An **annotation symbol** is the flowchart symbol used to hold comments; it is represented by a three-sided box connected with a dashed line to the step it explains. Figure 1-4 shows a flowchart and pseudocode for the number-doubling program, each with an added comment.

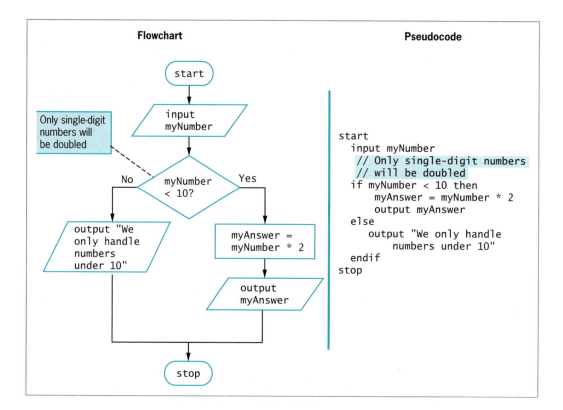

Figure 1-4 Flowchart and pseudocode with comments

Understanding Programming and User Environments

There are many ways to write and execute a computer program. When you plan a program's logic, you can use a flowchart or pseudocode, or a combination of the two. When you code the program, you can type statements into a variety of text editors. When your program executes, it might accept input from a keyboard, mouse, microphone, or any other input device, and when you provide a program's output, you might use text, images, or sound. This section describes the most common environments you will encounter as a new programmer.

Understanding Programming Environments

When you plan the logic for a computer program, you can use paper and pencil to create a flowchart, or you might use software that allows you to manipulate flowchart shapes. If you choose to write pseudocode, you can do so by hand or by using a word-processing program. To enter the program into a computer so you can translate and execute it, you usually use a keyboard to type program statements into an editor. You can type a program into one of the following:

- A plain text editor
- A text editor that is part of an integrated development environment

A **text editor** is a program that you use to create simple text files. It is similar to a word processor, but without as many features. You can use a text editor such as Notepad that is included with Microsoft Windows. Figure 1-5 shows a C# program in Notepad that accepts a number and doubles it. An advantage to using a simple text editor to type and save a program is that the completed program does not require much disk space for storage. For example, the file shown in Figure 1-5 occupies only 314 bytes of storage.

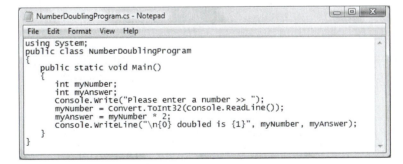

Figure 1-5   A C# number-doubling program in Notepad

You also can use the editor of an **integrated development environment (IDE)** to enter a program. An IDE is a software package that provides an editor, compiler, and other programming tools. For example, Figure 1-6 shows a C# program in the Microsoft Visual Studio IDE, an environment that contains tools useful for creating programs in Visual Basic, C++, and C#.

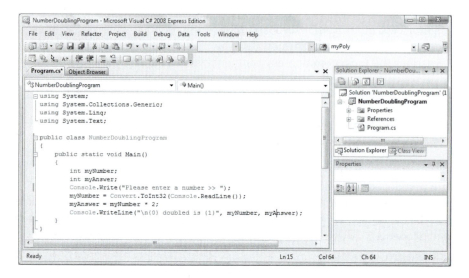

Figure 1-6   A C# number-doubling program in Visual Studio

Using an IDE is helpful to programmers because IDEs usually provide features similar to those you find in many word processors. In particular, an IDE's editor usually provides such features as the following:

- It uses different colors to display various language components, making built-in language elements easier to identify.

- It highlights syntax errors visually for you.

- It employs automatic statement completion; when you start to type a statement, the IDE suggests a likely completion, which you can accept with a keystroke.

- It provides tools that allow you to step through a program's execution one statement at a time so you can more easily follow the program's logic and determine the source of any errors.

When you use the IDE to create and save a program, the program occupies much more disk space than when you use a plain text editor. For example, the program in Figure 1-6 occupies more than 49,000 bytes of disk space. Additionally, installing and starting the IDE can be complex and time-consuming.

Although programming environments might look different and offer different features, the process of using them is very similar. Your logic and written instructions are the same no matter what programming environment you use.

Understanding User Environments

A user might execute a program you have written in any number of environments. For example, a user might execute the number-doubling program from a command line like the one shown in Figure 1-7. A **command line** is a location on your computer screen at which you type text entries to communicate with the computer's operating system. In the program in Figure 1-7, the user is asked for a number, and the results are displayed.

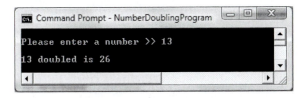

Figure 1-7 Executing a number-doubling program in a command-line environment

Many programs are not run at the command line in a text environment, but are run using a graphical user interface, which allows users to interact with a program in a graphical environment. When running a GUI program, the user might type input into a text box or use a mouse or other pointing device to select options on the screen. Figure 1-8 shows a number-doubling program that performs exactly the same task as the one in Figure 1-7, but this program uses a GUI.

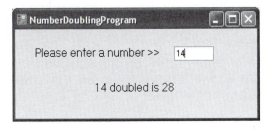

Figure 1-8 Executing a number-doubling program in a GUI environment

A command-line program and a GUI program might be written in the same programming language. (For example, the programs shown in Figures 1-7 and 1-8 were both written using C#.) However, no matter which environment is used to write or execute a program, the logical process is the same. The two programs in Figures 1-7 and 1-8 both accept input, perform multiplication, and perform output. In this book, you will not concentrate on which environment is used to type a program's statements, nor will you care about the type of environment the user sees. Instead, you will be concerned with the logic that applies to all programming situations.

Chapter Summary

- Together, computer hardware (physical devices) and software (instructions) accomplish three major operations: input, processing, and output. You write computer instructions in a computer programming language that requires specific syntax; the instructions are translated into machine language by a compiler or interpreter. When both the syntax and logic of a program are correct, you can run, or execute, the program to produce the desired results.

- For a program to work properly, you must develop correct logic. Logical errors are much more difficult to locate than syntax errors.

- Procedural programming focuses on the procedures that programmers create to manipulate data. Object-oriented programming (OOP) focuses on objects, or "things." OOP describes these objects' features (or attributes) and their behaviors.

- Developing a system involves analyzing the system, designing it, and writing the programs. Writing the programs involves planning the logic, coding the program, translating the program into machine language, and testing it.

- When programmers plan the logic for a solution to a programming problem, they often use pseudocode or a flowchart. Pseudocode is an English-like representation of a program's logical steps; a flowchart is a pictorial representation of the same thing.

- Program comments are nonexecuting statements that you add to a program for the purpose of documentation. You can indicate comments in pseudocode by starting a line with two forward slashes. You can add comments to a flowchart using an annotation symbol.

- You can type a program into a plain text editor or one that is part of an integrated development environment. When a program's data values are entered from a keyboard, they can be entered at the command line in a text environment or in a GUI. Either way, the logic is similar.

Key Terms

A **computer system** is a combination of all the components required to process and store data using a computer.

Hardware is the set of physical devices in a computer system.

Software is the set of programs that tell a computer what to do.

Programs are the sets of executable instructions written by programmers.

Programming is the act of developing and writing software instructions.

Application software comprises all the programs you apply to a task.

System software comprises the programs that you use to manage your computer, including operating systems such as Windows or UNIX and other utility programs not directly used by end users.

Input describes the entry of data into a system using hardware devices such as keyboards and mice.

Computer memory is a computer's temporary, internal storage.

Data items include all the text, numbers, and other raw material that are processed by a computer.

Processing data items may involve organizing or sorting them, checking them for accuracy, or performing calculations with them. Processing turns data into information.

The **central processing unit**, or **CPU**, is the hardware component that processes data.

Output describes the operation of retrieving information from memory and sending it to a device, such as a monitor or printer, so that people can view, interpret, and use the results.

Information is processed data.

Storage devices are hardware, such as disks or flash media, on which you can store data.

Program code is written computer instructions.

Coding the program is the act of writing program instructions.

The **syntax** of a language consists of its rules.

A **syntax error** is an error in language or grammar.

RAM is internal computer memory; it is an acronym for *random access memory*.

To **run** a program is to carry out a program's instructions.

To **execute** a program is to carry out a program's instructions.

Executable statements are the statements that carry out a program's actions.

High-level describes programming languages that are English-like.

Low-level describes languages that more closely reflect computer circuitry than high-level languages; the lowest-level language is the set of statements made up of 1s and 0s that the computer understands.

Machine language is a computer's on-off circuitry language.

A **compiler** translates a high-level language into machine language and indicates if you have used a programming language incorrectly. A compiler translates an entire program at once.

An **interpreter** translates a high-level language into machine language and indicates if you have used a programming language incorrectly. An interpreter translates a program one instruction at a time.

Binary language consists of 1s and 0s; it is machine language.

Source code is the statements you write in a programming language before they are translated to object code.

Object code is machine language statements that have been translated from source code.

A **logical error** occurs when incorrect instructions are performed, or when instructions are performed in the wrong order.

The **logic** of a computer program is developed when you give instructions to the computer in a specific sequence, without leaving any instructions out or adding extraneous instructions.

Semantic errors are logical program errors.

Procedural programming is a technique that focuses on the procedures programmers create to manipulate data.

Object-oriented programming (**OOP**) is a technique that focuses on objects, or "things." OOP describes the objects' features (or attributes) and their behaviors.

An **object** is a "thing" or entity used in an object-oriented program.

The **attributes of an object** are the features it "has."

The **state of an object** is made up of its attributes' values.

The **behaviors of an object** are the things it "does."

An **object-oriented approach** to a problem involves defining the objects needed to accomplish a task and developing the objects so that each maintains its own data and carries out tasks when another object requests them.

Computer simulations attempt to mimic real-world activities so that their processes can be improved or so that users can better understand how the real-world processes operate.

Users (or **end users**) are the people or entities for whom programs are written and who benefit from using them.

A **graphical user interface**, or **GUI** (pronounced *gooey*), allows users to interact with a program in a graphical environment.

Software testers evaluate programs by running them under a variety of conditions.

Black box tests are software tests in which the tester does not know how the software works internally but verifies that correct output is derived from various input values.

White box tests are software tests in which the tester understands how the software works internally.

Object-oriented analysis, or **OOA**, is analyzing a system using an object-oriented approach.

Object-oriented design, or **OOD**, is designing a system using an object-oriented approach.

Relationships describe how objects communicate with and react to each other.

A **class** is a general category of objects.

An **algorithm** is the sequence of steps necessary to solve any problem.

Desk-checking is the process of walking through a program's logic on paper without using a computer.

To **test a program** is to execute it on a computer to determine if the output is correct.

Conversion is the entire set of actions an organization must take to switch over to using a new program or set of programs.

Maintenance is the act of making changes to programs that are already finished and in production.

Pseudocode is an English-like representation of the logical steps it takes to solve a problem.

A **flowchart** is a pictorial representation of the logical steps it takes to solve a problem.

Conventions are standards of format and style that are selected for consistency while acknowledging that other customs might be used by others and be equally as correct.

An **input symbol** in a flowchart contains an input statement and is represented by a parallelogram.

A **processing symbol** in a flowchart contains a processing statement and is represented by a rectangle.

An **output symbol** in a flowchart contains an output statement and is represented by a parallelogram.

An **input/output symbol**, or **I/O symbol**, is a parallelogram used to diagram both input and output operations.

A **terminal symbol** in a flowchart marks the beginning or end of a segment, and is represented by a lozenge.

A **decision symbol** in a flowchart holds a question that allows program logic to follow divergent paths, and is represented by a diamond.

Flowlines are the arrows in a flowchart that show the sequence of steps carried out.

Program comments are nonexecuting statements that you add to a program for the purpose of documentation.

An **annotation symbol** is a flowchart symbol that is used to hold comments; it is represented by a three-sided box connected with a dashed line to the step it explains.

A **text editor** is a program that you use to create simple text files; it is similar to a word processor, but without as many features.

An **integrated development environment** (**IDE**) is a software package that provides an editor, compiler, and other programming tools.

A **command line** is a location on your computer screen at which you type text entries to communicate with the computer's operating system.

Review Questions

1. The two major components of any computer system are its _____.

   a. input and output   c. hardware and software
   b. data and programs   d. memory and disk drives

2. The major computer operations include _____.

   a. hardware and software
   b. input, processing, and output
   c. sequence and looping
   d. spreadsheets, word processing, and data communications

3. Another term meaning "computer instructions" is _____.

   a. hardware   c. queries
   b. software   d. data

4. Visual Basic, C++, and Java are all examples of computer _____.

   a. operating systems   c. machine languages
   b. hardware   d. programming languages

5. A programming language's rules are its _____.

   a. syntax   c. format
   b. logic   d. options

6. The most important task of a compiler or interpreter is to _____.

   a. create the rules for a programming language
   b. translate English statements into a language such as Java
   c. translate programming language statements into machine language
   d. execute machine language programs to perform useful tasks

7. Which of the following terms is most closely related to machine language?

   a. high-level   c. binary language
   b. source code   d. all of the above

8. Which of the following is true about newer programming languages as opposed to older ones?

    a. Newer languages do not require that you understand logic.
    b. Newer languages do not have specific syntax rules.
    c. Programs in newer languages tend to be written as one set of steps instead of being broken into modules.
    d. Newer languages allow you to use reasonable names for memory locations instead of referencing memory addresses.

9. Object-oriented programming focuses most on _____ .

    a. data
    b. objects
    c. procedures
    d. arithmetic

10. The attributes of an object are the things that it _____ .

    a. has
    b. does
    c. influences
    d. understands

11. In object-oriented programming, each object _____ .

    a. maintains its own data
    b. carries out tasks when another object requests them
    c. both of these
    d. none of these

12. Originally, object-oriented programming was used most frequently for two major types of applications. These were _____ .

    a. payroll and inventory
    b. input and storage
    c. computer simulations and graphical user interfaces
    d. public and private applications

13. Identifying all the objects you want to manipulate and how they relate to each other is known as _____ .

    a. object programming
    b. object-oriented design
    c. method manipulation
    d. relating

14. Writing a program in a language such as C++ or Java is known as _____ the program.

    a. translating
    b. coding
    c. interpreting
    d. compiling

15. A compiler would find all of the following programming errors *except* _____ .

    a. the misspelled word *prrint* in a language that includes the word *print*

    b. the use of an *X* for multiplication in a language that instead requires an asterisk

    c. a newBalanceDue calculated by adding a customerPayment to an oldBalanceDue instead of subtracting it

    d. an arithmetic statement written as regularSales + discountedSales = totalSales

16. Two tools that are commonly used for planning a program's logic are _____ .

    a. flowcharts and pseudocode

    b. ASCII and EBCDIC

    c. Java and Visual Basic

    d. word processors and spreadsheets

17. In a flowchart, input is represented by a(n) _____ .

    a. rectangle

    b. arrow

    c. diamond

    d. parallelogram

18. In a flowchart, processing is represented by a(n) _____ .

    a. rectangle

    b. arrow

    c. diamond

    d. parallelogram

19. When you use an IDE instead of a simple text editor to develop a program, _____ .

    a. the logic is more complicated

    b. the logic is simpler

    c. the syntax is different

    d. some help is provided

20. When you write a program that will run in a GUI environment as opposed to a command-line environment, _____ .

    a. the logic is very different

    b. some syntax is different

    c. you do not need to plan the logic

    d. users are more confused

Exercises

1. Which of the following are examples of hardware? Which are examples of software?

    a. Microsoft Word

    b. iTunes

    c. a laser printer

    d. a USB flash drive

    e. a laptop battery

    f. Super Mario Bros. game

    g. Facebook

2. Suppose that Donna has called her friends Carlos and Ramona to ask them over for dinner. Which of the following are similar to syntax errors, and which are like logic errors?

   a. Donna asked Carlos to lunch.

   b. Donna asked Carlos to dinner.

   c. Ramona asked Donna to dinner.

   d. Donna ast Ramona to dinner.

   e. Carlos and Donna are friends.

   f. Carlos and Ramona are friends.

3. Of each of the following pairs of tasks, which one should be completed first?

   a. testing a program or translating a program

   b. developing the logic for a program or coding a program

   c. coding a program or translating a program

   d. translating a program or developing the logic for a program

4. Using pseudocode or a flowchart, develop the logic for a program that accepts a number as input and displays the value that is 10 more than the number.

5. Using pseudocode or a flowchart, develop the logic for a program that accepts two numbers as input and displays the product of the numbers.

6. Using pseudocode or a flowchart, develop the logic for a program that accepts a number as input and displays the number five times.

Case Projects

Case: Cost Is No Object

1. Cost Is No Object is a car rental service that specializes in lending antique and luxury cars to clients on a short-term basis. A typical customer might rent a vintage convertible to transport out-of-town clients to a business meeting, or rent a luxury car to transport a wedding party. The service currently has three employees and ten vehicles that it rents. List the objects, attributes, behaviors, and relationships needed to write a program that could simulate one day's business activity.

Case: Classic Reunions

2. Classic Reunions provides services for organizers of high school class reunions. A typical customer might need help locating former classmates, deciding on a theme, selecting a venue, entertainment, and decorations, and so on. The service currently has two employees. List the objects, attributes, behaviors, and relationships needed to write a program that could simulate serving one client's reunion needs.

Case: The Barking Lot

3. The Barking Lot is a dog boarding facility. It provides boarding for any number of days and additional services such as grooming and walking. The Barking Lot currently has three employees, a list of 40 dog clients, and room to board 8 dogs at any one time. List the objects, attributes, behaviors, and relationships needed to write a program that could simulate one day's business activity.

Up for Discussion

1. Use an Internet search engine to find at least three definitions of object-oriented programming. (Try searching with and without the hyphen in *object-oriented*.) Compare the definitions and compile them into one "best" definition.

2. What is the image of the computer programmer in popular culture? Is the image different in books than in TV shows and movies? Would you like a programmer's image for yourself, and if so, which one?

CHAPTER 2

Applications and Data

In this chapter, you will learn about:

◎ Creating an application class with a `main()` method

◎ Literals, variables, and named constants

◎ Assigning values to variables

◎ Arithmetic operations

◎ Features of good program design

◎ Structure and creating a complete program

Creating an Application Class with a `main()` Method

An **application** is a program that you execute to accomplish some task, such as preparing a paycheck, placing a customer order, or playing a game. In everyday conversation, most people use the term *program* synonymously with *application*. *Application* is short for *application software*, which is software that helps you accomplish tasks.

In purely object-oriented programming languages, such as Java, every statement you make must be part of a class. In other languages, such as C++, you can write programs that contain class objects, yet are not classes themselves. This book will use the "pure view"—that every object-oriented application resides in a class.

 In Chapters 2 through 5, you will learn about application classes; in Chapter 6, you will learn to create classes that are not applications themselves but are used by applications.

Within a class, all actions, or executable statements, must take place within a method. A **method** is a named set of statements that performs some task or group of tasks. Most classes contain methods, although they are not required to do so. Application classes must contain at least one method called the **main method**; they also can contain additional methods. The main method in most programming languages has a name similar to `main()`. If a class contains a `main()` method, then it is an application. If an application contains multiple methods, the `main()` method executes first.

One of the simplest programs you can write is one that displays a message on the screen. Figure 2-1 shows the flowchart and pseudocode for a simple application that displays the word *Hello*.

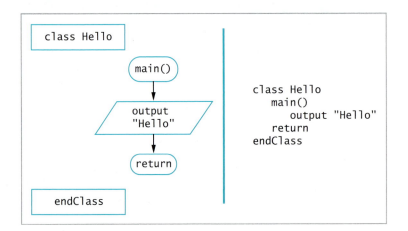

```
class Hello
    main()
        output "Hello"
    return
endClass
```

Figure 2-1   Flowchart and pseudocode for a class with a `main()` method that displays *Hello*

In both the flowchart and pseudocode in Figure 2-1, the class begins with the word `class`, followed by the class name. The class ends with `endClass`. Although no major object-oriented programming language uses the term `endClass`, this book will use it to emphasize where a class ends. As a design tool, flowcharts predate object-oriented programming by many years. Therefore, there is no consistent way to express `class` and `endClass`. This book will follow the convention of showing the class stop and start points in two rectangular boxes, as in Figure 2-1.

A class name can be any legal identifier you choose. An **identifier** is the name of a programming object—for example, a class, method, or variable. Every computer programming language has its own set of rules and conventions for creating identifiers. Identifiers usually conform to the following rules, so they are the conventions used in this book:

- An identifier can contain both letters and digits. Some languages allow hyphens, underscores, dollar signs, or other special characters in identifiers; others allow foreign-alphabet characters such as π or Ω. Most popular languages do not allow an identifier to start with a digit.

- An identifier cannot contain any **white space**, which is space that appears to be "empty"; that is, no spaces, tabs, or line breaks can be embedded between the characters in an identifier.

- When you use an identifier in a programming language, the identifier cannot be a keyword in that language. Each programming language has 80 to 100 reserved **keywords** that are predefined in the language and cannot be used as identifiers. Although different languages contain different keywords, there is a lot of overlap among languages. For example, no matter what language you use, you can be fairly certain that `class`, `if`, and `while` are keywords. When you learn a programming language, you will learn its list of keywords.

- In most modern languages, identifiers are case sensitive, so `Hello`, `hello`, and `HELLO` represent three separate identifiers. The case used in any identifier must be consistent throughout a program.

An individual programming language might have more rules. You must learn the rules for creating identifiers in each programming language you use.

 Identifiers in this text are shown using **camel casing**, a style that increases readability by capitalizing the first letter of new words. The format is so named because identifiers appear to have "humps" in the middle. Class names typically use an initial uppercase letter; this style is known as **upper camel casing** or **Pascal casing**. For example, class names such as `Hello`, `HelloClass`, `DisplayHello`, and `MyHelloClass` are all legal and conventional. Later you will see that other identifiers, such as those for variables and methods, use a style called **lower camel casing** in which identifiers start with a lowercase letter. For example, a variable might use the identifier `firstName`.

When you write a class that displays the word *Hello*, the computer does not care if you call the class `G`, `U84`, or `Fred`. As long as the correct result appears, the name of the class doesn't really matter. However, it's much easier to keep track of classes that have reasonable names. When you look at an application several months after completing it, you and your fellow programmers will appreciate clear, descriptive identifiers.

The first line on each side of Figure 2-1, `class Hello`, is the **class header**. In the last line of the class, `endClass` shows where the class ends. The class header and the `endClass` statement align vertically to show they are a pair—there will always be only one header and one endClass statement for each class. When you learn more about classes in Chapter 7, you will add more information at the start of class headers.

Understanding the `main()` Method

In Figure 2-1, the class contains one method, the `main()` method. An application or executable program must have a class that contains a `main()` method. In Chapter 6, you will learn that classes can have additional methods but that each class can have one `main()` method at most. You will learn in Chapter 7 that not all classes contain a `main()` method, but those that do are executable programs.

The terminal shape in the flowchart in Figure 2-1 and the second line of the pseudocode contain the `main()` **method header**. A set of parentheses always follows a method name; this helps you recognize method names as different from other program elements. Method identifiers must follow the same basic naming rules as class identifiers. That is, they can contain letters and digits, but they must not start with a digit and cannot contain white space. Programmers who use different languages follow different conventions when naming their methods. By convention, most Java and C++ programmers begin their method names with a lowercase letter, but C# and Visual Basic programmers use an uppercase letter to start method names. In this book, method names begin with a lowercase letter to help distinguish them from class names. When multiple words appear in a method header, subsequent words will begin with an uppercase letter for readability. Therefore, `main()`, `computePaycheck()`, and `startTheGame()` are all legal and conventional method headers.

In Chapters 2 through 5 of this book, all classes will have only a `main()` method. When you learn to create additional methods in Chapter 6, you will add more details to method headers, including placing items within their parentheses.

In this book, every method will end with a `return` statement, which is the convention in many programming languages. In most languages, however, methods end normally even if you omit the `return` statement. In some circumstances, you will need to add more information to a method's `return` statement, but nothing else is needed in Figure 2-1. In the flowchart representation of the logic, the `main()` method header and the method's `return` statement appear in lozenges; in the pseudocode, they are vertically aligned to show they are a pair. They are also indented more than the `class` and `endClass` statements, but less than the executable statements in the program. Writing pseudocode with these indentation conventions makes the program easier to read.

Between the `main()` method header and the method's `return` statement, you place all the executable statements of the `main()` method. In this case, the desired action is to output *Hello*.

Watch the video *The `main()` Method.*

Understanding How Programming Languages Reflect Logic

Figures 2-2, 2-3, and 2-4 show how the Hello class looks when implemented in Java, C#, and Visual Basic, respectively. Although these programs contain different and perhaps confusing syntax and punctuation that are not used in the pseudocode in Figure 2-1, see whether you can discern the pieces of code in each language that correspond to each part of the logic.

```
public class Hello
{
    public static void main(String[] args)
    {
        System.out.println("Hello");
    }
}
```

Figure 2-2   The Hello class written in the Java programming language

```
public class Hello
{
    static void Main()
    {
        System.Console.WriteLine("Hello");
    }
}
```

Figure 2-3   The Hello class written in the C# programming language

```
Class Hello
    Sub Main()
        System.Console.WriteLine("Hello")
    End Sub
End Class
```

Figure 2-4   The Hello class written in the Visual Basic programming language

Using Literals, Variables, and Named Constants

As you learned in Chapter 1, data items include all the text, numbers, and other information that are processed by a computer. Data can be input using any number of hardware devices. For example, **interactive programs** frequently ask a user to enter data by typing it from a keyboard or selecting options with a mouse. **Batch programs**, which operate on large quantities of data without human intervention for each record, accept data from a storage device such as a disk.

When you input data items into a computer, they are stored in **variables**, which are named memory locations with contents that can change. Data items stored in memory can be processed and converted to information that is output.

In object-oriented languages, sometimes variables reside within classes but outside any methods, and sometimes they reside within methods. In Chapters 2 through 5, all variables will reside within an application's `main()` method. In Chapter 6, you will add variables to other methods that you create, and in Chapter 7 you will add variables outside of methods (but within a class) that are attributes of class objects.

When you write programs, you work with data in three different forms:

- Literals, or unnamed constants
- Variables
- Named constants

Understanding Unnamed, Literal Constants and their Data Types

Computer programs deal with two basic types of data—text and numeric.

- When you use a specific numeric value, such as 43, within a program, you write it using digits and no quotation marks. A specific numeric value is often called a **numeric constant** (or **literal numeric constant**) because it does not change—43 always has the value 43.

- When you use a specific text value, or string of characters, such as "Amanda", you enclose the **string constant** (or **literal string constant**) within quotation marks. Literal string constants might contain digits, punctuation marks, or other characters. For example, the following is a valid literal string constant that contains letters, digits, punctuation, and spaces:

    "27 Elm St., Iowa City, Iowa"

    The constants 43, "Amanda", and "27 Elm St., Iowa City, Iowa" are examples of **unnamed constants**—they do not have identifiers like variables do, as you will learn in the next section. String values are also called **alphanumeric values** because they can contain alphabetic characters, numbers, and punctuation. Numeric values, however, cannot contain alphabetic characters.

When you store a numeric value in computer memory, additional characters such as dollar signs and commas typically are not input or stored. Those characters can be added to output for readability, but then the output is a string and not a number.

Working with Variables

Variables are named memory locations whose contents can vary or differ over time. For example, consider the number-doubling statements shown in pseudocode in Figure 2-5.

```
input myNumber
myAnswer = myNumber * 2
output myAnswer
```

Figure 2-5   Statements that input a number, double it, and display the results

In Figure 2-5, the statement myAnswer = myNumber * 2 contains the numeric constant 2. The value is constant because it will always be "worth" 2. The other elements in the statement, myAnswer and myNumber, are not constant—they are variables that might hold different values. At any moment in time, a variable holds just one value. Sometimes, myNumber holds 2 and myAnswer holds 4; at other times, myNumber holds 6 and myAnswer holds 12. The ability of memory variables to change in value is what makes computers and programming worthwhile. Because one memory location can be used repeatedly with different values, you can write program instructions once and then use them for thousands of separate calculations. *One* set of payroll instructions at your company produces each employee's paycheck, and *one* set of instructions at your electric company produces each household's bill.

In most programming languages, before you can use any variable, you must include a declaration for it. A **variable declaration** is a statement that provides a data type and an identifier for a variable. A data item's **data type** is a classification that describes the following:

- What values can be held by the item
- How the item is stored in computer memory
- What operations can be performed on the data item

In this book, two data types will be used: num and string. These two types represent the broad data types stored by computers. When you declare a variable, you provide both a data type and an identifier. Optionally, you can declare a starting value for any variable, which is known as **initializing the variable**. For example, each of the following statements is a valid declaration. Two of the statements include initializations, and two do not:

```
num mySalary
num yourSalary = 14.55
string myName
string yourName = "Juanita"
```

Variables must be declared before they are used in a program for the first time. Some languages require all variables to be declared at the beginning of a class or method; others allow variables to be declared anywhere before their first use. This book will follow the convention of declaring all variables together.

Figure 2-6 shows a complete number-doubling program. The start and stop statements begin and end the program. The figure and the rest of the book follow the convention of including a comment before a method's variable declarations so that you can more easily identify them as separate from a method's executable statements. The input, processing, and output statements do the actual work of the program. This program contains no string variables—just two numeric ones. Notice in this program that neither variable needs to be assigned a starting value because the value of the first variable is provided by a user as input, and the value of the second one is calculated after the input value is accepted.

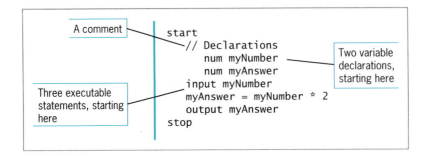

A comment

start
// Declarations
    num myNumber
    num myAnswer
input myNumber
myAnswer = myNumber * 2
output myAnswer
stop

Two variable declarations, starting here

Three executable statements, starting here

Figure 2-6   A complete number-doubling program

In many programming languages, if you declare a variable and do not initialize it, the variable contains an unknown value until it is assigned a value. A variable's unknown value commonly is called **garbage**. In many languages it is illegal to use a garbage-holding variable in an arithmetic statement or to display it as output. Even if you work with a language that allows you to display garbage, it serves no purpose to do so and constitutes a logical error. When you create a variable without assigning it an initial value, your intention is to assign a value later—as in the program in Figure 2-6, by receiving a value as input or assigning a value as the result of a calculation. Although some languages use a default value for some variables (such as assigning 0 to any unassigned numeric variable), this book will assume that an unassigned variable holds garbage.

Naming Variables

The number-doubling statements in Figure 2-6 require two variables: myNumber and myAnswer. Alternatively, these variables could be named userEntry and programSolution, or inputValue and twiceTheValue. As a programmer, you choose reasonable and descriptive names for your variables. The language interpreter then associates the names you choose with specific memory addresses. The names you choose for variables must follow the same general rules that you have learned for naming classes and methods—one-word names that start with a letter and contain no embedded spaces. In many languages, identifiers are case sensitive, so myNumber, Mynumber, and mYnUmBeR are three separate variable names. By convention, variable names in this book will begin with a lowercase letter and use camel casing.

Conventions differ in some languages, and your workplace might have specific naming conventions. Adopting a naming convention for variables and using it consistently will help make your programs easier to read and understand. Variable names should make sense and describe their purpose. For example, myNumber and inputNumber are reasonable identifiers for the number a user inputs, whereas corporationName makes no sense for an input number. Some programmers name variables after friends or create puns with them, but businesspeople consider such behavior unprofessional.

Understanding a Variable's Data Type

Like literals, each variable has a data type.

- A **numeric variable** is one that can hold digits and have mathematical operations performed on it. Also, you usually have the option of letting a numeric variable hold a decimal point and a plus or minus sign, indicating a positive or negative value. In the statement myAnswer = myNumber * 2, both myAnswer and myNumber are numeric variables; that is, their intended contents are numeric values, such as 6 and 3, 14.8 and 7.4, or −18 and −9.

Most programming languages allow for several specific types of numeric data. Languages such as C++, C#, Visual Basic, and Java distinguish between **integer** (whole number) numeric variables and **floating-point** (fractional) numeric variables that contain a decimal point. (Floating-point numbers are also called **real numbers**.) Thus, in some languages, the values 4 and 4.3 would be stored in different types of numeric variables.

- A **string variable** can hold text, such as letters of the alphabet, and other special characters, such as punctuation marks. If a working program contains the statement lastName = "Lincoln", then lastName is a string variable. A string variable also can hold digits either with or without other characters. For example, "235 Main Street" and "86" are both strings. A string like "86" is stored differently than the numeric value 86, and you cannot perform arithmetic with the string.

In object-oriented programming languages, you can create new data types. You will create classes that you can use as complex data types in Chapter 7. If a data item is not the correct type, most languages provide ways for you to convert it to the correct type. Data conversion is known as **type casting**.

You can assign data to a variable only if it is the correct type. If you declare taxRate as a numeric variable and inventoryItem as a string, then the following statements are valid:

```
taxRate = 2.5
inventoryItem = "monitor"
```

The following are invalid because the type of data being assigned does not match the variable type:

```
taxRate = "2.5"
inventoryItem = 2.5
```

> **Don't Do It**
> If taxRate is numeric and inventoryItem is a string, then these assignments are invalid.

In addition to setting a variable to a literal value, you can set it to the value of another variable of the same data type. If taxRate and oldRate are both numeric, and inventoryItem and orderedItem are both strings, then the following are valid:

```
taxRate = oldRate
orderedItem = inventoryItem
```

Declaring Named Constants

Besides variables, most programming languages allow you to create named constants. A **named constant** is similar to a variable, except that it can be assigned a value only once. You use a named constant to assign a useful name to a value that will never be changed during a program's execution. Using named constants makes your programs easier to understand by eliminating magic numbers. A **magic number** is an unnamed constant, like 0.06, whose purpose is not immediately apparent.

For example, if a program uses a sales tax rate of 6 percent, you might want to declare a named constant as follows:

```
num SALES_TAX = 0.06
```

You then might use SALES_TAX in a program statement similar to the following:

```
taxAmount = price * SALES_TAX
```

The way in which named constants are declared differs among programming languages. This book follows the convention of using all uppercase letters in constant identifiers, and using underscores to separate words for readability. These conventions make named constants easier to recognize.

 In many languages, a constant must be assigned its value when it is declared, but in some languages, a constant can be assigned its value later. In both cases, however, a constant's value can never be changed after the first assignment. This book follows the convention of initializing all constants when they are declared.

Declaring a named constant provides several benefits:

- Program maintenance becomes easier. If the value of a constant changes in the future (for example, if the sales tax rate is increased), then you only need to change the value assigned to the named constant at the beginning of the program and all references to it are automatically updated.

- Constant names provide clarity and a type of internal documentation for the program, so there is less chance that someone reading the program will misunderstand what the values represent.

- Using named constants helps prevent typographical errors. When a program with the SALES_TAX constant is written in a programming language and compiled, the translation software will issue an error statement if SALES_TAX is misspelled in the program. If the programmer uses constant numeric values instead and mistakenly types 0.05 instead of 0.06, for example, the compiler will not recognize an error, and incorrect tax amounts will be calculated.

 Sometimes, using unnamed literal constants is appropriate in a program, especially if their meaning is clear to most readers. For example, in a program that calculates half of a value by dividing by two, you might choose to use the literal 2 instead of incurring the extra time and memory costs of creating a named constant HALF and assigning 2 to it. Extra costs that result from adding variables or instructions to a program are known as **overhead**.

Assigning Values to Variables

When you create a flowchart or pseudocode for a program that doubles numbers, you can include a statement such as the following:

```
myAnswer = myNumber * 2
```

Such a statement is an **assignment statement**. This statement incorporates two actions. First, the computer calculates the arithmetic value of myNumber * 2. Second, the computed value is stored in the myAnswer memory location.

The equal sign is the **assignment operator**. The assignment operator is an example of a **binary operator**, meaning it requires two operands—one on each side. (An **operand** is a value that is manipulated by an operator.) The assignment operator always works from right to left; the value of the expression to the right of the operator is evaluated before the assignment to the operand on the left occurs. The operand to the right of an assignment operator can be a value, a formula, a named constant, or a variable. The operand to the left of an assignment operator must be a name that represents a memory address—the name of the location where the result will be stored. An operator that works from right to left, like the assignment operator, has **right-associativity** or **right-to-left associativity**.

For example, if you have declared a numeric variable named someNumber, then each of the following is a valid assignment statement:

```
someNumber = 2
someNumber = 3 + 7
```

Additionally, if you have declared another numeric variable named someOtherNumber and assigned a value to it, then each of the following is a valid assignment statement:

```
someNumber = someOtherNumber
someNumber = someOtherNumber * 5
```

In each case, the expression to the right of the assignment operator is evaluated and stored at the location referenced on the left side.

The following statements, however, are *not* valid:

```
2 + 4 = someNumber
someOtherNumber * 10 = someNumber
```

> **Don't Do It**
> The operand to the left of an assignment operator must represent a memory address.

In each of these cases, the value to the left of the assignment operator is not a memory address, so the statements are invalid. The result to the left of an assignment operator is an **lvalue**. The *l* is for *left*. Lvalues are always memory address identifiers. In other words, an lvalue is a location to which a value can be assigned, so lvalues can never be literal constants. An operand that can be used to the right of an operator is an **rvalue**. Rvalues can be constants, variables, or expressions.

 Watch the video *Literals, Variables, and Named Constants*.

Performing Arithmetic Operations

Most programming languages use the following standard arithmetic operators:

+ (plus sign)—addition

– (minus sign)—subtraction

* (asterisk)—multiplication

/ (slash)—division

Many languages also support operators that calculate the remainder after division (often the percent sign, %) and that raise a number to a higher power (often the carat, ^).

For example, the following statement adds two test scores and assigns the sum to a variable named `totalScore`:

```
totalScore = test1 + test2
```

The following adds 10 to `totalScore` and stores the result in `totalScore`:

```
totalScore = totalScore + 10
```

In other words, this example increases the value of `totalScore`. The last example looks odd in algebra because it might appear to indicate that the value of `totalScore` and `totalScore` plus 10 are equivalent. You must remember that the equal sign is the assignment operator, and that the statement is actually taking the original value of `totalScore`, adding 10 to it, and assigning the result to the memory address on the left of the operator, which is `totalScore`.

In programming languages, you can combine arithmetic statements. When you do, every operator follows **rules of precedence** (also called the **order of operations**) that dictate the order in which operations in the same statement are carried out. The rules of precedence for the basic arithmetic statements are as follows:

- Expressions within parentheses are evaluated first. If there are multiple sets of parentheses, the expression within the innermost parentheses is evaluated first.

- Multiplication and division are evaluated next, from left to right.

- Addition and subtraction are evaluated next, from left to right.

The assignment operator has a very low precedence. Therefore, in a statement such as `d = e * f + g`, the operations on the right of the assignment operator are always performed before the final assignment to the variable on the left.

Many languages support additional operators with specialized functions. When you learn a specific programming language, you will learn about all the operators that can be used in that language. Many programming language books contain a table that specifies the relative precedence of every operator used in the language. However, in all languages, parentheses take precedence over arithmetic operators, and multiplication and division take precedence over addition and subtraction.

For example, consider the following two arithmetic statements:

```
firstAnswer = 2 + 3 * 4
secondAnswer = (2 + 3) * 4
```

After these statements execute, the value of `firstAnswer` is 14. According to the rules of precedence, multiplication is carried out before addition, so 3 is multiplied by 4, giving 12, and then 2 and 12 are added, and 14 is assigned to `firstAnswer`. The value of secondAnswer, however, is 20, because the parentheses force the contained addition operation to be performed first. The 2 and 3 are added to produce 5, and then 5 is multiplied by 4, producing 20.

Forgetting about the rules of arithmetic precedence, or forgetting to add parentheses when you need them, can cause logical errors that are difficult to find in programs. For example, the following statement might appear to average two test scores:

```
average = score1 + score2 / 2
```

However, it does not. Because division has a higher precedence than addition, the preceding statement takes half of score2, adds it to score1, and stores the result in average. The correct statement is:

```
average = (score1 + score2) / 2
```

You are free to add parentheses even when you don't need them to force a different order of operations; sometimes you use them just to make your intentions clearer. For example, the following statements operate identically:

```
totalPriceWithTax = price + price * TAX_RATE
totalPriceWithTax = price + (price * TAX_RATE)
```

In both cases, price is multiplied by TAX_RATE first, then the result is added to price, and finally the result is stored in totalPriceWithTax. Because multiplication occurs before addition on the right side of the assignment operator, both statements are the same. However, if you think the statement with the parentheses makes your intentions clearer to someone reading your program, then you should use them.

All the arithmetic operators have **left-to-right associativity**. This means that operations with the same precedence take place from left to right. Consider the following statement:

```
answer = a + b + c * d / e - f
```

Multiplication and division have higher precedence than addition or subtraction, so the multiplication and division are carried out from left to right as follows:

c is multiplied by d, and the result is divided by e, giving a new result.

Therefore, the statement becomes:

```
answer = a + b + (temporary result just calculated) - f
```

Then, addition and subtraction are carried out from left to right as follows:

a and b are added, the temporary result is added, and then f is subtracted. The final result is then assigned to answer.

Another way to say this is that the following two statements are equivalent:

```
answer = a + b + c * d / e - f
answer = a + b + ((c * d) / e) - f
```

Table 2-1 summarizes the precedence and associativity of the five most frequently used operators.

Operator symbol	Operator name	Precedence (compared to other operators in this table)	Associativity
*	Multiplication	Highest	Left-to-right
/	Division	Highest	Left-to-right
+	Addition	Medium	Left-to-right
–	Subtraction	Medium	Left-to-right
=	Assignment	Lowest	Right-to-left

Table 2-1   Precedence and associativity of five common operators

 Watch the video *Arithmetic Operations.*

Features of Good Program Design

As your programs become larger and more complicated, the need for good planning and design increases. Think of an application you use, such as a word processor or a spreadsheet. The number and variety of user options are staggering. Not only would it be impossible for a single programmer to write such an application, but without thorough planning and design, the components would never work together properly. Such programs do not just contain a main() method; they contain dozens or even hundreds of methods. Just as a house with poor plumbing or a car with bad brakes is fatally flawed, a computer-based application can be highly functional only if each component is designed well. Walking through your program's logic on paper (called desk-checking, as you learned in Chapter 1) is an important step toward achieving superior programs. Additionally, you can implement several design features that can make programs easier to write and maintain:

- Use program comments where appropriate.
- Choose identifiers thoughtfully.
- Strive to design clear statements within your programs.
- Write clear prompts and echo input.
- Continue to maintain good programming habits as you develop your programming skills.

Using Program Comments

When you write programs, you often might want to insert program comments. In Chapter 1, you learned that program comments are written explanations that are not part of the program logic but serve as documentation for readers of the program. Program comments are a type of **internal documentation**. Internal documentation describes explanations and clarifications that appear within the same document as the program's source code. Supporting documents outside the program are called **external documentation**.

Including program comments is not necessary to create a working program, but comments can help you to remember the purpose of variables or to explain complicated calculations. Some students do not like to include comments in their programs because it takes time to type them and they aren't part of the "real" program, but the programs you write in the future will require some comments. When you acquire your first programming job and modify a program written by another programmer, you will appreciate well-placed comments that explain complicated sections of the code.

You probably will use program comments in your coded programs more frequently than you use them in pseudocode or flowcharts. For one thing, flowcharts and pseudocode are more English-like than the code in some languages, so your statements might be less cryptic. Also, your comments will remain in the program as part of the program documentation, but your planning tools are likely to be discarded once the program goes into production. A drawback to comments is that they must be kept current as a program is modified. Outdated comments can provide misleading information about a program's status.

Choosing Identifiers

The selection of good identifiers is an often overlooked element in program design. When you write programs, you choose identifiers for variables, constants, methods, and classes. Choosing good names for these components simplifies your programming job and makes it easier for others to understand your work.

Some general guidelines include the following:

- Although not required in any programming language, it usually makes sense to give a variable or constant a name that is a noun (or a combination of an adjective and noun) because it represents a thing. Similarly, it makes sense to give a method an identifier that is a verb, or a combined verb and noun, because a method takes action. (The main() method is an exception to this rule.)

- Use meaningful names. Creating a data item named someData or a class named Class2 makes a program cryptic. Not only will others find it hard to read your programs, but you will forget the purpose of these identifiers even within your own programs. All programmers occasionally use short, nondescriptive names such as x or temp in a quick program; however, in most cases, method and class names should be meaningful. Programmers refer to programs that contain meaningful names as **self-documenting**. This means that even without further documentation, the program code explains itself to readers.

- Use pronounceable names whenever possible. A variable name like pzf is neither pronounceable nor meaningful. A name that looks meaningful when you write it might not be as meaningful when someone else reads it; for instance, preparead() might mean "Prepare ad" to you, but "Prep a read" to others. Look at your names critically to make sure they can be pronounced. Very standard abbreviations do not have to be pronounceable. For example, most businesspeople would interpret ssn as Social Security number.

- Don't forget that not all programmers share your culture. An abbreviation whose meaning seems obvious to you might be cryptic to someone in a different part of the world.

- Be judicious in your use of abbreviations. You can save a few keystrokes when creating a class called St, but does it represent a state, a saint, a street, or a statistic? Similarly, is a variable named fn meant to hold a first name, file number, or something else?

To save typing time when you develop a program, you can use a short name like efn. After the program operates correctly, you can use a text editor's Search and Replace feature to replace your coded name with a more meaningful name such as employeeFirstName.

Many IDEs support an automatic statement-completion feature that saves typing time. After the first time you use a name like employeeFirstName, you need to type only the first few letters before the compiler editor offers a list of available names from which to choose. The list is constructed from all the names you have used that begin with the same characters.

- Usually, avoid digits in a name. Zeroes get confused with the letter O, and the lowercase letter *l* is misread as the numeral 1. Of course, use your judgment: budgetFor2014 probably will not be misinterpreted.

- Use the system your language allows to separate words in long, multiword identifiers. For example, if the programming language you use allows underscores, then a class name like My_first_application is easier to read than Myfirstapplication. If you use a language that is case sensitive, it is legal but confusing to use identifiers that differ only in case. For example, if a single program contains empName, EmpName, and Empname, confusion is sure to follow.

- Consider including a form of the verb *to be*, such as *is* or *are*, in names for variables that are intended to hold a status. For example, use isFinished as a variable that holds a "Y" or "N" to indicate whether an input file is exhausted. The shorter name finished is more likely to be confused with a method that executes when a program is done. Many languages support a Boolean data type, which you assign to variables meant to hold only true or false. Using a form of *to be* in identifiers for Boolean variables is appropriate.

- Many programmers follow the convention of naming constants using all uppercase letters, inserting underscores between words for readability. For example, WITHHOLDING_RATE is a conventional constant name. As mentioned earlier, this convention is used in the book.

- Organizations sometimes enforce different rules for programmers to follow when naming variables. It is your responsibility to learn the conventions used in your organization and adhere to them.

Programmers sometimes create a **data dictionary**, which is a list of every variable name used in a program, along with its type, size, and description. When a data dictionary is created, it becomes part of the program documentation.

When you begin to write programs, the process of determining what classes, methods, variables, and constants you need and what to name them might seem overwhelming. The design process is crucial, however. When you acquire your first professional programming assignment, the design process might very well be completed already. Most likely, your first assignment will be to write or modify one small member method of a much larger application. The more the original programmers stuck to these guidelines, the better the original design was, and the easier your modifications will be.

Designing Clear Statements

In addition to using program comments and selecting good identifiers, you can use the following tactics to contribute to the clarity of statements within your programs:

- Avoid confusing line breaks.
- Use temporary variables to clarify long statements.

Avoiding Confusing Line Breaks

Some older programming languages require that program statements be placed in specific columns. Most modern programming languages are free-form; you can arrange your lines of code any way you see fit. As in real life, with freedom comes responsibility; when you have flexibility in arranging your lines of code, you must make sure your meaning is clear. With free-form code, programmers are allowed to place two or three statements on a line, but this makes programs harder to read. Programmers also can spread a single statement across multiple lines, which can make a program easier to read because the reader does not have to scroll horizontally to view the complete statement when displayed on a screen. All the pseudocode examples in this book use appropriate, clear spacing and line breaks.

Using Temporary Variables to Clarify Long Statements

When you need several mathematical operations to determine a result, consider using a series of temporary variables to hold intermediate results. A **temporary variable** (or a **work variable**) is not used for input or output, but instead is just a working variable that you use during a program's execution. For example, Figure 2-7 shows two ways to calculate a value for a real estate salespersonCommission variable. Each pseudocode segment achieves the same result—the salesperson's commission is based on the square feet multiplied by the price per square foot, plus any premium for a lot with special features, such as woods or waterfront access. However, the second example uses two temporary variables: basePropertyPrice and totalSalePrice. When the computation is broken down into less complicated, individual steps, it is easier to see how the total sale price is part of the commission calculation. In calculations with even more computation steps, performing the arithmetic in stages would become increasingly helpful.

```
// Using a single statement to compute commission
salespersonCommission = (sqFeet * pricePerFoot + lotPremium) *
    commissionRate

// Using multiple statements to compute commission
basePropertyPrice = sqFeet * pricePerFoot
totalSalePrice = basePropertyPrice + lotPremium
salespersonCommission = totalSalePrice * commissionRate
```

Figure 2-7   Two ways of achieving the same `salespersonCommission` result

Another advantage to breaking a calculation into steps is that, if your final result is incorrect, you can display the temporary results after each step to help pinpoint the problem with the equation.

Programmers might say using temporary variables, like the second example in Figure 2-7, is *cheap*. When executing a lengthy arithmetic statement, even if you don't explicitly name temporary variables, the programming language compiler creates them behind the scenes (although without descriptive names), so declaring them yourself does not cost much in terms of program execution time.

Writing Clear Prompts and Echoing Input

When you write an interactive program that accepts user input, you almost always want to provide prompts. A **prompt** is a message that asks the user for a response and perhaps explains how that response should be formatted. Prompts are used both in command-line and GUI interactive programs. Prompts might appear on the user's screen, but prompts might also be spoken to the user from the computer's speaker system.

For example, suppose that a program asks a user to enter a catalog number for an item the user is ordering. The following prompt is not very helpful:

`Please enter a number.`

The following prompt is more helpful:

`Please enter a five-digit catalog order number.`

The following prompt might be even more helpful:

`The five-digit catalog order number appears to the right of the item's picture`
`in the catalog. Please enter it now.`

When program input comes from a stored file instead of a user, prompts are not needed. However, when a program expects a user response, prompts are valuable. For example, Figure 2-8 shows the flowchart and pseudocode for the beginning of a `main()` method that requires a name and balance as input data. If the input was coming from a data file, no prompt would be required, and the logic might look like that in Figure 2-8.

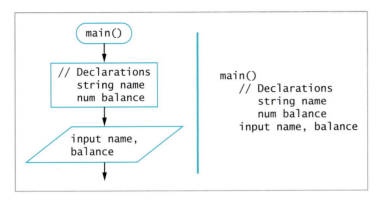

Figure 2-8 Beginning of a program that accepts a name and balance as input

However, if the input was coming from a user, including prompts would be helpful. You could supply a single prompt such as *Please enter a customer's name and balance due*, but inserting more requests into a prompt generally makes it less likely that the user can remember to enter all the parts or enter them in the correct order. It is almost always best to include a separate prompt for each item to be entered. Figure 2-9 shows an example.

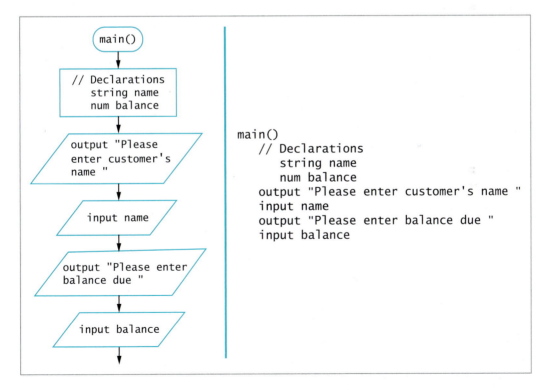

Figure 2-9 Beginning of a program that accepts a name and balance as input and uses a separate prompt for each item

Users also find it helpful when you echo their input. **Echoing input** is the act of repeating input back to a user either in a subsequent prompt or in output. For example, Figure 2-10 shows how the second prompt in Figure 2-9 can be improved by echoing the user's first piece of input data. When a user runs the program that is started in Figure 2-10 and enters *Green* for the customer name, the second prompt will not be *Please enter balance due.* Instead, it will be *Please enter balance due for Green.* For example, if a clerk was about to enter the balance for the wrong customer, the mention of *Green* might be enough to alert the clerk to the potential error.

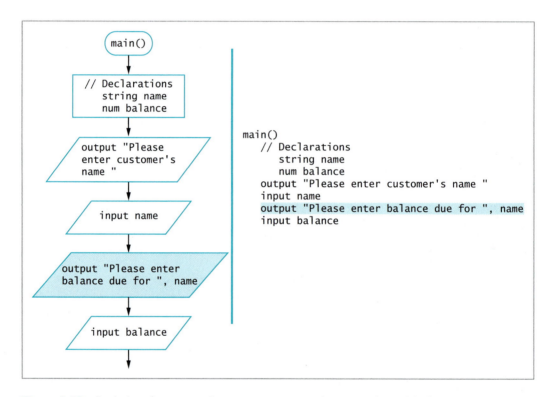

Figure 2-10   Beginning of a program that accepts a customer's name and uses it in the second prompt

In Figure 2-10, notice the space before each ending quotation mark in the two output statements. Each space makes the output more readable by separating the constant output from the last name.

Maintaining Good Programming Habits

When you learn a programming language and begin to write lines of program code, it is easy to forget the principles you have learned in this text. Having some programming knowledge and a keyboard at your fingertips can lure you into typing lines of code before you think things through. But every program you write will be better if you plan before you code.

Maintaining the habit of first drawing flowcharts or writing pseudocode, as you have learned here, will make your future programming projects go more smoothly. If you desk-check your program logic on paper before coding statements in a programming language, your programs will run correctly sooner. If you think carefully about the identifiers you choose, and design program statements to be easy to read and use, your programs will be easier to develop and maintain. Additionally, clear and correct programs adhere to rules of structure, as you will learn in the next section.

An Introduction to Structure

A **structure** is a basic unit of programming logic. The instructions contained in every method of every application are created using combinations of three structures. Each structure is one of the following:

- sequence
- selection
- loop

Figure 2-11 shows these structures. Some methods contain examples of all three types of structures; others contain only one or two. Any number of each of these structures might appear in any order within a method, and with these three structures alone, you can diagram any task, from doubling a number to performing brain surgery. You can diagram each structure with a specific configuration of flowchart symbols or describe it with pseudocode.

The simplest of these three basic structures is a sequence, as shown at the left side of Figure 2-11. With a **sequence structure**, you perform an action or task, and then you perform the next action, in order. A sequence can contain any number of tasks, but there is no option of branching to skip or repeat any of the tasks. (In other words, a flowchart or pseudocode that describes a sequence structure never contains a decision.) Once you start a series of actions in a sequence, you must continue step by step until the sequence ends.

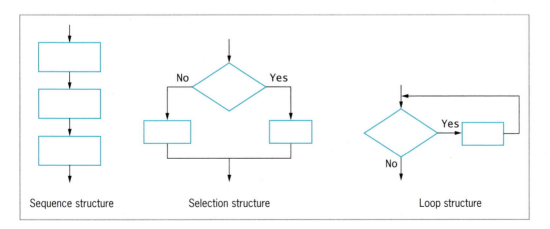

Sequence structure   Selection structure   Loop structure

Figure 2-11   The three structures

As an example, driving directions often are listed as a sequence. For example, to tell a friend how to get to your house from school, you might provide the following sequence, in which one step follows the other and no steps can be skipped:

```
go north on First Avenue for 3 miles
turn left on Washington Boulevard
go west on Washington for 2 miles
stop at 634 Washington
```

The other two structures shown in Figure 2-11 require decisions. In the **selection structure**, one of two branches of logic is followed based on a decision, and in the **loop structure**, instructions repeat based on a decision. You will learn much more about them in Chapters 3 and 4.

Figure 2-12 shows a flowchart for a complete application class. The class contains a `main()` method that contains only a sequence structure. The program determines an employee's net pay, which is calculated by multiplying the employee's hours worked by a standard pay rate and then subtracting a standard withholding percentage. The figure uses comments to point out many of the elements of logic and design you learned about in this chapter. You can use this figure as an example of good programming style. Figure 2-13 shows a typical execution of the program in a command-line environment.

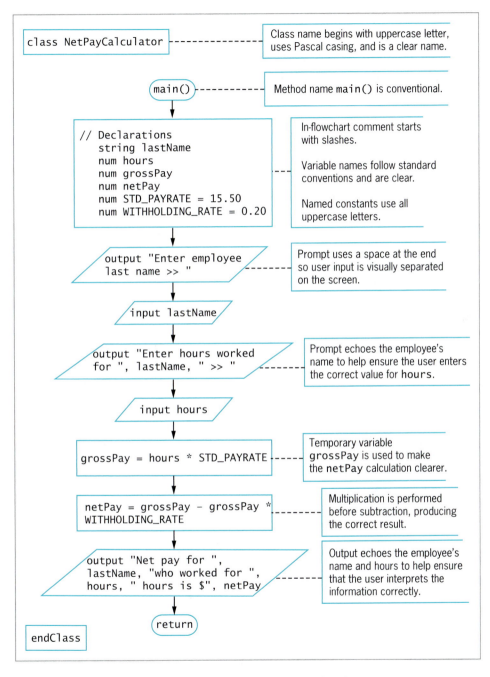

Figure 2-12   Flowchart of the NetPayCalculator application class

```
Command Prompt                                          □ ▣ X
Enter employee last name >> Bennett
Enter hours worked for Bennett >> 20
Net pay for Bennett who worked for 20 hours is $248.00
```

Figure 2-13   Typical execution of the `NetPayCalculator` program

 Watch the video *Understanding Structure*.

Chapter Summary

- An application is a program that accomplishes some task. In every object-oriented programming language, all of an application's actions must take place within a method. In most object-oriented languages, if a class contains only one method that executes, it is called the main method. Classes and methods require identifiers. Every computer programming language has its own set of rules and conventions for naming identifiers, but identifiers typically start with a letter and contain no spaces.

- Data values are stored as literals, variables, and named constants. Each of these can be numeric or a string. Variables are named memory locations whose contents can vary or differ over time. A declaration is a statement that provides a data type and an identifier for a variable. A data item's data type describes the values that can be held in the data item, the amount of memory it occupies, and the types of operations that can be performed with it. A named constant is similar to a variable, except that it can be assigned a value only once.

- The equal sign is the assignment operator; it is used in an assignment statement. The assignment operator has right-to-left associativity.

- Most programming languages use +, −, *, and / as the four standard arithmetic operators. Every operator follows rules of precedence that dictate the order in which operations in the same statement are carried out; multiplication and division always take precedence over addition and subtraction. The rules of precedence can be overridden by using parentheses.

- As your programs become larger and more complicated, the need for good planning and design increases. You should use program comments where appropriate. Choose identifiers wisely, strive to design clear statements within your programs, write clear prompts and echo input, and continue to maintain good programming habits as you develop your programming skills.

- A structure is a basic unit of programming logic; each structure is a sequence, selection, or loop. With these three structures alone, you can diagram any task. The simplest of these three basic structures is a sequence that performs tasks in order with no decisions or branches.

Key Terms

An **application** is a program that you execute to accomplish some task.

A **method** is a named set of statements that performs some task or group of tasks within an application.

The **main method** is an application's primary method.

An **identifier** is the name of a programming object such as a class, method, or variable.

White space describes any character that appears to be empty, such as a space or tab.

Keywords constitute the limited word set that is reserved in a language.

Camel casing is the format for naming identifiers in which multiple-word names are run together, and each new word within the identifier begins with an uppercase letter.

Upper camel casing is the format for naming identifiers in which the initial letter is uppercase, multiple-word names are run together, and each new word within the identifier begins with an uppercase letter. Also called *Pascal casing*.

Pascal casing is the format for naming identifiers in which the initial letter is uppercase, multiple-word names are run together, and each new word within the identifier begins with an uppercase letter. Also called *upper camel casing*.

Lower camel casing is the format for naming identifiers in which the initial letter is lowercase, multiple-word names are run together, and each new word within the identifier begins with an uppercase letter.

A **class header** starts a class; it contains the word `class` and an identifier.

A **method header** starts a method. It contains an identifier followed by parentheses.

Interactive programs execute with frequent intervention from a user with an input device such as a keyboard or a mouse.

Batch programs execute on large quantities of data without human intervention for each record; they accept data from a storage device such as a disk.

Variables are named memory locations whose contents can vary or differ over time.

A **numeric constant** (or **literal numeric constant**) is a specific numeric value.

A **string constant** (or **literal string constant**) is a specific group of characters enclosed within quotation marks.

An **unnamed constant** is a literal numeric or string value.

Alphanumeric values can contain alphabetic characters, numbers, and punctuation.

A **variable declaration** is a statement that provides a data type and identifier for a variable.

A **data type** describes what values can be held by an item, how the item is stored in computer memory, and what operations can be performed on the data item.

To **initialize a variable** is to provide a first value for it.

Garbage describes the unknown values that reside in variables that have not been initialized.

A **numeric variable** is one that can hold digits, have mathematical operations performed on it, and usually can hold a decimal point and a plus or minus sign, indicating a positive or negative value.

An **integer** is a whole number.

A **floating-point** number is a number with decimal places.

Real numbers are floating-point numbers.

A **string variable** can hold text that includes letters, digits, and special characters such as punctuation marks.

Type casting is the act of converting data from one type to another.

A **named constant** is similar to a variable, except that its value cannot change after the first assignment.

A **magic number** is an unnamed constant whose purpose is not immediately apparent.

Overhead describes the extra resources a task requires.

An **assignment statement** assigns a value from the right of an assignment operator to the variable or constant on the left of the assignment operator.

The **assignment operator** is the equal sign; it is used to assign a value to the variable or constant on its left.

A **binary operator** is an operator that requires two operands—one on each side.

An **operand** is a value that is manipulated by an operator.

Right-associativity and **right-to-left associativity** describe operators that evaluate the expression to the right first.

An **lvalue** is the memory address identifier to the left of an assignment operator.

An **rvalue** is an operand to the right of an assignment operator.

Rules of precedence dictate the order in which operations in the same statement are carried out.

The **order of operations** describes the rules of precedence.

Left-to-right associativity describes operators that evaluate the expression to the left first.

Internal documentation is documentation within a coded program that helps explain the meaning and purpose of program elements.

External documentation is documentation that is outside a coded program in separate documents.

Self-documenting programs contain meaningful data, method, and class names that describe their purposes.

A **data dictionary** is a list of every variable name used in a program, along with its type, size, and description.

A **temporary variable** (or a **work variable**) is a working variable that you use to hold intermediate results during a program's execution.

A **prompt** is a message that is displayed on a monitor to ask the user for a response and perhaps explain how that response should be formatted.

Echoing input is the act of repeating input back to a user either in a subsequent prompt or in output.

A **structure** is a basic unit of programming logic.

A **sequence structure** contains steps that execute in order with no option of branching to skip or repeat any of the tasks.

A **selection structure** contains a decision in which the logic can break in one of two paths.

A **loop structure** repeats instructions based on a decision.

Review Questions

1. Which of the following is true in object-oriented programming?
    a. All classes are applications.
    b. All applications are system applications.
    c. All applications are programs.
    d. All classes contain multiple methods.

2. In object-oriented programming, a main method _____.
    a. is automatically created by the compiler
    b. is the name of the method that executes first in an application
    c. is the method that does most of the work or contains the most instructions
    d. exists in every class

3. In object-oriented programming, the identifier for a class, method, or variable _____.
    a. always uses all lowercase letters
    b. always begins with a lowercase letter
    c. can contain white space
    d. none of the above

4. A set of parentheses always follows a _____ .

   a. method name   c. variable name

   b. class name   d. all of the above

5. Which of the following is a literal numeric constant?

   a. 12   c. "fourteen"

   b. `myNumber`   d. all of the above

6. What does a declaration provide for a variable?

   a. a name   c. both of the above

   b. a data type   d. none of the above

7. A variable's data type describes all of the following *except* _____ .

   a. what values the variable can hold

   b. how the variable is stored in memory

   c. what operations can be performed with the variable

   d. the parts of the program in which the variable can be used

8. In many languages, the value stored in an uninitialized variable is _____ .

   a. garbage   c. compost

   b. null   d. its identifier

9. The value "house" is a _____ .

   a. numeric variable   c. string variable

   b. numeric constant   d. string constant

10. If `size` has been declared to be a string variable, which of the following is legal?

   a. `size = 6`   c. `size = "6"`

   b. `size = "six"`   d. two of the above

11. Which of the following statements is true if a declaration has been made as follows:
`num count`

   a. `count` is an initialized variable

   b. `count` is a numeric variable

   c. `count` is a literal

   d. all of the above

12. Which of the following statements is true if a declaration has been made as follows:
`num count = 9`

   a. `count` is an uninitialized variable   c. `count` is a literal

   b. `count` is a numeric variable   d. all of the above

13. The assignment operator _____ .

    a. is a binary operator

    b. has left-to-right associativity

    c. is most often represented by a colon

    d. two of the above

14. Which of the following is true about arithmetic precedence?

    a. Multiplication has higher precedence than division.

    b. Operators with the lowest precedence always have left-to-right associativity.

    c. Division has higher precedence than subtraction.

    d. all of the above

15. Which of the following evaluates to 10?

    a. 3 + 5 * 2

    b. 5 + 20 / 4

    c. 25 / 2 + 3

    d. all of the above

16. What is the value of the expression 8 − 4 * 6 / 4?

    a. 2

    b. 4

    c. 6

    d. 8

17. Program comments are _____ .

    a. required to create an executable program

    b. a form of external documentation

    c. both of the above

    d. none of the above

18. Which of the following is valid advice for naming variables?

    a. To save typing, make most variable names one or two letters.

    b. To avoid conflict with names that others are using, use unusual or unpronounceable names.

    c. To make names easier to read, separate long phrases by using underscores or capitalization for each new word.

    d. To maintain your independence, shun the conventions of your organization.

19. A message that asks a user for input is a _____ .

    a. comment

    b. prompt

    c. echo

    d. declaration

20. Which of the following is a list of the three structures used in structured programming?

    a. sequence, skip, and go

    b. selection, choice, and if-then

    c. sequence, selection, and loop

    d. selection, loop, and method

Exercises

1. Using this book's conventions, identify each of the following as a class, method, or variable name:

   a. calculateInsurancePremium()   e. InsuranceRequirements

   b. premium   f. deductPremium()

   c. premiumValue   g. clientAge

   d. paymentAmount

2. Explain why each of the following names does or does not seem like a good variable name to you.

   a. p

   b. product

   c. productNumber

   d. product number

   e. pdtnbr

   f. sevenDigitProductNumberAssignedByManufacturer

   g. productionFor2014

   h. 2014Production

3. If deposit and rent are numeric variables, and landlordName is a string variable, which of the following statements are valid assignments? If a statement is not valid, explain why not.

   a. deposit = 200   j. landlordName = Garvey

   b. rent = deposit   k. landlordName = "Garvey"

   c. rent = landlordName   l. landlordName = 500

   d. rent = "landlordName"   m. landlordName = "500"

   e. 850 = rent   n. landlordName = rent * 100

   f. deposit = 150.50   o. landlordName = "deposit"

   g. deposit = rent * 0.33   p. 500 = landlordName

   h. deposit = landlordName   q. "Cooper" = landlordName

   i. landlordName = rent

4. Assume that `dependents` = 2 and `yearsOnJob` = 5. What is the value of each of the following expressions?

    a. `dependents + yearsOnJob * 3`

    b. `10 + dependents * yearsOnJob`

    c. `(yearsOnJob + 4) * dependents`

    d. `4 - 3 * 2 + dependents`

    e. `dependents * ((yearsOnJob - 1) * 4) - 6`

5. Draw the flowchart or write the pseudocode for an application that allows a user to enter the price of an item and computes 8 percent sales tax on the item.

6. Draw the flowchart or write the pseudocode for an application that allows a user to enter the number of text messages he or she sent last month and then displays the bill. Messages cost 25 cents each, and 9 percent tax is charged on the total.

7. Draw the flowchart or write the pseudocode for an application that allows a user to enter credits earned for the fall, spring, and summer semesters and then displays the total for the year.

8. Draw the flowchart or write the pseudocode for an application that allows a bowler to enter scores for three bowling games and then displays the numeric average.

9. Draw the flowchart or write the pseudocode for an application that allows a user to enter an automobile loan balance. Assume that the user pays 1/36 of the balance each month, and display the new balance after one month and after two months.

Case Projects

 ## Case: *Cost Is No Object*

1. In Chapter 1, you thought about the objects needed for programs for Cost Is No Object—a car rental service that specializes in lending antique and luxury cars to clients on a short-term basis. One required application is a program that calculates customer bills. This month, cars are being rented for $35 per day, with a 9 percent tax applied. Draw a flowchart or write pseudocode for a program that accepts a client's name, the type of car the client wants to rent, and the number of rental days needed. Output the client's bill, including the name, type of car, number of days, total due before tax, tax, and total due with tax.

Case: Classic Reunions

2.   In Chapter 1, you thought about the objects needed for programs for Classic Reunions—a company that provides services for organizers of high school class reunions. One required program must be able to estimate the cost of a reunion event per person. This month, the company is charging $200 per hour for renting its on-site party room, $350 for its house band for the evening, and $40 a plate for dinner. Develop the logic for an application that accepts the number of guests expected for an event and the number of hours for the party as input, then calculates and outputs the total cost for the event as well as the cost per person.

Case: The Barking Lot

3.   In Chapter 1, you thought about the objects needed for programs for The Barking Lot—a dog boarding facility. One required program must be able to estimate profits for a day. The facility can board eight dogs at a time; it charges $25 a day for dogs that weigh more than 50 pounds and $20 a day for smaller dogs. The facility's expenses include $2 per day per dog for food (no matter the size of the dog), and $30 per day for utilities. Develop the logic for a program that allows a user to enter the number of large dogs boarded; assume that the rest are small dogs and that the facility is full. Output is the total revenue collected for the day, total expenses, and the difference.

Up for Discussion

1.   Many programming style guides are published on the Web. These guides suggest good identifiers, explain standard indentation rules, and identify style issues in specific programming languages. Find style guides for at least two languages (for example, C++, Java, Visual Basic, or C#) and list any differences you notice.

2.   What advantages are there to requiring variables to have a data type?

3.   Would you prefer to write a large program by yourself, or work on a team in which each programmer produces one or more methods? Why?

4.   Extreme programming is a system for rapidly developing software. One of its tenets is that all production code is written by two programmers sitting at one machine. Is this a good idea? Does working this way as a programmer appeal to you? Why or why not?

CHAPTER 3

Making Decisions

In this chapter, you will learn about:

- ◎ Evaluating Boolean expressions
- ◎ Relational comparison operators
- ◎ AND logic
- ◎ OR logic
- ◎ Making selections within ranges
- ◎ Precedence when combining AND and OR selections

Evaluating Boolean Expressions

People frequently think computers are smart because computer programs have the ability to make decisions. A medical diagnosis program that can decide if your symptoms fit various disease profiles seems quite intelligent, as does a program that can offer different potential driving routes based on your destination.

The selection structure (sometimes called a decision structure) is one of the basic structures you learned about in Chapter 2. You use a selection structure when a program's logic should take one of two paths based on a decision. This selection structure is also called an **if-then-else structure** because of the language used when describing it. For example, if you were giving a friend directions to your house, you might include a decision that the friend must make during the trip using the words *if*, *then*, and *else*:

```
go north on Third Street
if Ninth Avenue is closed for repairs then
    continue to Tenth Avenue and turn left
else
    turn left on Ninth Avenue
endif
turn right on Sixth Street
```

In these directions, the question of whether Ninth Avenue is closed for repairs is a **Boolean expression**—an expression whose value can be only true or false. That is, either Ninth Avenue is closed for repairs or it isn't. Every decision you make in a computer program involves evaluating a Boolean expression while the program executes. True/false evaluation is "natural" from a computer's standpoint, because computer circuitry consists of two-state on-off switches, often represented by 1 or 0. Every computer decision yields a true-or-false, yes-or-no, 1-or-0 result.

George Boole was a mathematician who lived from 1815 to 1864. He approached logic more simply than his predecessors did, by expressing logical selections with common algebraic symbols. He is considered the founder of mathematical logic, and Boolean (true/false) expressions are named for him.

Figure 3-1 shows how a selection structure looks in both flowchart and pseudocode formats. In the flowchart, you can see that when a question is asked, the logic takes one of two paths based on the answer, and then, no matter which path was taken, the logic continues. In the pseudocode, the word if starts the selection, and the action that should be taken when the tested Boolean expression is **true** is indented. The word **else** aligns with **if**, and the action that is taken when the Boolean expression is **false** follows. In pseudocode, an **endif** statement is used to clearly show where the structure ends. The choices in a selection structure are mutually exclusive; that is, the logic can flow only to one of the two alternatives, never to both. When different actions occur based on the tested Boolean value, the structure can be called a **dual-alternative selection**.

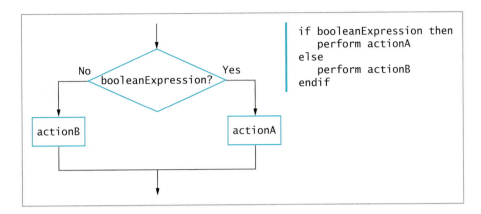

if booleanExpression then
    perform actionA
else
    perform actionB
endif

Figure 3-1 The selection structure

This book follows the convention that the two logical paths emerging from a decision in a flowchart are drawn to the right and left of a diamond, and that the *yes*, or *true*, logical path proceeds to the right. Some programmers might draw one of the flowlines emerging from the bottom of the diamond, or make the *yes* path go to the left. The exact format of the diagram is not as important as the idea that one logical path flows into a selection and two possible outcomes emerge.

Figure 3-2 shows an example of a **single-alternative selection** in which action is required for only one outcome of the question. You call this form of the selection structure an **if-then**, because no alternative or else action is necessary.

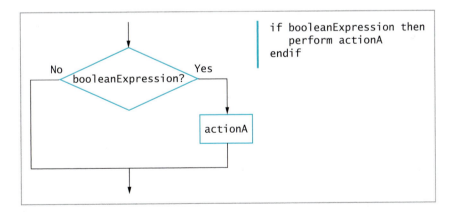

if booleanExpression then
    perform actionA
endif

Figure 3-2 The single-alternative selection structure

For example, the directions to your house might include a single-alternative selection, as in the following:

```
if the grocery store on the corner is open then
    stop and pick up some potato chips
endif
```

In this example, there is no action to be taken if the tested expression is false. A single-alternative selection can always be expressed as a dual-alternative selection. For example:

```
if the grocery store on the corner is open then
    stop and pick up some potato chips
else
    do nothing
endif
```

Figure 3-3 shows the flowchart and pseudocode for a program that contains a typical if-then-else decision in a business program. Many organizations pay employees time and a half (one and one-half times their usual hourly rate) for hours worked in excess of 40 per week. The program decides whether the employee qualifies for the extra pay.

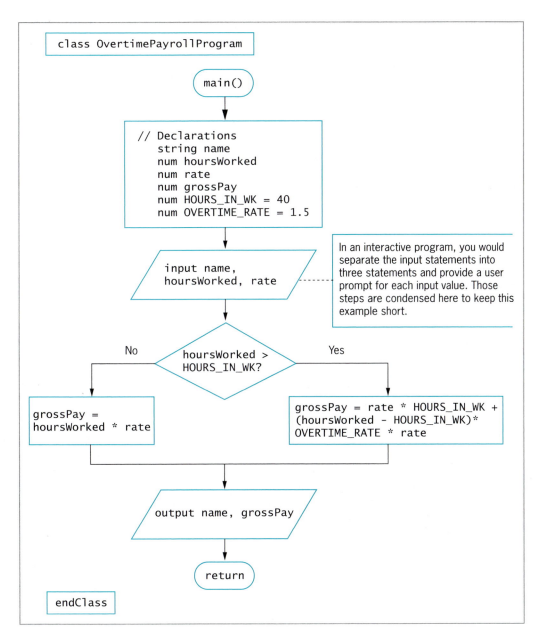

Figure 3-3 Flowchart and pseudocode for overtime payroll program

```
class OvertimePayrollProgram
   main()
      // Declarations
         string name
         num hoursWorked
         num rate
         num grossPay
         num HOURS_IN_WK = 40
         num OVERTIME_RATE = 1.5
      input name, hoursWorked, rate
      if hoursWorked > HOURS_IN_WK then
         grossPay = rate * HOURS_IN_WK +
            (hoursWorked - HOURS_IN_WK) *
            OVERTIME_RATE * rate
      else
         grossPay = hoursWorked * rate
      endif
      output name, grossPay
   return
endClass
```

Figure 3-3   Flowchart and pseudocode for overtime payroll program (continued)

Throughout this book, you will see many examples presented in both flowchart and pseudocode form. When you analyze a solution, you might find it easier to concentrate on just one of the two design tools at first. When you understand how the program works using one tool (for example, a flowchart), you can confirm that the solution is identical using the other tool.

In the program in Figure 3-3, several variables and constants are declared. The variables include those that will be retrieved from input (name, which is a string, and hoursWorked and rate, which are numbers) and one that will be calculated from the input values (grossPay, which is a number). The program in Figure 3-3 also uses two named constants: HOURS_IN_WK, which represents the number of hours in a standard workweek, and OVERTIME_RATE, which represents a multiplication factor for the premium rate at which an employee is paid after working more than the standard number of hours in a week.

After the input data is retrieved in the program in Figure 3-3, a decision is made about the value of hoursWorked. The longer calculation that adds a time-and-a-half factor to an employee's gross pay executes only when the expression hoursWorked > HOURS_IN_WK is true. The long calculation exists in the **if clause**, which is the part of the decision that holds the action or actions that execute when the decision's tested expression is true. The shorter calculation, which produces grossPay by multiplying hoursWorked by rate, constitutes the **else clause** of the decision—the part that executes only when the tested condition in the decision is false.

Suppose that an employee's paycheck should be reduced if the employee participates in the company dental plan and that no action is taken if the employee is not a dental plan participant. Figure 3-4 shows how this decision might be added to the payroll program. The additions to Figure 3-3 are shaded.

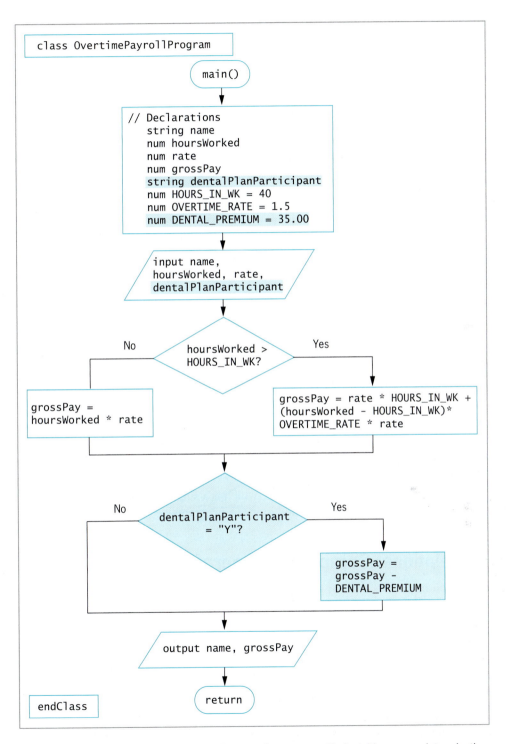

Figure 3-4 Flowchart and pseudocode for payroll program with dental insurance determination

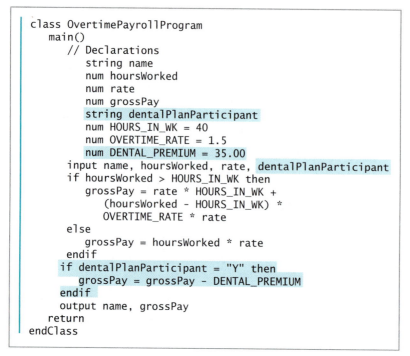

```
class OvertimePayrollProgram
   main()
      // Declarations
         string name
         num hoursWorked
         num rate
         num grossPay
         string dentalPlanParticipant
         num HOURS_IN_WK = 40
         num OVERTIME_RATE = 1.5
         num DENTAL_PREMIUM = 35.00
      input name, hoursWorked, rate, dentalPlanParticipant
      if hoursWorked > HOURS_IN_WK then
         grossPay = rate * HOURS_IN_WK +
            (hoursWorked - HOURS_IN_WK) *
            OVERTIME_RATE * rate
      else
         grossPay = hoursWorked * rate
      endif
      if dentalPlanParticipant = "Y" then
         grossPay = grossPay - DENTAL_PREMIUM
      endif
      output name, grossPay
   return
endClass
```

Figure 3-4　Flowchart and pseudocode for payroll program with dental insurance determination (continued)

The two selection structures in Figure 3-4 are **stacked structures**. That means that one is "on top of" and completely separate from the other. You can stack any of the three structures—sequence, selection, and loop—in any order. In the program in Figure 3-4, a sequence that makes the declarations and gets the input data is stacked on top of two selection structures, which finally are stacked on another sequence (which is a single statement that produces the output). In Chapter 4, you will learn to add loops to programs.

Using Relational Comparison Operators

Frequently, you make selections in programs by comparing two values. You could ask every question in a program by using one of only three types of operations in a Boolean expression. For any two values, you can decide whether:

- The two values are equal.

- The first value is greater than the second value.

- The first value is less than the second value.

You are used to thinking of numeric values as equal to, less than, or greater than each other, but computer programs can compare string values, too. In some programming languages, you must write special instructions to compare strings, but this book assumes that the standard relational operators work. Strings are compared based on their character values, from left to right. For example, "hello" is greater than "goodbye" because "h" follows "g" in the alphabet. Usually, string values are not considered to be equal unless they are identical, including the spacing and whether they appear in uppercase or lowercase. For example, "black pen" is not equal to "blackpen", "BLACK PEN ", "Black Pen", or even "black pen ", which contains an extra space just before the closing quotation mark.

For convenience, six types of **relational comparison operators** are available in all modern programming languages. (The term *relational comparison operators* is somewhat redundant. You also can call these operators **relational operators** or **comparison operators**.) Table 3-1 describes them; three are composed of one character, and the other three are composed of two characters. (When an operator requires two keystrokes, you never insert a space between them.) Each of these operators is binary—that is, each requires two operands.

Operator	Name	Discussion
=	Equivalency operator	Evaluates as true when its operands are equivalent. Many languages use a double equal sign (==) to avoid confusion with the assignment operator.
>	Greater-than operator	Evaluates as true when the left operand is greater than the right operand.
<	Less-than operator	Evaluates as true when the left operand is less than the right operand.
>=	Greater-than or equal-to operator	Evaluates as true when the left operand is greater than or equivalent to the right operand.
<=	Less-than or equal-to operator	Evaluates as true when the left operand is less than or equivalent to the right operand.
<>	Not-equal-to operator	Evaluates as true when its operands are not equivalent. Some languages use an exclamation point followed by an equal sign to indicate not equal to (!=).

Table 3-1 Relational comparison operators

When you construct an expression using two operands and one of the operators described in Table 3-1, the expression evaluates to true or false based on the operands' values. Usually, both operands in a comparison must be the same data type; that is, you can compare a numeric value to another numeric value, and a string to another string. Some programming languages allow you to compare a character to a number using the character's numeric code value in the comparison. Appendix C contains more information on coding systems and characters' numeric values. In some languages, the operators shown in Table 3-1 are used only with numbers, and different techniques are used to compare strings. This book will assume that these standard operators work with either strings or numbers.

In any Boolean expression, the two values compared can be either variables or constants. For example, the expression currentTotal > 100 compares a variable, currentTotal, to a numeric constant, 100. Depending on the currentTotal value, the expression's value is true or false. In the expression currentTotal > previousTotal, both values are variables, and the result is also true or false, depending on the values stored in each of the two variables. Although it's legal, you would never use expressions in which you compare two constants— for example, 20 < 20 or 30 < 40. Such expressions are **trivial expressions** because each will always evaluate to the same result: false for 20 < 20 and true for 30 < 40.

Any relational situation can be expressed using just three types of comparisons: equal, greater than, and less than. You never need the three additional comparisons (greater than or equal, less than or equal, or not equal), but using them often makes decisions more convenient. For example, assume that you need to issue a 10 percent discount to any customer whose age is 65 or greater, and charge full price to other customers. You can use the greater-than-or-equal-to symbol to write the logic as follows:

```
if customerAge >= 65 then
    discount = 0.10
else
    discount = 0
endif
```

As an alternative, if you want to use the < operator instead of the >= operator, you can express the same logic by writing:

```
if customerAge < 65 then
    discount = 0
else
    discount = 0.10
endif
```

In any expression for which a >= b is true, then a < b is false. Conversely, if a >= b is false, then a < b is true. By rephrasing the question and swapping the actions taken based on the outcome, you can make the same decision in multiple ways. The clearest route is often to ask a question so the positive or true outcome results in the action that is your motivation for making the test. When your company policy is to "provide a discount for those who are 65 and older," the phrase *greater than or equal to 65* comes to mind, so it is the most natural to use. Conversely, if your policy is to "charge full price for those under 65," then it is more natural to use the *less than 65* syntax. Either way, the same people receive a discount.

Comparing two values to determine if they are *not* equal to each other is the most confusing of all the comparisons. Using "not equal to" in decisions involves thinking in double negatives, which makes you prone to include logical errors in your programs. For example, consider the logic in Figure 3-5.

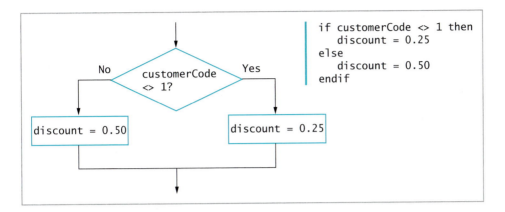

```
if customerCode <> 1 then
    discount = 0.25
else
    discount = 0.50
endif
```

Figure 3-5 Using a negative comparison

In Figure 3-5, if the value of `customerCode` *is* equal to 1, the logical flow follows the false branch of the selection. If `customerCode not equal to 1` is true, the `discount` is 0.25; if `customerCode not equal to 1` is not true, it means `customerCode` *is* 1, and the `discount` is 0.50. Even reading the phrase *customerCode not equal to 1 is not true* is awkward.

Figure 3-6 shows the same decision, this time asked in a positive way. Making the decision `if customerCode is 1` is clearer than trying to determine what `customerCode` is *not*.

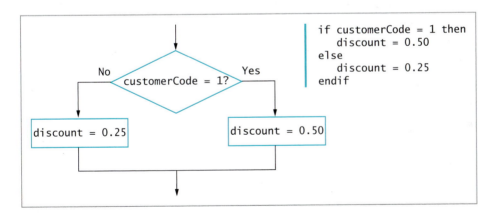

```
if customerCode = 1 then
    discount = 0.50
else
    discount = 0.25
endif
```

Figure 3-6 Using the positive equivalent of the negative comparison in Figure 3-5

Although negative comparisons can be awkward to use, your meaning is sometimes clearest if you use one. Frequently, this occurs when you use an if without an else, taking action only when some comparison is false. Examples might include the following:

```
if customerZipCode <> localZipCode then
    add deliveryCharge to total
endif
if customerResponse <> "Exempt" then
    taxDue = STANDARD_TAX_AMOUNT
endif
```

Besides being awkward to use, the "not equal to" comparison operator is the one most likely to be different in various programming languages. Visual Basic and Pascal use a less-than sign followed immediately by a greater-than sign (<>); C#, C++, C, and Java use an exclamation point followed by an equal sign (!=). In a flowchart or in pseudocode, you can use the symbol that mathematicians use to mean "not equal," an equal sign with a slash through it (≠). When you program, you will not be able to use this symbol because no single key on the keyboard produces it.

Most programming languages support a NOT operator. You use the **NOT operator** to reverse the meaning of a Boolean expression. For example, the following two expressions are equivalent:

```
age <> 21
NOT (age = 21)
```

The NOT operator is unary instead of binary—that is, you do not use it between two expressions, but you use it in front of a single expression.

In C++, Java, and C#, the exclamation point is the symbol used for the NOT operator. In Visual Basic, the operator is Not.

Pitfall: Using the Wrong Relational Operator

A common error that occurs with relational operators is using the wrong one and missing the boundary or limit required for a selection. If you use the > symbol to make a selection when you should have used >=, all the cases in which the operands are equal will go unselected. Unfortunately, people who request programs do not always speak as precisely as a computer. If, for example, your boss says, "Write a program that selects all employees over 65," does she mean to include employees who are 65 or not? In other words, is the comparison age > 65 or age >= 65? Although the phrase *over 65* implies *greater than 65*, people do not always say what they mean, and the best course of action is to double-check the intended meaning with the person who requested the program—for example, the end user, your supervisor, or your instructor. Similar phrases that can cause misunderstandings are *no more than*, *at least*, and *not under*.

 Watch the video *Boolean Expressions and Decisions*.

Understanding *AND* Logic

Often, you need more than one selection structure to determine whether an action should take place. When you ask multiple questions before an outcome is determined, you create a **compound condition**. For example, suppose that you work for a cell phone company that charges customers as follows:

- The basic monthly service bill is $30.

- An additional $20 is billed to customers who make more than 100 calls and use more than 500 minutes.

The logic needed for this billing program includes an **AND decision**—a decision in which more than one condition must be true for an action to take place. In this case, both a minimum number of calls must be made *and* a minimum number of minutes must be used before the customer is charged the additional amount. An AND decision can be constructed using a **nested decision** (also called a **nested selection** or a **nested if**). A nested decision contains a decision "inside of" another decision. The flowchart and pseudocode for the program that determines the charges for customers is shown in Figure 3-7.

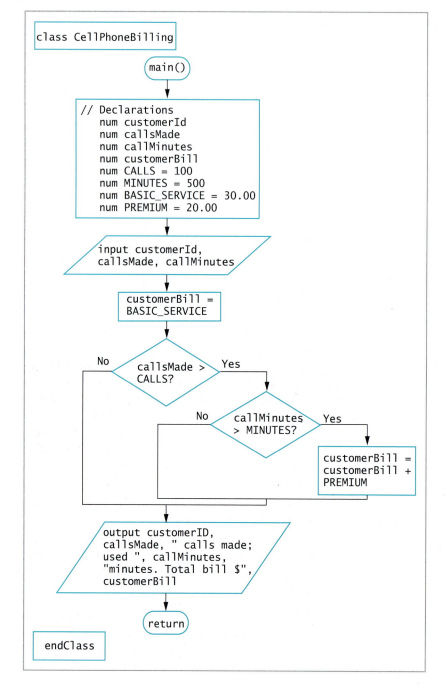

Figure 3-7 Flowchart and pseudocode for cell phone billing program

```
class CellPhoneBilling
    main()
        // Declarations
            num customerID
            num callsMade
            num callMinutes
            num customerBill
            num CALLS = 100
            num MINUTES = 500
            num BASIC_SERVICE = 30.00
            num PREMIUM = 20.00
        input customerId, callsMade, callMinutes
        customerBill = BASIC_SERVICE
        if callsMade > CALLS then
            if callMinutes  > MINUTES then
                customerBill = customerBill + PREMIUM
            endif
        endif
        output customerID, callsMade, " calls made; used ",
            callMinutes, " minutes. Total bill $", customerBill
    return
endClass
```

Figure 3-7   Flowchart and pseudocode for cell phone billing program (continued)

In Figure 3-7, the appropriate variables and constants are declared, and then the customer's data is entered. The customer's bill is set to the standard fee, and then the nested decision executes. In the nested if structure in Figure 3-7, the expression callsMade > CALLS is evaluated first. If this expression is true, only then is the second Boolean expression callMinutes > MINUTES evaluated. If that expression is also true, then the $20 premium is added to the customer's bill. If neither of the tested conditions is true, the customer's bill value is never altered, retaining the initially assigned value of $30.

In the flowchart in Figure 3-7, notice how the second decision falls within one branch of the first decision. In the pseudocode, notice how the second if statement and its corresponding endif are indented more than the first if. Because of these relationships, programmers call the first selection the **outer selection** of the nested statements. Similarly, the second selection, which is asked only after the first one is evaluated and found to be true, is the **inner selection**. Because of the indentation in the pseudocode, a series of nested if statements is also called a **cascading if statement**.

Most languages allow you to use a variation of the decision structure called the *case structure* when you must nest a series of decisions about a single variable. Appendix D contains information about the case structure.

Nesting *AND* Decisions for Efficiency

When you nest decisions because the resulting action requires that two conditions be true, you must decide which of the two decisions to make first. Logically, either selection in an AND decision can come first. However, when there are two selections, you often can improve your program's performance by correctly choosing which selection to make first.

For example, Figure 3-8 shows two ways to design the nested decision structure that assigns a premium to customers' bills if they make more than 100 cell phone calls and use more than 500 minutes in a billing period. The program can ask about calls made first, eliminate customers who have not made more than the minimum, and ask about the minutes used only for customers who "pass" the minimum calls test. Or, the program could ask about the minutes first, eliminate those who do not qualify, and ask about the number of calls only for customers who "pass" the minutes test. Either way, only customers who exceed both limits must pay the premium. Does it make a difference which question is asked first? As far as the result goes, no. Either way, the same customers pay the premium—those who qualify on the basis of both criteria. As far as program efficiency goes, however, it *might* make a difference which question is asked first.

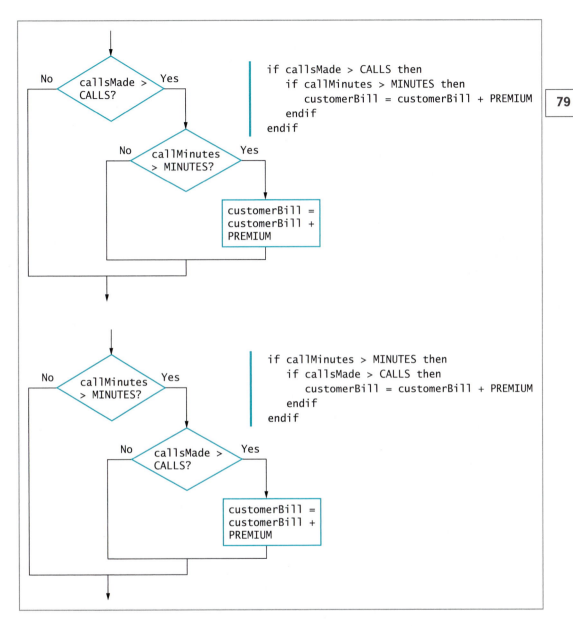

Figure 3-8 Two ways to produce cell phone bills using identical criteria

Assume that you know that out of 1000 cell phone customers, about 90 percent, or 900, make more than 100 calls in a billing period. Assume that you also know that only about half the 1000 customers, or 500, use more than 500 minutes of call time.

If you use the logic shown first in Figure 3-8, and you need to produce 1000 phone bills, the first Boolean expression, `callsMade > CALLS`, will be evaluated 1000 times. For approximately

90 percent of the customers, or 900 of them, the answer is `true`, so 100 customers are eliminated from the premium assignment, and 900 proceed to the next question about the minutes used. Only about half the customers use more than 500 minutes, so 450 of the 900 pay the premium, and it takes 1900 questions to identify them.

Using the alternate logic shown second in Figure 3-8, the first expression, `callMinutes > MINUTES`, will also be evaluated 1000 times—once for each customer. Because only about half the customers use the high number of minutes, only 500 will "pass" this test and proceed to the question for number of calls made. Then, about 90 percent of the 500, or 450 customers, will pass the second test and be billed the premium amount. It takes 1500 questions to identify the 450 premium-paying customers.

Whether you use the first or second decision order in Figure 3-8, the same 450 customers who satisfy both criteria pay the premium. The difference is that when you ask about the number of calls first, the program must make 400 more decisions than when you ask about the minutes used first.

The 400-decision difference between the two approaches used in Figure 3-8 doesn't take much evaluation time on most computers. But it does take *some* time, and if a corporation has hundreds of thousands of customers instead of only 1000, or if many such decisions have to be made within a program, performance time can be significantly improved by asking questions in the more efficient order.

Often when you must make nested decisions, you have no idea which event is more likely to occur; in that case, you can legitimately ask either question first. However, if you do know the probabilities of the conditions, or can make a reasonable guess, the general rule is: *In an AND decision, first ask the question that is less likely to be true.* This eliminates as many evaluations of the second decision as possible, which speeds up processing time.

Using the AND Operator

Most programming languages allow you to evaluate two or more expressions in a single statement by using a **conditional AND operator**, or more simply, an **AND operator** that joins comparisons in a single statement. For example, if you want to bill an extra amount to cell phone customers who make more than 100 calls that total more than 500 minutes in a billing period, you can use nested decisions, as shown in the previous section, or you can include both decisions in a single statement by writing the following expression:

```
callsMade > CALLS AND callMinutes > MINUTES
```

When you use one or more AND operators to combine two or more Boolean expressions, each Boolean expression must be true for the entire expression to be evaluated as true. For example, if you ask, "Are you a native-born U.S. citizen and are you at least 35 years old?", the answer to both parts of the question must be "yes" before the response can be a single, summarizing "yes." If either part of the expression is false, then the entire expression is false.

The conditional **AND** operator in Java, C++, and C# consists of two ampersands, with no spaces between them (&&). In Visual Basic, you use the word **And**.

Using a Truth Table

One tool that can help you understand the AND operator is a truth table. **Truth tables** are diagrams used in mathematics and logic to help describe the truth of an entire expression based on the truth of its parts. Table 3-2 shows a truth table that lists all the possibilities with an AND decision. As the table shows, for any two expressions x and y, the expression x AND y is true only if both x and y are individually true. If either x or y alone is false, or if both are false, then the expression x AND y is false.

x	y	x AND y
True	True	True
True	False	False
False	True	False
False	False	False

Table 3-2   Truth table for the AND operator

If the programming language you use allows an AND operator, you must realize that the question you place first (to the left of the operator) is the one that will be asked first, and cases that are eliminated based on the first question will not proceed to the second question. In other words, each part of an expression that uses an AND operator is evaluated only as far as necessary to determine whether the entire expression is true or false. This feature is called **short-circuit evaluation**. The computer can ask only one question at a time; even when your pseudocode looks like the first example in Figure 3-9, the computer will execute the logic shown in the second example.

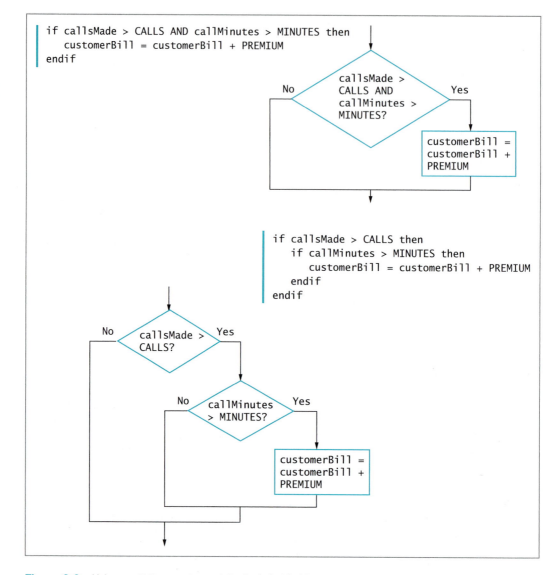

Figure 3-9   Using an AND operator and the logic behind it

You are never required to use the AND operator because using nested if statements can always achieve the same result, but using the AND operator often makes your code more concise, less error-prone, and easier to understand. Using an AND operator does not eliminate your responsibility for determining which condition to test first. Even when you use an AND operator, the computer makes decisions one at a time and makes them in the order you ask them. If the first question in an AND expression evaluates to false, then the entire expression is false, and the second question is not even tested.

Avoiding Common Errors in an *AND* Selection

New programmers make a few common errors when making AND selections. For example, errors include:

- Performing an action when only one of two criteria is satisfied because of incorrect nesting

- Performing an action twice that should occur only once because of incorrect nesting

- Failing to include a complete Boolean expression on each side of an AND operator

Pitfall: Taking Action Without Meeting All Necessary Conditions

When you need to satisfy two or more criteria to initiate an event in a program, you must make sure that the second decision is nested entirely within the first decision. For example, if a program's objective is to add a $20 premium to the bill of cell phone customers who exceed both 100 calls and 500 minutes in a billing period, then the program segment shown in Figure 3-10 is incorrect.

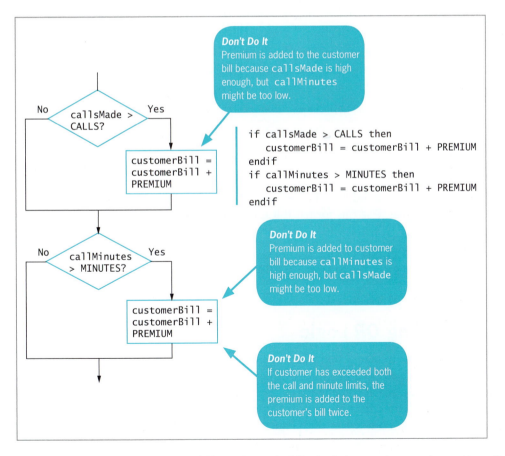

Figure 3-10   Incorrect logic to add a $20 premium to the bills of cell phone customers who meet two criteria

The first decision in Figure 3-10 shows that $20 is added to the bill of a customer who makes too many calls. This customer should not necessarily be billed extra because even though the customer has made too many calls, the customer has not necessarily used too many minutes.

In addition, according to the program requirements, a customer who has made 100 calls or fewer should never be charged the extra $20. However, in Figure 3-10, all customers are subjected to the minutes question no matter how many calls they have made, and some are assigned the extra charge even though they made few calls.

Pitfall: Performing an Action Twice When it Should Occur Once

Because the selection structures in Figure 3-10 are not nested, any customer who has exceeded both the calls and minutes limits has the premium added to his bill twice. Therefore, the logic shown in Figure 3-10 is *not* correct for this problem.

Pitfall: Forgetting to Use a Complete Boolean Expression on Each Side of the AND Operator

When you use the AND operator in most languages, you must provide a complete Boolean expression on each side of the operator. In other words, the following is a valid expression to select callMinutes between 100 and 200:

callMinutes > 100 AND callMinutes < 200

However, the following is not valid because the data after the AND operator is not a complete Boolean expression:

callMinutes > 100 AND < 200

For clarity, you can surround each Boolean expression in a compound expression with its own set of parentheses. Use this format if it is clearer to you. For example, you might write the following:

```
if (callMinutes > MINUTES) AND (callsMade > CALLS)
    customerBill = customerBill + PREMIUM
endif
```

Understanding *OR* Logic

Sometimes you want to take action when one *or* the other of two conditions is true. This is called an **OR decision** because either one condition *or* some other condition must be met for an event to take place. If someone asks, "Do you have a blue or green shirt I can borrow?," only one of the two conditions has to be true for the answer to the whole question to be "yes"; only if the answers to both halves of the question are false is the value of the entire expression false.

For example, suppose you want to add $20 to the bills of cell phone customers who *either* make more than 100 calls *or* use more than 500 minutes. Figure 3-11 shows the altered module of the billing program that accomplishes this objective.

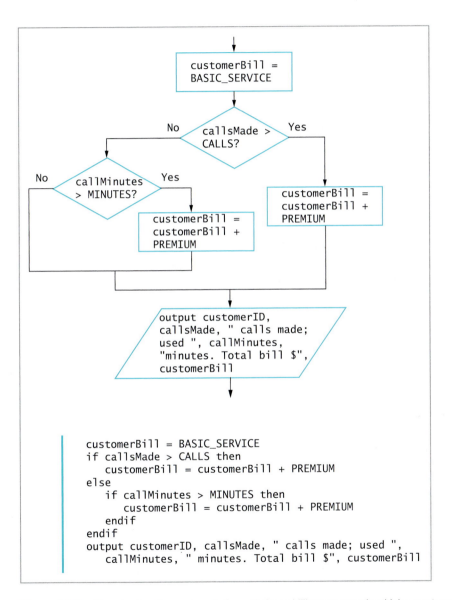

```
customerBill = BASIC_SERVICE
if callsMade > CALLS then
    customerBill = customerBill + PREMIUM
else
    if callMinutes > MINUTES then
        customerBill = customerBill + PREMIUM
    endif
endif
output customerID, callsMade, " calls made; used ",
    callMinutes, " minutes. Total bill $", customerBill
```

Figure 3-11 Flowchart and pseudocode for cell phone billing program in which a customer must meet one or both of two criteria to be billed a premium

The program segment in Figure 3-11 evaluates the expression callsMade > CALLS, and if the result is true, the extra amount is added to the customer's bill. Because making many calls is enough for the customer to incur the premium, there is no need for further questioning. If the customer has not made more than 100 calls, only then does the program need to ask whether too many minutes have been used.

Writing *OR* Decisions for Efficiency

As with an AND selection, when you use an OR selection, you can choose to ask either question first. For example, you can add an extra $20 to the bills of customers who meet one or the other of two criteria using the logic in either part of Figure 3-12.

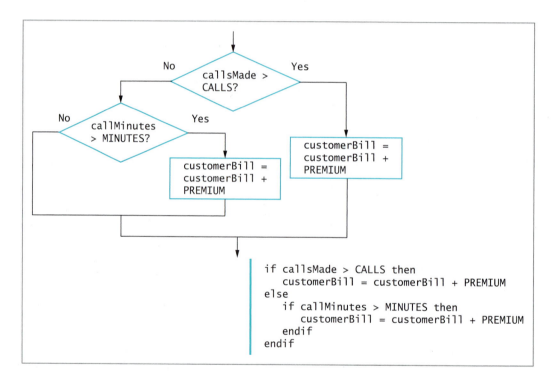

```
if callsMade > CALLS then
    customerBill = customerBill + PREMIUM
else
    if callMinutes > MINUTES then
        customerBill = customerBill + PREMIUM
    endif
endif
```

Figure 3-12   Two ways to assign a premium to bills of customers who meet one of two criteria

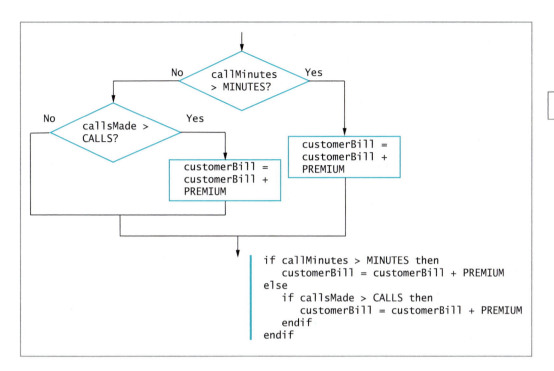

Figure 3-12 Two ways to assign a premium to bills of customers who meet one of two criteria (continued)

You might have guessed that one of these selections is superior to the other when you have some background information about the relative likelihood of each condition being tested. For example, let's say you know that out of 1000 cell phone customers, about 90 percent, or 900, make more than 100 calls in a billing period. You also know that only about half the 1000 customers, or 500, use more than 500 minutes of call time.

When you use the logic shown in the first half of Figure 3-12, you first ask about the calls made. For 900 customers the answer is true, and you add the premium to their bills. Only about 100 sets of customer data continue to the next question regarding the call minutes, where about 50 percent of the 100, or 50, are billed the extra amount. In the end, you have made 1100 decisions and correctly added premium amounts for 950 customers.

If you use the OR logic in the second half of Figure 3-12, you ask about minutes used first—1000 times, once each for 1000 customers. The result is true for 50 percent, or 500 customers, whose bill is increased. For the other 500 customers, you ask about the number of calls made. For 90 percent of the 500, the result is true, so premiums are added for 450 additional people. In the end, the same 950 customers are billed an extra $20—but this approach required executing 1500 decisions, 400 more decisions than when using the first decision logic.

The general rule is: *In an OR decision, first ask the question that is more likely to be true.* This approach eliminates as many executions of the second decision as possible, and the time it takes to process all the data is decreased. As with the AND situation, in an OR situation, it is more efficient to eliminate as many extra decisions as possible.

Using the OR Operator

If you need to take action when either one or the other of two conditions is met, you can use two separate, nested selection structures, as in the previous examples. However, most programming languages allow you to evaluate two or more Boolean expressions in a single comparison by using a **conditional OR operator** (or simply the **OR operator**). For example, you can evaluate the following expression:

```
callsMade > CALLS OR callMinutes > MINUTES
```

As with the AND operator, most programming languages require a complete Boolean expression on each side of the OR operator. When you use the OR operator, only one of the listed conditions must be met for the resulting action to take place. Table 3-3 shows the truth table for the OR operator. As you can see, the entire expression x OR y is false only when x and y each are false individually.

C#, C++, C, and Java use the symbol || as the OR operator. In Visual Basic, the operator is Or.

x	y	x OR y
True	True	True
True	False	True
False	True	True
False	False	False

Table 3-3   Truth table for the OR operator

If the programming language you use supports the OR operator, you still must realize that the question you place first is the question that will be asked first, and cases that pass the first test will not proceed to the second one. As with the AND operator, this feature is called short-circuiting. The computer can evaluate only one expression at a time; even when you write code as shown at the top of Figure 3-13, the computer will execute the logic shown at the bottom.

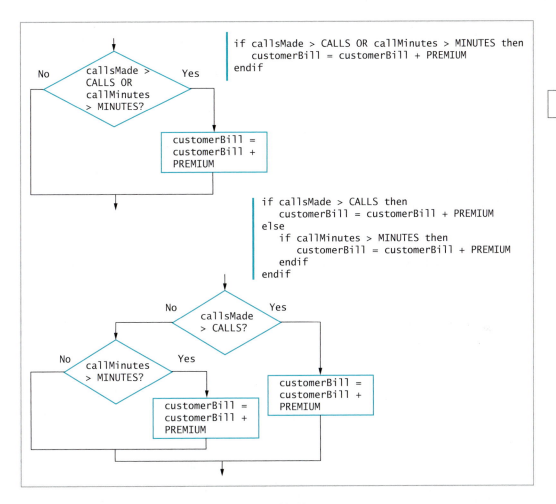

Figure 3-13 Using an OR operator and the logic behind it

Avoiding Common Errors in an *OR* Selection

When you make decisions using OR logic, it is easy to make errors such as the following:

- Creating unstructured logic
- Using AND logic when OR logic is needed
- Using OR logic when AND logic is needed

Pitfall: Creating Unstructured Logic

You might have noticed that the assignment statement `customerBill = customerBill + PREMIUM` appears twice in the decision-making processes in Figures 3-12 and 3-13. When you create a flowchart, the temptation is to draw the logic to look like Figure 3-14. Logically, you might argue that the flowchart in Figure 3-14 is correct because the correct customers are billed the extra $20. However, this flowchart is not structured.

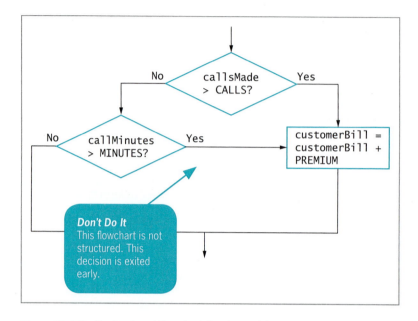

Figure 3-14   Unstructured flowchart for determining customer cell phone bill

When you create a structured selection, the logic must diverge in one of two directions that represent the true and false results of the selection-controlling question. Then, the diverging paths must join together before proceeding to the next steps in the program. In other words, a structured selection must have one entry point at the decision, and one exit point when the two logical paths rejoin. The second question in Figure 3-14 is not a self-contained structure with one entry and exit point; instead, the flowline "breaks out" of the inner selection structure to join the true side of the outer selection structure.

Pitfall: Using AND Logic When OR Logic is Needed

The OR selection has additional potential for errors because of the differences in the way people and computers use language. When your boss wants to add an extra amount to the bills of customers who make more than 100 calls or use more than 500 minutes, she is likely to say, "Add $20 to the bill of anyone who makes more than 100 calls and to anyone who has used more than 500 minutes." Her request contains the word *and* between two types of people—those who made many calls and those who used many minutes—placing the emphasis on the people.

However, each decision you make is for a single customer who has met one criterion *or* the other *or* both. In other words, the OR condition is between each customer's attributes, and not between different customers. Instead of the manager's previous statement, it would be clearer if she said, "Add $20 to the bill of anyone who has made more than 100 calls or has used more than 500 minutes," placing the emphasis on the two billing criteria for a single customer. However, you can't count on people to speak like computers. As a programmer, you have the job of clarifying what really is being requested. Often, a casual request for A *and* B logically means a request for A *or* B.

The way we use English can cause another type of error when you are required to find whether a value falls between two other values. For example, a movie theater manager might say, "Provide a discount to patrons who are under 13 years old and to those who are over 64 years old; otherwise, charge the full price." Because the manager has used the word *and* in the request, you might be tempted to create the decision shown in Figure 3-15; however, this logic will not provide a discounted price for any movie patron. You must remember that every time the decision is made in Figure 3-15, it is made for a single movie patron. If `patronAge` contains a value lower than 13, then it cannot possibly contain a value over 64. Similarly, if `patronAge` contains a value over 64, there is no way it can contain a lesser value. Therefore, no value could be stored in `patronAge` for which both parts of the AND question could be true—and the price will never be set to the discounted price for any patron. Figure 3-16 shows the correct logic.

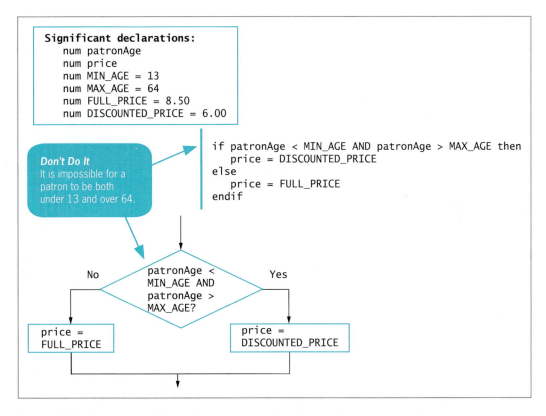

Figure 3-15 Incorrect logic that attempts to provide a discount for young and old movie patrons

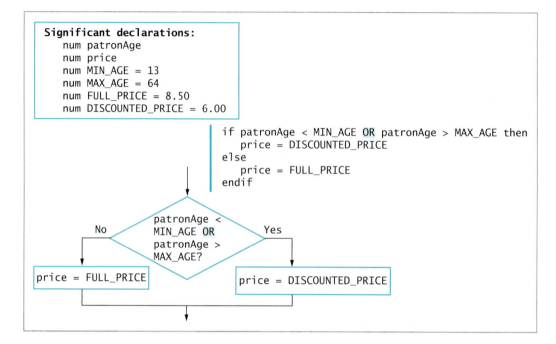

```
Significant declarations:
    num patronAge
    num price
    num MIN_AGE = 13
    num MAX_AGE = 64
    num FULL_PRICE = 8.50
    num DISCOUNTED_PRICE = 6.00
```

```
if patronAge < MIN_AGE OR patronAge > MAX_AGE then
    price = DISCOUNTED_PRICE
else
    price = FULL_PRICE
endif
```

```
                          patronAge <
         No               MIN_AGE OR          Yes
                          patronAge >
                          MAX_AGE?

 price = FULL_PRICE                    price = DISCOUNTED_PRICE
```

Figure 3-16   Correct logic that provides a discount for young and old movie patrons

Pitfall: Using OR Logic When AND Logic is Needed

A similar error can occur in your logic if the theater manager says something like, "Don't give a discount—that is, charge full price—if a patron is over 12 or under 65." Because the word *or* appears in the request, you might plan your logic to resemble Figure 3-17. No patron ever receives a discount, because every patron is either over 12 or under 65. Remember, in an OR decision, only one of the conditions needs to be true for the entire expression to be evaluated as true. So, for example, because a patron who is 10 is under 65, the full price is charged, and because a patron who is 70 is over 12, the full price also is charged. Figure 3-18 shows the correct logic for this decision.

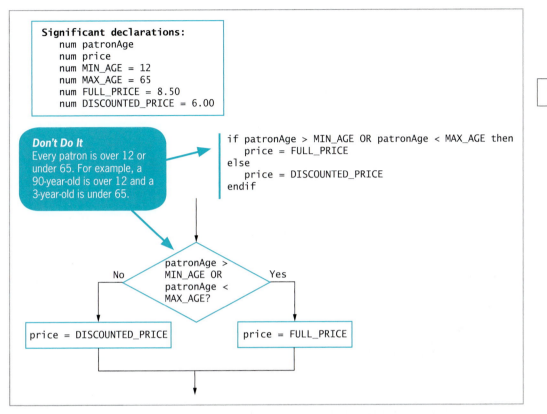

Significant declarations:
```
num patronAge
num price
num MIN_AGE = 12
num MAX_AGE = 65
num FULL_PRICE = 8.50
num DISCOUNTED_PRICE = 6.00
```

Don't Do It
Every patron is over 12 or under 65. For example, a 90-year-old is over 12 and a 3-year-old is under 65.

```
if patronAge > MIN_AGE OR patronAge < MAX_AGE then
    price = FULL_PRICE
else
    price = DISCOUNTED_PRICE
endif
```

patronAge > MIN_AGE OR patronAge < MAX_AGE?

No

Yes

price = DISCOUNTED_PRICE

price = FULL_PRICE

Figure 3-17 Incorrect logic that attempts to charge full price for patrons whose age is over 12 and under 65

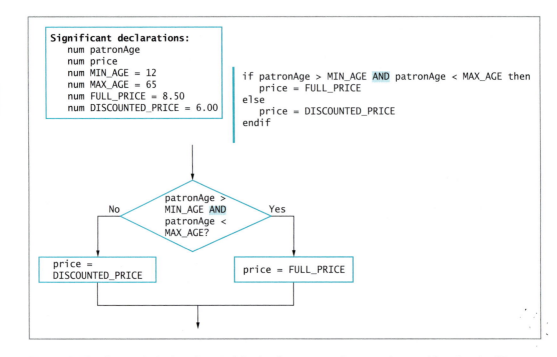

Significant declarations:
```
num patronAge
num price
num MIN_AGE = 12
num MAX_AGE = 65
num FULL_PRICE = 8.50
num DISCOUNTED_PRICE = 6.00
```

```
if patronAge > MIN_AGE AND patronAge < MAX_AGE then
    price = FULL_PRICE
else
    price = DISCOUNTED_PRICE
endif
```

Figure 3-18   Correct logic that charges full price for patrons whose age is over 12 and under 65

 Watch the video *Looking in Depth at AND and OR Decisions.*

Making Selections within Ranges

You often need to make selections based on a variable falling within a range of values. A **range of values** is any series of contiguous values that fall between specified limits. For example, in many courses you earn an A for any test score greater than or equal to 90, a B for any score greater than or equal to 80, and so on. As another example, suppose that your company provides various customer discounts based on the number of items ordered, as shown in Figure 3-19.

When you write the program that determines a discount rate based on the number of items, you could evaluate hundreds of expressions, such as itemQuantity = 1, itemQuantity = 2, and so on. However, it is more convenient to find the correct discount rate by using a range check.

Items Ordered	Discount Rate (%)
0 to 10	0
11 to 24	10
25 to 50	15
51 or more	20

When you use a **range check**, you compare a variable to a series of values that mark the limiting ends of ranges. To perform a range check, make comparisons using either the lowest or highest value in each range of values. For example, to find each discount rate listed in Figure 3-19, you can use one of the following techniques:

Figure 3-19 Discount rates based on items ordered

95

- Make comparisons using the low ends of the ranges.

  - You can ask: Is itemQuantity less than 11? If not, is it less than 25? If not, is it less than 51? (If it's possible the value is negative, you would also check for a value less than 0 and take appropriate action if it is.)

  - You can ask: Is itemQuantity greater than or equal to 51? If not, is it greater than or equal to 25? If not, is it greater than or equal to 11? (If it's possible the value is negative, you would also check for a value greater than or equal to 0 and take appropriate action if it is not.)

- Make comparisons using the high ends of the ranges.

  - You can ask: Is itemQuantity greater than 50? If not, is it greater than 24? If not, is it greater than 10? (If there is a maximum allowed value for itemQuantity, you would also check for a value greater than that limit and take appropriate action if it is.)

  - You can ask: Is itemQuantity less than or equal to 10? If not, is it less than or equal to 24? If not, is it less than or equal to 50? (If there is a maximum allowed value for itemQuantity, you would also check for a value less than or equal to that limit and take appropriate action if it is not.)

Figure 3-20 shows the flowchart and pseudocode that represent the logic to determine the correct discount for each order quantity. In the decision-making process, itemsOrdered is compared to the high end of the lowest-range group (RANGE1). If itemsOrdered is less than or equal to that value, then you know the correct discount, DISCOUNT1; if not, you continue checking. If itemsOrdered is less than or equal to the high end of the next range (RANGE2), then the customer's discount is DISCOUNT2; if not, you continue checking, and the customer's discount eventually is set to DISCOUNT3 or DISCOUNT4.

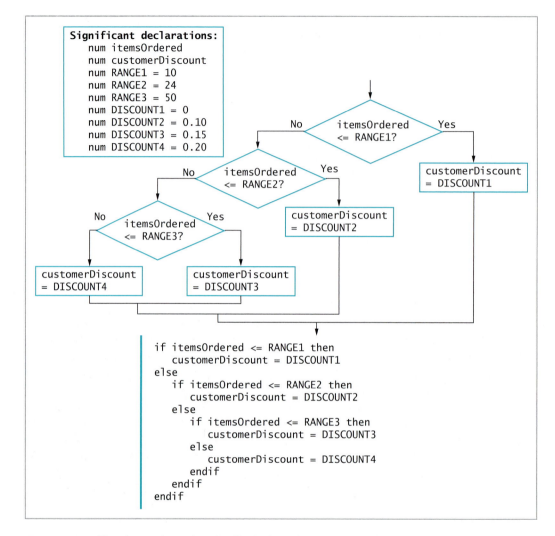

Significant declarations:
```
num itemsOrdered
num customerDiscount
num RANGE1 = 10
num RANGE2 = 24
num RANGE3 = 50
num DISCOUNT1 = 0
num DISCOUNT2 = 0.10
num DISCOUNT3 = 0.15
num DISCOUNT4 = 0.20
```

```
if itemsOrdered <= RANGE1 then
    customerDiscount = DISCOUNT1
else
    if itemsOrdered <= RANGE2 then
        customerDiscount = DISCOUNT2
    else
        if itemsOrdered <= RANGE3 then
            customerDiscount = DISCOUNT3
        else
            customerDiscount = DISCOUNT4
        endif
    endif
endif
```

Figure 3-20   Flowchart and pseudocode of logic that selects correct discount based on items ordered

In the pseudocode in Figure 3-20, notice how each `if`, `else`, and `endif` group aligns vertically.

In Chapter 2 you learned that punctuation such as dollar signs and commas are not stored in memory with numeric values, but can be used as explanatory output. Similarly, a percent sign (%) is not stored with a value that represents a percentage. Instead, the mathematical equivalent is stored. For example, 15% is stored as 0.15.

For example, consider an order for 30 items. The expression itemsOrdered <= RANGE1 evaluates as false, so the else clause of the decision executes. There, itemsOrdered <= RANGE2 also evaluates to false, so its else clause executes. The expression itemsOrdered <= RANGE3 is true, so customerDiscount becomes DISCOUNT3, which is 0.15. Walk through the logic with other values for itemsOrdered and verify for yourself that the correct discount is applied each time.

Avoiding Common Errors When Using Range Checks

When new programmers perform range checks, they are prone to including logic that has too many decisions, entailing more work than is necessary. When you make too many decisions, the incorrect result might be caused by one of the following:

- The logic might incorrectly contain an unreachable path.
- You might incorrectly ask questions when the answers are irrelevant.

Pitfall: Creation of an Unreachable Path

Figure 3-21 shows a program segment that contains a range check in which the programmer has asked one question too many—the shaded question in the figure. If you know that itemsOrdered is not less than or equal to RANGE1, not less than or equal to RANGE2, and not less than or equal to RANGE3, then itemsOrdered must be greater than RANGE3. Asking whether itemsOrdered is greater than RANGE3 is a waste of time; no customer order can ever travel the logical path on the far left of the flowchart. You might say such a path is a **dead** or **unreachable path**, and that the statements written there constitute dead or unreachable code. Although a program that contains such logic will execute and assign the correct discount to customers who order more than 50 items, providing such a path is inefficient. When you ask questions of human beings, you sometimes already know the answers. For example, a good trial lawyer seldom asks a question in court if the answer will be a surprise. With computer logic, however, such questions are an inefficient waste of time.

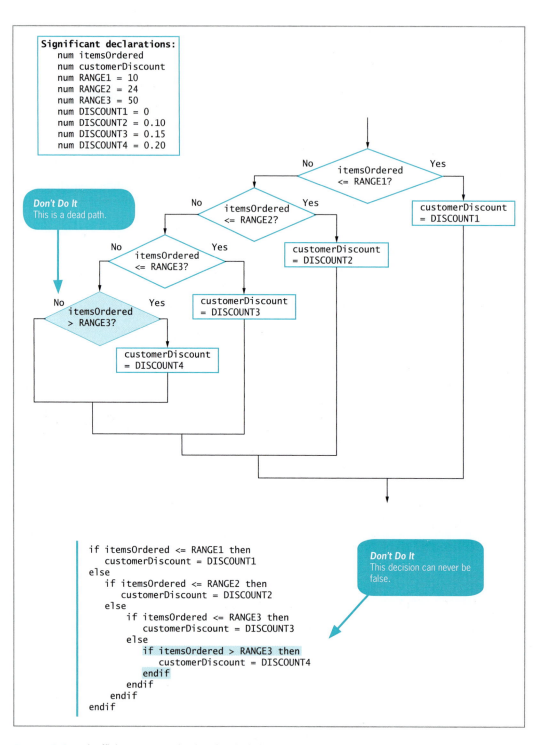

Figure 3-21 Inefficient range selection that includes an unreachable path

In Figure 3-21, it is easier to see the useless path in the flowchart than in the pseudocode representation of the same logic. However, anytime you use an if without an else, you are doing nothing when the question's answer is false.

Pitfall: Performing Comparisons When the Results are Irrelevant

Another error that programmers make when writing the logic to perform a range check also involves asking unnecessary questions. You should never ask a question if there is only one possible answer or outcome. Figure 3-22 shows an inefficient range selection that asks two unneeded questions. If itemsOrdered is less than or equal to RANGE1, customerDiscount is set to DISCOUNT1. If itemsOrdered is not less than or equal to RANGE1, then it must be greater than RANGE1, so the next decision (shaded in the figure) is unnecessary. The computer logic will never execute the shaded decision unless itemsOrdered is already greater than RANGE1— that is, unless the logic follows the false branch of the first selection. If you use the logic in Figure 3-22, you are wasting computer time asking a question that has previously been answered. The same logic applies to the second shaded decision. Beginning programmers sometimes justify their use of unnecessary questions as "just making really sure," but such caution is unnecessary when writing computer logic.

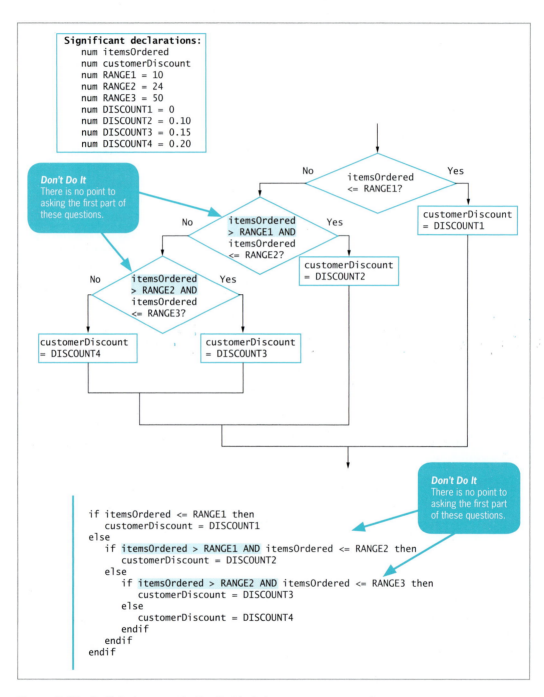

Figure 3-22   Inefficient range selection that includes unnecessary questions

Watch the video *Making Range Selections.*

Understanding Precedence When Combining AND and OR Operators

Most programming languages allow you to combine as many AND and OR operators in an expression as you need. For example, assume that you need to achieve a score of at least 75 on each of three tests to pass a course. You can declare a constant MIN_SCORE equal to 75 and test the multiple conditions with a statement like the following:

```
if score1 >= MIN_SCORE AND score2 >= MIN_SCORE AND score3 >= MIN_SCORE then
    classGrade = "Pass"
else
    classGrade = "Fail"
endif
```

On the other hand, if you need to pass only one of three tests to pass a course, then the logic is as follows:

```
if score1 >= MIN_SCORE OR score2 >= MIN_SCORE OR score3 >= MIN_SCORE then
    classGrade = "Pass"
else
    classGrade = "Fail"
endif
```

The logic becomes more complicated when you combine AND and OR operators within the same statement. When you do, the AND operators take **precedence**, meaning their Boolean values are evaluated first.

In Chapter 2 you learned that in every programming language, multiplication has precedence over addition in an arithmetic statement. That is, the value of 2 + 3 * 4 is 14 because the multiplication occurs before the addition. Similarly, in every programming language, AND has precedence over OR because computer circuitry treats the AND operator as multiplication and the OR operator as addition.

For example, consider a program that determines whether a movie theater patron can purchase a discounted ticket. Assume that discounts are allowed for children and senior citizens who attend G-rated movies. The following code looks reasonable, but it produces incorrect results because the expression that contains the AND operator (see shading) evaluates before the one that contains the OR operator.

```
if age <= 12 OR age >= 65 AND rating = "G" then
  output "Discount applies"
endif
```

Don't Do It
The AND evaluates first, which is not the intention.

For example, assume that a movie patron is 10 years old and the movie rating is R. The patron should not receive a discount (or be allowed to see the movie!). However, within the if statement, the part of the expression that contains the AND operator, age >= 65 AND rating = "G", is evaluated first. For a 10-year-old and an R-rated movie, the question is false (on both counts), so the entire if statement becomes the equivalent of the following:

```
if age <= 12 OR aFalseExpression then
    output "Discount applies"
endif
```

Because the patron is 10, age <= 12 is true, so the original if statement becomes the equivalent of:

```
if aTrueExpression OR aFalseExpression then
    output "Discount applies"
endif
```

The combination true OR false evaluates as true. Therefore, the string "Discount applies" is output when it should not be.

Many programming languages allow you to use parentheses to correct the logic and force the OR expression to be evaluated first, as shown in the following pseudocode.

```
if (age <= 12 OR age >= 65) AND rating = "G" then
    output "Discount applies"
endif
```

With the added parentheses, if the patron's age is 12 or under OR the age is 65 or over, the expression is evaluated as:

```
if aTrueExpression AND rating = "G" then
    output "Discount applies"
endif
```

When the age value qualifies a patron for a discount, then the rating value must also be acceptable before the discount applies. This was the original intention.

You can use the following techniques to avoid confusion when mixing AND and OR operators:

- You can use parentheses to override the default order of operations, as in the movie discount example.

- You can use parentheses for clarity even though they do not change what the order of operations would be without them. For example, if a customer should be between 12 and 19 or have a school ID to receive a high school discount, you can use the expression (age > 12 AND age < 19) OR validId = "Yes", even though the evaluation would be the same without the parentheses.

- You can use nesting if statements instead of combining AND and OR operators in a single expression. With the flowchart and pseudocode shown in Figure 3-23, it is clear which movie patrons receive the discount. In the flowchart, you can see that the OR is nested entirely within the Yes branch of the rating = "G" selection. Similarly, in the pseudocode in Figure 3-23, you can see by the alignment that if the rating is not G, the logic proceeds directly to the last endif statement, bypassing any checking of age at all.

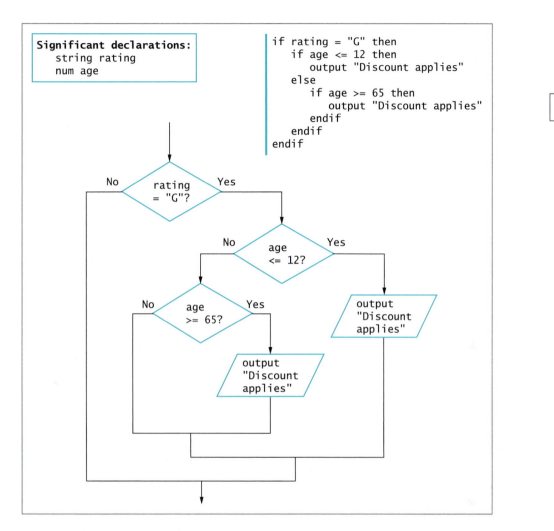

```
Significant declarations:        if rating = "G" then
  string rating                    if age <= 12 then
  num age                              output "Discount applies"
                                   else
                                       if age >= 65 then
                                           output "Discount applies"
                                       endif
                                   endif
                               endif
```

Figure 3-23   Nested decisions that determine movie patron discount

Chapter Summary

- Every decision in a computer program involves evaluating a Boolean expression. You can use if-then-else structures when action is required whether the selection is true or false, and if-then structures when there is only one outcome for the question for which action is required.

- For any two values that are the same type, you can use relational comparison operators to decide whether the two values are equal, the first value is greater than the second value, or the first value is less than the second value. The two values used in a Boolean expression can be either variables or constants.

- An AND decision occurs when two conditions must be true for a resulting action to take place. In an AND decision, you can use a nested decision, or a nested if. In an AND decision, first ask the question that is less likely to be true. Most programming languages allow you to evaluate two or more expressions in a single statement by using an AND operator.

- An OR decision occurs when you want to take action when at least one of two conditions is true. Errors occur in OR decisions when programmers do not maintain structure. An additional source of errors stems from people using the word AND to express OR requirements. In an OR decision, first ask the question that is more likely to be true. Most programming languages allow you to evaluate two or more expressions in a single comparison by using an OR operator.

- To perform a range check, make comparisons with either the lowest or highest value in each range of values you are using. Common errors that occur when programmers perform range checks include asking unnecessary and previously answered questions.

- AND operators have higher precedence than OR operators.

Key Terms

An **if-then-else structure** is a selection structure.

A **Boolean expression** is an expression whose value can be only true or false.

A **dual-alternative selection** is a selection structure that includes separate actions when an expression is true and when it is false.

A **single-alternative selection** is a selection structure that includes an action only when an expression is true or when it is false—in other words, when action is required for only one outcome of the question.

An **if-then** structure is a single-alternative selection structure.

An **if clause** of a decision holds the action that results when the Boolean expression in the decision is true.

The **else clause** of a decision holds the action or actions that execute only when the Boolean expression in the decision is false.

Stacked structures are structures that are linked end to end so that one follows the other.

Relational comparison operators are the symbols that express Boolean comparisons. Examples include =, >, <, >=, <=, and <>. These operators can be more simply called **relational operators** or **comparison operators**.

A **trivial expression** is one that always evaluates to the same result.

The **NOT operator** is a symbol that reverses the meaning of a Boolean expression.

A **compound condition** is constructed when you need to ask multiple questions before determining an outcome.

An **AND decision** is one in which two or more conditions must both be true for an action to take place.

A **nested decision**, or **nested selection** or **nested if**, is a decision "inside of" another decision.

An **outer selection** is the first one made in a nested decision; it is the one whose outcome determines whether a subsequent decision will be made.

An **inner selection** is the decision structure nested within one branch of an outer selection in a nested selection.

A **cascading if statement** contains a series of nested if statements.

A **conditional AND operator** (or more simply, an **AND operator**) is a symbol that combines decisions when all must be true to execute a resulting action.

Truth tables are diagrams used in mathematics and logic to help describe the truth of an entire expression based on the truth of its parts.

Short-circuit evaluation is a logical feature in which each part of a larger expression is evaluated only as far as necessary to determine the final outcome.

An **OR decision** is one in which at least one of two (or more) conditions must be true for a resulting action to take place.

A **conditional OR operator** (or more simply, an **OR operator**) is a symbol that combines decisions when only one condition must be true to execute a resulting action.

A **range of values** is any series of contiguous values that fall between specified limits.

A **range check** compares a variable to a series of values that mark the limiting ends of ranges.

A **dead** or **unreachable path** is a logical path that can never be traveled.

Precedence is the set of rules that defines the priority or order of operations.

Review Questions

1. The selection statement if quantity > 100 then discountRate = RATE is an example of a _____ .

    a. single-alternative selection
    b. dual-alternative selection
    c. binary selection
    d. all of the above

2. The selection statement `if dayOfWeek = "Sunday" then price = LOWER_PRICE else price = HIGHER_PRICE` is an example of a _____ .

    a. unary selection   c. dual-alternative selection

    b. single-alternative selection   d. all of the above

3. All selection statements must have _____ .

    a. an `if` clause   c. both of the above

    b. an `else` clause   d. none of the above

4. An expression like `amount < 10` is a(n) _____ expression.

    a. Gregorian   c. Machiavellian

    b. Boolean   d. Edwardian

5. Usually, you compare only variables that have the same _____ .

    a. value   c. name

    b. size   d. type

6. Symbols like > and < are known as _____ operators.

    a. arithmetic   c. sequential

    b. relational comparison   d. scripting accuracy

7. If you could use only three relational comparison operators, you could most easily get by with _____ .

    a. greater than, less than, and greater than or equal to

    b. less than, less than or equal to, and not equal to

    c. equal to, less than, and greater than

    d. equal to, not equal to, and greater than or equal to

8. If `a > b` is false, then which of the following is always true?

    a. `a < b`   c. `a = b`

    b. `a <= b`   d. `a >= b`

9. The comparison operator that tends to cause the most logical errors is _____ .

    a. equal to   c. less than

    b. greater than   d. not equal to

10. Which of the lettered choices is equivalent to the following decision?

```
if x > 10 then
   if y > 10 then
      output "X"
   endif
endif
```

a. if x > 10 AND y > 10 then output "X"

b. if x > 10 OR y > 10 then output "X"

c. if x > 10 AND x > y then output "X"

d. if y > x then output "X"

11. The Acme Computer Company operates in all 50 of the United States. The Midwest Sales region consists of five states—Illinois, Indiana, Iowa, Missouri, and Wisconsin. Suppose that you have input records containing Acme customer data, including state of residence. To most efficiently select and display all customers who live in the Midwest Sales region, you would use _____ .

a. five completely separate unnested if statements

b. nested if statements using AND logic

c. nested if statements using OR logic

d. Not enough information is given.

12. The Midwest Sales region of Acme Computer Company consists of five states— Illinois, Indiana, Iowa, Missouri, and Wisconsin. About 50 percent of the regional customers reside in Illinois, 20 percent in Indiana, and 10 percent in each of the other three states. Suppose that you have input records containing Acme customer data, including state of residence. To most efficiently select and display all customers who live in the Midwest Sales region, you would ask first about residency in _____ .

a. Illinois

b. Indiana

c. either Iowa, Missouri, or Wisconsin—it does not matter which one of these three is first

d. any of the five states; it does not matter which one is first

13. The Boffo Balloon Company makes helium balloons. Large balloons cost $13.00 a dozen, medium-sized balloons cost $11.00 a dozen, and small balloons cost $8.60 a dozen. About 60 percent of the company's sales are of the smallest balloons, 30 percent are medium, and large balloons constitute only 10 percent of sales. Customer order records include customer information, quantity ordered, and size. For the most efficient decision when you write a program to determine price based on size, you should ask first whether the size is _____ .

a. large

b. medium

c. small

d. It does not matter.

14. The Boffo Balloon Company makes helium balloons in three sizes, 12 colors, and with a choice of 40 imprinted sayings. As a promotion, the company is offering a 25-percent discount on orders of large, red "Happy Valentine's Day" balloons. To most efficiently select the orders to which a discount applies, you would use _____ .

 a. three completely separate unnested if statements

 b. nested if statements using AND logic

 c. nested if statements using OR logic

 d. Not enough information is given.

15. Radio station FM 99 keeps a record of every song played on the air in a week. Each record contains the day, hour, and minute the song started, and the title and artist of the song. The station manager wants a list of every title played during the important 8 a.m. commute hour on the two busiest traffic days, Monday and Friday. Which logic would select the correct titles?

```
a. if day = "Monday" OR day = "Friday" OR hour = 8 then
       output title
   endif
```

```
b. if day = "Monday" then
       if hour = 8 then
           output title
       else
           if day = "Friday" then
               output title
           endif
       endif
   endif
```

```
c. if hour = 8 AND day = "Monday" OR day = "Friday" then
       output title
   endif
```

```
d. if hour = 8 then
       if day = "Monday" OR day = "Friday" then
           output title
       endif
   endif
```

16. In the following pseudocode, what percentage raise will an employee in Department 5 receive?

```
if department < 3 then
   raise = SMALL_RAISE
else
   if department < 5 then
      raise = MEDIUM_RAISE
   else
      raise = BIG_RAISE
   endif
endif
```

   a.   SMALL_RAISE   c.   BIG_RAISE

   b.   MEDIUM_RAISE   d.   impossible to tell

17. In the following pseudocode, what percentage raise will an employee in Department 8 receive?

```
if department < 5 then
   raise = SMALL_RAISE
else
   if department < 14 then
      raise = MEDIUM_RAISE
   else
      if department < 9 then
         raise = BIG_RAISE
      endif
   endif
endif
```

   a.   SMALL_RAISE   c.   BIG_RAISE

   b.   MEDIUM_RAISE   d.   impossible to tell

18. In the following pseudocode, what percentage raise will an employee in Department 10 receive?

```
if department < 2 then
   raise = SMALL_RAISE
else
   if department < 6 then
      raise = MEDIUM_RAISE
   else
      if department < 10 then
         raise = BIG_RAISE
      endif
   endif
endif
```

   a.   SMALL_RAISE   c.   BIG_RAISE

   b.   MEDIUM_RAISE   d.   impossible to tell

19. In the following pseudocode, what percentage raise will an employee in Department 3 receive?

```
if department < 2 then
    raise = SMALL_RAISE
endif
if department < 6 then
    raise = MEDIUM_RAISE
endif
if department < 10 then
    raise = BIG_RAISE
endif
```

  a. SMALL_RAISE   c. BIG_RAISE
  b. MEDIUM_RAISE   d. impossible to tell

20. Which of the following is true?

  a. The AND operator has higher precedence than the OR operator.
  b. The OR operator has higher precedence than the AND operator.
  c. The AND and OR operators have the same precedence.
  d. The precedence of AND and OR operators depends on the programming language.

Exercises

1. Assume that the following variables contain the values shown:
   ```
   lowestA = 90
   lowestB = 80
   lowestC =70
   name = "Louis "
   school = "Washington"
   street = "Oak"
   ```

   For each of the following Boolean expressions, decide whether the statement is true, false, or illegal.

   a. lowestA = lowestB   f. name = school

   b. lowestA <= lowestB   g. name < school

   c. lowestC > lowestA   h. lowestB = "80"

   d. lowestA < name   i. street = "90"

   e. name = "Louis"   j. street > school

2. The Happy Cow Ice Cream Company manufactures several types of ice cream. Design a flowchart or pseudocode for a program that accepts an ice cream flavor (for example, "triple chocolate"), price per gallon, and number of gallons sold in

the average year. Display a message that indicates whether the ice cream is a bestseller, which is defined as a flavor that sells more than 40,000 gallons per year.

3. The Romance World Cruise Line provides special gifts and celebrations for passengers who are newlyweds, as well as for those who have been married more than 40 years. Design a flowchart or pseudocode for a program that accepts a couple's last name, ship cabin number, and number of years married. Display a couple's data with the message *Newlywed Gift* if the couple has been married one year or less, *Deluxe Anniversary Package* if the couple has been married 40 years or more, and no message if the couple has been married between 2 and 39 years inclusive.

4. The *Daily Gazette* accepts classified ads in several categories. For most ads, the newspaper charges 10 cents per word for the first 50 words, and 8 cents per word for every word after that. Design a flowchart or pseudocode for a program that accepts data about an ad: customer name, ad category (for example, *Apartment for rent*), and number of words. Display all the input data and the price for the ad.

    a. Modify the newspaper ad program to provide a 10 percent discount for ads over 300 words.

    b. Modify the newspaper ad program to display the details of the ad only if it is in the *Used cars* category.

    c. Modify the newspaper ad program so the ad rates are the same as in the original program unless the ad is in the *Found* category, in which case it is free, or in the *Business services* category, in which case the charge is 20 cents per word.

    d. Modify the newspaper ad program to accept the ad data, then to prompt the user for and accept an ad category. Display the data only if the ad is in the specified category.

5. The Parasol Insurance Group sells a variety of insurance policy types. Design a flowchart or pseudocode for a program that accepts a client's name and "Y" or "N" string answers to questions about whether the client wants each of the following policy types: homeowners ($800 annually), renters ($300 annually), and automobile ($1000 annually per car). If the client wants automobile insurance, add a question to determine the number of vehicles covered. Display all the details, as well as the client's annual bill.

    a. Modify the insurance program to display a client's data only if the client selects automobile insurance.

    b. Modify the insurance program to display a client's data only if the client will pay more than $1200 annually.

6. Lakeside Cottages accepts guests during the summer and early fall. Design a flowchart or pseudocode for a program that accepts a guest's last name, month and day the guest's stay will start, and the number of nights for the stay. If the month is

not 5 through 9 inclusive, then display a message that indicates the cottages are not available. Otherwise, if the number of nights is more than 14, display a message that indicates reservations are not accepted for more than 14 nights. Otherwise, display the total fee for the guest, which is $600 total for any number of days through 7, and then $75 per day for any additional days through 14.

a. Modify the cottage rental program to display the guest's data only if the stay starts in month 9 and lasts more than 10 days.

b. Modify the cottage rental program to display the guest's data only if the total bill is more than $1000.

c. Modify the cottage rental program to prompt the user for a month and day after the guest's rental data has been entered. Display the guest's data only if the specified date falls within the guest's stay.

7. Rick Hammer is a carpenter who wants an application to compute the price of any desk a customer orders, based on the following: desk length and width in inches, type of wood, and number of drawers. The price is computed as follows:

- The charge for all desks is a minimum $200.

- If the surface (length * width) is over 750 square inches, add $50.

- If the wood is mahogany, add $150; for oak, add $125. No charge is added for pine.

- For every drawer in the desk, there is an additional $30 charge.

Design a flowchart or pseudocode for a program that accepts data for an order number, customer name, length and width of the desk ordered, type of wood, and number of drawers. Display all the entered data and the final price for the desk.

8. Black Dot Printing is attempting to organize carpools to save energy. Each input record contains an employee's name and town of residence. Ten percent of the company's employees live in Wonder Lake. Thirty percent of the employees live in Woodstock. Because these towns are both north of the company, the company wants to encourage employees who live in either town to drive to work together. Design a flowchart or pseudocode for a program that accepts an employee's data and displays it with a message that indicates whether the employee is a candidate for the carpool.

9. The Dorian Gray Portrait Studio charges its customers based on the number of subjects who pose for a portrait. The fee schedule is as follows:

Subjects in Portrait	Base Price
1	$100
2	$130
3	$150
4	$165
5	$175
6	$180
7 or more	$185

Table 3-4 Portrait prices

Portrait sittings on Saturday or Sunday cost 20 percent more than the base price.

Design a flowchart or pseudocode for a program that accepts the following data: the last name of the family sitting for the portrait, the number of subjects in the portrait, and the scheduled day of the week. Display all the input data as well as the calculated sitting fee.

Case Projects

 Case: Cost Is No Object

1. In Chapter 2, you designed a program for Cost Is No Object—a car rental service that specializes in lending antique and luxury cars to clients on a short-term basis. Design a flowchart or pseudocode for a program that accepts rental contract data and displays a completed rental contract ready for a customer's signature.

   Accept the following as input:

   - Contract number
   - Customer's first and last names
   - Automobile's vehicle identification number
   - Starting date for the rental agreement stored as three separate variables—month, day, and year
   - Length, in days, of the rental agreement
   - Indicator of whether the customer bought the optional insurance policy

Display output as follows:

- If the contract number is not between 10000 and 99999 inclusive, issue an error message and end the program.

- If the starting date for the rental agreement is invalid, issue an error message and end the program. (In other words, make sure the month is between 1 and 12 inclusive. If the month is 1, 3, 5, 7, 8, 10, or 12, the day must be between 1 and 31 inclusive. If the month is 2, the day must be between 1 and 28 inclusive. You do not need to check for leap years. If the month is 4, 6, 9, or 11, the day must be between 1 and 30 inclusive.)

- If the length of the rental agreement is not between 1 and 30 days inclusive, issue an error message and end the program. Otherwise, calculate the ending month, day, and year based on the starting date and length of the agreement.

- The insurance indicator must be "Y" or "N" (for "Yes" or "No"); otherwise, display an error message and assume "Y".

- If all the entered data is valid, display it along with the fee for the rental, which is calculated as follows:

  - $25 per day for 10 days or fewer

  - $18 per day for each day over 10 days

  - $2.50 per day for insurance, regardless of the number of days in the contract

Case: Classic Reunions

2. In Chapter 2, you designed a program for Classic Reunions—a company that provides services for organizers of high school class reunions. Design a flowchart or pseudocode for a program that accepts reunion contract data and displays a completed contract ready for a customer's signature.

Accept the following as input:

- Contract number

- Contact person's first and last names

- Month, day, and year of the reunion party

- Number of guests expected at the reunion

- Indicators of whether selected options include cocktails, appetizers, dinner, and a band

Display output as follows:

- If the contract number is not between 10000 and 99999 inclusive, issue an error message and end the program.

- If the reunion date is invalid, issue an error message and end the program. (In other words, make sure the month is between 1 and 12 inclusive. If the month is 1, 3, 5, 7, 8, 10, or 12, the day must be between 1 and 31 inclusive. If the month is 2, the day must be between 1 and 28 inclusive. You do not need to check for leap years. If the month is 4, 6, 9, or 11, the day must be between 1 and 30 inclusive.)

- The indicator values for cocktails, appetizers, dinner, and the band must each be "Y" or "N" (for "Yes" or "No"); otherwise, display an error message and assume "Y".

- Display all the entered data along with the total fee for the reunion, which is calculated as follows:

  - $5 per person base price

  - An additional $12 per person for appetizers only, $15 per person for cocktails only, and $19 per person for dinner only. If the customer selects appetizers and cocktails, but no dinner, the cost is $22 per person. If the customer selects cocktails and dinner, but no appetizers, the cost is $26 per person. If the customer selects appetizers and dinner, but no cocktails, the cost is $24 per person. If the customer selects appetizers, cocktails, and dinner, the cost is $36 per person.

  - The charge for the band is $500 no matter how many people attend the reunion.

Case: The Barking Lot

3. In Chapter 2, you designed a program for The Barking Lot—a dog-boarding facility. Design a flowchart or pseudocode for a program that accepts contract data and displays a completed contract ready for a client's signature.

Accept the following as input:

- Contract number
- Dog owner's first and last names
- Dog's name
- Dog's weight
- Month, day, and year of the first day of boarding

- Number of days for boarding

- Indicators of whether selected options include a daily walk, a daily ice cream treat, and a bath on the last boarding day

Display output as follows:

- If the contract number is not between 10000 and 99999 inclusive, issue an error message and end the program.

- If the start boarding date is invalid, issue an error message and end the program. (In other words, make sure the month is between 1 and 12 inclusive. If the month is 1, 3, 5, 7, 8, 10, or 12, the day must be between 1 and 31 inclusive. If the month is 2, the day must be between 1 and 28 inclusive. You do not need to check for leap years. If the month is 4, 6, 9, or 11, the day must be between 1 and 30 inclusive.)

- The indicator values for walking, treat, and bath options must be "Y" or "N" (for "Yes" or "No"); otherwise, display an error message and assume "N".

- Display all the entered data along with the total fee for boarding, which is calculated as follows:

  - $15 per day base price

  - An additional $4 per day for dogs over 50 pounds; an additional $7 per day for dogs over 100 pounds

  - Additional fees include $3 per day for a walk, $1 per day for ice cream, and $20 for a bath on the last boarding day. If the client selects walks and treats, provide one treat for free. If the client selects walks, treats, and a bath, provide one walk for free.

Up for Discussion

1. Computer programs can be used to make decisions about your insurability, as well as the rates you will be charged for health and life insurance policies. For example, certain preexisting conditions may raise your insurance premiums considerably. Is it ethical for insurance companies to access your health records and then make insurance decisions about you?

2. Job applications are sometimes screened by software that makes decisions about a candidate's suitability based on keywords in the applications. Is such screening fair to applicants?

3. Medical facilities often have more patients waiting for organ transplants than there are available organs. Suppose that you have been asked to write a computer program that selects which candidates should receive an available organ. What data would you want on file to be able to use in your program, and what decisions would you make based on the data? What data do you think others might use that you would choose not to use?

CHAPTER 4

Looping

In this chapter, you will learn about:

- ◎ The loop structure
- ◎ Using a loop control variable
- ◎ Nested loops
- ◎ Avoiding common loop mistakes
- ◎ Using a `for` loop
- ◎ Common loop applications

Understanding the Loop Structure

Although making decisions is what makes computers seem intelligent, looping makes computer programming both efficient and worthwhile. When you use a loop, you can write one set of instructions that operates on multiple data items. For example, a large company might use a single loop to produce thousands of paychecks, or a big-city utility company might use a single loop to process millions of customer bills. Using fewer instructions results in less time needed for design and coding, less compile time, and fewer errors.

Recall the loop structure that you learned about in Chapter 2. Along with sequence and selection, it is one of the three basic structures used in structured programming. Figure 4-1 shows a loop structure. This loop starts with a test of a Boolean expression. The statements within a loop constitute the **loop body**; the body executes as long as the loop-controlling Boolean expression remains true. The same loop-controlling question is asked following each execution of the loop body; the structure is exited only when the test expression is false. You may hear programmers refer to looping as **repetition** or **iteration**.

The loop structure in Figure 4-1 is also called a **while loop** because it fits the following statement:

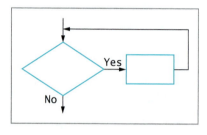

```
while testCondition continues to be true
    do someProcess
endwhile
```

In pseudocode for the while loop, the endwhile statement clearly shows where the looping structure ends. In Chapter 3, you learned to use endif to perform the same function for a selection structure.

Figure 4-1 The loop structure

All loops can be written as while loops. Most programming languages support an additional loop format called the do-while loop. Appendix D discusses this loop.

You encounter examples of looping every day, as in the following example:

```
while you continue to be hungry
    take another bite of food
endwhile
```

or

```
while an unread page remains in the reading assignment
    read another unread page
endwhile
```

In a business application, you might perform tasks like the following:

```
while quantity in inventory remains low
    continue to order items
endwhile
```

or

```
while there is another price on which to compute a discount
    compute a discount on the current price
endwhile
```

In Chapter 3, you learned that a structured selection has one entry point (at its tested Boolean expression) and one exit point (where the logical paths converge after the selection has split the logic into two paths). Similarly, a structured loop has one entry point and one exit point. The loop's entry point is at its tested Boolean expression. While the expression continues to be true, the loop body and the test of the expression repeat. The loop's exit point is where the logic emerges from the Boolean expression when the tested expression becomes false.

The body of a loop might contain any number of statements, including sequences, selections, and other loops. Once your logic enters the body of a structured loop, the entire loop body executes. Your program can leave a structured loop only at the point where the loop-controlling question is evaluated.

 Watch the video *A Quick Introduction to Loops.*

Using a Loop Control Variable

You can use a `while` loop to execute a body of statements continuously as long as some condition continues to be true. To make a `while` loop end correctly, you should declare a **loop control variable**, which is a variable whose value is tested to control the loop's execution. In a correct loop, three separate actions should occur:

- The loop control variable is initialized before entering the loop.

- The loop control variable is tested, and if the result is true, the loop body is entered.

- The body of the loop must take some action that alters the value of the loop control variable so that in a subsequent test, the `while` expression eventually evaluates as false.

When you write a loop, you must control the number of repetitions it performs; if you do not, you run the risk of creating an **infinite loop**, which is a loop with no end. Commonly, you can control a loop's repetitions in one of two ways:

- Use a counter to create a definite, counter-controlled loop.

- Use a sentinel value to create an indefinite loop.

Using a Definite Loop with a Counter

Figure 4-2 shows an application with a `main()` method that contains a loop that displays *Hello* four times before it displays *Goodbye*. The variable `count` is the loop control variable. This loop is a **definite loop** because it executes a definite, predetermined number of times—in this case, four. The loop is a **counted loop** or **counter-controlled loop** because the program keeps track of the number of loop repetitions by counting them.

120

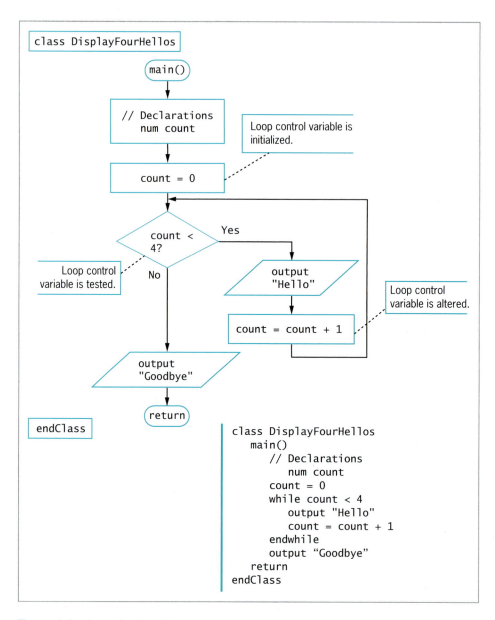

Figure 4-2 An application with a counted `while` loop

The loop in Figure 4-2 executes as follows:

- The loop control variable is initialized to 0.
- The `while` expression compares `count` to 4.

- The value of count is less than 4, so the loop body executes. The loop body shown in Figure 4-2 consists of two statements. The first statement displays *Hello* and the second statement adds 1 to count.

- The next time count is evaluated, its value is 1, which is still less than 4, so the loop body executes again. *Hello* is displayed a second time and count becomes 2, *Hello* is displayed a third time and count becomes 3, then *Hello* is displayed a fourth time and count becomes 4. Now when the expression count < 4 evaluates, it is false, so the loop ends, and the logic proceeds to the statement that follows the loop.

Within the body of a correctly functioning loop, you can change the value of the loop control variable in a number of ways. Many loop control variable values are altered by **incrementing**, or adding to them, as in Figure 4-2. Other loops are controlled by reducing, or **decrementing**, a variable and testing whether the value remains greater than some benchmark value. For example, the loop in Figure 4-2 could be rewritten so that count is initialized to 4 and reduced by 1 on each pass through the loop. The loop should then continue while count remains greater than 0. Loops are also controlled by adding or subtracting values other than 1. For example, to display company profits at five-year intervals for the next 50 years, you would want to add 5 to a loop control variable during each iteration.

 Because programmers so frequently need to increment a variable, many programming languages contain a shortcut operator for incrementing. You will learn about these shortcut operators when you study a programming language that uses them.

The looping logic shown in Figure 4-2 uses a counter. A **counter** is any numeric variable you use to count the number of times an event has occurred. In everyday life, people usually count things starting with 1. Many programmers prefer starting their counted loops with a variable that contains a 0 value. When you learn about arrays in Chapter 5, you will discover that array manipulation naturally lends itself to 0-based loops.

Using an Indefinite Loop with a Sentinel Value

Often, the value of a loop control variable is not altered by arithmetic, but instead is altered by input. For example, perhaps you want to continue performing some task while the user indicates a desire to continue. In that case, you do not know when you write the program whether the loop will be executed 2 times, 200 times, or not at all. This type of loop is an **indefinite loop**.

Consider an interactive program that displays *Hello* repeatedly as long as the user wants to continue. The loop is indefinite because each time the program executes, the loop might be performed a different number of times depending on the user's choices. The program appears in Figure 4-3.

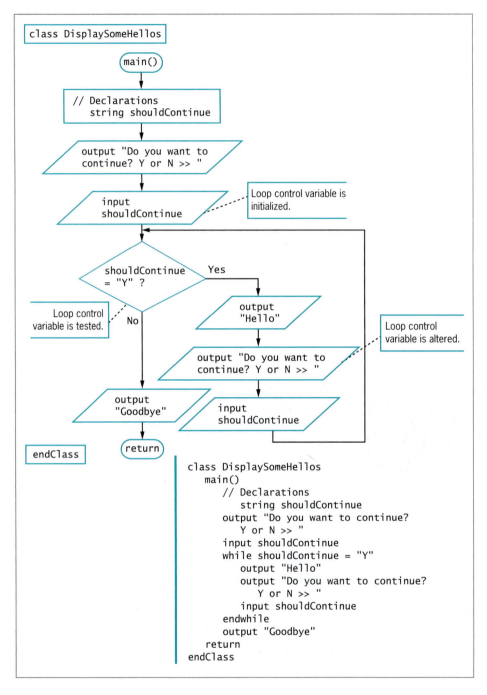

Figure 4-3 An application with an indefinite `while` loop

In the program in Figure 4-3, the loop control variable is shouldContinue. The program executes as follows:

- The loop control variable is initialized by the user's first response. The first response is an example of a priming input. A **priming input** is a first input that gets a loop control variable's first value before the loop starts.

- The while expression compares the loop control variable to "Y". A value like "Y" that signals a stop to a loop is called a **sentinel value**.

- If the user has entered Y, then *Hello* is output and the user is asked whether the program should continue.

- At any point, if the user enters anything other than Y, the loop ends. In most programming languages, comparisons are case sensitive. If a program tests shouldContinue = "Y", a user response of y will result in a false evaluation.

Figure 4-4 shows how the program might look when it is executed at the command line and in a graphical user interface (GUI) environment. The screens in Figure 4-4 show programs that perform exactly the same tasks using different environments. In each environment, the user can continue to choose to see *Hello* messages or can choose to quit the program and display *Goodbye*.

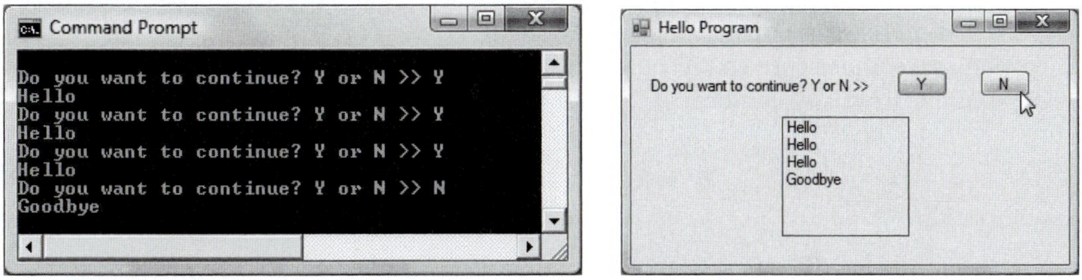

Figure 4-4   Typical executions of the program in Figure 4-3 in two environments

Using Nested Loops

Program logic gets more complicated when you must use loops within loops, or **nested loops**. When one loop appears inside another, the loop that contains the other loop is the **outer loop**, and the loop that is contained is the **inner loop**. You need to create nested loops when the values of two or more variables repeat to produce every combination of values. Usually, when you create nested loops, each loop has its own loop control variable.

For example, suppose that you want to write a program that produces a quiz answer sheet like the one shown in Figure 4-5. The answer sheet is for a quiz that has five parts with three questions in each part, and you want a fill-in-the-blank line for each question. You could write a program that uses 21 separate output statements to produce the 21 lines on the answer sheet, but it is more efficient to use nested loops.

Figure 4-6 shows the logic for the program that produces an answer sheet. Two loop control variables are declared for the program:

- partCounter controls the outer loop that keeps track of the answer sheet parts.

- questionCounter controls the inner loop that keeps track of the questions and answer lines within each part section on each answer sheet.

Four named constants are also declared. Two of these constants (PARTS and QUESTIONS) hold the sentinel values for the loops in the program. The other two hold the text that will be output (the word *Part* that precedes each part number, and the period-space-underscore combination that forms a fill-in line for each question).

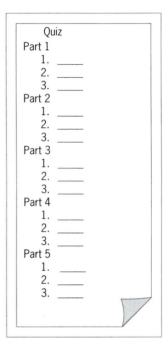

Figure 4-5   Quiz answer sheet

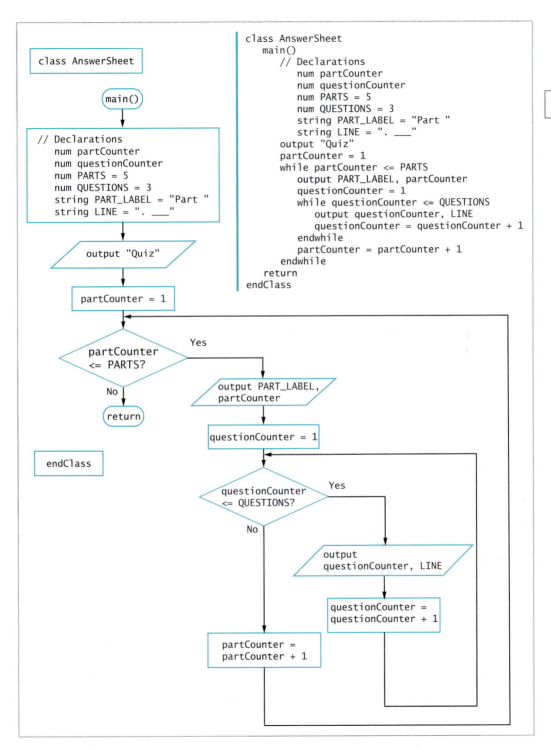

```
class AnswerSheet
    main()
        // Declarations
            num partCounter
            num questionCounter
            num PARTS = 5
            num QUESTIONS = 3
            string PART_LABEL = "Part "
            string LINE = ". ___"
        output "Quiz"
        partCounter = 1
        while partCounter <= PARTS
            output PART_LABEL, partCounter
            questionCounter = 1
            while questionCounter <= QUESTIONS
                output questionCounter, LINE
                questionCounter = questionCounter + 1
            endwhile
            partCounter = partCounter + 1
        endwhile
        return
endClass
```

Figure 4-6 Flowchart and pseudocode for program that produces an answer sheet

When the program starts, the quiz title is output, and then `partCounter` is initialized to 1. The `partCounter` variable is the loop control variable for the outer loop. The outer loop continues while `partCounter` is less than or equal to `PARTS`. The last statement in the outer loop adds 1 to `partCounter`. In other words, the outer loop will execute when `partCounter` is 1, 2, 3, 4, and 5.

In the outer loop in Figure 4-6, the word *Part* and the current `partCounter` value are output. The following steps then execute:

- The loop control variable for the inner loop is initialized by setting `questionCounter` to 1.

- The loop control variable `questionCounter` is evaluated by comparing it to `QUESTIONS`, and while `questionCounter` does not exceed `QUESTIONS`, the loop body executes: The value of `questionCounter` is output, followed by a period and a fill-in-the-blank line.

- At the end of the loop body, the loop control variable is altered by adding 1 to `questionCounter` and the `questionCounter` comparison is made again.

In other words, when `partCounter` is 1, the part heading is output and underscore lines are output for questions 1, 2, and 3. Then `partCounter` becomes 2, the part heading is output, and underscore lines are created for another set of questions 1, 2, and 3. Then `partCounter` becomes 3, 4, and 5 in turn, and three underscore lines are created for each part. In the program in Figure 4-6, it is important that `questionCounter` is reset to 1 within the outer loop, just before entering the inner loop. If this step was omitted, Part 1 would contain questions 1, 2, and 3, but subsequent parts would be empty.

 Watch the video *Nested Loops*.

Avoiding Common Loop Mistakes

Beginning and experienced programmers make logical errors when writing loops. The mistakes programmers make most often with loops are:

- Neglecting to initialize the loop control variable

- Neglecting to alter the loop control variable

- Using the wrong comparison with the loop control variable

- Including statements inside the loop that belong outside the loop

The following sections explain these common mistakes in more detail.

Mistake: Neglecting to Initialize the Loop Control Variable

Failing to initialize a loop's control variable is a mistake. For example, consider the program in Figure 4-7. It prompts the user for a name, and while the name continues to be something other than the sentinel value *ZZZ*, it outputs a greeting that uses the name and asks for the next name. This program works correctly.

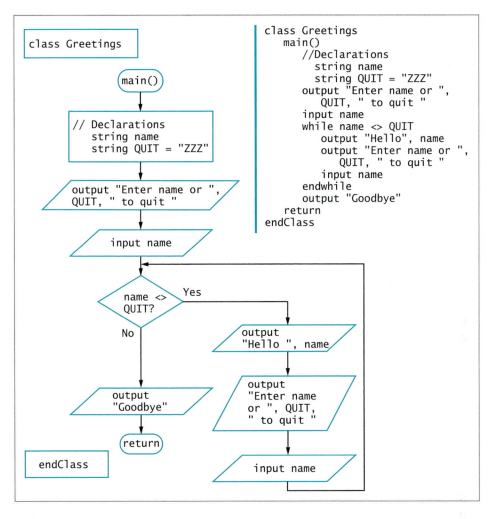

```
class Greetings
    main()
        //Declarations
            string name
            string QUIT = "ZZZ"
        output "Enter name or ",
            QUIT, " to quit "
        input name
        while name <> QUIT
            output "Hello", name
            output "Enter name or ",
                QUIT, " to quit "
            input name
        endwhile
        output "Goodbye"
    return
endClass
```

Figure 4-7 Correct logic for greeting program

Figure 4-8 shows an incorrect program in which the loop control variable is not assigned a starting value. If the name variable is not set to a starting value, then when the name is compared to QUIT, there is no way to predict whether the result will be true. If the user does not enter a value for name, the garbage value originally held by that variable might or might not be *ZZZ*. So, one of two scenarios follows:

- Most likely, the uninitialized value of name is not *ZZZ*, so the first greeting output will include garbage—for example, *Hello 12BGr5*.

- By a remote chance, the uninitialized value of name *is ZZZ*, so the program ends immediately before the user can enter any names.

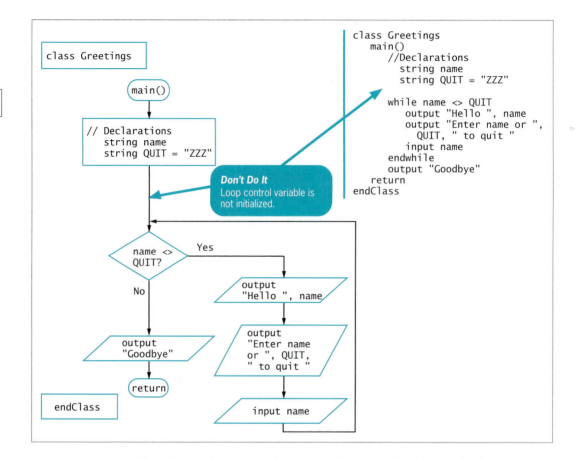

Figure 4-8   Incorrect logic for greeting program because the loop control variable initialization is missing

Mistake: Neglecting to Alter the Loop Control Variable

Different sorts of errors will occur if you fail to alter a loop control variable within the loop. For example, in the program in Figure 4-7 that accepts and displays names, you create such an error if you don't accept names within the loop. Figure 4-9 shows the resulting incorrect logic.

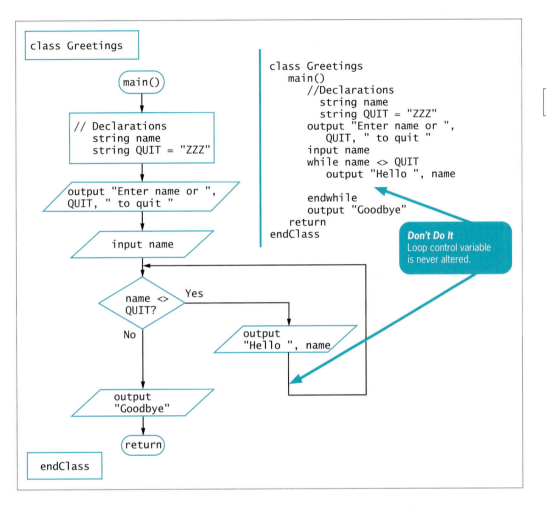

Figure 4-9 Incorrect logic for greeting program because the loop control variable is not altered

If you remove the `input name` instruction from the end of the loop in the program, no name is ever entered after the first one. For example, assume that when the program starts, the user enters *Fred*. The name will be compared to the sentinel value, and the loop will be entered. After a greeting is output for Fred, no new name is entered, so when the logic returns to the loop-controlling question, the `name` will still not be *ZZZ*, and greetings for Fred will continue to be output infinitely. You never want to create a loop that cannot terminate.

Mistake: Using the Wrong Comparison with the Loop Control Variable

Programmers must be careful to use the correct comparison in the statement that controls a loop. A comparison is correct only when the correct operands and operator are used. For example, although only one keystroke differs between the original greeting program in

Figure 4-7 and the one in Figure 4-10, the original program correctly produces named greetings and the second one does not.

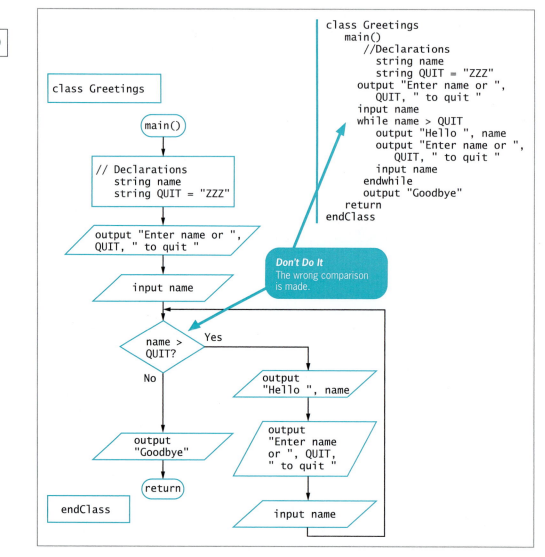

Figure 4-10 Incorrect logic for greeting program because the wrong test is made with the loop control variable

In Figure 4-10, a greater-than comparison (>) is made instead of a not-equal-to (<>) comparison. Suppose that when the program executes, the user enters *Fred* as the first name. In most programming languages, when the comparison between *Fred* and *ZZZ* is made, the values are compared alphabetically. *Fred* is not greater than *ZZZ*, so the loop is never entered, and the program ends.

Using the wrong comparison can have serious effects. For example, in a counted loop, if you use <= instead of < to compare a counter to a sentinel value, the program will perform one loop execution too many. If the loop only displays greetings, the error might not be critical, but if such an error occurred in a loan company application, each customer might be charged a month's additional interest. If the error occurred in an airline's application, it might overbook a flight. If the error occurred in a pharmacy's drug-dispensing application, each patient might receive one extra (and possibly harmful) unit of medication.

Mistake: Including Statements Inside the Loop that Belong Outside the Loop

Suppose that you write a program for a store manager who wants to discount every item he sells by 30 percent. The manager wants 100 new price label stickers for each item. The user enters a price, the new discounted price is calculated, 100 stickers are printed, and the next price is entered. Figure 4-11 shows a program that performs the job inefficiently because the same value, newPrice, is calculated 100 separate times for each price that is entered.

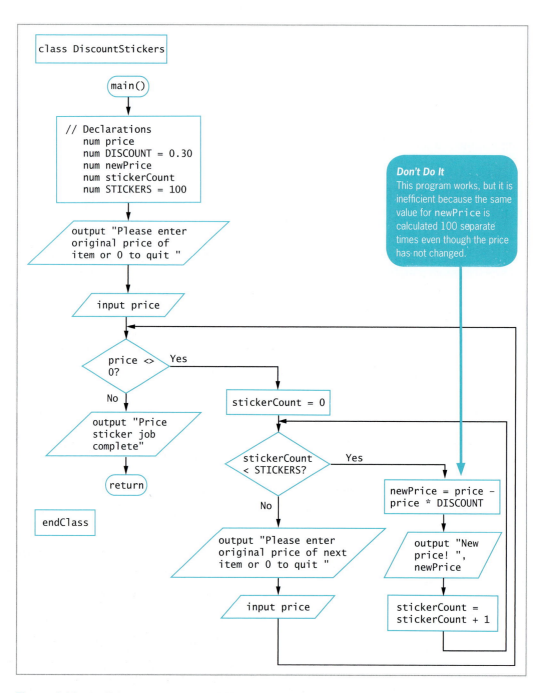

Figure 4-11   Inefficient way to produce 100 discount price stickers for differently priced items

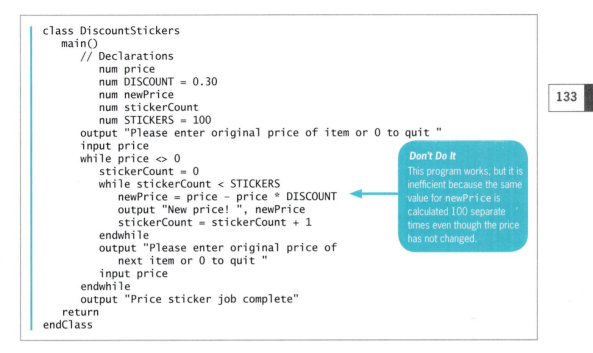

```
class DiscountStickers
    main()
        // Declarations
            num price
            num DISCOUNT = 0.30
            num newPrice
            num stickerCount
            num STICKERS = 100
        output "Please enter original price of item or 0 to quit "
        input price
        while price <> 0
            stickerCount = 0
            while stickerCount < STICKERS
                newPrice = price - price * DISCOUNT
                output "New price! ", newPrice
                stickerCount = stickerCount + 1
            endwhile
            output "Please enter original price of
                next item or 0 to quit "
            input price
        endwhile
        output "Price sticker job complete"
    return
endClass
```

Don't Do It
This program works, but it is inefficient because the same value for newPrice is calculated 100 separate times even though the price has not changed.

Figure 4-11   Inefficient way to produce 100 discount price stickers for differently priced items
(continued)

Figure 4-12 shows the same program, in which the newPrice value that is output on the sticker is calculated only once per new price; the calculation has been moved to a better location. The programs in Figures 4-11 and 4-12 do the same thing, but the second program does it more efficiently. As you become more proficient at programming, you will recognize many opportunities to perform the same tasks in alternate, more elegant, and more efficient ways.

When you describe people or events as *elegant*, you mean they possess a refined gracefulness. Similarly, programmers use the term *elegant* to describe programs that are well designed and easy to understand and maintain.

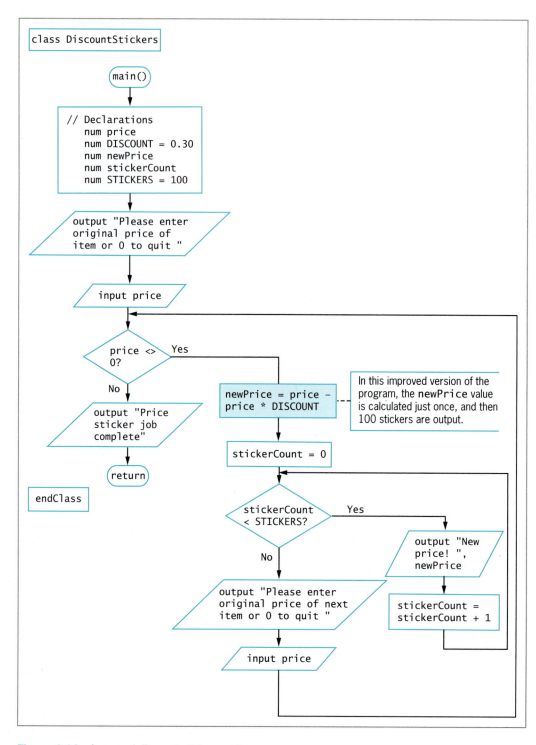

Figure 4-12   Improved discount sticker-making program

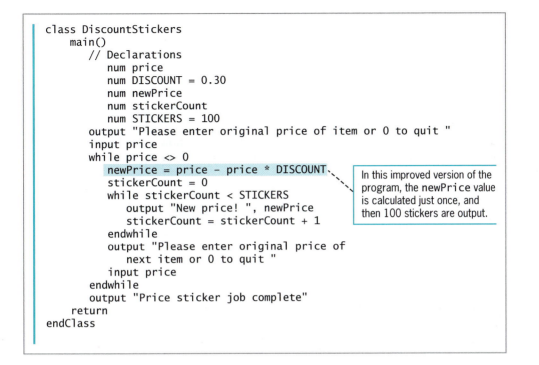

```
class DiscountStickers
    main()
        // Declarations
            num price
            num DISCOUNT = 0.30
            num newPrice
            num stickerCount
            num STICKERS = 100
        output "Please enter original price of item or 0 to quit "
        input price
        while price <> 0
            newPrice = price - price * DISCOUNT
            stickerCount = 0
            while stickerCount < STICKERS
                output "New price! ", newPrice
                stickerCount = stickerCount + 1
            endwhile
            output "Please enter original price of
                next item or 0 to quit "
            input price
        endwhile
        output "Price sticker job complete"
    return
endClass
```

In this improved version of the program, the newPrice value is calculated just once, and then 100 stickers are output.

Figure 4-12 Improved discount sticker-making program (continued)

 Watch the video *Avoiding Common Loop Mistakes.*

Using a for Loop

Every high-level programming language contains a while statement that you can use to code any loop, including both indefinite and definite loops. In addition to the while statement, most computer languages support a **for statement**, or **for loop**. You use a for statement with definite loops—those that will loop a specific number of times—when the program knows exactly how many times the loop will repeat.

The for statement provides you with three actions in one compact statement. In a for statement, a loop control variable is:

- Initialized

- Evaluated

- Altered

135

The statement takes the following form, where `lcv` is a loop control variable:

```
for lcv = initialValue to finalValue step stepValue
   do something
endfor
```

The `for` statement looks slightly different in various modern programming languages. In several languages, the three actions in the `for` statement are separated with semicolons. Figure 4-13 shows three possible ways to write pseudocode that displays *Hello* four times—using a `while` loop, using pseudocode that resembles how a `for` loop looks in Visual Basic, and using pseudocode that represents how a `for` loop looks in Java, C++, and C#.

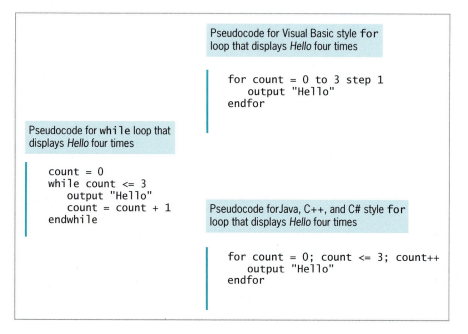

Figure 4-13   Comparable `while` and `for` statements that each output *Hello* four times

The code segments in Figure 4-13 each accomplish the same tasks:

- The variable `count` is initialized to 0.

- The `count` variable is compared to the limit value 3; while `count` is less than or equal to 3, the loop body executes. In the `for` loop version that is most like Visual Basic, you can think of the expression `count = 0 to 3` as meaning that `count` takes on values *through* 3. In the version of the `for` loop that is more like Java, C++, or C#, the expression `count <= 3` appears between semicolons that separate it from the first and last sections, and the comparison is similar to the one used in the `while` statement.

- As the last statement in the loop execution, the value of `count` increases by 1. In the version that is similar to Visual Basic, the expression `step 1` means to increase the loop control variable by 1 each time. In the version that is similar to Java, C++, and C#, the expression count++ means to add 1 to count; you could also write count = count + 1, but the shorthand version is preferred by many programmers.

- After the loop control variable is increased, the comparison to the limit value is made again.

The while loop and for loop execute the same iterations; the for loop simply can express the same logic in a more compact form.

The amount by which a for loop control variable changes after the body executes is often called a **step value**. The step value can be positive or negative, and it does not have to be 1. For example, the following loop also displays *Hello* four times:

```
for count = 12 to 6 step -2
    output "Hello"
endfor
```

In this loop, the loop control variable is initialized to 12, and the body executes when the loop control variable value is 12, 10, 8, and 6. Of course, writing a loop using these values makes it harder for someone reading your program to immediately understand your intentions, but the loop would work.

You never are required to use a for statement for any loop; a while statement can always be used instead. However, when a loop's execution is based on a loop control variable progressing from a known starting value to a known ending value in equal steps, the for loop provides you with a convenient shorthand. It is easy for others to read, and because the loop control variable's initialization, testing, and alteration are all performed in one location, you are less likely to leave out one of these crucial elements.

The programmer doesn't need to know the starting value, ending value, or step value for the loop control variable when the program is written; only the application must know those values while the program is running. For example, any of the values might be entered by the user or might be the result of a calculation.

The for loop is particularly useful when processing arrays. You will learn about arrays in Chapter 5.

Both the while loop and the for loop are examples of *pretest loops*. That means the loop control variable is tested before each iteration. Most languages allow you to use a variation of the looping structure known as a *posttest loop*, which tests the loop control variable after each iteration. Appendix D contains information about posttest loops.

Common Loop Applications

Although every computer program is different, many techniques are common to a variety of applications. Loops, for example, are frequently used to accumulate totals and to validate data.

Using a Loop to Accumulate Totals

Business reports often include totals. The supervisor who requests a list of employees in the company dental plan is often as interested in the total premiums paid as in who the participants are. When you receive your telephone bill at the end of the month, you usually check the total as well as the charges for the individual calls.

For example, a real estate broker might want to see a list of all properties sold in the last month, as well as the total value for all the properties. A program might read sales data that includes the street address of the property sold and its selling price. The data records might be entered by a clerk as each sale is made and stored in a file until the end of the month; subsequently, they can be used in a monthly report. Figure 4-14 shows an example of such a report.

```
            MONTH–END SALES REPORT

      Address                Price

      287 Acorn St          150,000
      12 Maple Ave          310,000
      8723 Marie Ln          65,500
      222 Acorn St          127,000
      29 Bahama Way         450,000

      Total               1,102,500
```

Figure 4-14   Month-end real estate sales report

To create the sales report, you must output the address and price for each property sold and add its value to an accumulator. An **accumulator** is a variable that you use to gather or accumulate values. An accumulator is very similar to a counter that you use to count loop iterations. However, usually you add just one to a counter, whereas you add some other value to an accumulator. If the real estate broker wants to know how many listings the company holds, you *count* them. When she wants to know the total real estate value, you *accumulate* it.

To accumulate total real estate prices, you declare a numeric variable such as accumValue and initialize it to 0. As you get each real estate transaction's data, you output it and add its value to the accumulator accumValue, as shown shaded in Figure 4-15.

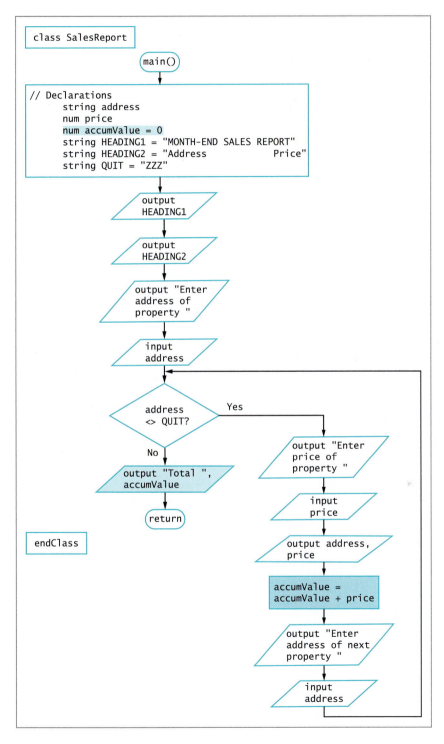

Figure 4-15 Flowchart and pseudocode for real estate sales report program

```
class SalesReport
   main()
      // Declarations
         string address
         num price
         num accumValue = 0
         string HEADING1 = "MONTH-END SALES REPORT"
         string HEADING2 = "Address          Price"
         string QUIT = "ZZZ"
      output HEADING1
      output HEADING2
      output "Enter address of property "
      input address
      while address <> QUIT
         output "Enter price of property "
         input price
         output address, price
         accumValue = accumValue + price
         output "Enter address of next property "
         input address
      endwhile
      output "Total ", accumValue
   return
endClass
```

Figure 4-15   Flowchart and pseudocode for real estate sales report program (continued)

The output in Figure 4-14 shows a blank line after the top heading and the column headings. When the real estate sales program is coded in a programming language, instructions will be created to produce the blank lines. The procedure to accomplish this varies among languages.

Some programming languages assign 0 to a numeric variable you fail to initialize explicitly, but many do not—when you try to add a value to an uninitialized variable, they either issue an error message or let you incorrectly start with an accumulator that holds garbage. The safest and clearest course of action is to assign the value 0 to accumulators before using them.

After the program in Figure 4-15 gets and displays the last real estate transaction, the user enters the sentinel value and loop execution ends. At that point, the accumulator will hold the grand total of all the real estate values. Just before the program ends, it displays the word *Total* and the accumulated value `accumValue`.

Figure 4-15 highlights the three actions you usually must take with an accumulator:

- Accumulators are initialized to 0.
- Accumulators are altered, usually once for every data set processed.
- At the end of processing, accumulators are output.

After outputting the value of `accumValue`, new programmers often want to reset it to 0. Their argument is that they are "cleaning up after themselves." Although you can take this step without harming the execution of the program, it does not serve any useful purpose. You cannot set `accumValue` to 0 in anticipation of having it ready for the next program, or even for the next time you execute this program. Variables exist only during an execution of the program, and even if a future application happens to contain a variable named `accumValue`, the variable will not necessarily occupy the same memory location as this one. Even if you run the same application a second time, the variables might occupy physical memory locations different from those they occupied during the first run. At the beginning of any method, it is the programmer's responsibility to initialize all variables that must start with a specific value. There is no benefit to changing a variable's value when it will never be used again during the current execution.

Some business reports list only totals, with no individual item details. Such reports are called **summary reports**. For example, in Figure 4-15, if the statement that outputs the address and price of each property were removed from the program (just above where `price` is added to `accumValue`), then no individual records would be listed on output, but the summary would still appear at the end.

Using a Loop to Validate Data

Incorrect user entries are by far the most common source of computer errors. The programs you write will be improved if you employ **defensive programming**, which means trying to prepare for all possible errors before they occur. Loops are frequently used as a defensive programming mechanism to **validate data**—that is, to make sure it is meaningful and useful. For example, validation might ensure that a value is the correct type or that it falls within an acceptable range.

Invalid data can make parts of a program worthless. Programmers employ the acronym **GIGO** for *garbage in, garbage out*. It means that if your input is incorrect, your output is worthless. For example, suppose that part of a program you are writing asks a user to enter a number that represents his or her birth month. If the user types a number lower than 1 or greater than 12, the month is obviously invalid, and you might want to take some sort of corrective action. For example:

- You could display an error message and stop the program.

- You could choose to assign a default value for the month (for example, 1) before proceeding.

- You could reprompt the user for valid input.

If you choose this last course of action, at least two approaches could be used. You could use a selection, and if the month is invalid, you can ask the user to reenter a number, as shown in Figure 4-16.

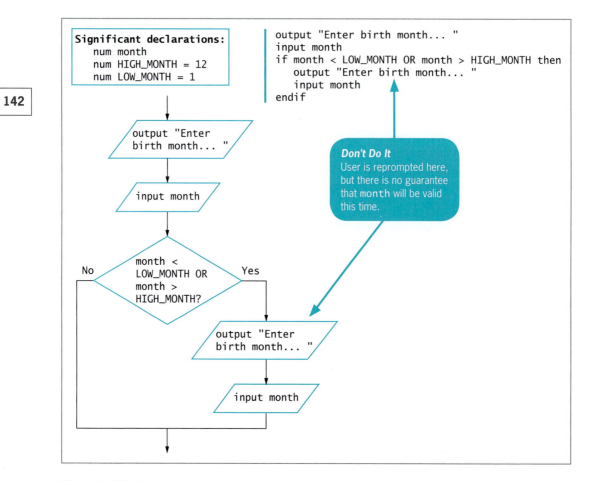

Significant declarations:
    num month
    num HIGH_MONTH = 12
    num LOW_MONTH = 1

```
output "Enter birth month... "
input month
if month < LOW_MONTH OR month > HIGH_MONTH then
    output "Enter birth month... "
    input month
endif
```

output "Enter
birth month... "

input month

month <
LOW_MONTH OR
month >
HIGH_MONTH?

No   Yes

Don't Do It
User is reprompted here,
but there is no guarantee
that month will be valid
this time.

output "Enter
birth month... "

input month

Figure 4-16   Reprompting a user once after an invalid month is entered

The problem with the logic in Figure 4-16 is that the user still might not enter valid data on the second attempt to enter a month. Of course, you could add a third decision, but you still couldn't control what the user enters.

The superior solution is to use a loop to continuously prompt a user for a month until the user enters it correctly. Figure 4-17 shows this approach.

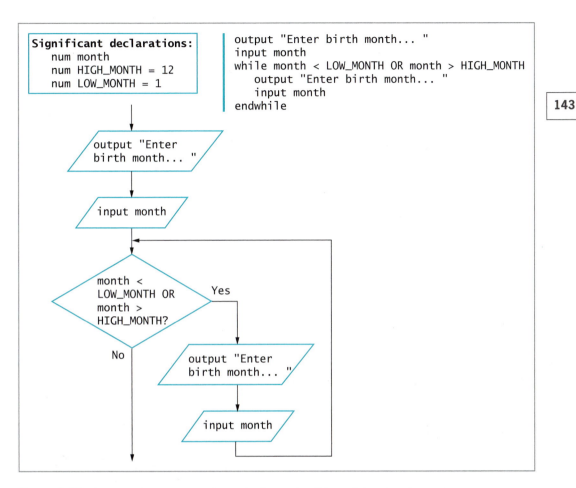

```
Significant declarations:
   num month
   num HIGH_MONTH = 12
   num LOW_MONTH = 1
```

```
output "Enter birth month... "
input month
while month < LOW_MONTH OR month > HIGH_MONTH
   output "Enter birth month... "
   input month
endwhile
```

Figure 4-17   Reprompting a user continuously after an invalid month is entered

Most languages provide a built-in way to check whether an entered value is numeric or not. When you rely on user input, you frequently accept each piece of input data as a string and then attempt to convert it to a number. The procedure for accomplishing numeric checks is slightly different in different programming languages.

Just because a data item is valid does not mean that it is correct. For example, a program can determine that 5 is a valid birth month, but not that your birthday actually falls in month 5. If entering a correct month is crucial, you might ask the user to enter the value twice and then check to make sure the entered values match. Alternatively, you might display the entered number and ask the user whether the value is correct, or you might ask the user to type the name of the month to ensure it matches the entered number. In situations where the data is extremely crucial, such as in a security program, you might even employ more sophisticated technology, such as using a device that scans the user's birth date from an ID card.

Limiting a Reprompting Loop

Reprompting a user is a good way to ensure valid data, but it can be frustrating to a user if it continues indefinitely. For example, suppose that the user must enter a valid birth month from 1 through 12, but has used another application in which January was month 0, and keeps entering 0 no matter how many times you repeat the prompt. One helpful addition to the program would be to use the limiting values as part of the prompt. In other words, instead of the statement output "Enter birth month... ", the following statement, which uses constants for the highest and lowest valid values, might be clearer:

```
output "Enter birth month between ", LOW_MONTH, ",
    and ", HIGH_MONTH, " ... "
```

Still, the user might not understand the prompt or not read it carefully, so you might want to employ the tactic used in Figure 4-18, in which a count of the number of reprompts is maintained. In this example, a constant named ATTEMPTS is set to 3. While a count of the user's attempts at correct data entry remains below this limit, and the user enters invalid data, the user continues to be reprompted. If the user exceeds the limited number of allowed attempts, the loop ends. The next action depends on the application. If count equals ATTEMPTS after the data-entry loop ends, you might want to force the invalid data to a default value. **Forcing** a data item means you override incorrect data by setting the variable to a specific value. For example, you might decide that if a month value does not fall between 1 and 12, you will force the month to 0 or 99, which indicates to users that no valid value exists. In a different application, you might just choose to end the program. In an interactive, Web-based program, you might choose to have a customer service representative start a chat session with the user to offer help. You want to make it easy for your users to enter correct data. Programs that frustrate users can result in lost revenue for a company. For example, if a company's Web site is difficult to navigate, users might just give up and not do business with the organization.

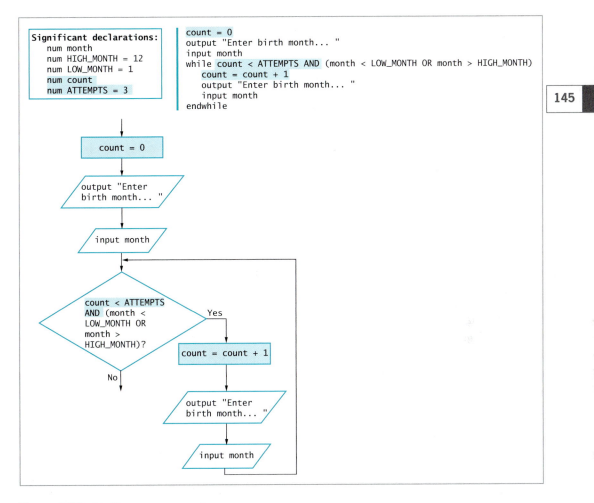

Figure 4-18 Limiting user reprompts

Validating a Data Type

The data you use within computer programs is varied. It stands to reason that validating data requires a variety of methods. For example, some programming languages allow you to check data items to make sure they are the correct data type. This book uses the data types string and num. Most programming languages provide additional, more specific data types. Although the techniques for validating a data type vary from language to language, a common approach is to use a statement like the one shown in Figure 4-19. In this program segment, isNumeric() represents a call to a prewritten method; it is used to check whether the entered employee salary falls within the category of numeric data. You check to ensure that a value is numeric for many reasons—an important one is that only numeric values can be used correctly in arithmetic statements. A method such as isNumeric() is most often provided with the language translator you use to write your programs; you must check your chosen language's documentation to find the exact name of the method in that language. Such a method operates as a black box; in other words, you can use the method's results without understanding its internal statements.

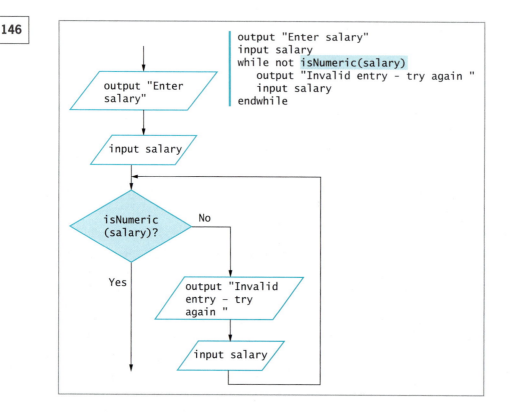

```
output "Enter salary"
input salary
while not isNumeric(salary)
    output "Invalid entry - try again "
    input salary
endwhile
```

Figure 4-19 Checking data for correct type

Besides allowing you to check whether a value is numeric, some languages contain methods such as isChar(), which checks whether a value is a character data type; isWhitespace(), which checks whether a value is a nonprinting character, such as a space or tab; and isUpper() or isLower(), which checks whether a value is an uppercase or lowercase alphabetic character.

In many languages, input statements are used to accept all user data as strings of characters. Then, you can use built-in methods to attempt to convert the characters to the correct data type for your application. When the conversion methods succeed, you have useful data. When the conversion methods fail because the user has entered the wrong data type, you can take appropriate action, such as issuing an error message, reprompting the user, or forcing the data to a default value.

When a data item is an incorrect type, you can avoid errors in many object-oriented languages using a technique called *exception handling*. Exception handling is described in Chapter 10.

Validating Reasonableness and Consistency of Data

Data items can be the correct type and within range but still be incorrect. You have experienced this problem yourself if anyone has ever misspelled your name or overbilled you. The data might have been the correct type—that is, alphabetic letters were used in your name—but the name itself was incorrect. Many data items cannot be checked for reasonableness; for example, the names Catherine, Katherine, and Kathryn are equally reasonable, but only one spelling is correct for a particular woman.

However, many data items can be checked for reasonableness. If you make a purchase on May 3, 2014, then the payment cannot possibly be due prior to that date. Perhaps within your organization, you cannot make more than $20.00 per hour if you work in Department 12. If your zip code is 90201, your state of residence cannot be New York. If your store's cash on hand was $3000 when it closed on Tuesday, the value should not be different when the store opens on Wednesday. If a customer's title is *Ms.*, the customer's gender should be *F*. Each of these examples involves comparing two data items for reasonableness or consistency. You should consider making as many such comparisons as possible when writing your own programs. Frequently, testing for reasonableness and consistency involves using additional data files. For example, to check that a user has entered a valid county of residence for a state, you might use a file that contains every county name within every state in the United States and check the user's county against those contained in the file.

Good defensive programs try to foresee all possible inconsistencies and errors. The more accurate your data, the more useful information you will produce as output from your programs. In school, your grade depends on the accuracy of your programs. When you become a professional programmer, you want your programs to work correctly as a source of professional pride as well as job security. On a more basic level, you do not want to be called in to work at 3 a.m. when the overnight run of your program fails because of errors you created.

Chapter Summary

- When you use a loop in a computer program, you can write one set of instructions that operates on multiple, separate sets of data.

- Three steps must occur in every loop: You must initialize a loop control variable, compare the variable to some value that controls whether the loop continues or stops, and alter the variable that controls the loop.

- When you must use loops within loops, you use nested loops. When nesting loops, you must maintain two individual loop control variables and alter each at the appropriate time.

- Common mistakes that programmers make when writing loops include neglecting to initialize the loop control variable, neglecting to alter the loop control variable, using the wrong comparison with the loop control variable, and including statements inside the loop that belong outside the loop.

- Most computer languages support a for statement or for loop that you can use with definite loops when you know how many times a loop will repeat. The for statement uses a loop control variable that it automatically initializes, evaluates, and increments.

- Loops are used in many applications—for example, to accumulate totals in business reports. Loops also are used to ensure that user data entries are valid by continuously reprompting the user.

Key Terms

A **loop body** contains the statements that execute as long as the loop's controlling Boolean expression remains true.

Repetition is an alternate name for looping.

Iteration is an alternate name for looping.

A **while loop** tests a Boolean expression, and as long as the expression continues to be true, the loop body executes.

A **loop control variable** is a variable that determines whether a loop will continue.

An **infinite loop** is one with no end.

A **definite loop** is one for which the number of repetitions is a predetermined value.

A **counted loop** or **counter-controlled loop** is a loop whose repetitions are managed by a counter.

Incrementing a variable is adding a constant value to it, frequently 1.

Decrementing a variable is decreasing it by a constant value, frequently 1.

A **counter** is any numeric variable you use to count the number of times an event has occurred.

An **indefinite loop** is one for which you cannot predetermine the number of executions.

A **priming input** is a first input that gets a loop control variable's first value before the loop begins.

A **sentinel value** is a value that is tested to determine whether a loop continues or ends.

Nested loops occur when a loop structure exists within another loop structure.

An **outer loop** contains another when loops are nested.

An **inner loop** is contained within another when loops are nested.

A **for statement**, or **for loop**, can be used to code definite loops. The `for` statement contains a loop control variable that it automatically initializes, evaluates, and increments.

A **step value** is a number you use to alter a loop control variable on each pass through a loop.

An **accumulator** is a variable that you use to gather or accumulate values.

A **summary report** lists only totals, without individual detail records.

Defensive programming is a technique with which you try to prepare for all possible errors before they occur.

To **validate data** is to ensure that data items are meaningful and useful.

GIGO ("garbage in, garbage out") means that if your input is incorrect, your output is worthless.

Forcing a data item means you override incorrect data by setting it to a specific value.

Review Questions

1. The structure that allows you to write one set of instructions that operates on multiple, separate sets of data is the _____ .

    a. sequence   c. loop
    b. selection   d. case

2. Every structured loop _____ .

    a. has one entry point
    b. has two exit points
    c. refers to a counter that increases on each pass through the loop
    d. contains a body that must execute at least one time

3. Which of the following is *not* a step that must occur with every correctly working loop?

    a. Initialize a loop control variable before the loop starts.
    b. Set the loop control value equal to a sentinel during each iteration.
    c. Compare the loop control value to a sentinel during each iteration.
    d. Alter the loop control variable during each iteration.

4. The statements executed within a loop are known collectively as the _____ .

    a. loop body   c. sequences
    b. loop controls   d. sentinels

5. A counter keeps track of _____ .

   a. the number of times an event has occurred
   b. the number of machine cycles required by a segment of a program
   c. the number of loop structures within a program
   d. the number of times software has been revised

6. Adding 1 to a variable is also called _____ it.

   a. digesting
   b. resetting
   c. decrementing
   d. incrementing

7. Which of the following is a definite loop?

   a. a loop that executes as long as a user continues to enter valid data
   b. a loop that executes 1000 times
   c. both of the above
   d. none of the above

8. Which of the following is an indefinite loop?

   a. a loop that executes exactly 10 times
   b. a loop that follows a prompt that asks a user how many repetitions to make and uses that value to control the loop
   c. both of the above
   d. none of the above

9. When you decrement a variable, you _____ .

   a. set it to 0
   b. reduce it by one-tenth
   c. subtract 1 from it
   d. remove it from a program

10. When two loops are nested, the loop that is contained by the other is the _____ loop.

    a. captive
    b. unstructured
    c. inner
    d. outer

11. When loops are nested, _____ .

    a. they typically share a loop control variable
    b. one must end before the other begins
    c. both must be the same type—definite or indefinite
    d. none of the above

12. The chief advantage to using a `for` loop is _____ .

    a. infinite loops are prevented

    b. unlike a `while` loop, a `for` loop can be nested

    c. its syntax is concise

    d. unlike a `while` loop, a `for` loop can have multiple entry and exit points

13. A report that lists only totals, with no details about individual records, is a(n) _____ report.

    a. accumulator

    b. final

    c. summary

    d. detailless

14. Typically, the value added to a counter variable is _____ .

    a. 0

    b. 1

    c. 10

    d. 100

15. Typically, the value added to an accumulator variable is _____ .

    a. 0

    b. 1

    c. the same for each iteration

    d. different in each iteration

16. After an accumulator or counter variable is displayed at the end of a program, it is best to _____ .

    a. delete the variable from the program

    b. reset the variable to 0

    c. subtract 1 from the variable

    d. none of the above

17. When you _____ , you make sure data items are the correct type and fall within the correct range.

    a. validate data

    b. employ offensive programming

    c. use object orientation

    d. count loop iterations

18. Overriding a user's entered value by setting it to a predetermined value is known as _____ .

    a. forcing

    b. accumulating

    c. validating

    d. pushing

19. To ensure that a user's entry is the correct data type, frequently you _____ .

    a. prompt the user to verify that the type is correct

    b. use a method built into the programming language

    c. include a statement at the beginning of the program that lists the data types allowed

    d. all of the above

20. Variables might hold incorrect values even when they are _____.

 a. the correct data type

 b. within a required range

 c. coded by the programmer rather than input by a user

 d. all of the above

Exercises

1. What is output by each of the pseudocode segments in Figure 4-20?

a.
```
a = 3
b = 4
c = 10
while a < c
     a = a + 2
     b = b * 2
endwhile
output a, b, c
```

b.
```
d = 3
e = 5
f = 7
while d > f
     d = d + 1
     e = e + 1
endwhile
f = f + 1
output d, e, f
```

c.
```
g = 5
h = 9
while g < h
     g = g + 1
endwhile
output g, h
```

d.
```
j = 2
k = 4
m = 0
n = 7
while j < k
     m = 5
     while m < n
          output "X"
          m = m + 1
     endwhile
     j = j + 1
endwhile
output j, k, m, n
```

e.
```
p = 0
q = 3
r = 6
while p < 5
     p = p + 1
     output p, q, r
     while q < r
          q = q + 1
          output p, q, r
     endwhile
endwhile
output p, q, r
```

f.
```
s = 1
t = 4
u = 6
while s < t
     s = s + 1
     output "Y"
     while s < u
          output "Z"
          u = u - 1
     endwhile
endwhile
output s, t, u
```

Figure 4-20 Pseudocode segments for Exercise 1

2. Design the logic for a program that outputs every number from 0 through 8.

3. Design the logic for a program that outputs every number from 0 through 8 along with its square and cube.

4. Design the logic for a program that outputs every even number from 2 through 20.

5. Design the logic for a program that outputs numbers in reverse order from 8 down to 0.

6. Design the logic for a program that allows a user to enter a number. Display the sum of every number from 1 through the entered number.

7. a. Honest Ralph's Used Car Company allows customers to purchase cars over a 24-month period by making 24 equal payments and charging no interest. Design an application that gets customer data, including an account number, customer name, and purchase price. Output the account number and name, then output the customer's projected balance each month for the next 24 months after the payment is made.

   b. Modify the car payment application so it executes continuously for any number of customers until a sentinel value is supplied for the account number.

8. a. Sneaky Sam's Used Car Company provides car loans to customers at 2 percent interest per month. Design an application that gets customer data, including an account number, customer name, and purchase price. Output the account number and name, then output the customer's projected balance each month for the next 24 months. Assume that when the balance reaches $25 or less, the customer can pay off the account. At the beginning of every month, 2 percent interest is added to the balance, and then the customer makes a payment equal to 1/24 of the current balance.

   b. Modify the car payment application so it executes continuously for any number of customers until a sentinel value is supplied for the account number.

9. Yabe Online Auctions requires its sellers to post items for sale for a six-week period during which the price of any unsold item drops 12 percent each week. For example, an item that costs $10.00 during the first week costs 12 percent less, or $8.80, during the second week. In the third week, the same item is 12 percent less than $8.80, or $7.74. Design an application that allows a user to input prices until an appropriate sentinel value is entered. Program output is the price of each item during each week, one through six.

10. The Howell Bank provides savings accounts that compound interest on a yearly basis. In other words, if you deposit $100 for two years at 4 percent interest, at the end of one year you will have $104. At the end of two years, you will have the $104 plus 4 percent of that, or $108.16. Design a program that accepts an account number, the account owner's first and last names, and a balance. The program operates continuously until an appropriate sentinel value is entered for the account number. Output the projected running total balance for each account for each of the next 20 years.

11. Mr. Roper owns 20 apartment buildings. Each building contains 15 units that he rents for $800 per month each. Design the application that would output 12 payment coupons for each of the 15 apartments in each of the 20 buildings. Each coupon should contain the building number (1 through 20), the apartment number (1 through 15), the month (1 through 12), and the amount of rent due.

12. Design a retirement planning calculator for Skulling Financial Services. Allow a user to enter a number of working years remaining in the user's career and the annual amount of money the user can save. Assume that the user earns three percent simple interest on savings annually. Program output is a schedule that lists each year number in retirement starting with year 0 and the user's savings at the start of that year. Assume that the user spends $50,000 per year in retirement and then earns three percent interest on the remaining balance. End the list after 40 years, or when the user's balance is 0 or less, whichever comes first.

13. Ellison Private Elementary School has three classrooms in each of nine grades, kindergarten (grade 0) through grade 8, and allows parents to pay tuition over the nine-month school year. Design the application that outputs nine tuition payment coupons for each of the 27 classrooms. Each coupon should contain the grade number (0 through 8), the classroom number (1 through 3), the month (1 through 9), and the amount of tuition due. Tuition for kindergarten is $80 per month. Tuition for the other grades is $60 per month times the grade level.

14. a. Design a program for the *Hollywood Movie Rating Guide*, which can be installed in a kiosk in theaters. Each theater patron enters a value from 0 to 4 indicating the number of stars that the patron awards to the guide's featured movie of the week. If a user enters a star value that does not fall in the correct range, reprompt the user continuously until a correct value is entered. The program executes continuously until the theater manager enters a negative number to quit. At the end of the program, display the average star rating for the movie.

    b. Modify the movie-rating program so that a user gets three tries to enter a valid rating. After three incorrect entries, the program issues an appropriate message and continues with a new user.

15. The Café Noir Coffee Shop wants some market research on its customers. When a customer places an order, a clerk asks for the customer's zip code and age. The clerk enters that data as well as the number of items the customer orders. The program operates continuously until the clerk enters a 0 for zip code at the end of the day. When the clerk enters an invalid zip code (more than 5 digits) or an invalid age (defined as less than 10 or more than 110), the program reprompts the clerk continuously. When the clerk enters fewer than 1 or more than 12 items, the program reprompts the clerk two more times. If the clerk enters a high value on the third attempt, the program accepts the high value, but if the clerk enters zero or a negative value on the third attempt, an error message is displayed and the order is not counted. At the end of the program, display a count of the number of items ordered by customers from the same zip code as the coffee shop (54984), and a count from other zip codes. Also display the average customer age as well as counts of the number of items ordered by customers under 30 and by customers 30 and older.

Case Projects

 Case: Cost Is No Object

1. In earlier chapters, you developed classes needed for Cost Is No Object—a car rental service that specializes in lending antique and luxury cars to clients on a short-term basis. The rental service produces computerized paychecks for its employees every week. Write a program that gets data for each of the following:

   - An employee ID number
   - A first name
   - A last name
   - A street address
   - A zip code
   - An hourly pay rate
   - Number of hours worked this week
   - An insurance plan code

   Create an application that prompts the user for employee data; the application continues to accept data for new employees until the user enters 0 for an ID number to quit. While the ID number is not zero, prompt the user for a value for each field in turn. Any time the user enters an invalid value, continue to reprompt the user for the same data. Continue with the next data item only when the previous item is valid, as follows:

   - An employee ID must be between 100 and 999 inclusive.
   - A zip code must not be greater than 99999.
   - An hourly pay rate must be between $6.00 and $25.00 inclusive.
   - The number of hours worked in a week cannot be negative or more than 70.
   - An insurance plan code must be 1 or 2.

   When all the needed data has been entered correctly for an employee, display a copy of all the data fields for the employee as well as the following:

   - Gross pay, calculated as hours worked times pay rate
   - Income tax, which is calculated as 15% of the gross pay if the gross pay is $400 or less; otherwise, it is 20% of the gross pay
   - An insurance premium, which is $60 for insurance plan code 1 and $100 for insurance plan code 2

- Net pay, which is calculated as gross pay minus income tax, minus insurance premium; if the net pay is negative (the employee did not earn enough to cover the tax and insurance), then the net pay should be $0

Case: Classic Reunions

2. In earlier chapters, you developed classes needed for Classic Reunions—a company that provides services for organizers of high school class reunions. The reunion service collects data for each reunion and creates invitations that can be mailed to each attendee. Write a program that gets data for each of the following:

- The name of the school

- The year of the graduating class

- The month, day, and year of the reunion

- The location of the reunion

- The cost per person

Create an application that prompts the user for reunion data. Any time the user enters an invalid value for the reunion data, continue to reprompt the user for the same data. Continue with the next data item only when the previous item is valid, as follows:

- The class year is 1920 to 2010 inclusive.

- The month of the reunion is between 1 and 12 inclusive.

- The day of the reunion is appropriate for the month.

- The cost per person is between $20 and $100 inclusive.

When all the needed reunion data has been entered correctly, continuously prompt the user for the name of an attendee until the user enters *ZZZ* to quit. Create an invitation for each attendee that includes the following:

- The attendee's name

- The school, year, location, date of the reunion, and cost per person

Case: The Barking Lot

3. In earlier chapters, you developed classes needed for The Barking Lot—a dog-boarding facility. A report card is created for each dog that stays in the facility. Staff members enter data about each day of a dog's stay and print the

report for the owner when the dog is picked up. Write a program that gets data for each of the following:

- A dog's name

- The number of days in the stay

Create an application that prompts the user for the boarding data; the application continues to accept data for dogs until the user enters *ZZZ* for the dog's name to quit. While the dog's name is not *ZZZ*, prompt the user for the number of days in the stay. If the number is not between 1 and 21 inclusive, reprompt the user for a valid number.

Then once for each day, enter the following scores:

- A score from 1 to 5 inclusive that rates the dog's appetite

- A score from 1 to 5 that rates the dog's general appearance

- A score from 1 to 5 that rates the dog's attitude and general demeanor

When any of the entered scores is out of range, reprompt the user to enter a valid score.

When all the scores have been entered, output the dog's name and the dog's total score for the entire stay.

Up for Discussion

1. Suppose that you wrote a program that you suspect is in an infinite loop because it keeps running for several minutes with no output and without ending. What would you add to your program to help you discover the origin of the problem?

2. Suppose that you know that every employee in your organization has a seven-digit ID number used for logging on to the computer system. A loop would be useful to guess every combination of seven digits in an ID. Are there any circumstances in which you should try to guess another employee's ID number?

3. If every employee in an organization had a seven-digit ID number, guessing all the possible combinations would be a relatively easy programming task. How could you alter the format of employee IDs to make them more difficult to guess?

CHAPTER 5

Arrays

In this chapter, you will learn about:

◎ Storing data in arrays

◎ How an array can replace nested decisions

◎ Using constants with arrays

◎ Searching an array for an exact match

◎ Using parallel arrays

◎ Searching an array for a range match

◎ Remaining within array bounds

◎ Using a `for` loop to process arrays

Storing Data in Arrays

Suppose that you wanted to write a program in which a user inputs three values and you output them in reverse order. You might write a segment of pseudocode similar to the following:

```
// Declarations
    num value1
    num value2
    num value3
input value1
input value2
input value3
output value3
output value2
output value1
```

Now suppose that you wanted to modify the logic to do the same thing for 3000 values instead of 3. The task of declaring 3000 variables with individual names, inputting them, and then outputting them in reverse order would be time-consuming, tedious, and prone to error. When you work with large volumes of data, using individual variables becomes unwieldy. To relieve programmers of the cumbersome process of dealing with multiple data items that can be better used as a unit, all modern high-level programming languages allow you to create data structures. A **data structure** is a collection of data items that is grouped and organized so it can be used more efficiently. One of the most useful data structures is an array.

An **array** is a data structure that consists of a series or list of values in computer memory. Usually, all the values in an array have something in common; for example, they might represent a list of employee ID numbers or a list of prices for items sold in a store.

Whenever you require multiple storage locations for objects, you can use a real-life counterpart of a programming array. If you store important papers in a series of file folders and label each folder with a consecutive letter of the alphabet, then you are using the equivalent of an array. When you look down the left side of a tax table to find your income level before looking to the right to find your income tax obligation, you are using an array. Similarly, if you look down the left side of a train schedule to find your station before looking to the right to find the train's arrival time, you also are using an array. Because arrays correspond so closely to printed tables, some programmers refer to an array as a *table*; they also use the term *matrix*.

Each of these real-life arrays helps you organize objects or information. You *could* store all your papers or mementos in one huge cardboard box, or find your tax rate or train's arrival time if they were printed randomly in one large book. However, using an organized storage and display system makes your life easier in each case. Using a programming array will accomplish the same results for your data.

How Arrays Occupy Computer Memory

When you declare an array, you declare a structure that contains multiple data items, each of which is the same data type. Each data item is one **element** of the array, and occupies an area in memory next to, or contiguous to, the others. You can indicate the number of elements an array will hold—the **size of the array**—when you declare the array along with your other variables and constants; every array has a fixed size. For example, you might declare an uninitialized, three-element numeric array named someVals as follows:

```
num someVals[3]
```

 Organizations follow different conventions when naming arrays. Some programmers prefer to start each array name with a lowercase *a*. Others prefer to use a plural noun such as *someVals* or *scores*. Still others add *List* to array names, as in *valsList* or *scoreList*.

Each array element is differentiated from the others with a unique **subscript**, also called an **index**, which is a number that indicates the position of a particular item within an array. All array elements have the same group name, but each individual element also has a unique subscript indicating how far away it is from the first element. Therefore, any array's subscripts are always a sequence of integers such as 0 through 4 or 0 through 9. In all languages, subscript values must be sequential integers (whole numbers). In most modern languages, such as Visual Basic, Java, C++, and C#, the first array element is accessed using subscript 0, and this book follows that convention. A common error made by beginning programmers is to forget that array subscripts start with 0. If you assume that an array's first subscript is 1, you will always be "off by one" in your array manipulation. Additionally, when you forget that the first element's subscript is 0, you might forget that the last element's subscript is one less than the array size. For example, the allowed subscripts for a five-element array are 0 through 4.

To use an array element, you place its subscript within parentheses or square brackets (depending on the programming language) after the group name. This book will use square brackets to hold array subscripts so that you don't mistake array names for method names. Many newer programming languages such as C++, Java, and C# also use the bracket notation.

After you declare an array, you can assign values to some or all of the elements individually. Providing array values sometimes is called **populating the array**. The following code shows a three-element array declaration, followed by three separate statements that populate the array:

```
// Declarations
   num someVals[3]
someVals[0] = 25
someVals[1] = 36
someVals[2] = 47
```

Figure 5-1 shows an array named someVals that contains three elements, so the elements are someVals[0], someVals[1], and someVals[2]. The array elements have been assigned the values 25, 36, and 47, respectively. The value stored in someVals[0] is 25; someVals[1] holds 36, and someVals[2] holds 47. The element someVals[0] is zero numbers away from the beginning of the array. The element someVals[1] is one number away from the beginning of the array and someVals[2] is two numbers away.

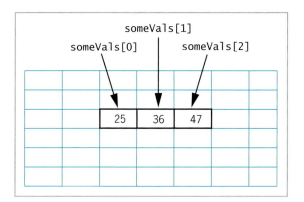

Figure 5-1   Appearance of a three-element array in computer memory

If appropriate, you can declare and initialize array elements in one statement. Most programming languages use a statement similar to the following to declare a three-element array and assign values to it:

num someVals[3] = 25, 36, 47

When you use a list of values to initialize an array, the first value you list is assigned to the first array element, and the subsequent values are assigned in order, starting with the element in position 0. Many programming languages allow you to initialize an array with fewer values than there are array elements declared, but no language allows you to initialize an array using more starting values than the number of positions declared.

After an array has been declared and appropriate values have been assigned to specific elements, you can use an individual element in the same way you would use any other data item of the same type. For example, you can input values to array elements and output the values, and if the elements are numeric, you can perform arithmetic with them.

    Watch the video *Understanding Arrays.*

How an Array Can Replace Nested Decisions

Consider an application requested by a company's human resources department to produce statistics on employees' claimed dependents. The department wants a report that lists the number of employees who have claimed 0, 1, 2, 3, 4, or 5 dependents. (Assume that you know that no employees have more than five dependents.) For example, Figure 5-2 shows a typical report.

Without using an array, you could write the application that produces counts for the six categories of dependents (0 through 5) by using a series of decisions. Figure 5-3 shows the pseudocode and flowchart for the decision-making part of such an application. Although this logic works, its length and complexity are unnecessary once you understand how to use an array.

Dependents	Count
0	43
1	35
2	24
3	11
4	5
5	7

Figure 5-2   Typical Dependents report

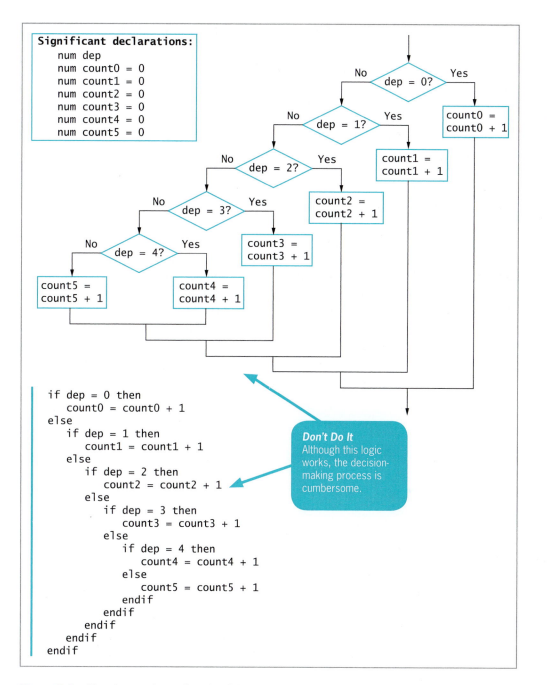

Significant declarations:
    num dep
    num count0 = 0
    num count1 = 0
    num count2 = 0
    num count3 = 0
    num count4 = 0
    num count5 = 0

Don't Do It
Although this logic works, the decision-making process is cumbersome.

```
if dep = 0 then
    count0 = count0 + 1
else
    if dep = 1 then
        count1 = count1 + 1
    else
        if dep = 2 then
            count2 = count2 + 1
        else
            if dep = 3 then
                count3 = count3 + 1
            else
                if dep = 4 then
                    count4 = count4 + 1
                else
                    count5 = count5 + 1
                endif
            endif
        endif
    endif
endif
```

Figure 5-3   Flowchart and pseudocode of decision-making process using a series of decisions—the hard way

The decision-making process in Figure 5-3 accomplishes its purpose, and the logic is correct, but the process is cumbersome and certainly not recommended. This logic requires far more work than is necessary. Follow the logic here so that you understand how the application works. In the next pages, you will see how to make the application more elegant.

In Figure 5-3, the variable dep is compared to 0. If it is 0, 1 is added to count0. If it is not 0, then dep is compared to 1. Based on the result, 1 is either added to count1 or dep is compared to 2, and so on. Each time the application executes this decision-making process, 1 ultimately is added to one of the six variables that acts as a counter. The dependent-counting logic in Figure 5-3 works, but even with only six categories of dependents, the decision-making process is unwieldy. What if the number of dependents might be any value from 0 to 10, or 0 to 20? With either of these scenarios, the basic logic of the program would remain the same; however, you would need to declare many additional variables to hold the counts, and you would need many additional decisions.

Using an array provides an alternate approach to this programming problem and greatly reduces the number of statements you need. When you declare an array, you provide a group name for a number of associated variables in memory. For example, the six dependent count accumulators can be redefined as a single array named count. The individual elements become count[0], count[1], count[2], count[3], count[4], and count[5], as shown in the revised decision-making process in Figure 5-4.

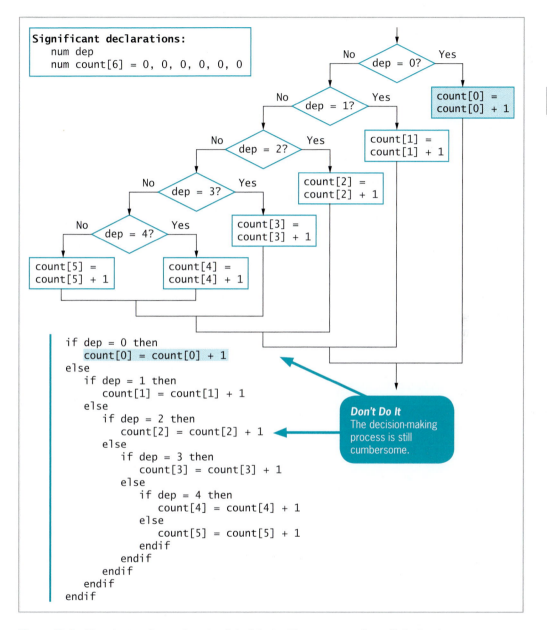

Figure 5-4   Flowchart and pseudocode of decision-making process—but still the hard way

The shaded statement in Figure 5-4 shows that when dep is 0, 1 is added to count[0]. You can see similar statements for the rest of the count elements; when dep is 1, 1 is added to count[1], when dep is 2, 1 is added to count[2], and so on. When the dep value is 5, this means that it was not 1, 2, 3, or 4, so 1 is added to count[5]. In other words, 1 is added to one of the elements of the count array instead of to an individual variable named count0, count1, count2, count3, count4, or count5. Is this version a big improvement over the original in Figure 5-3? Of course it isn't. You still have not taken advantage of the benefits of using the array in this application.

The true benefit of using an array lies in your ability to use a variable as a subscript to the array, instead of using a literal constant such as 0 or 5. Notice in the logic in Figure 5-4 that within each decision, the value compared to dep and the constant that is the subscript in the resulting *Yes* process are always identical. That is, when dep is 0, the subscript used to add 1 to the count array is 0; when dep is 1, the subscript used for the count array is 1, and so on. Therefore, you can just use dep as a subscript to the array. You can rewrite the decision-making process as shown in Figure 5-5.

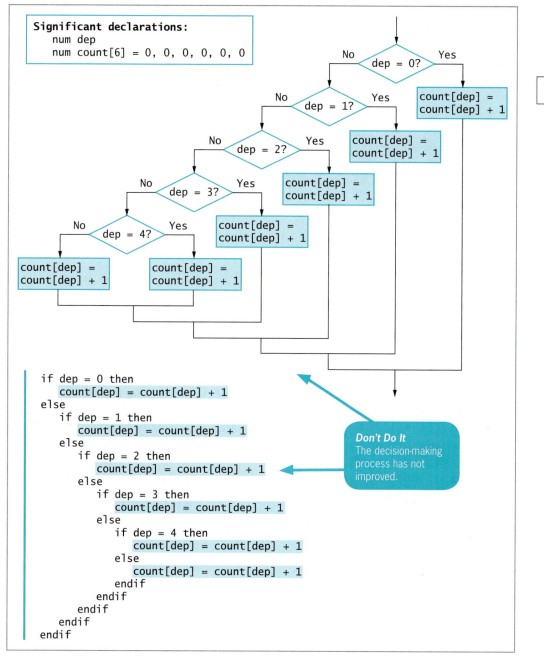

Significant declarations:
```
num dep
num count[6] = 0, 0, 0, 0, 0, 0
```

```
if dep = 0 then
    count[dep] = count[dep] + 1
else
    if dep = 1 then
        count[dep] = count[dep] + 1
    else
        if dep = 2 then
            count[dep] = count[dep] + 1
        else
            if dep = 3 then
                count[dep] = count[dep] + 1
            else
                if dep = 4 then
                    count[dep] = count[dep] + 1
                else
                    count[dep] = count[dep] + 1
                endif
            endif
        endif
    endif
endif
```

Don't Do It
The decision-making process has not improved.

Figure 5-5 Flowchart and pseudocode of decision-making process using an array—but still a hard way

The code segment in Figure 5-5 looks no more efficient than the one in Figure 5-4. However, notice the shaded statements in Figure 5-5—the process that occurs after each decision is exactly the same. In each case, no matter what the value of **dep** is, you always add 1 to count[dep]. If you always will take the same action no matter what the answer to a question is, there is no need to ask the question. Instead, you can rewrite the decision-making process as shown in Figure 5-6.

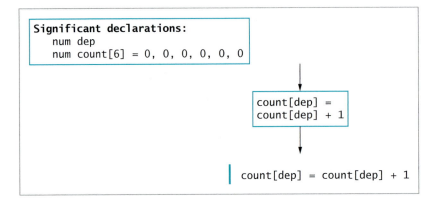

Figure 5-6   Flowchart and pseudocode of an efficient decision-making process using an array

The example in Figure 5-6 is simple and elegant, and saves the programmer work. The single statement in the figure eliminates the *entire* decision-making process that was the original highlighted section in Figure 5-5! When **dep** is 2, 1 is added to count[2]; when **dep** is 4, 1 is added to count[4], and so on. *Now* you have significantly improved the original logic. What's more, this process does not change whether there are 20, 30, or any other number of possible categories. To use more than five accumulators, you would declare additional **count** elements in the array, but the categorizing logic would remain the same as it is in Figure 5-6.

Figure 5-7 shows an entire program that takes advantage of the array to produce the report that shows counts for dependent categories. Variables and constants are declared and a first value for **dep** is entered into the program. Then, 1 is added to the appropriate element of the count array and the next value is input. The first loop in Figure 5-7 is an indefinite loop; it continues as long as the user does not enter the sentinel value.

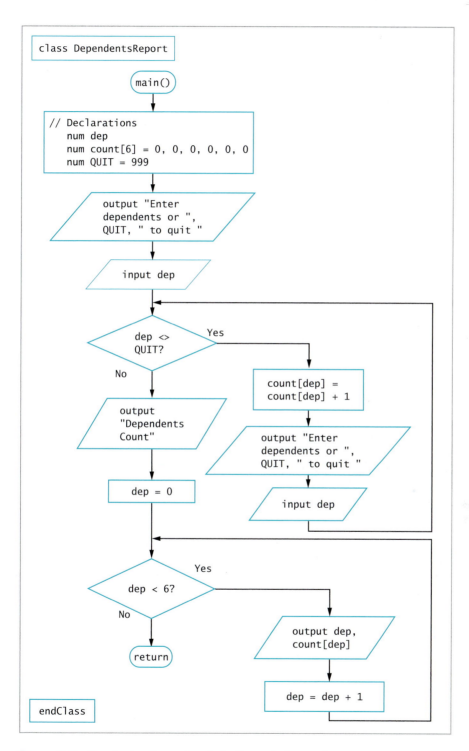

Figure 5-7 Flowchart and pseudocode for Dependents report program

```
class DependentsReport
   main()
      // Declarations
         num dep
         num count[6] = 0, 0, 0, 0, 0, 0
         num QUIT = 999
      output "Enter dependents or ", QUIT, " to quit "
      input dep
      while dep <> QUIT
         count[dep] = count[dep] + 1
         output "Enter dependents or ", QUIT, " to quit "
         input dep
      endwhile
      output "Dependents    Count"
      dep = 0
      while dep < 6
         output dep, count[dep]
         dep = dep + 1
      endwhile
   return
endClass
```

Figure 5-7 Flowchart and pseudocode for Dependents report program (continued)

When data entry is complete, the report is displayed. First, the heading is output, then **dep** is reset to 0, and then each **dep** and **count[dep]** are output in a loop. The first output statement contains 0 (as the number of dependents) and the value stored in **count[0]**. Then, 1 is added to **dep** and the same set of instructions is used again to display the counts for each number of dependents. The second loop in Figure 5-7 is a definite loop; it executes precisely six times.

The logic in Figure 5-7 assumes that the user will enter a value between 0 and 5 inclusive for the number of dependents. Otherwise, an error will occur. Later in this chapter you will learn about staying within appropriate boundary values for an array.

The dependent-counting program would have *worked* if it contained a long series of decisions and output statements, but the program is easier to write when you use an array and access its values using the number of dependents as a subscript. Additionally, the new program is more efficient, easier for other programmers to understand, and easier to maintain. Arrays are never mandatory, but often they can drastically cut down on your programming time and make your logic easier to understand. Learning to use arrays properly can make many programming tasks far more efficient and professional. When you understand how to use arrays, you will be able to provide elegant solutions to problems that otherwise would require tedious programming steps.

Watch the video *Accumulating Values in an Array*.

Using Constants with Arrays

In Chapter 2, you learned that named constants hold values that do not change during a program's execution. When working with arrays, you can use constants in several ways:

- To hold the size of an array
- As the array values
- As a subscript

Using a Named Constant as the Size of an Array

The program in Figure 5-7 still contains one minor flaw. In Chapter 2, you learned to avoid *magic numbers*—that is, unnamed constants. As the totals are output in the loop at the end of the program in Figure 5-7, the array subscript is compared to the constant 6. The program can be improved if you use a named constant instead. Using a named constant makes your code easier to modify and understand. In most programming languages, you can take one of two approaches:

- You can declare a named numeric constant such as `ARRAY_SIZE = 6`. Then, you can use this constant every time you access the array, always making sure any subscript you use remains less than the constant value.

- In many languages, a constant that represents the array size is automatically provided for each array you create. For example, in Java, after you declare an array named `count`, its size is stored in a field named `count.length`. In both C# and Visual Basic, the array size is `count.Length`, with an uppercase *L*. Using the automatically supplied constant reduces errors and makes program modifications easier because the constant is assigned a new value automatically if you change the size of the array.

Using Constants as Array Element Values

Sometimes the values stored in arrays should be constants because they are not changed during program execution. For example, suppose that you create an array that holds names for the months of the year. Don't confuse the array identifier with its contents—the convention in this book is to use all uppercase letters in constant identifiers, but not necessarily in array values. The array can be declared as follows:

```
string MONTH[12] = "January", "February", "March", "April",
    "May", "June", "July", "August", "September", "October",
    "November", "December"
```

Using a Constant as an Array Subscript

Occasionally you will want to use an unnamed numeric constant as a subscript to an array. For example, to display the first value in an array named salesArray, you might write a statement that uses an unnamed literal constant as follows:

```
output salesArray[0]
```

You might also have occasion to use a named constant as a subscript. For example, if salesArray holds sales values for each of 20 states served by your company, and Indiana is state 5, you could output the value for Indiana as follows:

```
output salesArray[5]
```

However, if you declare a named constant as num INDIANA = 5, then you can display the same value using this statement:

```
output salesArray[INDIANA]
```

An advantage to using a named constant in this case is that the statement becomes self-documenting—anyone who reads your statement more easily understands that your intention is to display the sales value for Indiana.

Searching an Array for an Exact Match

In the dependent-counting application in this chapter, the array's subscript variable conveniently held small whole numbers—the number of dependents allowed was 0 through 5—and the dep variable directly accessed the array. Unfortunately, real life doesn't always happen in small integers. Sometimes you don't have a variable that conveniently holds an array position; sometimes you have to search through an array to find a value you need.

Consider a mail-order business in which customers place orders that contain a name, address, item number, and quantity ordered. Assume that the item numbers from which a customer can choose are three-digit numbers, but perhaps they are not consecutively numbered 001 through 999. For example, let's say that you offer only six items: 106, 108, 307, 405, 457, and 688, as shown in the shaded VALID_ITEM array declaration in Figure 5-8. (The array is declared as constant because the item numbers do not change during program execution.) When a customer orders an item, a clerical worker can tell whether the order is valid by looking down the list and manually verifying that the ordered number is on it. In a similar fashion, a computer program can use a loop to test the ordered item number against each VALID_ITEM, looking for an exact match. When you search through a list from one end to the other, you are performing a **linear search** or a **sequential search**.

172

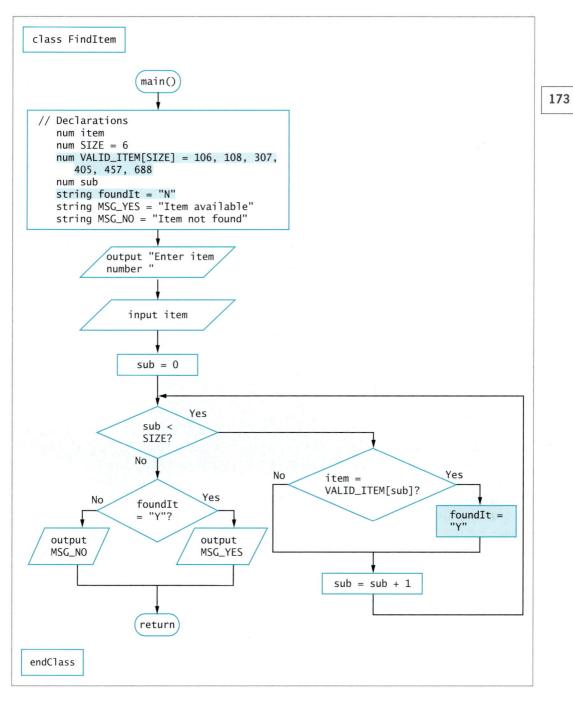

Figure 5-8 Flowchart and pseudocode for program that verifies item availability

```
class FindItem
   main()
      // Declarations
         num item
         num SIZE = 6
         num VALID_ITEM[SIZE] = 106, 108, 307,
            405, 457, 688
         num sub
         string foundIt = "N"
         string MSG_YES = "Item available"
         string MSG_NO = "Item not found"
      output "Enter item number "
      input item
      sub = 0
      while sub < SIZE
         if item = VALID_ITEM[sub] then
            foundIt = "Y"
         endif
         sub = sub + 1
      endwhile
      if foundIt = "Y" then
         output MSG_YES
      else
         output MSG_NO
      endif
   return
endClass
```

Figure 5-8   Flowchart and pseudocode for program that verifies item availability (continued)

To determine if an ordered item number is valid, you could use a series of six decisions to compare the number to each of the six allowed values. However, the superior approach shown in Figure 5-8 is to create an array that holds the list of valid item numbers and then to search through the array for an exact match to the ordered item. If you search through the entire array without finding a match for the item the customer ordered, it means the ordered item number is not valid.

The program in Figure 5-8 takes the following steps to verify that an item number exists:

- A flag variable named foundIt is initialized to "N". A **flag** is a variable that is set to indicate whether some event has occurred. In this example, "N" indicates that the item number has not yet been found in the list. (See the second shaded statement in the declarations in Figure 5-8.)

- After an item number is entered, a subscript, sub, is initialized to 0. This subscript is a loop control variable that will be used to access each VALID_ITEM element.

- A loop executes, varying sub from 0 through one less than the size of the array. Within the loop, the customer's ordered item number is compared to each item number in the array. If the customer-ordered item matches any item in the array, the flag variable is assigned "Y". (See the last shaded statement in Figure 5-8.) After all six valid item numbers have been compared to the ordered item, if the customer item matches none of them, then the flag variable foundIt will still hold the value "N".

- If the flag variable value is "Y" after the entire list has been searched, then the item is valid, and an appropriate message is displayed. However, if the flag has not been assigned "Y", the item was not found in the array of valid items. In this case, an error message is output and 1 is added to a count of bad item numbers.

Instead of using the string foundIt variable in Figure 5-8, you might prefer to use a numeric variable that you set to 1 or 0 to represent true or false. Most programming languages also support a Boolean data type that you can use for foundIt; when you declare a variable to be Boolean, you can set its value to true or false.

Using Parallel Arrays

When you accept an item number into a mail-order company program, you usually want to accomplish more than simply verifying the item's existence. For example, you might want to determine the name, price, or available quantity of the ordered item. Tasks like these can be completed efficiently using parallel arrays. **Parallel arrays** are two or more arrays in which each element in one array is associated with the element in the same relative position in the other array. Although each array can contain just one data type, each array in a set of parallel arrays might be a different type.

Suppose that you have a list of item numbers and their associated prices. One array named VALID_ITEM contains six elements; each element is a valid item number. Its parallel array also has six elements. The array is named VALID_PRICE; each element is a price of an item. Each price in the VALID_PRICE array is conveniently and purposely in the same position as the corresponding item number in the VALID_ITEM array. Figure 5-9 shows how the parallel arrays might look in computer memory.

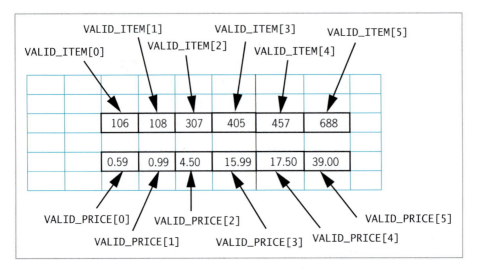

Figure 5-9   Parallel arrays in memory

The two arrays in Figure 5-9 are aligned to illustrate the parallel relationship between their values. However, the arrays might be located anywhere in memory, and one might immediately follow the other.

When you use parallel arrays:

- Two or more arrays contain related data.
- A subscript relates the arrays. That is, elements at the same position in each array are logically related.

Figure 5-10 shows a program that declares parallel arrays. The VALID_PRICE array is shaded; each element in it corresponds to a valid item number.

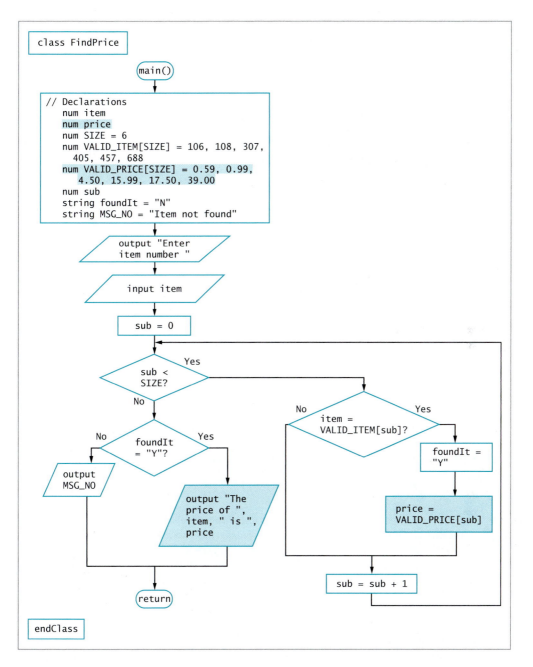

Figure 5-10 Flowchart and pseudocode of program that finds an item price using parallel arrays

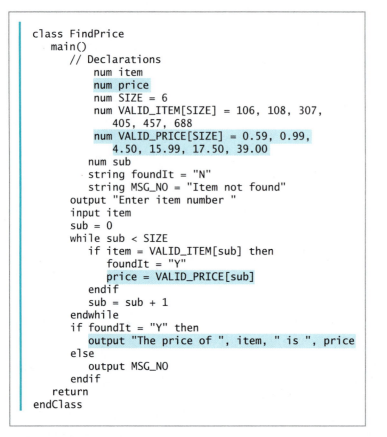

```
class FindPrice
   main()
      // Declarations
         num item
         num price
         num SIZE = 6
         num VALID_ITEM[SIZE] = 106, 108, 307,
            405, 457, 688
         num VALID_PRICE[SIZE] = 0.59, 0.99,
            4.50, 15.99, 17.50, 39.00
         num sub
         string foundIt = "N"
         string MSG_NO = "Item not found"
      output "Enter item number "
      input item
      sub = 0
      while sub < SIZE
         if item = VALID_ITEM[sub] then
            foundIt = "Y"
            price = VALID_PRICE[sub]
         endif
         sub = sub + 1
      endwhile
      if foundIt = "Y" then
         output "The price of ", item, " is ", price
      else
         output MSG_NO
      endif
   return
endClass
```

Figure 5-10   Flowchart and pseudocode of program that finds an item price using parallel arrays (continued)

Some programmers object to using a cryptic variable name for a subscript, such as `sub` in Figure 5-10, because such names are not descriptive. These programmers would prefer a name like `priceIndex`. Others approve of short names when the variable is used only in a limited area of a program, as it is used here, to step through an array. Programmers disagree on many style issues like this one. As a programmer, it is your responsibility to find out what conventions are used among your peers in an organization.

As the program in Figure 5-10 receives a customer's order, it looks through each of the `VALID_ITEM` values separately by varying the subscript `sub` from 0 to the number of items available. When a match for the item number is found, the program pulls the corresponding parallel price out of the list of `VALID_PRICE` values and stores it in the `price` variable. (See shaded statements in Figure 5-10.)

The relationship between an item's number and its price is an **indirect relationship**. That means you don't access a price directly by knowing the item number. Instead, you determine the price by knowing an item number's array position. Once you find a match for the ordered item number in the VALID_ITEM array, you know that the price of the item is in the same position in the other array, VALID_PRICE. When VALID_ITEM[sub] is the correct item, VALID_PRICE[sub] must be the correct price, so sub links the parallel arrays.

Parallel arrays are most useful when value pairs have an indirect relationship. If values in your program have a direct relationship, you probably don't need parallel arrays. For example, if items were numbered 0, 1, 2, 3, and so on consecutively, you could use the item number as a subscript to the price array instead of using a parallel array to hold item numbers. Even if the items were numbered 200, 201, 202, and so on consecutively, you could subtract a constant value (200) from each and use that as a subscript instead of using a parallel array.

Suppose that a customer orders item 457. Walk through the logic yourself to see if you come up with the correct price per item, $17.50. Then, suppose that a customer orders item 458. Walk through the logic and see whether the appropriate *Item not found* message is displayed.

Improving Search Efficiency

The mail-order program in Figure 5-10 is still a little inefficient. When a customer orders item 106 or 108, a match is found on the first or second pass through the loop, and continuing to search provides no further benefit. However, even after a match is made, the program in Figure 5-10 continues searching through the item array until sub reaches the value SIZE. One way to stop the search when the item has been found and foundIt is set to "Y" is to change the loop-controlling question. Instead of simply continuing the loop while the number of comparisons does not exceed the highest allowed array subscript, you should continue the loop while the searched item is not found *and* the number of comparisons has not exceeded the maximum. Leaving the loop as soon as a match is found improves the program's efficiency. The larger the array, the more beneficial it becomes to exit the searching loop as soon as you find the desired value.

Figure 5-11 shows the improved version of the loop that finds an item's price; the altered loop-controlling question is shaded.

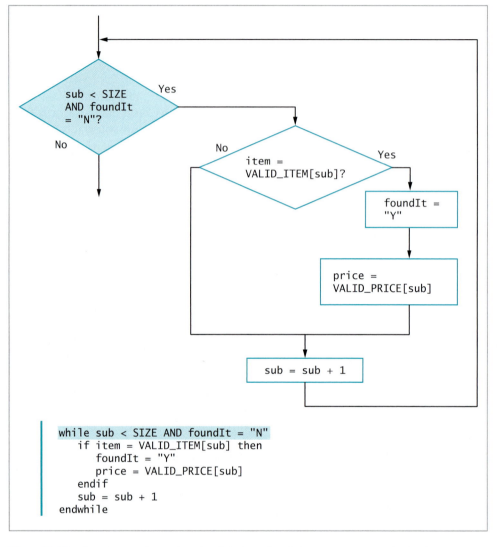

```
while sub < SIZE AND foundIt = "N"
    if item = VALID_ITEM[sub] then
        foundIt = "Y"
        price = VALID_PRICE[sub]
    endif
    sub = sub + 1
endwhile
```

Figure 5-11   Flowchart and pseudocode of the loop that finds an item price and exits the loop as soon as it is found

Notice that the price-finding program offers the greatest efficiency when the most frequently ordered items are stored at the beginning of the array so that only the seldom-ordered items require many loops before finding a match. Often, you can improve search efficiency by rearranging array elements.

 As you study programming, you will learn other search techniques. For example, a **binary search** starts looking in the middle of a sorted list and then determines whether it should continue higher or lower.

Watch the video *Using Parallel Arrays.*

Searching an Array for a Range Match

Customer order item numbers need to match available item numbers exactly to determine the correct price of an item. Sometimes, however, programmers want to work with ranges of values in arrays. In Chapter 3, you learned that a range of values is any series of contiguous values between specified limits—for example, 1 through 5 or 20 through 30.

Suppose that a company decides to offer quantity discounts when a customer orders multiple items, as shown in Figure 5-12.

Quantity	Discount %
0–8	0
9–12	10
13–25	15
26 or more	20

Figure 5-12 Discounts on orders by quantity

You want to be able to read in customer order data and determine a discount percentage based on the value in the quantity field. For example, if a customer has ordered 20 items, you want to be able to output *Your discount is 15 percent.* One ill-advised approach might be to set up an array with as many elements as any customer might ever order, and store the appropriate discount for each possible number, as shown in Figure 5-13. This array is set up to contain the discount for 0 items, 1 item, 2 items, and so on. This approach has at least three drawbacks:

- It requires a very large array that uses a lot of memory.

- You must store the same value repeatedly. For example, each of the first nine elements receives the same value, 0, and each of the next four elements receives the same value, 10.

- How do you know you have enough array elements? Is a customer order quantity of 75 items enough? What if a customer orders 100 or 1000 items? No matter how many elements you place in the array, there's always a chance that a customer will order more.

182

```
num DISCOUNT[76]
  = 0, 0, 0, 0, 0, 0, 0, 0, 0,
    0.10, 0.10, 0.10, 0.10,
    0.15, 0.15, 0.15, 0.15, 0.15,
    0.15, 0.15, 0.15, 0.15, 0.15,
    0.15, 0.15, 0.15,
    0.20, 0.20, 0.20, 0.20, 0.20,
    0.20, 0.20, 0.20, 0.20, 0.20,
    0.20, 0.20, 0.20, 0.20, 0.20,
    0.20, 0.20, 0.20, 0.20, 0.20,
    0.20, 0.20, 0.20, 0.20, 0.20,
    0.20, 0.20, 0.20, 0.20, 0.20,
    0.20, 0.20, 0.20, 0.20, 0.20,
    0.20, 0.20, 0.20, 0.20, 0.20,
    0.20, 0.20, 0.20, 0.20, 0.20,
    0.20, 0.20, 0.20, 0.20, 0.20
```

Don't Do It
Although this array is usable, it is repetitious, prone to error, and difficult to use.

Figure 5-13   Usable—but inefficient—discount array

A better approach is to create two parallel arrays, each with four elements, as shown in Figure 5-14. Each discount rate is listed once in the DISCOUNT array, and the low end of each quantity range is listed in the QUAN_LIMIT array.

```
num DISCOUNT[4]   =   0, 0.10, 0.15, 0.20
num QUAN_LIMIT[4] = 0,    9,   13,   26
```

Figure 5-14   Parallel arrays to use for determining discount

To find the correct discount for any customer's ordered quantity, you can start with the *last* quantity range limit (QUAN_LIMIT[3]). If the quantity ordered is at least that value, 26, the loop is never entered and the customer gets the highest discount rate (DISCOUNT[3], or 20 percent). If the quantity ordered is not at least QUAN_LIMIT[3]—that is, if it is less than 26—then you reduce the subscript and check to see if the quantity is at least QUAN_LIMIT[2], or 13. If so, the customer receives DISCOUNT[2], or 15 percent, and so on. Figure 5-15 shows a program that accepts a customer's quantity ordered and determines the appropriate discount rate.

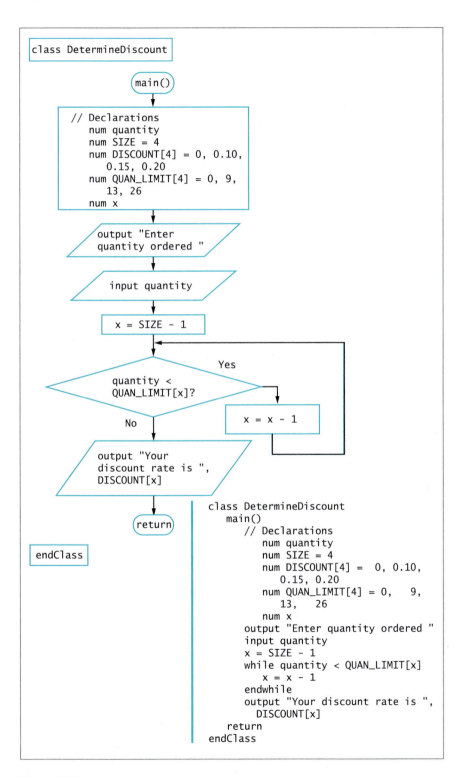

class DetermineDiscount
    main()
        // Declarations
            num quantity
            num SIZE = 4
            num DISCOUNT[4] = 0, 0.10,
                0.15, 0.20
            num QUAN_LIMIT[4] = 0,   9,
                13,   26
            num x
        output "Enter quantity ordered "
        input quantity
        x = SIZE - 1
        while quantity < QUAN_LIMIT[x]
            x = x - 1
        endwhile
        output "Your discount rate is ",
            DISCOUNT[x]
    return
endClass

Figure 5-15 Program that determines discount rate

An alternate approach to the one taken in Figure 5-15 is to store the high end of every range in an array. Then, you start with the lowest element and check for values less than or equal to each array element value.

When using an array to store range limits, you use a loop to make a series of comparisons that would otherwise require many separate decisions. The program that determines customer discount rates in Figure 5-15 requires fewer instructions than one that does not use an array, and modifications will be easier to make in the future.

Remaining within Array Bounds

Every array has a finite size. You can think of an array's size in one of two ways—either by the number of elements in the array or by the number of bytes in the array. Arrays are always composed of elements of the same data type, and elements of the same data type always occupy the same number of bytes of memory, so the number of bytes in an array is always a multiple of the number of elements in an array. For example, in Java, integers occupy 4 bytes of memory, so an array of 10 integers occupies exactly 40 bytes.

In every programming language, when you access data stored in an array you must use a subscript containing a value that accesses a location within the area of memory occupied by the array. An array's name represents a memory address. When you use a subscript, it is multiplied by the size of the data type in bytes, and that value is added to the address of the array to find the address of the appropriate element. For example, if you are working in a system in which numbers occupy four memory bytes, then element 2 in an array is 8 bytes from the array address and element 10 is 40 bytes from the array address. So, if you use a subscript that is too large or too small, the program will attempt to access an address that is not part of the array's space.

For example, examine the program in Figure 5-16. The method accepts a numeric value for mon and displays the name associated with that month. The logic in Figure 5-16 makes a questionable assumption: that every number entered by the user is a valid month number.

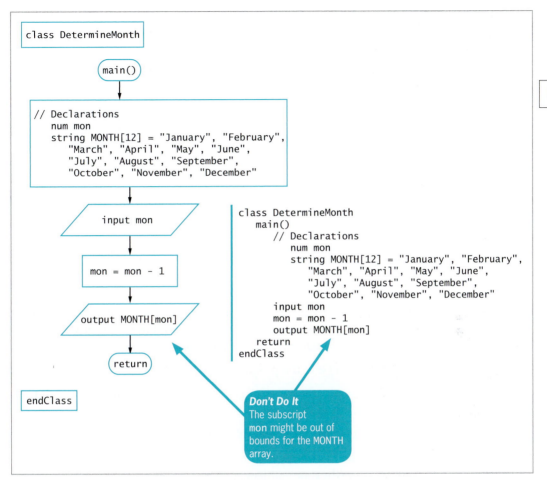

Figure 5-16 Determining the month string from a user's numeric entry

In the program in Figure 5-16, notice that 1 is subtracted from **mon** before it is used as a subscript. Although January is the first month of the year, its name occupies the location in the array with the 0 subscript. With values that seem naturally to start with 1, like month numbers, some programmers would prefer to create a 13-element array and simply never use the zero-position element. That way, each "natural" month number would be the correct value to access its data without subtracting. Other programmers dislike wasting memory by creating an extra, unused array element. Although workable programs can be created with or without the extra array element, professional programmers should follow the conventions and preferences of their colleagues and managers.

In Figure 5-16, if the user enters a number that is too small or too large, one of two things will happen depending on the programming language. When you use a subscript value that is negative or higher than the highest allowed subscript:

- Some programming languages will stop execution of the program and issue an error message.

- Other programming languages will not issue an error message but will access a value in a memory location that is outside the area occupied by the array. That area might contain garbage, or worse, it accidentally might contain the name of an incorrect month.

Either way, a logical error occurs. When you use a subscript that is not within the range of acceptable subscripts, it is said to be **out of bounds**. Users enter incorrect data frequently; a good program should be able to handle the mistake and not allow the subscript to be out of bounds.

A user might enter an invalid number or might not enter a number at all. In Chapter 4, you learned that many languages have a built-in method with a name like isNumeric() that can test for such mistakes.

You can improve the program in Figure 5-16 by adding a test that ensures the subscript used to access the array is within the array bounds. If you find that the input value is not between 1 and 12 inclusive, you might take one of the following approaches:

- Display an error message and end the program.

- Use a default value for the month. For example, when an entered month is invalid, you might want to assume that it is December.

- Continuously reprompt the user for a new value until it is valid.

The way you handle an invalid month depends on the requirements of your program as spelled out by your user, supervisor, or company policy.

Using a for Loop to Process Arrays

In Chapter 4, you learned about the for loop—a loop that, in a single statement, initializes a loop control variable, compares it to a limit, and alters it. The for loop is a particularly convenient tool when working with arrays because you frequently need to process every element of an array from beginning to end. As with a while loop, when you use a for loop, you must be careful to stay within array bounds, remembering that the highest usable array subscript is one less than the size of the array. Figure 5-17 shows a for loop that correctly displays all of a company's department names that are stored in an array declared as DEPTS. Notice that dep is incremented through one less than the number of departments because with a five-item array, the subscripts you can use are 0 through 4.

```
class DisplayDepartments
    main()
        //Declarations
            num dep
            num SIZE = 5
            string DEPTS[SIZE] = "Accounting", "Personnel",
                "Technical", "Customer Service", "Marketing"
        for dep = 0 to SIZE - 1 step 1
            output DEPTS[dep]
        endfor
    return
endClass
```

Figure 5-17   Pseudocode that uses a **for** loop to display an array of department names

The loop in Figure 5-17 is slightly inefficient because, as it executes five times, the subtraction operation that deducts 1 from SIZE occurs each time. Five subtraction operations do not consume much computer power or time, but in a loop that processes thousands or millions of array elements, the program's efficiency would be compromised. Figure 5-18 shows a superior solution. A new constant called LIMIT is calculated once, then used repeatedly in the comparison operation to determine when to stop cycling through the array.

```
class DisplayDepartments
    main()
        //Declarations
            num dep
            num SIZE = 5
            num LIMIT = SIZE - 1
            string DEPTS[SIZE] = "Accounting", "Personnel",
                "Technical", "Customer Service", "Marketing"
        for dep = 0 to LIMIT step 1
            output DEPTS[dep]
        endfor
    return
endClass
```

Figure 5-18   Pseudocode that uses a more efficient **for** loop to output department names

You will learn much more about arrays in Chapter 12, including how to sort data in arrays and how to use multidimensional arrays.

Chapter Summary

- An array is a data structure that is a named series or list of values in computer memory, whose members have the same data type but are differentiated by subscripts. Each array element occupies an area in memory next to, or contiguous to, the others.

- When you use a variable as a subscript to an array, you can replace multiple nested decisions with many fewer statements.

- Constants can be used to hold an array's size or to represent its values. Using a named constant for an array's size makes the code easier to understand and less likely to contain an error. Array values are declared as constant when they should not change during program execution.

- Searching through an array to find a value you need involves initializing a subscript, using a loop to test each array element, and setting a flag when a match is found.

- With parallel arrays, each element in one array is associated with the element in the same relative position in the other array.

- When you need to compare a value to a range of values in an array, you can store either the low- or high-end value of each range for comparison.

- When you access data stored in an array, it is important to use a subscript containing a value that accesses memory occupied by the array. When you use a subscript that is not within the defined range of acceptable subscripts, your subscript is said to be out of bounds.

- The for loop is a particularly convenient tool when working with arrays because you frequently need to process every element of an array from beginning to end.

Key Terms

A **data structure** is a collection of data items that are grouped and organized so they can be used more efficiently.

An **array** is a data structure that consists of a series or list of values in computer memory, whose members have the same name but are differentiated by special numbers called subscripts.

An **element** is a single data item in an array.

The **size of the array** is the number of elements it can hold.

A **subscript**, also called an **index**, is a number that indicates the position of a particular item within an array.

Populating an array is the act of assigning values to the array elements.

A **linear search** is a search through a list from one end to the other.

A **sequential search** is a linear search.

A **flag** is a variable that you set to indicate whether some event has occurred.

In **parallel arrays**, each element in one array is associated with the element in the same relative position in the other array(s).

An **indirect relationship** describes the relationship between parallel arrays in which an element in the first array does not directly access its corresponding value in the second array.

A **binary search** is one that starts in the middle of a sorted list, and then determines whether it should continue higher or lower to find a target value.

Out of bounds describes an array subscript that is not within the range of acceptable subscripts for the array—usually 0 through one less than the array size.

Review Questions

1. A subscript is a(n) ——————.

    a. element in an array
    b. alternate name for an array
    c. number that represents the highest value stored within an array
    d. number that indicates the position of an array element

2. Each variable in an array must have the same ——————— as the others.

    a. data type   c. value
    b. subscript   d. memory location

3. Each data item in an array is called a(n) ——————.

    a. data type   c. component
    b. subscript   d. element

4. The subscripts of any array are always ——————.

    a. integers   c. characters
    b. fractions   d. strings of characters

5. Suppose that you have an array named number, and two of its elements are number[1] and number[4]. You know that ——————.

    a. the two elements hold the same value
    b. the array holds exactly four elements
    c. there are exactly two elements between those two elements
    d. the two elements are at the same memory location

6. Suppose that you want to write a program that inputs customer data including name, zipCode, balanceDue, and regionNumber. The program counts the number of high-balance customers in each of 12 sales regions. A high-balance customer is defined as one who owes more than $1000. During record processing, you sometimes would add 1 to an array element whose subscript would be represented by _____ .

    a. name

    b. zipCode

    c. balanceDue

    d. regionNumber

7. The most useful type of subscript for manipulating arrays is a _____ .

    a. numeric constant

    b. variable

    c. character

    d. filename

8. At the start of a program, you declare a seven-element array that holds the names of the days of the week, and a single numeric variable named dayNum. Later, you display the names using dayNum as a subscript. Near the end of the program, you can display the same array values again by writing a loop that _____ as a subscript to the array.

    a. must use dayNum

    b. can use dayNum, but instead can use another variable

    c. must not use dayNum, and must use a different variable

    d. must use a numeric constant instead of a variable

9. Suppose that you have declared an array as follows: num values[4] = 0, 0, 0, 0. Which of the following is an allowed operation?

    a. values[2] = 17

    b. input values[0]

    c. values[3] = values[0] + 10

    d. all of the above

10. Filling an array with values during a program's execution is known as _____ the array.

    a. executing

    b. colonizing

    c. populating

    d. declaring

11. Using an array can make a program _____ .

    a. easier to understand

    b. illegal in some modern languages

    c. harder to maintain

    d. all of the above

12. A _____ is a variable that you set to indicate whether some event has occurred.

    a. subscript

    b. banner

    c. counter

    d. flag

13. What do you call two arrays in which each element in one array is associated with the element in the same relative position in the other array?

    a. cohesive arrays
    b. parallel arrays

    c. hidden arrays
    d. perpendicular arrays

14. In most modern programming languages, the highest subscript you should use with a 10-element array is _____ .

    a. 8
    b. 9

    c. 10
    d. 11

15. Parallel arrays _____ .

    a. frequently have an indirect relationship
    b. never have an indirect relationship
    c. must be the same data type
    d. must not be the same data type

16. Each element in a five-element array can hold _____ value(s).

    a. one
    b. five

    c. at least five
    d. an unlimited number of

17. After the annual dog show in which the Barkley Dog Training Academy awards points to each participant, the academy assigns a status to each dog based on the criteria in Table 5-1.

Points Earned	Level of Achievement
0–5	Good
6–7	Excellent
8–9	Superior
10	Unbelievable

Table 5-1 Barkley Dog Training Academy achievement levels

The academy needs a program that compares a dog's points earned with the grading scale, so that each dog can receive a certificate acknowledging the appropriate level of achievement. Of the following, which set of values would be most useful for the contents of an array used in the program?

    a. 0, 6, 9, 10
    b. 5, 7, 8, 10

    c. 5, 7, 9, 10
    d. any of the above

18. When you use a subscript value that is negative or higher than the number of elements in an array, _____ .

   a. execution of the program stops and an error message is issued

   b. a value in a memory location that is outside the area occupied by the array will be accessed

   c. Either of the above might happen, depending on the programming language used.

   d. Neither of the above happens in any modern programming language.

19. In every array, a subscript is out of bounds when it is _____ .

   a. negative   c. 1

   b. 0   d. 999

20. You can access every element of an array using a _____ .

   a. `while` loop   c. both of the above

   b. `for` loop   d. none of the above

Exercises

1. a. Design the logic for a program that allows a user to enter 15 numbers, then displays them in the reverse order of entry.

   b. Modify the reverse-display program so that the user can enter any amount of numbers up to 15 until a sentinel value is entered.

2. a. Design the logic for a program that allows a user to enter 10 numbers, then displays each number and its difference from the numeric average of the numbers entered.

   b. Modify the program in Exercise 2a so that the user can enter any amount of numbers up to 10 until a sentinel value is entered.

3. a. Registration workers at a conference for authors of children's books have collected data about conference participants, including the number of books each author has written and the target age of their readers. The participants have written from 1 to 40 books each, and target readers' ages range from 0 through 16. Design a program that continuously accepts the number of books written until a sentinel value is entered, and then displays a list of how many participants have written each number of books (1 through 40).

   b. Modify the author registration program so that a target age for each author's audience is input until a sentinel value is entered. The output is a count of the number of books written for each of the following age groups: under 3, 3 through 7, 8 through 10, 11 through 13, and 14 and older.

4. a. The Downdog Yoga Studio offers five types of classes, as shown in Table 5-2. Design a program that accepts a number representing a class and then displays the class name.

   b. Modify the Downdog Yoga Studio program so that numeric class requests can be entered continuously until a sentinel value is entered. Then, display each class number, name, and a count of the number of requests for each class.

Class Number	Class Name
1	Yoga 1
2	Yoga 2
3	Children's Yoga
4	Prenatal Yoga
5	Senior Yoga

Table 5-2 Downdog Yoga Studio classes

5. a. Watson Elementary School contains 30 classrooms numbered 1 through 30. Each classroom can contain any number of students up to 35. Each student takes an achievement test at the end of the school year and receives a score from 0 through 100. Write a program that accepts data for each student in the school—student ID, classroom number, and score on the achievement test. Design a program that lists the total points scored for each of the 30 classrooms.

   b. Modify the Watson Elementary School program so that the average of the test scores is output for each classroom, rather than total scores for each classroom.

6. The Jumpin' Jive coffee shop charges $2.00 for a cup of coffee and offers the add-ins shown in Table 5-3.

Product	Price ($)
Whipped cream	0.89
Cinnamon	0.25
Chocolate sauce	0.59
Amaretto	1.50
Irish whiskey	1.75

Table 5-3 Add-in list for Jumpin' Jive coffee shop

Design the logic for an application that allows a user to enter ordered add-ins continuously until a sentinel value is entered. After each item, display its price or the message *Sorry, we do not carry that* as output. After all items have been entered, output the total price for the order.

194

7. Design the application logic for a company that wants a report containing a breakdown of payroll by department. Input includes each employee's department number, hourly salary, and number of hours worked. The output is a list of the seven departments in the company and the total gross payroll (rate times hours) for each department. The department names are shown in Table 5-4.

Department Number	Department Name
1	Personnel
2	Marketing
3	Manufacturing
4	Computer Services
5	Sales
6	Accounting
7	Shipping

Table 5-4   Department numbers and names

8. Design a program that computes pay for employees. Allow a user to continuously input employee names until an appropriate sentinel value is entered. Also input each employee's hourly wage and hours worked. Compute each employee's gross pay (hours times rate), withholding tax percentage (based on Table 5-5), withholding tax amount, and net pay (gross pay minus withholding tax). Display all the results for each employee. After the last employee has been entered, display the sum of all the hours worked, the total gross payroll, the total withholding for all employees, and the total net payroll.

Weekly Gross Pay ($)	Withholding Percentage (%)
0.00–200.00	10
200.01–350.00	14
350.01–500.00	18
500.01 and up	22

Table 5-5   Withholding percentage based on gross pay

9. Countrywide Tours conducts sightseeing trips for groups from its home base in Iowa. Create an application that continuously accepts tour data, including a three-digit tour number; the numeric month, day, and year values representing the tour start date; the number of travelers taking the tour; and a numeric code that represents the destination. As data is entered for each tour, verify that the month, day, year, and destination code are valid; if necessary, continue to prompt the user until valid data is entered. The valid destination codes are shown in Table 5-6.

Code	Destination	Price per Person ($)
1	Chicago	300.00
2	Boston	480.00
3	Miami	1050.00
4	San Francisco	1300.00

Table 5-6   Countrywide Tours codes and prices

Design the logic for an application that outputs each tour number, validated start date, destination code, destination name, number of travelers, gross total price for the tour, and price for the tour after discount. The gross total price is the tour price per guest times the number of travelers. The final price includes a discount for each person in larger tour groups, based on Table 5-7.

Number of Tourists	Discount per Tourist ($)
1–5	0
6–12	75
13–20	125
21–50	200
51 and over	300

Table 5-7   Countrywide Tours discounts

10.   a.   *Daily Life Magazine* wants an analysis of the demographic characteristics of its readers. The marketing department has collected reader survey records containing the age, gender, marital status, and annual income of readers. Design an application that allows a user to enter reader data and, when data entry is complete, produces a count of readers by age groups as follows: under 20, 20–29, 30–39, 40–49, and 50 and older.

   b.   Modify the *Daily Life Magazine* program so that it produces a count of readers by gender within age group—that is, under-20 females, under-20 males, and so on.

   c.   Modify the *Daily Life Magazine* program so that it produces a count of readers by income groups as follows: under $30,000, $30,000–$49,999, $50,000–$69,999, and $70,000 and up.

11.   Glen Ross Vacation Property Sales employs seven salespeople, as shown in Table 5-8.

When a salesperson makes a sale, a record is created, including the date, time, and dollar amount of the sale. The time is expressed in hours and minutes, based on a 24-hour clock. The sale amount is expressed in whole dollars. Salespeople earn a commission that

ID Number	Salesperson Name
103	Darwin
104	Kratz
201	Shulstad
319	Fortune
367	Wickert
388	Miller
435	Vick

Table 5-8   Glen Ross salespeople

differs for each sale, based on the rate schedule in Table 5-9.

Design an application that produces each of the following:

a. A list of each salesperson number, name, total sales, and total commissions

b. A list of each month of the year as both a number and a word (for example, *01 January*), and the total sales for the month for all salespeople

Sale Amount ($)	Commission Rate (%)
0–50,999	4
51,000–125,999	5
126,000–200,999	6
201,000 and up	7

Table 5-9 Glen Ross commission schedule

c. A list of total sales as well as total commissions earned by all salespeople for each of the following time frames, based on hour of the day: 00–05, 06–12, 13–18, and 19–23

12. Design an application in which the number of days for each month in the year is stored in an array. (For example, January has 31 days, February has 28, and so on. Assume that the year is not a leap year.) Prompt a user to enter a birth month and day, and continue to prompt until the day entered is in range for the month. Compute the day's numeric position in the year. (For example, February 2 is day 33.) Then, using parallel arrays, find and display the traditional Zodiac sign for the date. For example, the sign for February 2 is Aquarius.

13. For games to hold your interest, they almost always include some random, unpredictable behavior. For example, a game in which you shoot asteroids loses some of its fun if the asteroids follow the same, predictable path each time you play. Therefore, generating random values is a key component in creating most interesting computer games. Many programming languages come with a built-in method you can use to generate random numbers. The syntax varies in each language, but it is usually something like the following:

```
myRandomNumber = random(10)
```

In this statement, `myRandomNumber` is a numeric variable you have declared and the expression `random(10)` means "call a built-in method that generates and returns a random number between 1 and 10." By convention, in a flowchart, you would place a statement like this in a processing symbol with two vertical stripes at the edges, as shown in Figure 5-19.

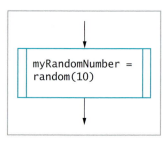

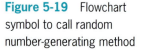

Figure 5-19 Flowchart symbol to call random number-generating method

Create the logic for a Magic 8 Ball game in which the user enters a question such as *What does my future hold?* The computer randomly selects one of eight possible vague answers, such as *It remains to be seen.*

 In Chapter 6 you will learn much more about calling built-in methods like the random number-generating method.

14. Create the logic for an application that contains an array of 10 multiple-choice questions related to your favorite hobby. Each question contains three answer choices. Also create a parallel array that holds the correct answer to each question—A, B, or C. Display each question and verify that the user enters only A, B, or C as the answer—if not, keep prompting the user until a valid response is entered. If the user responds to a question correctly, display *Correct!*; otherwise, display *The correct answer is* and the letter of the correct answer. After the user answers all the questions, display the number of correct and incorrect answers.

15. a. Create the logic for a dice game. The application randomly "throws" five dice for the computer and five dice for the player. After each random throw, store the results in an array. The application displays all the values, which can be from 1 to 6 inclusive for each die. Decide the winner based on the following hierarchy of die values. Any higher combination beats a lower one; for example, five of a kind beats four of a kind.

    ◆ Five of a kind

    ◆ Four of a kind

    ◆ Three of a kind

    ◆ A pair

    For this game, the numeric dice values do not count. For example, if both players have three of a kind, it's a tie, no matter what the values of the three dice are. Additionally, the game does not recognize a full house (three of a kind plus two of a kind). Figure 5-20 shows how the game might be played in a command-line environment.

    Figure 5-20 Typical execution of the dice game

    b. Improve the dice game so that when both players have the same number of matching dice, the higher value wins. For example, two 6s beats two 5s.

16. Design the logic for the game Hangman, in which the user guesses letters in a hidden word. Store the letters of a word in an array of characters. Display a dash for each missing letter. Allow the user to continuously guess a letter until all the letters in the word are guessed correctly. As the user enters each guess,

display the word again, filling in the guessed letter if it was correct. For example, if the hidden word is *computer*, first display a series of eight dashes: --------. After the user guesses *p*, the display becomes ---p----. Make sure that when a user makes a correct guess, all the matching letters are filled in. For example, if the word is *banana* and the user guesses *a*, all three *a* characters should be filled in.

17. Create two parallel arrays that represent a standard deck of 52 playing cards. One array is numeric and holds the values 1 through 13 (representing Ace, 2 through 10, Jack, Queen, and King). The other array is a string array that holds suits (Clubs, Diamonds, Hearts, and Spades). Create the arrays so that all 52 cards are represented. Then, create a War card game that randomly selects two cards (one for the player and one for the computer) and declares a winner or a tie based on the numeric value of the two cards. The game should last for 26 rounds and use a full deck with no repeated cards. For this game, assume that the lowest card is the Ace. Display the values of the player's and computer's cards, compare their values, and determine the winner. When all the cards in the deck are exhausted, display a count of the number of times the player wins, the number of times the computer wins, and the number of ties.

    Here are some hints:

    - Start by creating an array of all 52 playing cards.

    - Select a random number for the deck position of the player's first card and assign the card at that array position to the player.

    - Move every higher-positioned card in the deck "down" one to fill in the gap. In other words, if the player's first random number is 49, select the card at position 49 (both the numeric value and the string), move the card that was in position 50 to position 49, and move the card that was in position 51 to position 50. Only 51 cards remain in the deck after the player's first card is dealt, so the available-card array is smaller by one.

    - In the same way, randomly select a card for the computer and "remove" the card from the deck.

Case Projects

Case: Cost Is No Object

1. In earlier chapters, you developed programs for Cost Is No Object—a car rental service. Create an application that produces employee information for Cost Is No Object. The application prompts the user for an employee ID number, first and last names, street address, zip code, and job description code.

Any time the user enters an invalid value, continue to reprompt the user for the same data. Invalid values are:

- An employee ID number that is negative or greater than 999
- A zip code that is not in the list of allowed zip codes
- A job description code that is not between 10 and 19 inclusive

Determine the employee's city and state based on the zip code, as described in Table 5-10. Determine the employee's job title based on the values in Table 5-11. Determine the employee's hourly pay rate based on the values in Table 5-12.

Zip Code	City	State
53115	Delavan	WI
53125	Fontana	WI
53147	Lake Geneva	WI
53184	Walworth	WI
53585	Sharon	IL
60001	Alden	IL
60033	Harvard	IL
60034	Hebron	IL
61012	Capron	IL

Table 5-10 Zip codes for Cost Is No Object

Job Code	Title
10	Desk clerk
11	Credit checker
12	Billing clerk
13	Car cleaner
14	Chauffeur
15	Marketer
16	Accountant
17	Mechanic
18	CEO
19	Contractor

Table 5-11 Job titles for Cost Is No Object

Job Code	Hourly Pay Rate ($)
10–13	9.00
14–15	14.50
16–17	20.00
18	65.00
19	0.00

Table 5-12 Hourly pay rates for Cost Is No Object

When all the needed data has been entered correctly for an employee, output the ID number, first and last names, street address, city, state, zip code, job code, job title, and hourly pay rate.

Case: Classic Reunions

2. In earlier chapters, you developed programs for Classic Reunions—a reunion planning service. Create an application that prompts the user for an ID number for a reunion party, the reunion school's name, number of guests, menu selection, and entertainment selection.

Any time the user enters an invalid value, continue to reprompt the user for the same data. Invalid values are:

- An ID number for the reunion that is negative or greater than 999

- A number of guests that is not between 10 and 600 inclusive

- A menu selection that is not between 1 and 5 inclusive

- An entertainment selection that is not between 1 and 3 inclusive

Determine the base price per person for the event based on the values in Table 5-13. Determine the menu description and additional price per person based on the menu selection code, as described in Table 5-14. Determine the entertainment description and price based on the values in Table 5-15.

Number of Guests	Rate per Person ($)
10–24	20.00
25–49	17.50
50–99	15.00
100–199	12.00
200 and up	10.00

Table 5-13   Base rates for Classic Reunions

Meal Code	Meal	Price per Person over Base Cost ($)
1	Roast beef dinner	5.00
2	Seafood extravaganza	9.00
3	Casual buffet	4.50
4	Formal buffet	6.50
5	Appetizers only	0.00

Table 5-14   Meal selections for Classic Reunions

Entertainment Code	Entertainment	Price for the Event ($)
1	DJ	0.00
2	Piano player	150.00
3	Four-piece band	600.00

Table 5-15   Entertainment selections for Classic Reunions

When all the needed data has been entered correctly for a reunion party, output all the data for the reunion, including the ID number, school name, number of guests, rate per person, meal description, price of the meal per person, and the entire cost (which is the base cost for the party plus the cost of the meal per person plus the cost of the selected entertainment).

Case: The Barking Lot

3. In earlier chapters, you developed programs for The Barking Lot—a dog-boarding facility. Create an application that prompts the user for a dog's ID number and the number of days the dog will be boarded.

Any time the user enters an invalid value, continue to reprompt the user for the same data. Invalid values are:

- An ID number for the dog that is less than 1000 or greater than 1999
- A number of days for boarding that is not between 1 and 31 inclusive

When the user enters a dog's ID, determine the dog's name and weight from Table 5-16. If the dog's ID does not appear in the table, prompt the user for the name and weight. Use Table 5-17 to determine the base price for boarding the dog based on the length of stay. Then determine the additional fee per day based on the dog's weight, as shown in Table 5-18.

ID	Dog	Weight
1001	Bowser	130
1003	Ginger	80
1007	Molly	45
1008	Tyler	18
1012	Roxy	70

Table 5-16   Dog IDs and weights for The Barking Lot

Length of Stay in Days	Price per Day ($)
1–3	28.00
4–8	24.00
9–20	20.00
21 and up	17.50

Table 5-17   Price per day of boarding based on length of stay for The Barking Lot

Dog's Weight in Pounds	Additional Price ($)
Under 15	0.00
16–40	2.00
41–80	3.00
81 and over	3.50

Table 5-18   Additional price per day based on weight of dog

When all the needed data has been entered correctly for a dog, output all the data, including the ID number, dog's name and weight, length of stay, base price per day, additional price per day based on weight, and total amount due.

Up for Discussion

1. A train schedule is an everyday, real-life example of an array. Identify at least four more.

2. Every element in an array always has the same data type. Why is this necessary?

Using Methods

In this chapter, you will learn about:

◎ The advantages of modularization

◎ Modularizing a program

◎ Declaring local and global variables and constants

◎ Methods that require parameters

◎ Methods that return a value

◎ Passing an array to a method

◎ Overloading methods

◎ Using predefined methods

Understanding the Advantages of Modularization

Programmers seldom write programs as one long series of steps. Instead, they break down the programming problem into reasonable units, called **modules**, and tackle one small task at a time. Programmers tend to use different names for modules, depending on the programming language they use. For example, Visual Basic programmers use **procedure** or **subprocedure**. C and C++ programmers call their modules **functions**, whereas programmers in COBOL, RPG, and BASIC (all older languages) are most likely to use **subroutine**. Programmers who use C#, Java, and other object-oriented languages are more likely to use *method*, so this book will do the same.

You have already seen many examples of application classes that contain a `main()` method. In this chapter, you will learn to break down `main()` method tasks into more easily manageable units. The process of converting a large program into a set of shorter methods is called **modularization**. (Reducing a large program into more manageable methods is sometimes called **functional decomposition**.) You are never required to modularize a large program to make it run on a computer, but there are several reasons for doing so:

- Modularization provides abstraction.

- Modularization simplifies the logic.

- Modularization allows multiple programmers to work on a problem.

- Modularization allows you to reuse work more easily.

Modularization Provides Abstraction

One reason modularized programs are easier to understand is that they enable a programmer to see the "big picture." **Abstraction** is the process of paying attention to important properties while ignoring nonessential details. Abstraction is selective ignorance. Life would be tedious without abstraction. For example, you can create a list of things to accomplish today:

```
Do laundry
Call Aunt Nan
Start term paper
```

Without abstraction, the list of chores would begin:

```
Pick up laundry basket
Put laundry basket in car
Drive to Laundromat
Get out of car with basket
Walk into Laundromat
Set basket down
Find quarters for washing machine
...and so on.
```

You might list a dozen more steps before you finish the laundry and move on to the second chore on your original list. If you had to consider every small, low-level detail of every task in your day, you would probably never make it out of bed in the morning. Using a higher-level, more abstract list makes your day manageable. Abstraction makes complex tasks look simple.

 Abstract artists create paintings in which they see only the big picture—color and form—and ignore the details. Abstraction has a similar meaning among programmers.

Likewise, some level of abstraction occurs in every computer program. Fifty years ago, a programmer had to understand the low-level circuitry instructions the computer used. Now, however, newer high-level programming languages allow you to use English-like vocabulary in which one broad statement corresponds to dozens of machine instructions. No matter which high-level programming language you use, you can display a message on the monitor without knowing how a monitor works to create each pixel on the screen. You write an instruction like output message and the details of the hardware operations are handled for you.

Methods provide another way to achieve abstraction. For example, a payroll program can call a method named computeFederalWithholdingTax(). When you call this method from your program, you use one statement; the method itself might contain dozens of statements. You can write the mathematical details of the method later, someone else can write them, or you can purchase them from an outside source. When you plan the main payroll program, your only concern is that a federal withholding tax will have to be calculated; you save the details for later.

Modularization Simplifies the Logic

When you modularize a program, each method is smaller and easier to follow. Most well-written methods execute a single, finite task, which makes them easier to understand than a large program. It also makes errors easier to find, and makes methods easier to revise in the future. Smaller methods are less complex and therefore more reliable.

Modularization Allows Multiple Programmers to Work on a Problem

When you dissect any large task into methods, you gain the ability to more easily divide the task among various people. Rarely does a single programmer write a commercial program that you buy. Consider any word-processing, spreadsheet, or database program you have used. Each program has so many options, and responds to user selections in so many possible ways, that it would take years for a single programmer to write all the instructions. Professional software developers can write new programs in weeks or months, instead of years, by dividing large programs into methods and assigning each to an individual programmer or team.

Modularization Allows You to Reuse Work

If a method is useful and well written, you may want to use it more than once within a program or to use it in other programs. For example, a method that verifies the validity of dates is useful in many business programs. (Verifying a date might include ensuring that a month value is not lower than 1 or higher than 12, that a day value is not lower than 1 or higher than 31 when the month is 1, and so on.) If a computerized personnel file contains each employee's birth date, hire date, last promotion date, and termination date, the date-validation method can be used four times with each employee record. Other programs in an organization can also use the method, including programs that ship customer orders, plan employees' birthday parties, and calculate when loan payments should be made. If you write the date-checking instructions so they are entangled with other statements in a program, they are difficult to extract and reuse. On the other hand, if you place the instructions in their own method, the unit is easy to use and portable to other applications. The feature of modular programs that allows individual methods to be used in a variety of applications is known as **reusability**.

You can find many real-world examples of reusability. When you build a house, you don't invent plumbing and heating systems; you incorporate systems with proven designs. This certainly reduces the time and effort it takes to build a house. The plumbing and heating systems you choose are in service in other houses, so they also improve the reliability of your house's systems—they have been tested under a variety of circumstances and shown to work. **Reliability** is the feature of programs and methods that assures you each has been tested and proven to function correctly. Reliable software saves time and money. If you create the functional components of your programs as stand-alone methods and test them in your current programs, much of the work will already be done when you use the methods in future applications.

Modularizing a Program

In many object-oriented programming languages, application classes contain a `main()` method—the first method that executes when you run the application. Optionally, application classes can contain additional methods that the `main()` method can use.

When you create a method, you include the following:

- A header—The **method header** includes the method identifier and possibly other necessary identifying information. In Chapter 2, you learned the general rules for creating identifiers in programs. Method names follow those rules, which means they must be a single word with no embedded spaces, and they must start with a letter. Although it is not a requirement of any programming language, it frequently makes sense to use a verb as all or part of a method's name, because a method performs an action. Typical method names begin with action words such as `set`, `calculate`, or `display`.

- A body—The **method body** contains all the statements in the method. A method can contain any number of statements, including variable and constant declarations, arithmetic statements, decisions, and loops.

- A `return` statement—The **method return statement** marks the end of the method and identifies the point at which control returns to the calling method. (In most programming languages, if you do not include a `return` statement at the end of a method, the logic will still return to the calling method. This book follows the convention of explicitly including a `return` statement with every method.)

When a method needs to use another method, it **calls the method** or **invokes** it, using the method's name. The flowchart symbol used to represent a method call is a rectangle with a bar across the top. You place the name of the method you are calling inside the rectangle. A method can call another method, and the called method can call another. The number of chained calls is limited only by the amount of memory available on your computer. When you call a method, the action is similar to putting a DVD player on pause. You abandon your primary action (watching a video), take care of some other task (for example, making a sandwich), and then return to the original task exactly where you left off.

Some programmers use a rectangle with stripes down each side to represent a method in a flowchart, but this book uses that convention only if a method is external to a program. For example, prewritten, built-in methods that generate random numbers, compute standard trigonometric functions, and sort values often are external to your programs. However, if the method is being created as part of the program, the book uses a rectangle with a single stripe across the top.

In a flowchart, you draw the `main()` method and every other method separately so that each has its own sentinel symbols. The first sentinel symbol contains the name of the method. This name must be identical to the name used by the calling method. The symbol that ends the method holds `return` and indicates that the logical progression of statements will exit the method and return to the calling method. Similarly, in pseudocode, you start each method with its name and end with a `return` statement; the method name and `return` statements are vertically aligned and all the method statements are indented between them.

For example, consider the program in Figure 6-1, which contains only a `main()` method. It accepts a customer's name and balance due as input and produces a bill. At the top of the bill, the company's name and address are displayed on three lines, which are followed by the customer's name and balance due. To display the company name and address, you can simply include three `output` statements in the `main()` method, as shown in Figure 6-1, or you can modularize the program by creating both the `main()` method and a `displayAddressInfo()` method that the `main()` method calls, as shown in Figure 6-2.

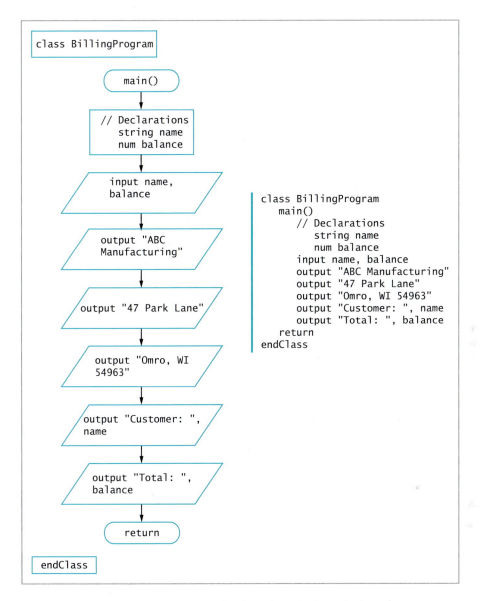

<figure>
class BillingProgram
    main()
        // Declarations
            string name
            num balance
        input name, balance
        output "ABC Manufacturing"
        output "47 Park Lane"
        output "Omro, WI 54963"
        output "Customer: ", name
        output "Total: ", balance
    return
endClass
</figure>

Figure 6-1 Program that produces a bill using only `main()` method

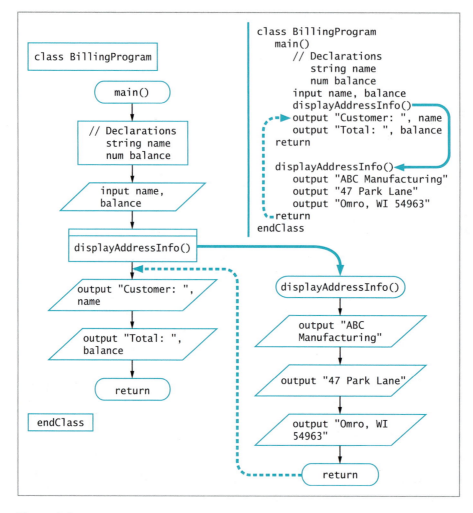

Figure 6-2 Program that produces a bill using `main()` method that calls `displayAddressInfo()` method

You place methods within a class but not within any other method. In most programming languages, methods can be written in any order within a class, although a few languages require that any calling method be placed after the method it calls. Therefore, in those languages, the `main()` method would always appear last.

In Figure 6-2, when the program starts, the `main()` method begins to execute. When the `displayAddressInfo()` method is called, logical control is transferred to it from the `main()` method, as shown by the solid arrow in both the flowchart and the pseudocode. There, each method statement executes in turn before logical control is transferred back to the `main()`

method, as shown by the dashed arrow. The logic continues in the `main()` method with the statement that follows the method call.

Neither of the programs in Figures 6-1 and 6-2 is superior to the other in terms of functionality; both perform exactly the same tasks in the same order. However, you may prefer the modularized version of the program for at least two reasons:

- In the modularized version, the `main()` method remains short and easy to follow because it contains just one statement to call the method, rather than three separate `output` statements to perform the work of the method.

- The method in the modularized version is easily reusable. After you create the address information method, you can use it in any application that needs the company's name and address. In other words, you do the work once, and then you can use the method many times. Programmers say the statements that are contained in a method have been **encapsulated**.

A potential drawback to creating multiple methods and moving between them is the overhead incurred. After executing a method, the computer keeps track of the correct memory address to which it should return by recording the memory address in a location known as the **stack**. This process requires a small amount of computer time and resources. In most cases, the advantage to creating methods far outweighs the small amount of overhead required.

The full name of the `displayAddressInfo()` method in Figure 6-2 is `BillingProgram.displayAddressInfo()`. The full name includes the class name, a dot, and the method name. When you use the `displayAddressInfo()` method within its own class, you do not need to use the full name (although you can); the method name alone is enough. However, if you want to use the `displayAddressInfo()` method in another class, the compiler will not recognize the method unless you use the full name; this format notifies the new class that the method is located in the `BillingProgram` class. Each of two different classes could have its own method named `displayAddressInfo()`. Such a method in the second class would be entirely distinct from the identically named method in the first class.

You can think of the class name as a family name. Within your own family, you might refer to a *family reunion*, but outside the family, people need to use a surname as well, as in *the Anderson family reunion*. Similarly, a method name alone is sufficient within a class, but outside the class, you need to use the fully qualified name.

Determining when to break down a program into methods does not depend on a fixed set of rules; it requires experience and insight. Programmers do follow some guidelines when deciding how far to break down methods, or how much to put in each of them. Some companies may have arbitrary rules, such as "a method's instructions should never take more than a page," or "a method should never have more than 30 statements," or "never have a method with only one statement." Rather than use such arbitrary rules, a better policy is to place together statements that contribute to one specific task. The more the statements contribute to the same job, the greater the **functional cohesion** of the method. A method that checks the validity of a date variable's value, or one that asks a user for a value and accepts it as input, is considered cohesive. A method that checks date validity, deducts insurance premiums, and computes federal withholding tax for an employee would be less cohesive.

 Watch the video *Modularizing a Program.*

Declaring Local and Global Variables and Constants

You can place any statements within methods, including variable and constant declarations. For example, you might decide to modify the billing program in Figure 6-2 so it looks like the one in Figure 6-3. In this version of the program, three named constants that hold the three lines of company data are declared within the `displayAddressInfo()` method. (See shading.)

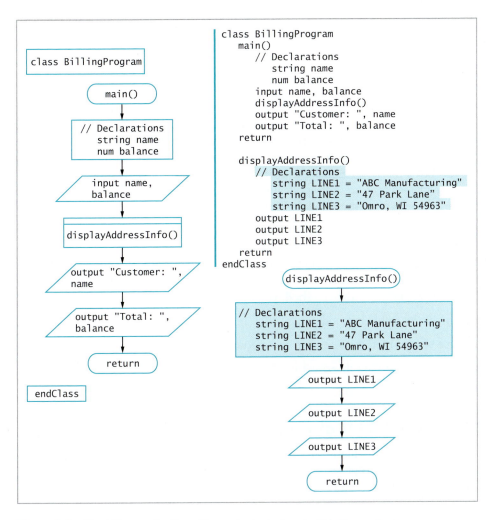

Figure 6-3 The billing application with constants declared within the method

Variables and constants declared in a method are usable only within that method. Programmers say the data items are **local** to the method in which they are declared, which means the program only recognizes them there. Programmers also use the terms **in scope** and **visible** to describe variables that are known to a method. In other words, when the strings LINE1, LINE2, and LINE3 are declared in the displayAddressInfo() method in Figure 6-3, they are not recognized and cannot be used by the main() method; they are visible and in scope only within their own method. When the displayAddressInfo() method ends, its locally declared variables die, or go **out of scope**. Similarly, the variables in the main() method, name and balance, are local to main() and are not recognized within the displayAddressInfo() method.

One of the motivations for creating methods is that separate methods are easily reusable in multiple programs. If the `displayAddressInfo()` method will be used by several programs within the organization, it makes sense that the definitions for its variables and constants must come with it. This makes the methods more **portable**; that is, they are self-contained units that are easily transported to other applications.

Besides local variables and constants, you can create **global** variables and constants that are known to the entire class. That means they are visible to and usable in all the methods used in a class. You declare global variables and constants inside a class, but outside of any methods. In this book, variables and constants declared in application classes will always be local to a method—either the `main()` method or another method. In Chapter 7, you will create classes that are not applications but are classes from which objects are created. These classes will contain global variables, which is conventional for such classes.

In the program in Figure 6-3, the `main()` method and the method it calls each contain only what is needed at the local level. However, two or more parts of a program sometimes require access to the same data. When methods must share data, you must pass the data into the methods and return the data out of them. In this chapter, you will learn that when you call a method from a program or other method, you must know three things:

- The name of the called method
- What type of information to send to the method, if any
- What type of return data to expect from the method, if any

Creating Methods that Require Parameters

Some methods require information to be sent in from the outside. A data item passed into a method from a calling program is called an **argument to the method**, or more simply, an argument. When the method receives the argument, it is stored in a **parameter** in the method header. *Argument* and *parameter* are closely related terms. A calling method sends an argument to a called method, and a called method accepts the value as its parameter. (Even more confusing, some programmers refer to arguments in a method call as *actual parameters* and to parameters in method headers as *formal parameters*.)

If a method could not receive parameters, you would have to write an infinite number of methods to cover every possible situation. As a real-life example, when you make a restaurant reservation, you do not need to employ a different method for every date of the year at every possible time of day. Rather, you can supply the date and time as information to the person who carries out the method. The method that records the reservation is carried out in the same manner, no matter what date and time are supplied. If you design a `square()` method that squares numeric values, you should supply the method with a parameter that represents the value to be squared, rather than developing a `square1()` method that squares the value 1, a `square2()` method that squares the value 2, and so on.

To call a square() method that accepts a parameter, you might write a statement like square(17) or square(86) and let the method use whatever argument you send.

For example, suppose that your supervisor asks you to modify the displayAddressInfo() method in the billing program so that when a customer's balance is over $1000, an attention-getting message precedes the company's name and address on the bill. In the original program, the balance is local to the main() method and therefore cannot be used in the displayAddressInfo() method. You could rewrite the program by taking several approaches:

- You could rewrite the program to eliminate the displayAddressInfo() method so that all statements are in the main()method. This approach would work, but you would not be taking advantage of the benefits provided by modularization. Those benefits include making the main() method more streamlined and abstract, and making the displayAddressInfo() method a self-contained unit that can easily be transported to other programs.

- You could retain the displayAddressInfo() method, but make at least the balance variable global by declaring it outside of any methods. If you took this approach, you would lose some of the portability of the displayAddressInfo() method because everything it used would no longer be contained within the method.

- You could retain the displayAddressInfo() method as is without access to the balance in the main() method, but add a local variable to displayAddressInfo() and prompt the user for the balance again within the method. The disadvantage to this approach is that the user must answer a balance question twice during one execution of the program. Not only does that require more work from the user, it also introduces the possibility that the user will enter different values, causing inconsistencies and confusion.

- You could store the balance variable in the main() method so that it could be used to display the customer's balance, but also pass the balance to the displayAddressInfo() method so that it could be used there as well. This is the best choice, and is illustrated in Figure 6-4.

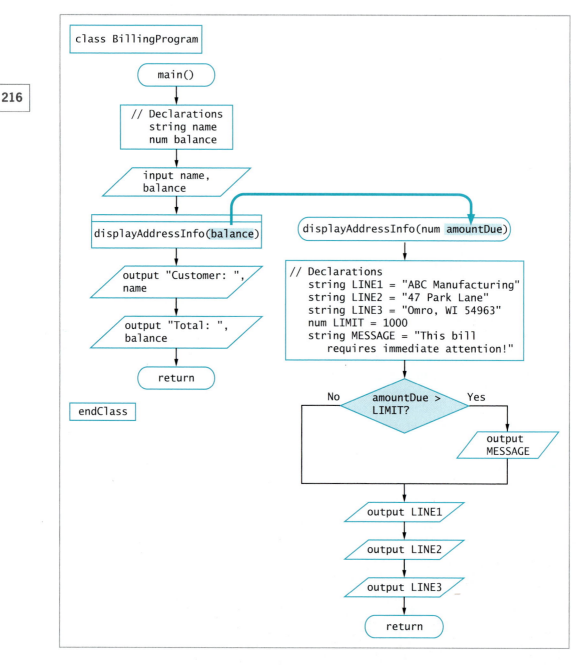

Figure 6-4   Billing application that passes an argument to a method

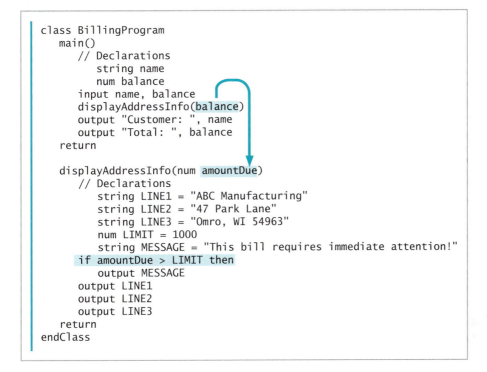

```
class BillingProgram
    main()
        // Declarations
            string name
            num balance
        input name, balance
        displayAddressInfo(balance)
        output "Customer: ", name
        output "Total: ", balance
    return

    displayAddressInfo(num amountDue)
        // Declarations
            string LINE1 = "ABC Manufacturing"
            string LINE2 = "47 Park Lane"
            string LINE3 = "Omro, WI 54963"
            num LIMIT = 1000
            string MESSAGE = "This bill requires immediate attention!"
        if amountDue > LIMIT then
            output MESSAGE
        output LINE1
        output LINE2
        output LINE3
    return
endClass
```

Figure 6-4   Billing application that passes an argument to a method (continued)

Figure 6-5 shows how the billing application in Figure 6-4 might look when prompts have been added for the customer data and the program is executed in a command-line environment.

```
Command Prompt                                    _  □  X

Enter customer name >> Al Zimmerman
Enter customer balance >> 1467.85


This bill requires immediate attention!
ABC Manufacturing
47 Park Lane
Omro, WI 54963

Customer: Al Zimmerman
Total: 1467.85
```

Figure 6-5   Typical execution of the BillingProgram application

In the main program in Figure 6-4, the numeric variable `balance` is declared and input in the `main()` method. The value then is passed to the `displayAddressInfo()` method. When you create a method that can receive a parameter, you must include the following items within the method header's parentheses:

- The type of the parameter

- A local name for the parameter

In the program in Figure 6-4, the value of the balance is stored in two places in memory:

- The `main()` method stores the balance in the variable `balance` and passes it to `displayAddressInfo()` as an argument.

- The `displayAddressInfo()` method accepts the parameter as `amountDue`. Within the method, `amountDue` takes on the value that `balance` had in the main program. In other words, `amountDue` holds a copy of the value in `balance`.

Understanding the Difference Between Passing Arguments by Value and by Reference

In most programming languages, an argument that is passed into a method can be passed in one of two ways:

- An argument can be **passed by value**, which means that a copy of its value is sent to the method and stored in a new memory location accessible to the method.

- An argument can be **passed by reference**, which means the address of the original variable is sent to the method.

Passing by Value

Most of the time, you pass an argument to a method by value, forcing the method to contain its own copy of the value. The `displayAddressInfo()` method could be called using any numeric value as an argument, whether it is a variable, a named constant, or a literal constant. If the value used as an argument in the method call is a variable, it might possess the same identifier as the parameter declared in the method header, or it might possess a different one. Within a method, the passed variable is simply a temporary placeholder; it makes no difference what name the variable "goes by" in the calling method. Each time a method executes, any parameter variables listed in the method header and passed by value are redeclared—that is, a new memory location is reserved and named. When the method ends at the `return` statement, the locally declared parameter variable ceases to exist.

For example, Figure 6-6 shows a `main()` method that declares a variable, assigns a value to it, displays it, and sends it to another method named `add86()`. Within `add86()`, the parameter is displayed, altered, and displayed again. When control returns to the `main()`

method, the original variable is displayed one last time. As the execution in Figure 6-7 shows, even though the variable in the second method was altered, the original variable in the first method retains its starting value because it never was altered; it occupies a different memory address from the variable in the second method.

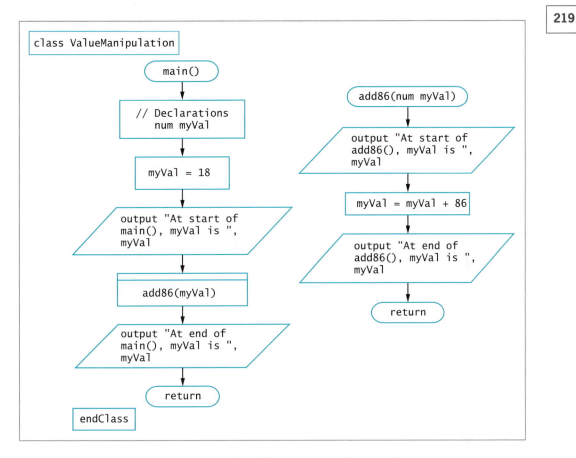

Figure 6-6 A program that calls a method in which the argument is passed by value

```
Command Prompt

At start of main(), myVal is 18
At start of add86(), myVal is 18
At end of add86(), myVal is 104
At end of main(), myVal is 18
```

Figure 6-7 Execution of the program in Figure 6-6

An important principle of object-oriented programming is the notion of **implementation hiding**, the encapsulation of method details within a class. With implementation hiding, you make a request to a method without knowing the details of how the method works. For example, when you make a restaurant reservation, you do not need to know how the reservation is actually recorded at the restaurant—perhaps it is written in a book, marked on a large chalkboard, or entered into a computerized database. The implementation details don't concern you as a patron, and if the restaurant changes its methods from one year to the next, the change does not affect your use of the reservation method—you still call and provide your name, a date, and a time.

The parameter types within parentheses in a method header are the method's **parameter list**. A method's name and parameter list constitute the method's **signature**. With well-written object-oriented methods, using implementation hiding means that a method that calls another must know the method's signature and what type of `return` data to expect (as you will see later in this chapter), but the program does not need to know how the method works internally; the implementation exists in a *black box*. The calling method needs to understand only the **interface to the method** that is called. In other words, the interface is the only part of a method that the **method's client** (or method's caller) sees or with which it interacts. Additionally, you can substitute a new, improved method implementation, and as long as the interface to the method does not change, you won't need to make changes in any methods that call the altered method.

Passing by Reference

Some programming languages allow you to pass arguments by reference, which gives the receiving method the address of the original variable rather than a copy of its value. The way you accomplish this differs among programming languages, but usually it involves placing a special symbol or specified keyword within the parentheses in the method header. Some programmers disapprove of passing a variable's reference from one method to another because some independence of the methods is lost and implementation hiding is reduced. Later in this chapter, you will learn that special structures such as arrays are passed by reference.

 When your instructor distributes copies of the course syllabus, they are passed by value. That is, each student can make changes to his own copy and the original is not altered. When the instructor submits the syllabus to her department chairman for approval, the syllabus is passed by reference. That is, the chairman can make changes that persist.

Creating Methods that Require Multiple Parameters

A method can require more than one parameter. You create and use a method with multiple parameters by doing the following:

- You list the arguments within the method call, separated by commas.

- You list a data type and local identifier for each parameter within the method header's parentheses, separating each declaration with a comma.

For example, suppose that you want to create a `computeTax()` method that calculates a tax on any value passed into it. You can create a method to which you pass two values—the amount to be taxed, as well as a percentage figure by which to tax it. Figure 6-8 shows a method that accepts two such parameters.

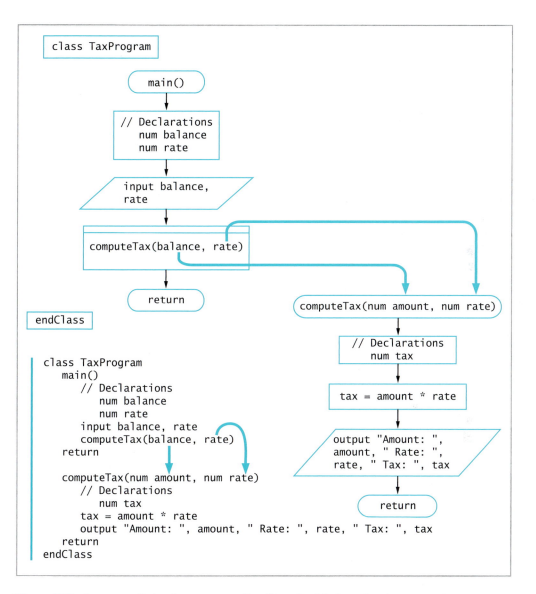

Figure 6-8   A program that calls a `computeTax()` method that requires two parameters

In Figure 6-8, two parameters (`num amount` and `num rate`) appear within the parentheses in the method header. A comma separates each parameter, and each requires its own declared type (in this case, both are numeric) as well as its own identifier. In Figure 6-8, notice that one of the arguments to the method has the same name as the corresponding method parameter, and the other has a different name from its corresponding parameter. Each could have the same identifier as its counterpart, or all could be different. Each identifier is local to its own method.

When multiple values are passed to a method, they are accepted by the parameters in the order in which they are passed. Arguments must be passed in the correct order. A call of `computeTax(rate, balance)` instead of `computeTax(balance, rate)` would result in incorrect values being displayed in the output statement. You can write a method so that it takes any number of parameters in any order. However, when you call a method, the arguments you send to the method must match in order—both in number and in type—the parameters listed in the method declaration. If a method requires multiple arguments that are the same type—for example, two numeric arguments—passing them to a method in the wrong order results in a logical error; the program will compile and execute but produce incorrect results. If a method expects arguments of diverse types—for example, a number and a string—then passing arguments in the wrong order is a syntax error, and the program will not compile.

Watch the video *Methods with Parameters*.

Creating Methods that Return a Value

A variable declared within a method ceases to exist when the method ends—it goes out of scope. When you want to retain a value that exists when a method ends, you can return the value from the method to the calling method. When a method returns a value, the method must have a return type that matches the data type of the returned value. The **return type** for a method indicates the data type of the value that the method will send back to the location where the method call was made. A return type can be any type, which includes numeric and string, as well as other more specific types in the programming language you are using. A method can also return nothing, in which case the return type is `void`, and the method is a **void method**. (The term *void* means "nothing" or "empty.") A method's return type is known more succinctly as a **method's type**. A method's type is listed in the method header in front of the method name when the method is defined; a return type and signature form a complete **method declaration**.

Up to this point, this book has not included return types for methods because all the methods have been void. From this point forward, a return type is included with every method. The `main()` method will have a `void` return type.

For example, a method that returns the number of hours an employee has worked might have the following header or declaration:

```
num getHoursWorked()
```

This method returns a numeric value, so its type is num.

A method's `return` statement can return one value at most. The value can be a simple data type or it can be a more complex type—for example, a structure or an object. You will learn to create objects in Chapter 7. The value returned from a method often is a variable, but it can be constant. For example, you might write a method that always returns a 1 to prove it executed completely, or you might call a method that returns a company's name or address, which would be defined as constants.

When a method returns a value, you usually want to use the returned value in the calling method, although this is not required. As an example of when you might call a method but not use its returned value, consider a method that gets a character from the keyboard and returns its value to the calling program. If you wanted to tell the user to "Press any key," you could call the method to accept the character from the keyboard, but you would not care which key was pressed or which key value was returned. However, you usually call a method with a return value because your program will use the value.

For example, Figure 6-9 shows how a program might use the value returned by the `getHoursWorked()` method. A variable named `hours` is declared in the `main()` method. The `getHoursWorked()` method call is part of an assignment statement. When the method is called, the logical control is transferred from the `main()` method to the `getHoursWorked()` method, which contains a variable named `workHours`. A value is obtained for this variable, which is returned to the `main()` method where it is assigned to `hours`. After the logical control returns to `main()` from `getHoursWorked()`, the latter method's local variable `workHours` no longer exists. However, its value has been stored in the `main()` method where, as `hours`, it can be displayed and used in a calculation.

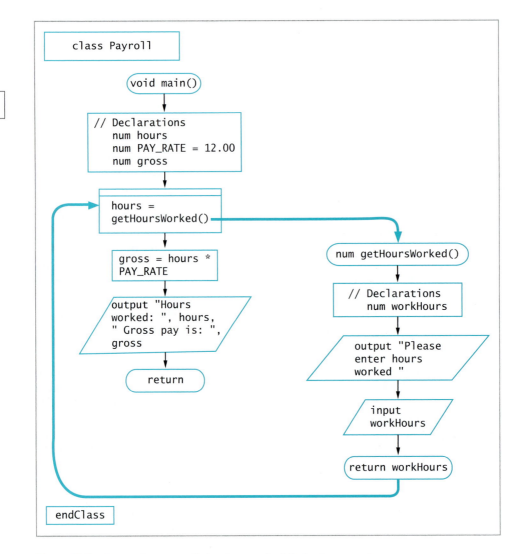

Figure 6-9   A payroll program that calls a method that returns a value

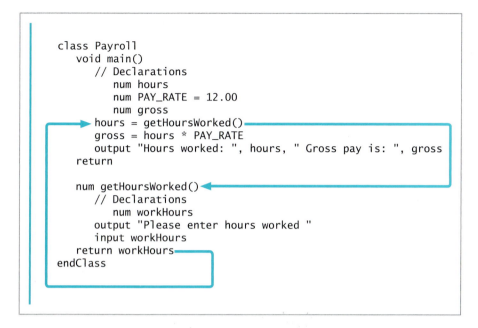

```
class Payroll
   void main()
      // Declarations
         num hours
         num PAY_RATE = 12.00
         num gross
      hours = getHoursWorked()
      gross = hours * PAY_RATE
      output "Hours worked: ", hours, " Gross pay is: ", gross
   return

   num getHoursWorked()
      // Declarations
         num workHours
      output "Please enter hours worked "
      input workHours
   return workHours
endClass
```

Figure 6-9   A payroll program that calls a method that returns a value (continued)

In Figure 6-9, notice the return type num that precedes the method name in the getHoursWorked() method header. A method's declared return type must match the type of the value used in the return statement; if it does not, the program will not compile. A numeric value is correctly included in the return statement—the last statement within the getHoursWorked() method. When you place a value in a return statement, the value is sent from the called method back to the calling method.

 Along with an identifier and parameter list, a return type is part of a method's declaration. Some programmers claim a method's return type is part of its signature, but this is not the case. Only the method name and parameter list constitute the signature.

You are not required to assign a method's return value to a variable in order to use the value. Instead, you can use a method's returned value directly, without storing it. You use a method's value in the same way you would use any variable of the same type. For example, you can output a return value in a statement such as the following:

`output "Hours worked is ", getHoursWorked()`

Because getHoursWorked() returns a numeric value, you can use the method call getHoursWorked() in the same way that you would use any simple numeric value. Figure 6-10 shows an example of a program that uses a method's return value directly without storing it. The value of the shaded workHours variable returned from the method is used directly in the calculation of gross in the main program.

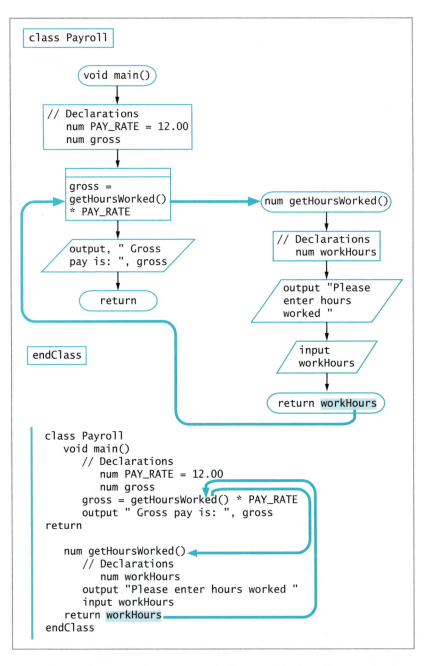

Figure 6-10 A program that uses a method's returned value without storing it

Style and efficiency determine whether you want to store a method's return value in a variable before using it or to use the method call directly as a value. When a program needs to use a method's returned value in more than one place, it makes sense to store the returned value in a variable instead of calling the method multiple times. A program statement that calls a method requires more computer time and resources than a statement that does not call any outside methods. However, the most important consideration is usually to make your programs clear and easy to understand.

In most programming languages, you technically are allowed to include multiple `return` statements in a method, although this practice is not recommended. For example, consider the `findLargest()` method in Figure 6-11. The method accepts three parameters and returns the largest of the values. Although this method works correctly (and you might see this technique used), you should not place more than one `return` statement in a method. In earlier chapters, you learned that each of the three basic logic structures—sequence, selection, and loop—has one entry point and one exit point. The `return` statements in Figure 6-11 violate this convention by leaving decision structures before they are complete. Figure 6-12 shows the superior and recommended way to handle the problem. In Figure 6-12, the largest value is stored in a variable. Then, when the nested decision structure is complete, the stored value is returned.

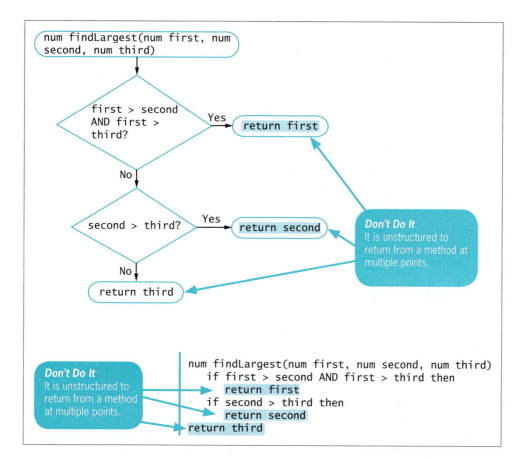

Figure 6-11 Unrecommended approach to returning one of several values

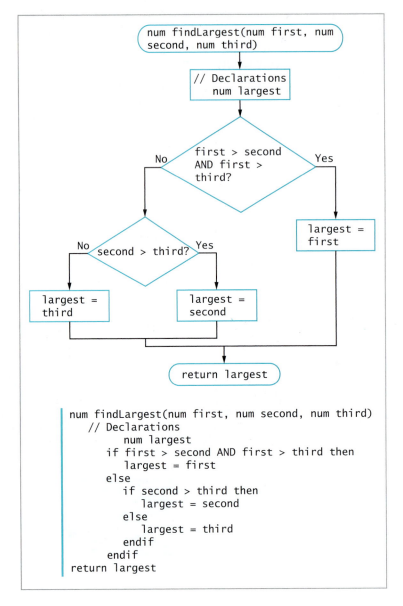

Figure 6-12   Recommended approach to returning one of several values

Passing an Array to a Method

In Chapter 5, you learned that you can declare an array to create a list of elements, and that you can use any individual array element in the same manner you would use any single variable of the same type. For example, suppose that you declare a numeric array as follows:

```
num someNums[12]
```

You can subsequently output someNums[0] or perform arithmetic with someNums[11], just as you would for any simple variable that is not part of an array. Similarly, you can pass a single array element to a method in exactly the same manner you would pass a variable or constant. A passed array element is passed by value; the receiving method receives a copy.

Instead of passing a single array element to a method, you can pass an entire array as an argument. You can indicate that a method parameter must be an array by placing square brackets after the data type in the method's parameter list. When you pass an array to a method, changes you make to array elements within the method are permanent; that is, they are reflected in the original array that was sent to the method. In Chapter 5 you learned that the name of an array represents a memory address, and the subscript used with an array name represents an offset from that address. So, when you use an array name, you are using an address. Arrays, unlike simple built-in types, are passed by reference; a method that receives an array receives the actual memory address of the array, and the method therefore has access to the actual values in the array elements.

The program shown in Figure 6-13 sends a four-element numeric array to methods three times as follows (see shaded method calls):

- The array is sent to a method named displayArray() that displays each array element. This produces the first line of output in Figure 6-14.

- The array is sent to a method named tenTimes() that multiples each array element by 10. The method produces no output and returns nothing to the main() method.

- The array is sent again to the displayArray() method. Even though the tenTimes() method returns nothing to main(), the array values have been altered as shown in the second output line in Figure 6-14. The values in the main() method have been altered because the tenTimes() method has access to the original array. Because arrays are passed by reference, the tenTimes() method "knows" the address of the array declared in the calling method and makes its changes directly to the array.

230

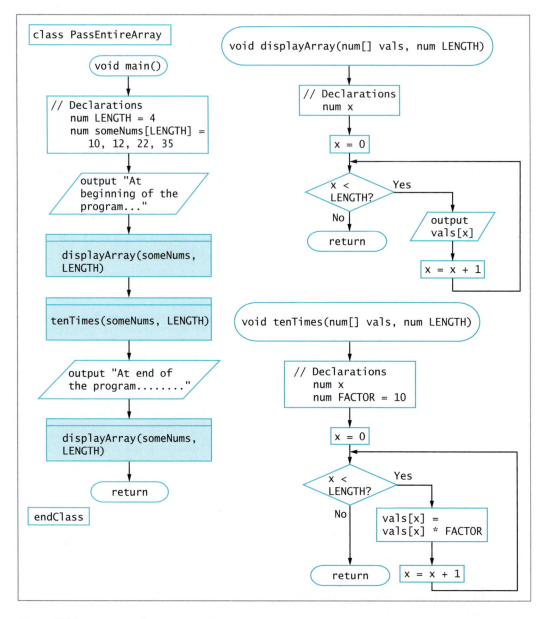

Figure 6-13   PassEntireArray program

```
class PassEntireArray
    void main()
        // Declarations
            num LENGTH = 4
            num someNums[LENGTH] = 10, 12, 22, 35
        output "At beginning of the program..."
        displayArray(someNums, LENGTH)
        tenTimes(someNums, LENGTH)
        output "At end of the program........"
        displayArray(someNums, LENGTH)
    return

    void displayArray(num[] vals, num LENGTH)
        // Declarations
            num x
        x = 0
        while x < LENGTH
            output vals[x]
            x = x + 1
        endwhile
    return

    void tenTimes(num[] vals, num LENGTH)
        // Declarations
            num x
            num FACTOR = 10
        x = 0
        while x < LENGTH
            vals[x] = vals[x] * FACTOR
            x = x + 1
        endwhile
    return
endClass
```

Figure 6-13 PassEntireArray program (continued)

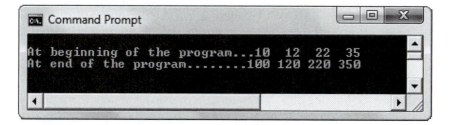

Figure 6-14 Output of the PassEntireArray program

When an array is a method parameter, the square brackets in the method header remain empty and do not hold a size. The array name that is passed is a memory address that indicates the start of the array. Depending on the language you are using, you can control the values you use for a subscript to the array in different ways. In some languages, you might also want to pass a constant that indicates the array size to the method, as in Figure 6-13. In other languages, you can access the automatically created length field for the array. Either way, the array size itself is never implied when you use the array name. The array name only indicates the starting point from which subscripts will be used.

Overloading Methods

In programming, **overloading** involves supplying diverse meanings for a single identifier. When you use the English language, you frequently overload words. When you say *break a window*, *break bread*, *break the bank*, and *take a break*, you describe four very different actions that use different methods and produce different results. However, anyone who speaks English well comprehends your meaning because *break* is understood in the context of the discussion.

In most programming languages, some operators are overloaded. For example, a + between two values indicates addition, but a single + to the left of a value means the value is positive. In many languages, a + between two strings links them end to end (an operation called *concatenation*). The + sign has different meanings based on the operands used with it.

A method's name and parameter list compose the method's signature. When you **overload a method**, you write multiple methods with a shared name but different parameter lists. In other words, overloaded methods have different signatures. When you call an overloaded method, the language translator understands which version of the method to use based on the arguments you use. Overloading a method is an example of **polymorphism**—the ability of a method to act appropriately according to the context. Literally, *polymorphism* means *many forms*.

For example, suppose that you create a method to output a message and the amount due on a customer bill, as shown in Figure 6-15. The method receives a numeric parameter that represents the customer's balance and produces two lines of output. Assume that you also need a method that is similar to `printBill()`, except the new method applies a discount to the customer bill. One solution to this problem would be to write a new method with a different name—for example, `printBillWithDiscount()`. A downside to this approach is that a programmer who uses your methods must remember the names of each slightly different version. It is more natural for your methods' clients to use a single well-designed method name for the task of printing bills, but to be able to provide different arguments as appropriate. In this case, you can overload the `printBill()` method so that, besides the version that takes a single numeric argument, you can create a version that takes two numeric arguments—one that represents the balance and one that represents the discount rate. Figure 6-15 shows the two versions of the `printBill()` method.

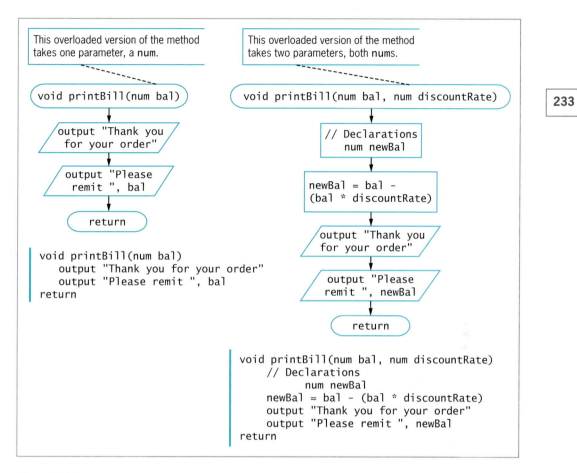

Figure 6-15 Two overloaded versions of the `printBill()` method

If both versions of `printBill()` are included in a program and you call the method using a single numeric argument, as in `printBill(custBalance)`, the first version of the method in Figure 6-15 executes. If you use two numeric arguments in the call, as in `printBill(custBalance, rate)`, the second version of the method executes.

If it suited your needs, you could provide more versions of the `printBill()` method, as shown in Figure 6-16. The first version in the figure accepts a numeric parameter that holds the customer's balance and a string parameter that holds an additional message that can be customized for the bill recipient and displayed on the bill. For example, if a program makes a method call such as the following, this version of `printBill()` will execute:

```
printBill(custBal, "Due in 10 days")
```

The second version of the method in Figure 6-16 accepts three parameters, providing a balance, discount rate, and customized message. For example, the following method call would use this version of the method:

```
printBill(balanceDue, discountRate, specialMessage)
```

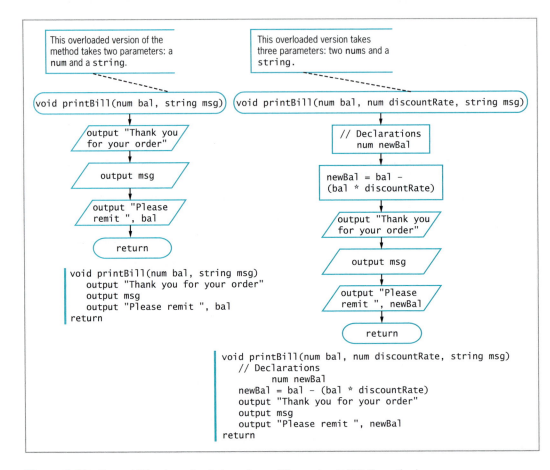

Figure 6-16   Two additional overloaded versions of the `printBill()` method

Overloading methods is never required in a program. Instead, you could create multiple methods with unique identifiers such as `printBill()` and `printBillWithDiscountAndMessage()`. Overloading methods does not reduce your work when creating a program; you need to write each method individually. The advantage is provided to your method's clients; those who use your methods need to remember just one appropriate name for all related tasks.

In many programming languages, the `output` statement is actually an overloaded method that you call. It is convenient that you use a single name, such as `output`, whether you want to output a number, a `string`, or any combination of the two.

Even if you write two or more overloaded versions of a method, many program clients will use just one version. For example, suppose that you develop a bill-creating program that contains all four versions of the `printBill()` method just discussed, and then sell it to different companies. An organization that adopts your program and its methods might only want to use one or two versions of the method. You probably own many devices for which only some of the features are meaningful to you; for example, some owners of microwave ovens only use the Popcorn button or never use Defrost.

Avoiding Ambiguous Methods

When you overload a method, you run the risk of creating **ambiguous** methods—a situation in which the compiler cannot determine which method to use. Every time you call a method, the compiler decides whether a suitable method exists; if so, the method executes, and if not, you receive an error message. For example, suppose that you write two versions of a `printBill()` method, as shown in the program in Figure 6-17. One version of the method is intended to accept a customer balance and a discount rate, and the other is intended to accept a customer balance and a discount amount expressed in dollars.

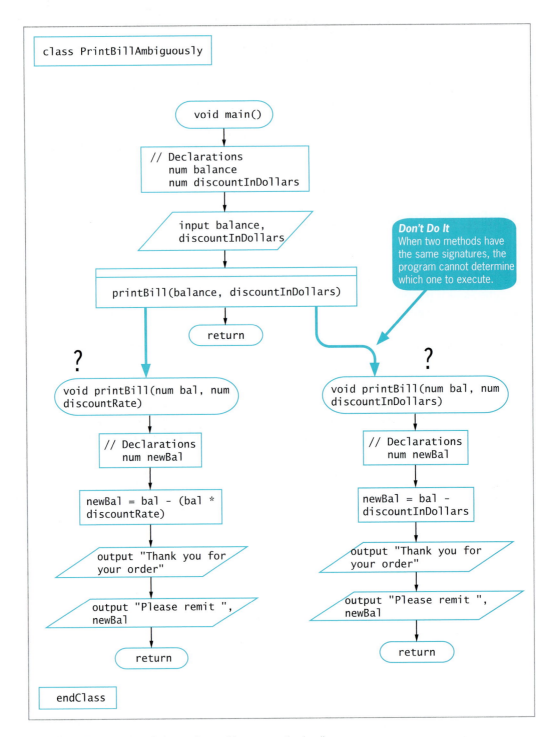

Figure 6-17   Program that contains ambiguous method call

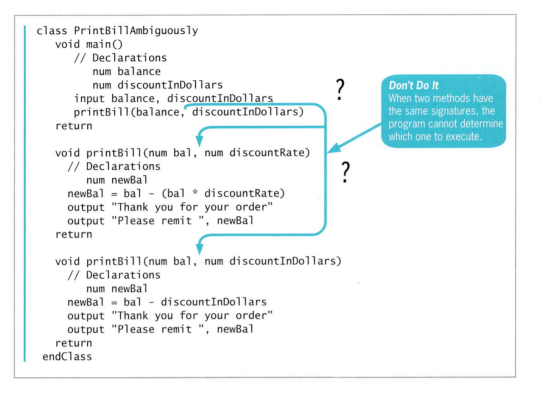

```
class PrintBillAmbiguously
    void main()
        // Declarations
            num balance
            num discountInDollars
        input balance, discountInDollars
        printBill(balance, discountInDollars)
    return

    void printBill(num bal, num discountRate)
        // Declarations
            num newBal
        newBal = bal - (bal * discountRate)
        output "Thank you for your order"
        output "Please remit ", newBal
    return

    void printBill(num bal, num discountInDollars)
        // Declarations
            num newBal
        newBal = bal - discountInDollars
        output "Thank you for your order"
        output "Please remit ", newBal
    return
endClass
```

Don't Do It
When two methods have the same signatures, the program cannot determine which one to execute.

237

Figure 6-17 Program that contains ambiguous method call (continued)

Each of the two versions of printBill() in Figure 6-17 is a valid method on its own. However, when the two versions exist in the same program, a problem arises. When the main program calls printBill() using two numeric arguments, the compiler cannot determine which version to call. You might think that the version with a parameter named discountInDollars would execute, because the method call uses the identifier discountInDollars. However, which version of a method to call is based on argument data types only, not their identifiers. Because both versions of the printBill() method could accept two numeric parameters, the method version cannot be determined and the program does not execute.

In some programming languages, an overloaded method is not ambiguous on its own—it becomes ambiguous only if you make a method call that matches multiple method signatures. In languages that allow it, a program with potentially ambiguous methods will run without problems if you don't make any method calls that match more than one method. However, creating such methods is still incorrect because none of the ambiguous methods can ever be used.

Methods can be overloaded correctly by providing different parameter lists for methods with the same name. Methods with identical names that have identical parameter lists but different return types are not overloaded—they are ambiguous. For example, the following two method headers create ambiguity.

```
string aMethod(num x)
num aMethod(num y)
```

The compiler determines which version of a method to call based on parameter lists, not return types. When the method call `aMethod(17)` is made, the compiler will not know which method to execute because both possible choices take a numeric argument.

All the popular object-oriented programming languages support multiple numeric data types. For example, Java, C#, C++, and Visual Basic all support integer (whole number) data types, which are different from floating-point (decimal place) data types. Many languages have even more specialized numeric types, such as signed and unsigned. Methods that accept different specific types are correctly overloaded.

Watch the video *Overloading Methods*.

Using Predefined Methods

All modern programming languages contain many methods that have already been written for you. Predefined methods might originate from several sources:

- Some prewritten methods are built into a language. For example, methods that perform input and output are almost always predefined for you. Most languages include many prewritten mathematical methods such as those that compute a number's square root or absolute value. Other methods retrieve the current date and time from the operating system or select a random number to use in a game application.

- When you work on a program in a team, each programmer might be assigned specific methods to create, and your methods will interact with methods written by others.

- If you work for a company, many standard methods may already have been written and you will be required to use them. For example, the company might have a standard method that displays its logo.

Predefined methods save you time and effort. For example, in most languages, displaying a message on the screen involves using a built-in method. When you want to display *Hello* on the command prompt screen in C#, you write the following:

```
Console.WriteLine("Hello");
```

In Java, you write:

```
System.out.println("Hello");
```

In these statements, you can recognize `WriteLine()` and `println()` as method names because they are followed by parentheses; the parentheses hold an argument that represents the message to display. If these methods were not written for you, you would have to know the low-level details of how to manipulate pixels on a screen to get the characters to display. Instead, by using the prewritten methods, you can concentrate on the higher-level task of displaying a useful and appropriate message.

In C#, the convention is to begin method names with an uppercase letter. In Java, method names conventionally begin with a lowercase letter. The `WriteLine()` and `println()` methods follow their respective language's convention. The `WriteLine()` and `println()` methods are both overloaded in their respective languages. For example, if you pass a string to either method, the version of the method that accepts a string parameter executes, but if you pass a number, another version that accepts a numeric parameter executes.

239

A language's prewritten methods were created as a convenience for you—computing a square root and generating random numbers are complicated tasks, so it is convenient to have methods already written, tested, and available when you need them. The names of the methods that perform these functions differ among programming languages, so you need to research the language's documentation to use them. Many of a language's methods are described in introductory programming language textbooks, and you can also find language documentation online.

When you want to use a predefined method, you should understand what the method does in general. Then, you must find out the three details that you should understand about any method you use:

- The method's name—for example, it might be `sqrt()`

- The method's required parameters—for example, a square root method might require a single numeric parameter. There might be multiple overloaded versions of the method from which you can choose.

- The method's return type—for example, a square root method most likely returns a numeric value that is the square root of the argument passed to the method

You do not need to know how the method is implemented—that is, how the instruction statements are written within it. Like all methods, you can use built-in methods without worrying about their low-level implementation details.

Chapter Summary

- Programs can be broken down into reasonable units called modules, subroutines, procedures, functions, or methods. Modularization is the process of converting a large program into a set of shorter methods. Modularization provides abstraction, simplifies the logic, lets multiple programmers work on a problem, and allows you to reuse work more easily.

- In object-oriented programming languages, application classes contain a `main()` method and can contain additional methods that the `main()` method can use. When you create a method, you include a header, a body, and a `return` statement. When a method needs to use another method, it calls the method or invokes it, using the method's name. The flowchart symbol used to represent a method call is a rectangle with a bar across the top.

- You can include variable and constant declarations within methods. Variables and constants declared in a method are local to that method, and usable only within that method.

- When you pass a data item into a method from a calling program, it is called an argument to the method. When the method receives the data item, it is stored in a parameter. When you write the declaration for a method that can receive a parameter, you must include the data type and a local name for the parameter within the method declaration's parentheses. In most programming languages, an argument that is passed into a method can be passed by value or by reference. You indicate that a method requires multiple arguments by listing their data types and local identifiers within the method header's parentheses. When you call a method, the arguments you send to the method must match in order—both in number and in type—the parameters listed in the method declaration.

- When a method returns a value, the method must have a return type. A method's return type indicates the data type of the value that the method will send back to the location where the method call was made. A return type also is known as a method's type, and is indicated in front of the method name when the method is defined. When a method returns a value, you usually want to use the returned value in the calling method, although this is not required.

- You can pass a single array element to a method in exactly the same manner you would pass a variable or constant. Additionally, you can pass an entire array to a method. You can indicate that a method parameter must be an array by placing square brackets after the data type in the method's parameter list. When you pass an array to a method, it is passed by reference; that is, the method receives the actual memory address of the array and has access to the actual values in the array elements.

- When you overload a method, you write multiple methods with a shared name but different parameter lists. The compiler understands your meaning based on the arguments you use when you call the method. Overloading a method introduces the risk of creating ambiguous methods—a situation in which the compiler cannot determine which method to use. Every time you call a method, the compiler decides whether a suitable method exists; if so, the method executes, and if not, you receive an error message. Methods can be overloaded correctly by providing different parameter lists for methods with the same name.

- All modern programming languages contain many methods that have already been written for you. Methods are built into a language to save you time and effort.

Key Terms

Modules are small program units that are combined to make programs.

Procedures and **subprocedures** are modules; Visual Basic programmers frequently use this term.

Functions are modules; C programmers frequently use this term.

Subroutines are modules; programmers who use older languages frequently use this term.

Modularization is the process of converting a large program into a set of shorter methods.

Functional decomposition is the act of reducing a large program into more manageable methods.

Abstraction is the process of paying attention to important properties while ignoring nonessential details.

Reusability is the feature of modular programs that allows individual methods to be used in a variety of applications.

Reliability is the feature of programs and methods that assures you each has been tested and proven to function correctly.

A **method header** is the first line of a method. It is the entry point to a method, and it provides an identifier, parameter list, and frequently other information.

A **method body** contains all the statements in a method.

A **method return statement** marks the end of the method and identifies the point at which control returns to the calling method.

Calling a method invokes it, causing it to execute.

Invoking a method calls it, causing it to execute.

Encapsulation is the feature of methods that provides for their instructions and data to be contained in the method.

The **stack** holds the memory addresses to which method calls should return.

Functional cohesion describes the extent to which a method's statements contribute to the same task.

Local describes data items that are usable only within the method in which they are declared.

In scope describes items that are visible in a method.

Visible describes items that are in scope for a method.

Out of scope describes data items that are no longer visible to a method.

Portable program features are those that can more easily be reused in multiple programs.

Global variables and constants are known to an entire class.

Arguments to a method are the data items sent to methods.

Parameters are the data items received by methods.

Passed by value describes parameters received by a method as a copy.

Passed by reference describes parameters received by a method as memory addresses.

Implementation hiding is a principle of object-oriented programming that describes the encapsulation of method details within a class.

A **parameter list** is the list of parameters in a method header.

242

A **signature** is a method's name and parameter list.

The **interface to a method** includes the method's return type, name, and arguments. The interface is the part that a client sees and uses.

A **method's client** is a program or other method that uses the method.

A method's **return type** is the data type for any value it returns.

A **void method** returns no value.

A **method's type** is its return type.

A **method declaration** is composed of the method's return type and signature.

Overloading involves supplying diverse meanings for a single identifier.

To **overload a method** is to write multiple methods with a shared name but different parameter lists.

Polymorphism is the ability of a method to act appropriately according to the context.

Ambiguous methods are overloaded methods for which the compiler cannot determine which version to use.

Review Questions

1. Which of the following is true?

   a. A class can contain two methods at most.
   b. A class might contain a method that calls two other methods.
   c. A method might contain two or more other methods.
   d. All of the above are true.

2. Which of the following must every method have?

   a. a header   c. at least one local variable
   b. a parameter list   d. all of the above

3. Which of the following is most closely related to the concept of *local*?

   a. abstract   c. in scope
   b. object-oriented   d. class level

4. Although the terms *parameter* and *argument* are closely related, the difference between them is that *argument* refers to _____ .

    a. a passed constant

    b. a value in a method call

    c. a formal parameter

    d. a variable that is local to a method

5. The notion of _____ most closely describes the way a calling method is not aware of the statements within a called method.

    a. abstraction

    b. object-oriented

    c. implementation hiding

    d. encapsulation

6. A method's name and parameter list constitute its _____ .

    a. signature

    b. return type

    c. identifier

    d. class

7. Which of the following must be included in a method declaration for a method that receives a parameter?

    a. the name of the argument that will be used to call the method

    b. a local name for the parameter

    c. the return value for the method

    d. all of the above

8. When you use a variable name in a method call, it _____ the same name as the variable in the method header.

    a. can have

    b. cannot have

    c. must have

    d. The answer depends on the programming language.

9. Assume that you have written a method with the header
   `void myMethod(num a, string b)`. Which of the following is a correct method call?

    a. `myMethod(12)`

    b. `myMethod(12, "Hello")`

    c. `myMethod("Goodbye")`

    d. It is impossible to tell.

10. Assume that you have written a method with the header
    `num myMethod(string name, string code)`. The method's type is _____ .

    a. `num`

    b. `string`

    c. `character`

    d. It is impossible to determine.

11. Assume that you have written a method with the header
    `string myMethod(num score, string grade)`. Also assume that you have declared a numeric variable named `test`. Which of the following is a correct method call?

    a. `myMethod()`

    b. `myMethod(test)`

    c. `myMethod(test, test)`

    d. `myMethod(test,"A")`

12. If a method returns a value, you —————— the returned value when you call the method.

    a. must use
    c. usually will want to use

    b. must not use
    d. usually will not want to use

13. A void method ——————.

    a. returns nothing
    c. has an empty body

    b. accepts no arguments
    d. all of the above

14. When a method receives a copy of the value stored in an argument used in the method call, it means the variable was ——————.

    a. unnamed

    b. passed by value

    c. passed by reference

    d. assigned its original value when it was declared

15. When an array is passed to a method, it is ——————.

    a. passed by reference
    c. unnamed in the method

    b. passed by value
    d. unalterable in the method

16. When you overload a method, you write multiple methods with the same ——————.

    a. name
    c. number of parameters

    b. parameter list
    d. return type

17. A class contains a method with the header
`num calculateTaxes(num amount, string name)`. Which of the following methods can coexist in the same class with no possible ambiguity?

    a. `num calculateTaxes(string name, num amount)`

    b. `string calculateTaxes(num money, string taxpayer)`

    c. `num calculateTaxes(num annualPay, string taxpayerId)`

    d. All of these can coexist without ambiguity.

18. A class contains a method with the header
`void printData(string name, string address)`. Which of the following methods can coexist in the same class with no possible ambiguity?

    a. `string printData(string name, num amount)`

    b. `void printData(string name)`

    c. `void printData()`

    d. All of these can coexist without ambiguity.

19. Methods in the same class with identical names and identical parameter lists are _____ .

    a. overloaded   c. overwhelmed

    b. overworked   d. illegal

20. Methods in different classes with identical names and identical parameter lists are _____ .

    a. overloaded   c. both of the above

    b. illegal   d. none of the above

Exercises

1. a. Create the logic for a program that calculates and displays the amount of money you would have if you invested $5000 at 3 percent interest for one year. Create a separate method to do the calculation and display the result.

    b. Modify the interest-calculating program so the calculated value is returned to the main program where it is displayed.

2. Create the logic for a program that prompts the user for a 10-digit telephone number. Pass the number to a method that inserts dashes between the area code, exchange, and last four digits of the number.

3. Create an application class whose `main()` method holds two numeric variables. Prompt the user for values for the variables. In a loop that continues while the returned value is N, pass both variables to a method that determines whether the first number is larger than the second and appropriately returns a character Y or N. After the method returns Y, pass the two numbers to a method named `difference()` that computes the difference between its two parameters and displays the results.

4. Create the logic for a program that accepts input values for the projected cost of a vacation and the number of months until vacation. Pass both values to a method that displays the amount you must save per month to achieve your goal.

5. Create the logic for an application that contains a `main()` method that continuously prompts the user for a number of dollars until the user enters 0. Pass the amount to a conversion method that displays the breakdown of the passed amount into the fewest bills; in other words, the method calculates the number of 20s, 10s, 5s, and 1s needed.

6. Create the logic for a program that calculates the due date for a bill. Prompt the user for the month, day, and year a bill is received, and pass the data to a method that displays slashes between the parts of the date—for example, *6/24/2013*. Then, pass the parts of the date to a method that calculates the bill's due date,

which is 10 days after receipt. (A due date might be in the next month or even the next year. For this exercise, assume that February has 28 days.) This method displays the due date with slashes by calling the display method.

7. Jacobson Builders is constructing new homes in the Parkway subdivision. The company needs the logic for an application that calls a method that computes the final price for construction of a new home. The `main()` method prompts the user for the number of bedrooms and bathrooms in the home and for the salesperson's commission expressed as a percentage, and then displays the final price. Create a `calculatePrice()` method that determines the final price and returns the value to the calling method. The `calculatePrice()` method requires three arguments: bedrooms, baths, and salesperson commission rate. A home's final price is the sum of the base price of $100,000 plus $20,000 per bedroom, $30,000 per bathroom, and the salesperson commission amount.

8. Carlisle Carpets wants a program to compute carpet costs. Create the logic for a program that prompts the user for two numeric values that represent room dimensions in feet. The program then displays the room area in square feet and the carpet price, which is $15 per square foot. If the user enters two positive numbers, call a method that accepts two parameters and multiplies them to compute the room's area. If just one of the entered values is positive, pass the positive value to an overloaded version of the method that accepts one parameter and squares it to calculate the area. If neither of the entered values is positive, then display an error message.

9. Create the logic for an application that computes and displays the amount a user should save to reach a one-year savings goal. Prompt the user for a dollar goal, and ask whether the user is paid weekly. If the user is not paid weekly, prompt the user to enter the number of paychecks received per year. Include two overloaded methods named `computeSaveAmount()` and call the appropriate one. One version accepts the goal and computes the amount to save per pay period as 1/52 of the goal. The other accepts the goal and the number of pay periods and computes the savings goal per pay period by dividing the two values. Each version returns the savings goal per pay period to the calling method.

10. Create the logic for a program whose `main()` method prompts a user for three numbers and stores them in an array. Pass the array to a method that reverses the order of the numbers. In the `main()` method, display the numbers.

11. Create the logic for a program whose `main()` method contains an array of 10 numbers. Prompt the user for a value for each number. Pass the array to a method that calculates the arithmetic average of the numbers and returns the value to the calling program. Display each number and how far it is from the arithmetic average. Continue to prompt the user for additional sets of 10 numbers until the user indicates a desire to quit.

Case Projects

Case: Cost Is No Object

1. In earlier chapters, you have developed programs for Cost Is No Object—a car rental service that specializes in lending antique and luxury cars to clients on a short-term basis. Create a class whose `main()` method assigns cars and rental fees to customers for the current day. The program continuously prompts for input data until the user indicates that the end of the data has been reached.

   Input data includes the following:

   - Customer name

   - Code for desired car type—*A* for an antique car or *L* for a luxury car

   - Number of days for the rental

   In the `main()` method, create four parallel arrays. The first three contain car descriptions, daily rental fees, and the car-type code, as follows:

Description	Daily Fee	Code
1967 Ford Mustang	$65	A
1922 Ford Model T	$95	A
2008 Lincoln Continental	$135	L
2012 Lexus	$140	L
2007 BMW	$160	L
1910 Mercer Runabout	$165	A
2011 Mercedes Benz	$200	L
1930 Cadillac V-16	$205	A

Table 6-1   Car descriptions and codes

The fourth array contains an indicator that specifies whether the car is already rented. At the start of the program, none of the cars is rented.

After the user is prompted for the first customer's data, pass the customer's name, car type requested, and the four arrays of data to a method named `fulfillRequest()`. The method finds the first available car of the correct type, displays its description and rental fee, and changes the rental indicator to show the car is no longer available. If no cars are available of the type requested by the customer, display an appropriate message. The method returns the daily rental fee unless no cars of the correct type are available, in which case the method returns 0. The `main()` method displays the daily rental fee.

If a car of the correct type is available, the `main()` method should pass the daily rental fee, the number of rental days, and the car type requested to a method named `calculateContractAmount()`. The contract amount is the daily fee times the number of days plus tax. The tax is 6 percent of the rental price for an antique car and 8 percent of the price for a luxury car. The method returns the amount of the contract to the `main()` method, where the amount is displayed.

Before the user is prompted for data for any customer after the first one, determine whether any cars are still available for rent. If no more cars are available, display an appropriate message and end the program.

Case: Classic Reunions

2. In earlier chapters, you have developed programs for Classic Reunions—a service that specializes in organizing class reunions. Create a class whose `main()` method schedules events for the current week. The program continuously prompts for input data until the user indicates that the end of the data has been reached.

Input data includes the following:

- Event number, which is a letter followed by a four-digit number assigned by Classic Reunions

- Event name (for example, Washington High 25th reunion)

- Day of the event in the current week (for example, 3 for Wednesday)

- Coordinator for the event, which is a numeric code. Currently the service employs only two coordinators, but the owner hopes to expand in the future.

Prompt the user for data for the first event, and prompt for the letter that begins the event number. Because Classic Reunions is in its first year of business, all events begin with *A*, so reprompt the user if *A* is not entered. When the user enters *Z* for the first character in the event number, data entry is complete.

Call a method that prompts the user for the four digits in the event number. Within the method, continue to reprompt the user if the number is not between 1000 and 9999 inclusive. Return the valid number to the `main()` method.

Call additional methods that prompt the user for and return the event name, day, and coordinator. The user should be reprompted continuously if the entered day code is not 1 through 7 inclusive and the coordinator code is not 1 or 2.

Create four 7-element arrays. Each element represents a day of the week. Two parallel arrays store the event number and name at the appropriate day position for coordinator 1, and the other two store the event number and name at the appropriate position for coordinator 2.

Each coordinator can handle only one event per day. Before the user is prompted for data for any event after the first one, determine whether the indicated coordinator is free on the available day. You do this by passing the coordinator's schedule to a method named determineAvailability(). If the requested coordinator is available, schedule the event for that coordinator. If the requested coordinator is not available, issue a warning and use the determineAvailability() method to determine whether the other coordinator is available. If the other coordinator is available, display a message that the coordinator is being changed and schedule the event for the new coordinator. If neither coordinator is available, issue an error message and do not schedule the event.

When data entry is complete, pass each coordinator's schedule in turn to a displaySchedule() method, and display each coordinator's schedule for the week.

Case: The Barking Lot

3. In earlier chapters, you have developed programs for The Barking Lot—a dog-boarding service. Create a class whose main() method schedules kennel assignments for the current night. The program continuously prompts for a four-digit dog ID number until the user indicates that the end of the data has been reached by entering 9999.

After a valid dog ID number has been entered, pass it to a method that identifies the dog based on the following list of current dog clients:

ID	Dog	Weight
1001	Bowser	130
1003	Ginger	80
1007	Molly	45
1008	Murphy	18
1012	Roxy	70
1034	Samantha	12
1038	Duke	90
1087	Pookie	16
1088	Abby	35
1120	Barney	65
1129	Autumn	20
1145	Hershey	100
1200	King	110
1211	Bosco	70
1222	Daisy	55

Table 6-2   Dog information

If the dog ID number is on the list, display the dog's name and return its weight to the main() method; if the dog is not on the list, display an error message and return 0 to the main() method.

From the main() method, call a method that assigns a dog to one of the eight kennels available each night. The kennels are available as follows:

Kennel Number	Weight Range
1	under 50 pounds
2	under 50 pounds
3	up to 99 pounds
4	up to 99 pounds
5	up to 99 pounds
6	up to 99 pounds
7	100 pounds and over
8	100 pounds and over

Table 6-3   Dog kennel information

Assign a dog to the first available kennel based on the dog's weight. If no kennels are available for a dog, display a message.

When the user enters 9999 for a dog ID number to quit, or when all eight kennels are filled, call a method that displays the eight kennel numbers and the dog ID assigned to each.

Up for Discussion

1. Name any device you use every day. Discuss how implementation hiding is demonstrated in the way this device works. Is it a benefit or a drawback to you that implementation hiding exists for this device?

2. One advantage to writing a program that is subdivided into methods is that the methods are easily transported to other applications. Describe some nonprogramming situations in which modular construction is beneficial.

CHAPTER 7

Object-Oriented Programming Concepts

In this chapter, you will learn about:

- ◎ The principles of object-oriented programming
- ◎ Classes and class diagrams
- ◎ Public and private access
- ◎ Ways to organize classes
- ◎ Instance methods
- ◎ Static methods
- ◎ Using objects
- ◎ Composition
- ◎ Using GUI components as predefined objects
- ◎ The advantages of object-oriented programming

Principles of Object-Oriented Programming

Object-oriented programming (OOP) focuses on an application's data and the methods you need to manipulate that data. With OOP, you consider the objects that a program will manipulate—for example, a customer invoice, a loan application, or a menu from which a user selects an option. You define the characteristics of those objects and the methods that each object will use; you also define the information that must be passed to those methods.

OOP uses all of the familiar concepts of modular procedural programming, such as declaring variables and passing values to methods. Methods in object-oriented programs continue to use sequence, selection, and looping structures and make use of arrays. However, OOP adds several new concepts to programming and involves a different way of thinking. A considerable amount of new vocabulary is involved as well.

Five important features of object-oriented languages are:

- Classes
- Objects
- Polymorphism
- Inheritance
- Encapsulation

Classes and Objects

In object-oriented terminology, a **class** describes objects with common attributes. An **object** is one **instance** of a class. Object-oriented programmers sometimes say an object is one **instantiation** of a class; this word is just another form of *instance*. For example, your `redChevroletAutomobileWithTheDent` is an instance of the class that is made up of all automobiles, and your `GoldenRetrieverDogNamedGinger` is an instance of the class that is made up of all dogs. A class is like a blueprint from which many houses might be constructed, or like a recipe from which many meals can be prepared. One house and one meal are each an instance of their class; countless instances might be created eventually. For example, Figure 7-1 depicts a `Dog` class and two instances of it.

254

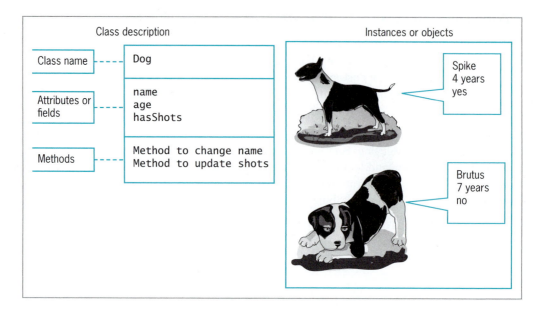

Class description | Instances or objects

Class name · · · · · Dog

Attributes or · · · · · name
fields   age
                          hasShots

Methods · · · · · Method to change name
                    Method to update shots

Spike
4 years
yes

Brutus
7 years
no

Figure 7-1   A Dog class and two instances

Since the beginning of this book, you have created application classes that could be used without creating instances. In this chapter, you will create additional types of classes that client programs will **instantiate**; that is, instances of the classes will be created.

Objects both in the real world and in object-oriented programming contain attributes and methods. **Attributes** are the characteristics that define an object as part of a class. For example, some of your automobile's attributes are its make, model, year, and purchase price. Other attributes include whether the automobile is currently running, its gear, its speed, and whether it is dirty. All automobiles possess the same attributes, but not the same values for those attributes. Similarly, your dog has the attributes of its breed, name, age, and whether its shots are current. Methods are the actions that can be taken on an object; methods often alter, use, or retrieve attributes. For example, an automobile has methods for changing and discovering its speed, and a dog has methods for setting and finding out its shot status.

Thinking of items as instances of a class allows you to apply your general knowledge of the class to its individual members. A particular instance of an object takes its attributes from the general category. If your friend purchases an Automobile, you know it has a model name, and if your friend gets a Dog, you know the dog has a breed. You might not know the current status of your friend's Automobile, such as its current speed, or the status of her Dog's shots, but you do know what attributes exist for the Automobile and Dog classes, which allows you to imagine these objects reasonably well before you see them. You know enough to ask the Automobile's model and not its breed; you know enough to ask the Dog's name and not its engine size. As another example, when you use a new application on your computer, you expect each component to have specific, consistent attributes, such as a button being clickable or a window being closable. Each component gains these attributes as a member of the general class of GUI (graphical user interface) components.

 Most programmers employ the format in which class names begin with an uppercase letter and multiple-word identifiers are run together, such as SavingsAccount. Each new word within the identifier starts with an uppercase letter. In Chapter 2, you learned that this format is known as *upper camel casing* or *Pascal casing*.

Much of your understanding of the world comes from your ability to categorize objects and events into classes. As a young child, you learned the concept of *animal* long before you knew the word. Your first encounter with an animal might have been with the family dog, a neighbor's cat, or a goat at a petting zoo. As you developed speech, you might have used the same term for all of these creatures, gleefully shouting "Doggie!" as your parents pointed out cows, horses, and sheep in picture books or along the roadside on drives in the country. As you grew more sophisticated, you learned to distinguish dogs from cows; still later, you learned to distinguish breeds. Your understanding of the class *animal* helps you see the similarities between dogs and cows, and your understanding of the class *dog* helps you see the similarities between a Great Dane and a Chihuahua. Understanding classes gives you a framework for categorizing new experiences. You might not know the term *okapi*, but when you learn it's an animal, you begin to develop a concept of what an okapi might be like.

When you think in an object-oriented manner, everything is an object. You can think of any inanimate physical item as an object—your desk, your computer, and your house are all called *objects* in everyday conversation. You can think of living things as objects, too—your houseplant, your pet fish, and your sister are objects. Events also are objects—the stock purchase you made, the mortgage closing you attended, and your graduation party are all objects.

Everything is an object, and every object is an instance of a more general class. Your desk is one tangible example of the class that includes all desks, and your pet fish is one example of the class that contains all fish. An object-oriented programmer would say that the desk in your office is an instance of the Desk class, and your fish is an instance of the Fish class.

The concept of a class is useful because of its reusability. For example, if you invite me to a graduation party, I automatically know many things about the object (the party). I assume there will be attributes such as a starting time, a number of guests, some quantity of food, and gifts. I understand this party because of my previous knowledge of the Party class, of which all parties are members. I don't know the number of guests or the date or time of this particular party, but I understand that because all parties have a date and time, then this one must as well. Similarly, even though every stock purchase is unique, each must have a dollar amount and a number of shares. All objects have predictable attributes because they are members of certain classes.

The data components of a class that belong to every instantiated object are the class's **instance variables**. Also, object attributes often are called **fields** to help distinguish them from other variables you might use. The set of all the values or contents of an object's instance variables is known as its **state**. For example, the current state of a particular party might be 8 p.m. and Friday; the state of a particular stock purchase might be $10 and five shares.

In addition to their attributes, objects have methods associated with them, and every object that is an instance of a class possesses the same methods. For example, at some point you might want to issue invitations for a party. You might name the method issueInvitations(), and it might display some text as well as the values of the party's date and time fields. Your graduation party, then, might possess the identifier myGraduationParty. As a member of the Party class, it might have data members for the date and time, like all parties, and it might have a method to issue invitations. When you use the method, you might want to be able to send an argument to issueInvitations() that indicates how many copies to print. When you think of an object and its methods, it's as though you can send a message to the object to direct it to accomplish a particular task—you can tell the party object named myGraduationParty to print the number of invitations you request. Even though yourAnniversaryParty also is a member of the Party class, and even though it also has an issueInvitations() method, you will send a different argument value to yourAnniversaryParty's issueInvitations() method than I send to myGraduationParty's corresponding method. Within an object-oriented program, you continuously make requests to an object's methods, often including arguments as part of those requests.

> In grammar, a noun is equivalent to an object and the values of a class's attributes are adjectives—they describe the characteristics of the objects. An object also can have methods, which are equivalent to verbs.

When you program in object-oriented languages, you frequently create classes from which objects will be instantiated. You also write applications to use the objects, along with their data and methods. Often, you will write programs that use classes created by others; at other times, you might create a class that other programmers will use to instantiate objects within their own programs. A program or class that instantiates objects of another prewritten class is a **class client** or **class user**. For example, your organization might already have a class named Customer that contains attributes such as name, address, and phoneNumber, and you might create clients that include arrays of thousands of Customers. Similarly, in a GUI operating environment, you might write applications that include prewritten components that are members of classes like Window and Button. You expect each component on a GUI screen to have specific, consistent attributes, because each component gains these attributes as a member of its general class.

Polymorphism

The real world is full of objects. Consider a door. A door needs to be opened and closed. You open a door with an easy-to-use interface known as a doorknob. Object-oriented programmers would say you are *passing a message* to the door when you tell it to open by turning its knob. The same message (turning a knob) has a different result when applied to your radio than when applied to a door. As depicted in Figure 7-2, the procedure you use to open something—call it the open() method—works differently on a door than it does on a desk drawer, a bank account, a computer file, or your eyes. However, even though these procedures operate differently using the different objects, you can call each of these procedures open().

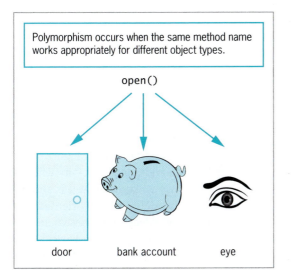

Figure 7-2   Examples of polymorphism

Within classes in object-oriented programs, you can create multiple methods with the same name, which will act differently and appropriately when used with different types of objects. In Chapter 6, you learned that this concept is *polymorphism*, and you learned to overload methods. For example, you might use a method named print() to print a customer invoice, loan application, or envelope. Because you use the same method name to describe the different actions needed to print these diverse objects, you can write statements in object-oriented programming languages that are more like English; you can use the same method name to describe the same type of action, no matter what type of object is being acted upon. Using the method name print() is easier than remembering printInvoice(), printLoanApplication(), and so on. Object-oriented languages understand verbs in context, just as people do.

As another example of the advantages to using one name for a variety of objects, consider a screen you might design for a user to enter data into an application you are writing. Suppose that the screen contains a variety of objects—some forms, buttons, scroll bars, dialog boxes, and so on. Suppose also that you decide to make all the objects blue. Instead of having to memorize the method names that these objects use to change color—perhaps changeFormColor(), changeButtonColor(), and so on—your job would be easier if the creators of all those objects had developed a setColor() method that works appropriately with each type of object.

Purists find a subtle difference between overloading and polymorphism. Some reserve the term *poly-morphism* (or **pure polymorphism**) for situations in which one method body is used with a variety of arguments. For example, a single method that can be used with any type of object is polymorphic. The term *overloading* is applied to situations in which you define multiple methods with a single name (for example, three methods, all named `display()`, that display a number, an employee, and a student, respectively). Certainly, the two terms are related; both refer to the ability to use a single name to communicate multiple meanings. For now, think of overloading as a primitive type of polymorphism.

258

Inheritance

Another important concept in object-oriented programming is **inheritance**, which is the process of acquiring the traits of one's predecessors. In the real world, a new door with a stained glass window inherits most of its traits from a standard door. It has the same purpose, it opens and closes in the same way, and it has the same knob and hinges. As Figure 7-3 shows, the door with the stained glass window simply has one additional trait—its window. Even if you have never seen a door with a stained glass window, you know what it is and how to use it because you understand the characteristics of all doors. With object-oriented programming, once you create an object, you can develop new objects that possess all the traits of the original object plus any new traits you desire. If you develop a `CustomerBill` class of objects, there is no need to develop an `OverdueCustomerBill` class from scratch. You can create the new class to contain all the characteristics of the already developed one, and simply add necessary new characteristics. This not only reduces the work involved in creating new objects, it makes them easier to understand because they possess most of the characteristics of already developed objects. You will learn much more about inheritance in Chapter 8.

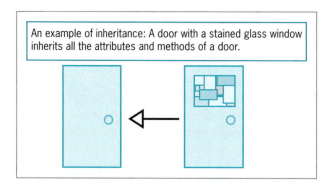

An example of inheritance: A door with a stained glass window inherits all the attributes and methods of a door.

Figure 7-3   An example of inheritance

Watch the video *An Introduction to Object-Oriented Programming.*

Encapsulation

Real-world objects often employ encapsulation and information hiding. **Encapsulation** is the process of combining all of an object's attributes and methods into a single package; the package includes data that is frequently hidden from outside classes and methods that are available to outside classes to access and alter the data. **Information hiding** is the concept that other classes should not alter an object's attributes—only the methods of an object's own class should have that privilege. Outside classes should only be allowed to make a request that an attribute be altered; it is then up to the class's methods to determine whether the request is appropriate. When using a door, you usually are unconcerned with the latch or hinge construction, and you don't have access to the interior workings of the knob. You care only about the functionality and the interface, the user-friendly boundary between the user and internal mechanisms of the device. When you turn a door's knob, you are interacting appropriately with the interface. Banging on the knob would be an inappropriate interaction, so the door would not respond. Similarly, the detailed workings of objects you create within object-oriented programs can be hidden from outside programs and modules if necessary, and the methods you write can control how the objects operate. When the details are hidden, programmers can focus on the functionality and the interface, as people do with real-life objects.

Information hiding is also called **data hiding**. In Chapter 6, you learned that encapsulating a method's instructions is known as *implementation hiding*. All these terms help emphasize the point that objects should be self-contained entities.

In summary, understanding object-oriented programming means that you must consider five of its integral components: classes, objects, polymorphism, inheritance, and encapsulation.

Defining Classes and Creating Class Diagrams

A class is a category of things; an object is a specific instance of a class. A **class definition** is a set of program statements that list the characteristics of each object and the methods each object can use.

A class definition can contain three parts:

- Every class has a name.
- Most classes contain data, although this is not required.
- Most classes contain methods, although this is not required.

The application classes you have studied and created in the first six chapters of this book have contained methods, but not their own data. The *methods* contained data, but the classes did not contain data at the class level.

For example, you can create a class named Employee. Each Employee object will represent one employee who works for an organization. Data members, or attributes of the Employee class, include fields such as lastName, hourlyWage, and weeklyPay.

The methods of a class include all the things its objects can do or have done to them. Appropriate methods for an Employee class might include setHourlyWage(), getHourlyWage(), and calculateWeeklyPay(). The job of setHourlyWage() is to provide values for an Employee's wage data field, the purpose of getHourlyWage() is to retrieve the wage value, and the purpose of calculateWeeklyPay() is to multiply the Employee's hourlyWage by the number of hours in a workweek to calculate a weekly salary. With object-oriented languages, you think of the class name, data, and methods as a single encapsulated unit.

Declaring a class does not create actual objects. A class is just an abstract description of what an object will be if any objects are actually instantiated. Just as you might understand all the characteristics of an item you intend to manufacture long before the first item rolls off the assembly line, you can create a class with fields and methods before you instantiate objects that are members of that class. After an object has been instantiated, its methods can be accessed using the object's identifier, a dot, and a method call. When you declare a simple variable that is a built-in data type, you write a statement such as one of the following:

```
num money
string name
```

When you write a program that declares an object that is a class data type, you write a statement such as the following:

```
Employee myAssistant
```

In some object-oriented programming languages, you need to add more to the declaration statement to actually create an Employee object. For example, in Java, you would write:

```
Employee myAssistant = new Employee();
```

You will understand more about the format of this statement when you learn about constructors in Chapter 8.

When you declare the myAssistant object, it contains all the data fields and has access to all the methods contained within its class. In other words, a larger section of memory is set aside than when you declare a simple variable, because an Employee contains several fields. You can use any of an Employee's methods with the myAssistant object. The usual syntax is to provide an object name, a dot (period), and a method name. For example, you can write a program that contains statements such as those shown in Figure 7-4.

```
class EmployeeDemo
    main()
        // Declarations
            Employee myAssistant
        myAssistant.setLastName("Reynolds")
        myAssistant.setHourlyWage(16.75)
        output "My assistant makes ",
            myAssistant.getHourlyWage(), " per hour"
    return
endClass
```

Figure 7-4   The EmployeeDemo application

The program segment in Figure 7-4 is very short. In a more useful real-life program, you might read employee data from a data file before assigning it to the object's fields, each Employee might contain dozens of fields, and your application might create hundreds or thousands of objects.

Besides referring to Employee as a class, many programmers would refer to it as a **user-defined type**, but a more accurate term is **programmer-defined type**. Object-oriented programmers typically refer to a class like Employee as an **abstract data type** (ADT); this term implies that the type's data can be accessed only through methods.

When you write a statement such as myAssistant.setHourlyWage(16.75), you are making a call to a method that is contained within the Employee class. Because myAssistant is an Employee object, it is allowed to use the setHourlyWage() method that is part of its class. You can tell from the method call that setHourlyWage() must accept a numeric parameter.

When you write the EmployeeDemo application in Figure 7-4, you do not need to know what statements are written within the Employee class methods, although you could make an educated guess based on the method names. Before you could execute the application in Figure 7-4, someone would have to write appropriate statements within the Employee class methods. If you wrote the methods, of course you would know their contents, but if another programmer has already written the methods, you could use the application without knowing the details contained in the methods. To use the methods, you only need to know their signatures—their names and parameter lists.

In Chapter 6, you learned that the ability to use methods as a black box without knowing their contents is a feature of encapsulation. The real world is full of many black-box devices. For example, you can use your television and microwave oven without knowing how they work internally—all you need to understand is the interface. Similarly, with well-written methods that belong to classes you use, you need not understand how they work internally to be able to use them; you need only understand the ultimate result when you use them.

In the client program segment in Figure 7-4, the focus is on the object—the `Employee` named `myAssistant`—and the methods you can use with that object. This is the essence of object-oriented programming.

In older object-oriented programming languages, simple numbers and characters are said to be **primitive data types**; this distinguishes them from objects that are class types. In the newest programming languages, every item you name, even one that is a numeric or string type, is an object that is a member of a class with both data and methods.

262

When you instantiate objects, their data fields are stored at separate memory locations. However, all members of the same class share one copy of the class's methods. You will learn more about this concept later in this chapter.

Creating Class Diagrams

A **class diagram** consists of a rectangle divided into three sections, as shown in Figure 7-5. The top section contains the name of the class, the middle section contains the names and data types of the attributes, and the bottom section contains the methods. This generic class diagram shows two attributes and three methods, but a given class might have any number of either, including none. Programmers often use a class diagram to plan or illustrate class features. Class diagrams also are useful for describing a class to nonprogrammers.

Class name
Attribute 1 : data type Attribute 2 : data type
Method 1() : data type Method 2() : data type Method 3() : data type

Figure 7-5 Generic class diagram

Figure 7-6 shows the class diagram for the `Employee` class. By convention, a class diagram lists the names of the data items first; each name is followed by a colon and the data type. Method names are listed next, and each is followed by its data type (return type). Listing the names first and the data types last emphasizes the purposes of the fields and methods.

Employee
lastName : string hourlyWage : num weeklyPay : num
setLastName(name : string) : void setHourlyWage(wage : num) : void getLastName() : string getHourlyWage() : num getWeeklyPay() : num calculateWeeklyPay() : void

Class diagrams are a type of Unified Modeling Language (UML) diagram. Chapter 11 covers the UML.

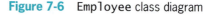

Figure 7-6 `Employee` class diagram

Figures 7-5 and 7-6 both show that a class diagram is intended to be only an overview of class attributes and methods. A class diagram shows *what* data items and methods the class will use, not the details of the methods nor *when* they will be used. It is a design tool that helps you see the big picture in terms of class requirements. Figure 7-6 shows the Employee class containing three data fields that represent an employee's name, hourly pay rate, and weekly pay amount. Every Employee object created in a program that uses this class will contain these three data fields. In other words, when you declare an Employee object, the single declaration statement allocates enough memory to hold all three fields.

Figure 7-6 also shows that the Employee class contains six methods. For example, the first method is defined as follows:

```
setLastName(name : string) : void
```

This notation means that the method name is setLastName(), that it takes a single string parameter named name, and that it returns nothing.

Various books, Web sites, and organizations use class diagrams that describe methods in different ways. For example, some developers use the method name only, and others omit parameter lists. This book will take the approach of being as complete as possible, so the class diagrams you see here will contain each method's identifier, parameter list with types, and return type.

The Employee class diagram shows that two of the six methods take parameters (setLastName() and setHourlyWage()). The diagram also shows the return type for each method—three void methods, two numeric methods, and one string method. The class diagram does not indicate what takes place inside the method, although you might be able to make an educated guess. Later, when you write the code that actually creates the Employee class, you include method implementation details. For example, Figure 7-7 shows some pseudocode you can use to list the details for the methods in the Employee class.

```
class Employee
   // Declarations
      string lastName
      num hourlyWage
      num weeklyPay

   void setLastName(string name)
      lastName = name
   return

   void setHourlyWage(num wage)
      hourlyWage = wage
      calculateWeeklyPay()
   return

   string getLastName()
   return lastName

   num getHourlyWage()
   return hourlyWage

   num getWeeklyPay()
   return weeklyPay

   void calculateWeeklyPay()
      // Declarations
         num WORK_WEEK_HOURS = 40
      weeklyPay = hourlyWage * WORK_WEEK_HOURS
   return
endClass
```

Figure 7-7   Pseudocode for `Employee` class described in the class diagram in Figure 7-6

In Figure 7-7, the `Employee` class attributes are identified with a data type and a field name. In addition to listing the required data fields, the figure shows the complete methods for the `Employee` class. The purposes of the methods can be divided into three categories:

- Two of the methods accept values from the outside world; these methods, by convention, have the prefix *set*. These methods are used to set the data fields in the class.

- Three of the methods send data to the outside world; these methods, by convention, have the prefix *get*. These methods return field values to a client program.

- One method performs work within the class; this method is named `calculateWeeklyPay()`. This method does not communicate with the outside; its purpose is to multiply `hourlyWage` by the number of hours in a week.

The Set Methods

In Figure 7-7, two methods begin with the word *set*; they are setLastName() and setHourlyWage(). The purpose of a **set method** or **mutator method** is to set the values of data fields within the class. There is no requirement that such methods start with *set*; the prefix is merely conventional and clarifies the intention of the methods. The method setLastName() is implemented as follows:

```
void setLastName(string name)
   lastName = name
return
```

In this method, a string name is passed in as a parameter and assigned to the field lastName. Because lastName is contained in the same class as this method, the method has access to the field and can alter it.

Similarly, the method setHourlyWage() accepts a numeric parameter and assigns it to the class field hourlyWage. This method also calls the calculateWeeklyPay() method, which sets weeklyPay based on hourlyWage. By writing the setHourlyWage() method to call the calculateWeeklyPay() method automatically, you guarantee that the weeklyPay field is updated any time hourlyWage changes.

When you create an Employee object with a statement such as Employee mySecretary, then you can use statements such as the following:

```
mySecretary.setLastName("Johnson")
mySecretary.setHourlyWage(15.00)
```

Instead of literal constants, you could pass variables or named constants to the methods as long as they were the correct data type. For example, if you write a program in which you make the following declaration, then the assignment in the next statement is valid.

```
// Declarations
   num PAY_RATE_TO_START = 8.00
mySecretary.setHourlyWage(PAY_RATE_TO_START)
```

In some languages—for example, Visual Basic and C#—you can create a **property** instead of creating a set method. Using a property provides a way to set a field value using a simpler syntax. By convention, if a class field is hourlyWage, its property would be HourlyWage, and in a program you could make a statement similar to mySecretary.HourlyWage = PAY_RATE_TO_START. The implementation of the property HourlyWage (with an uppercase initial letter) would be written in a format very similar to that of the setHourlyWage() method.

Like other methods, the methods that manipulate fields within a class can contain any statements you need. For example, a more complicated setHourlyWage() method might be written as in Figure 7-8. In this version, the wage passed to the method is tested against minimum and maximum values and is assigned to the class field hourlyWage only if it falls within the prescribed limits. If the wage is too low, the MINWAGE value is substituted, and if the wage is too high, the MAXWAGE value is substituted.

```
void setHourlyWage(num wage)
    // Declarations
        num MINWAGE = 6.00
        num MAXWAGE = 70.00
    if wage < MINWAGE then
        hourlyWage = MINWAGE
    else
        if wage > MAXWAGE then
            hourlyWage = MAXWAGE
        else
            hourlyWage = wage
        endif
    endif
    calculateWeeklyPay()
return
```

Figure 7-8   More complex `setHourlyWage()` method

Similarly, if the set methods in a class required them, the methods could contain output statements, loops, array declarations, or any other legal programming statements. However, if the main purpose of a method is not to set a field value, then for clarity the method should not be named with the *set* prefix.

The Get Methods

The purpose of a **get method** or **accessor method** is to return a value to the world outside the class. In the `Employee` class in Figure 7-7, the three get methods have the prefix *get*: `getLastName()`, `getHourlyWage()`, and `getWeeklyPay()`. The methods are implemented as follows:

```
string getLastName()
return lastName
```

```
num getHourlyWage()
return hourlyWage
```

```
num getWeeklyPay()
return weeklyPay
```

Each of these methods simply returns the value in the field implied by the method name. Like set methods, any of these get methods could also contain more complicated statements as needed. For example, in a more complicated class, you might return the hourly wage of an employee only if the user had also passed an appropriate access code to the method, or you might return the weekly pay value as a string with a dollar sign attached instead of as a numeric value.

When you declare an Employee object such as Employee mySecretary, you can then make statements in a program similar to the following:

```
// Declarations
    string employeeName
employeeName = mySecretary.getLastName()
output "Wage is ", mySecretary.getHourlyWage()
output "Pay for half a week is ", mySecretary.getWeeklyPay() * 0.5
```

In other words, the value returned from a get method can be used as any other variable of its type would be used. You can assign the value to another variable, output it, perform arithmetic with it, or make any other statement that works correctly with the returned data type.

In some languages—for example, Visual Basic and C#—instead of creating a get method, you can add statements to the property to return a value using simpler syntax. For example, if you created an HourlyWage property, you could write a program that makes the statement output mySecretary.HourlyWage.

Work Methods

The Employee class in Figure 7-7 contains one method that is neither a get nor a set method. This method, calculateWeeklyPay(), is a **work method** within the class. A work method is also known as a **help method** or **facilitator**. The method contains a locally named constant that represents the hours in a standard workweek, and it computes the weeklyPay field value by multiplying hourlyWage by the named constant. The method is written as follows:

```
void calculateWeeklyPay()
    // Declarations
        num WORK_WEEK_HOURS = 40
    weeklyPay = hourlyWage * WORK_WEEK_HOURS
return
```

No values need to be passed into this method, and no value is returned from it because the method does not communicate with the outside world. Instead, this method is called only from another method in the same class (the setHourlyWage() method), and that method is called from the outside world. Each time a program uses the setHourlyWage() method to alter an Employee's hourlyWage field, calculateWeeklyPay() is called to recalculate the weeklyPay field. No setWeeklyPay() method is included in this Employee class because the intention is that weeklyPay is set only inside the calculateWeeklyPay() method each time the setHourlyWage() method calls it. If you wanted programs to be able to set the weeklyPay field directly, you would have to write a method to allow it.

Programmers who are new to class creation often want to pass the hourlyWage value into the calculateWeeklyPay() method so that it can use the value in its calculation. Although this technique would work, it is not required. The calculateWeeklyPay() method has direct access to the hourlyWage field by virtue of being a member of the same class.

For example, Figure 7-9 shows a program that declares an Employee object and sets the hourly wage value. The program outputs the weeklyPay value. A new value is then assigned to hourlyWage and weeklyPay is output again. As you can see from the output in Figure 7-10, the weeklyPay value has been recalculated even though it was never set directly by the client program.

```
class EmployeeDemo2
    main()
        // Declarations
            num LOW = 9.00
            num HIGH = 14.65
            Employee myGardener
        myGardener.setLastName("Greene")
        myGardener.setHourlyWage(LOW)
        output "My gardener makes ",
            myGardener.getWeeklyPay(), " per week"
        myGardener.setHourlyWage(HIGH)
        output "My gardener makes ",
            myGardener.getWeeklyPay(), " per week"
    return
endClass
```

Figure 7-9   Program that sets and displays Employee data two times

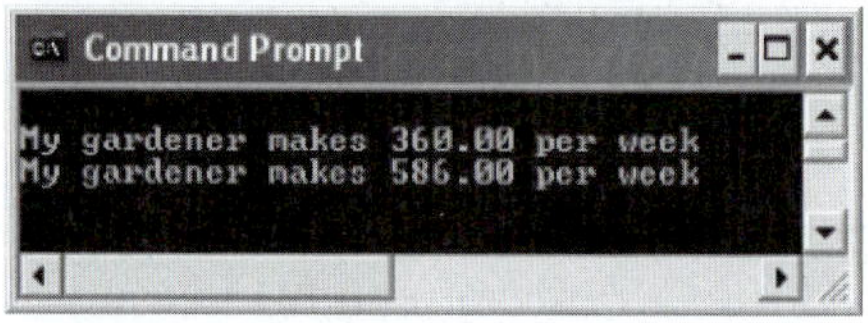

Figure 7-10   Execution of program in Figure 7-9

Understanding Public and Private Access

When you buy a new product, one of the usual conditions of its warranty is that the manufacturer must perform all repair work. For example, if your computer has a warranty and something goes wrong with its operation, you cannot open the system unit yourself, remove and replace parts, and then expect to get your money back for a device that does not work properly. Instead, when something goes wrong, you must take the computer to an approved technician. The manufacturer guarantees that your machine will work properly only if the manufacturer can control how the computer's internal mechanisms are modified.

Similarly, in object-oriented design, you do not want outside programs or methods to alter your class's data fields unless you have control over the process. For example, you might design a class that performs complicated statistical analysis on some data, and you would not want others to be able to alter your carefully crafted result. Or, you might design a class from which others can create an innovative and useful GUI screen object. In this case, you would not want anyone altering the dimensions of your artistic design.

To prevent outsiders from changing your data fields in ways you do not endorse, you force other programs and methods to use a method that is part of your class to alter data. (Earlier in this chapter, you learned that the principle of keeping data private and inaccessible to outside classes is called *information hiding* or *data hiding*.) To prevent unauthorized field modifications, object-oriented programmers usually specify that their data fields will have **private access**—the data cannot be accessed by any method that is not part of the class. The methods themselves, like setHourlyWage() in the Employee class, support public access. When methods have **public access**, other programs and methods may use the methods to get access to the private data.

Figure 7-11 shows a complete Employee class to which access specifiers have been added to describe each attribute and method. An **access specifier** is the adjective that defines the type of access outside classes will have to the attribute or method (public or private). In the figure, each access specifier is shaded.

```
class Employee
   // Declarations
      private string lastName
      private num hourlyWage
      private num weeklyPay

   public void setLastName(string name)
      lastName = name
   return

   public void setHourlyWage(num wage)
      hourlyWage = wage
      calculateWeeklyPay()
   return

   public string getLastName()
   return lastName

   public num getHourlyWage()
   return hourlyWage

   public num getWeeklyPay()
   return weeklyPay

   private void calculateWeeklyPay()
      // Declarations
         num WORK_WEEK_HOURS = 40
      weeklyPay = hourlyWage * WORK_WEEK_HOURS
   return
endClass
```

Figure 7-11   Employee class including `public` and `private` access specifiers

 In many object-oriented programming languages, if you do not declare an access specifier for a data field or method, then it is private by default. This book will follow the convention of explicitly specifying access for every class member.

In Figure 7-11, each of the data fields is private, which means each field is inaccessible to an object declared in a program. In other words, if a program declares an Employee object, such as Employee myAssistant, then the following statement is illegal:

myAssistant.hourlyWage = 15.00   ←

Don't Do It
You cannot assign a value to a private variable by using a statement in another class.

Instead, hourlyWage can be assigned only through a public method as follows:

myAssistant.setHourlyWage(15.00)

If you made `hourlyWage` public instead of private, then a direct assignment statement would work, but you would violate the important OOP principle of data hiding using encapsulation. Data fields should usually be private and a client application should be able to access them only through the public interfaces—in other words, through the class's public methods. That way, if you have restrictions on the value of `hourlyWage`, those restrictions will be enforced by the public method that acts as an interface to the private data field. Similarly, a public get method might control how a private value is retrieved. Perhaps you do not want clients to have access to an `Employee`'s `hourlyWage` if it is more than a specific value, or maybe you want to return the wage to the client as a string with a dollar sign attached. Even when a field has no data value requirements or restrictions, making data private and providing public set and get methods establishes a framework that makes such modifications easier in the future.

In the `Employee` class in Figure 7-11, only one method is not public; the `calculateWeeklyPay()` method is private. That means if you write a program and declare an `Employee` object such as `Employee myAssistant`, then the following statement is not permitted:

`myAssistant.calculateWeeklyPay()` ◄———

> **Don't Do It**
> The `calculateWeeklyPay()` method is not accessible outside the class.

Because it is private, the only way to call the `calculateWeeklyPay()` method is from another method that already belongs to the class. In this example, it is called from the `setHourlyWage()` method. This prevents a client program from setting `hourlyWage` to one value while setting `weeklyPay` to an incompatible value. By making the `calculateWeeklyPay()` method private, you ensure that the class retains full control over when and how it is used.

Classes most often contain private data and public methods, but as you have just seen, they can contain private methods; they can contain public data items as well. For example, an `Employee` class might contain a public constant data field named `MINIMUM_WAGE`; outside programs then would be able to access that value without using a method. Public data fields are not required to be named constants, but they frequently are.

In some object-oriented programming languages, such as C++, you can label a set of data fields or methods as public or private using the access specifier name just once, then following it with a list of the items in that category. In other languages, such as Java, you use the specifier public or private with each field or method. For clarity, this book will label each field and method as public or private.

Many object-oriented languages provide more specific access specifiers than just public and private. In Chapter 8, you will learn about the protected access specifier.

Many programmers like to specify in class diagrams whether each component in a class is public or private. Figure 7-12 shows the conventions that are typically used. A minus sign (−) precedes the items that are private; a plus sign (+) precedes those that are public.

```
Employee

-lastName : string
-hourlyWage : num
-weeklyPay : num

+setLastName(name : string) : void
+setHourlyWage(wage : num) : void
+getLastName() : string
+getHourlyWage() : num
+getWeeklyPay() : num
-calculateWeeklyPay() : void
```

Figure 7-12 Employee class diagram with public and private access specifiers

When you write an application program that contains a main() method, the method is virtually always defined as public. Therefore, when sample code includes a main() method from this point forward in the book, the public modifier will be used with it.

Watch the video *Creating a Class.*

Organizing Classes

The Employee class in Figure 7-12 contains just three data fields and six methods; most classes you create for professional applications will have many more. For example, in addition to a last name and pay information, real employees require an employee number, a first name, address, phone number, hire date, and so on, as well as methods to set and get those fields. As classes grow in complexity, deciding how to organize them becomes increasingly important.

Although it is not required, most programmers place data fields in some logical order at the beginning of a class. For example, an ID number is most likely used as a unique identifier for each employee, so it makes sense to list the employee ID number first in the class. An employee's last name and first name "go together," so it makes sense to store the two components adjacently. Despite these common-sense rules, you have a lot of flexibility when positioning your data fields within a class. For example, depending on the class, you might choose to store the data fields alphabetically, or you might group together all the fields that are the same data type. Alternatively, you might choose to store all public data items first, followed by private ones, or vice versa.

In some languages, you can organize data fields and methods in any order within a class. For example, you could place all the methods first, followed by all the data fields, or you could organize the class so that data fields are followed by methods that use them. This book will follow the convention of placing all data fields first so that you can see their names and data types before reading the methods that use them. This format also echoes the way data and methods appear in standard class diagrams.

For ease in locating a class's methods, some programmers store them in alphabetical order. Other programmers arrange them in pairs of get and set methods, in the same order as the data fields are defined. Another option is to list all accessor (get) methods together and all mutator (set) methods together. Depending on the class, you might decide to create other logically functional groupings. Of course, if your company distributes guidelines for organizing class components, you must follow those rules.

Understanding Instance Methods

Classes contain data and methods, and every instance of a class possesses the same data and has access to the same methods. For example, Figure 7-13 shows a class diagram for a simple Student class that contains just one private data field for a student's grade point average. The class also contains get and set methods for the field. Figure 7-14 shows the pseudocode for the Student class. This class becomes the model for a new data type named Student; when Student objects are created eventually, each will have its own gradePointAverage field and have access to methods to get and set it.

```
Student
-gradePointAverage : num
+setGradePointAverage(gpa : num) : void
+getGradePointAverage() : num
```

Figure 7-13   Class diagram for Student class

```
class Student
   // Declarations
      private num gradePointAverage

   public void setGradePointAverage(num gpa)
      gradePointAverage = gpa
   return

   public num getGradePointAverage()
   return gradePointAverage
endClass
```

Figure 7-14   Pseudocode for the Student class

If you create multiple Student objects using the class in Figure 7-14, you need a separate storage location in computer memory to store each Student's unique grade point average.

For example, Figure 7-15 shows a program that creates three Student objects and assigns values to their gradePointAverage fields. It also shows how the Student objects look in memory after the values have been assigned.

```
class StudentDemo
   main()
      // Declarations
         Student oneSophomore
         Student oneJunior
         Student oneSenior
      oneSophomore.setGradePointAverage(2.6)
      oneJunior.setGradePointAverage(3.8)
      oneSenior.setGradePointAverage(3.4)
   return
endClass
```

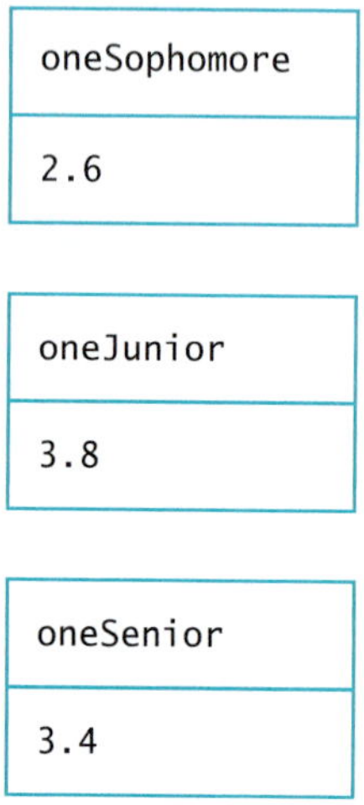

oneSophomore

2.6

oneJunior

3.8

oneSenior

3.4

Figure 7-15   StudentDemo program and how Student objects look in memory

It makes sense for each Student object in Figure 7-15 to have its own gradePointAverage field, but it does not make sense for each Student to have its own copy of the methods that get and set gradePointAverage. Creating identical copies of a method for each instance would be inefficient. Instead, even though every Student has its own gradePointAverage field, only one copy of each of the methods getGradePointAverage() and setGradePointAverage() is stored in memory; however, each instantiated object of the class can use the single method copy. A method that works appropriately with different objects is an **instance method**.

Although the StudentDemo class contains only one copy of the get and set methods, they work correctly for the fields contained in any number of specific instances. Therefore, methods like getGradePointAverage() and setGradePointAverage() are instance methods; they are methods that are called using an instance. Because only one copy of each instance method is stored, but the method works with multiple instances, the computer needs a way to determine which gradePointAverage is being set or retrieved when one of the methods is called. The mechanism that handles this problem is illustrated in Figure 7-16. When a method call such as oneSophomore.setGradePointAverage(2.6) is made, the true method call, which is invisible and automatically constructed, includes the memory address of the oneSophomore object. (These method calls are represented by the three narrow boxes in the center of Figure 7-16.)

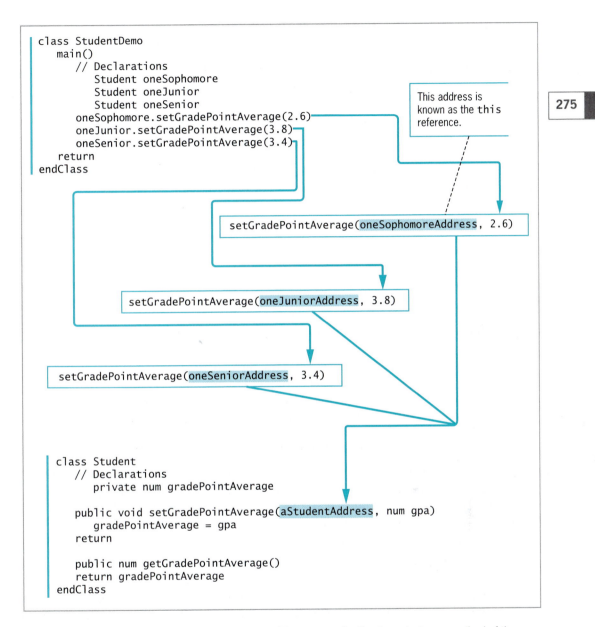

```
class StudentDemo
    main()
        // Declarations
            Student oneSophomore
            Student oneJunior
            Student oneSenior
        oneSophomore.setGradePointAverage(2.6)
        oneJunior.setGradePointAverage(3.8)
        oneSenior.setGradePointAverage(3.4)
    return
endClass
```

This address is
known as the this
reference.

```
setGradePointAverage(oneSophomoreAddress, 2.6)
```

```
setGradePointAverage(oneJuniorAddress, 3.8)
```

```
setGradePointAverage(oneSeniorAddress, 3.4)
```

```
class Student
    // Declarations
        private num gradePointAverage

    public void setGradePointAverage(aStudentAddress, num gpa)
        gradePointAverage = gpa
    return

    public num getGradePointAverage()
    return gradePointAverage
endClass
```

Figure 7-16 How Student addresses are passed from an application to an instance method of the Student class

Within the setGradePointAverage() method in the Student class, an invisible and automatically created parameter is added to the list. (For illustration purposes, this parameter is named aStudentAddress and is shaded in the Student class definition in Figure 7-16. In fact, no parameter is created with that name.) This parameter accepts the address of a

Student object because the instance method belongs to the Student class; if this method belonged to another class—Employee, for example—then the method would accept an address for that type of object. The shaded addresses are not written as code in any program—they are "secretly" sent and received behind the scenes. The address variable in Figure 7-16 is called a this reference. A **this reference** is an automatically created variable that holds the address of an object and passes it to an instance method whenever the method is called. It is called a this reference because it refers to "this particular object" that is using the method at the moment. In other words, an instance method is one that receives a this reference to a specific class instance. In the application in Figure 7-16, when oneSophomore uses the setGradePointAverage() method, the address of the oneSophomore object is contained in the this reference. Later in the program, when the oneJunior object uses the setGradePointAverage() method, the this reference will hold the address of that Student object.

The term *this reference* is used in many object-oriented programming languages, but not all of them. For example, in Lingo, the reference is called *me*.

Figure 7-16 shows each place the this reference is used in the Student class. It is implicitly passed as a parameter to each instance method. You never explicitly refer to the this reference when you write the method header for an instance method; Figure 7-16 just shows where it implicitly exists. Within each instance method, the this reference is implied any time you refer to one of the class data fields. For example, when you call setGradePointAverage() using a oneSophomore object, the gradePointAverage assigned within the method is the "*this* gradePointAverage", or the one that belongs to the oneSophomore object. The phrase "this gradePointAverage" usually is written as this, followed by a dot, followed by the field name—this.gradePointAverage.

The this reference exists throughout every instance method. You can explicitly use the this reference with data fields, but it is not required. Figure 7-17 shows two locations where the this reference can be used implicitly, or where you can (but do not have to) use it explicitly. Within an instance method, the following two identifiers mean exactly the same thing:

- any field name defined in the class

- this, followed by a dot, followed by the same field name

For example, within the setGradePointAverage() method, gradePointAverage and this.gradePointAverage refer to exactly the same memory location.

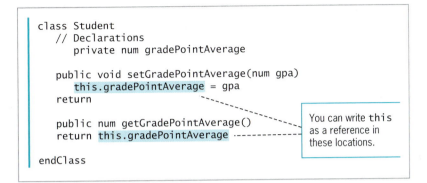

```
class Student
    // Declarations
        private num gradePointAverage

    public void setGradePointAverage(num gpa)
        this.gradePointAverage = gpa
    return

    public num getGradePointAverage()
        return this.gradePointAverage

endClass
```

You can write this as a reference in these locations.

Figure 7-17 Explicitly using this in the Student class

The this reference can be used only with identifiers that are field names. For example, in Figure 7-17 you can refer to this.gradePointAverage, but you cannot refer to this.gpa because gpa is not a class field—it is only a local variable.

The syntax for using this differs among programming languages. For example, within a class in C++, you can refer to the Student class gradePointAverage value as this->gradePointAverage or (*this).gradePointAverage, but in Java you refer to it as this.gradePointAverage. In Visual Basic, the this reference is named Me, so the variable would be Me.gradePointAverage.

Usually you do not need to use the this reference explicitly within the methods you write, but the this reference is always there, working behind the scenes, accessing the data field for the correct object.

You might work for an organization that requires explicit use of the this reference for clarity even though it is not needed to create a workable program. It is the programmer's responsibility to follow the conventions established at work or by clients.

As an example of when you might use the this reference explicitly, consider the following setGradePointAverage() method and compare it to the version in the Student class in Figure 7-17.

```
public void setGradePointAverage(num gradePointAverage)
    this.gradePointAverage = gradePointAverage
return
```

In this version of the method, the programmer has used the variable name gradePointAverage as the parameter to the method and as the instance field within the class. Therefore, gradePointAverage is the name of a local variable within the method whose value is received by passing, as well as the name of a class field. To differentiate the two, you explicitly use the this reference with the copy of gradePointAverage that is a member of the class. Omitting the this reference in this case would result in the local parameter gradePointAverage being assigned to itself, and the class's instance variable would not be set.

Any time a local variable in a method has the same identifier as a field, the field is hidden; you must use a `this` reference to distinguish the field from the local variable.

 Watch the video *The this Reference*.

Understanding Static Methods

Some methods do not require a `this` reference because it makes no sense for them either implicitly or explicitly. For example, the `displayStudentMotto()` method in Figure 7-18 does not use any data fields from the `Student` class, so it does not matter which `Student` object calls it. If you write a program in which you declare 100 `Student` objects, the `displayStudentMotto()` method executes in exactly the same way for each of them; it does not need to know whose motto is displayed and it does not need to access any specific object addresses. As a matter of fact, you might want to display the `Student` motto without instantiating any `Student` objects. Therefore, the `displayStudentMotto()` method can be written as a static method instead of an instance method.

```
public static void displayStudentMotto()
    output "Every student is an individual"
    output "in the pursuit of knowledge."
    output "Every student strives to be"
    output "a literate, responsible citizen."
return
```

Figure 7-18   `Student` class `displayStudentMotto()` method

When you write a class, you can indicate two types of methods:

- **Static methods**, also called **class methods**, are those for which no object needs to exist, like the `displayStudentMotto()` method in Figure 7-18. Static methods do not receive a `this` reference as an implicit parameter. Typically, static methods include the word `static` in the method header, as shown shaded in Figure 7-18.

- **Nonstatic methods** are methods that exist to be used with an object created from a class. These instance methods receive a `this` reference to a specific object. In most programming languages, you use the word `static` when you want to declare a static class member, but you do not use a special word when you want a class member to be nonstatic. In other words, methods in a class are nonstatic instance methods by default.

In everyday language, the word *static* means "stationary"; it is the opposite of *dynamic*, which means "changing." In other words, static methods are always the same for every instance of the class, whereas nonstatic methods act differently depending on the object used to call them.

In most programming languages, you use a static method with the class name, as in the following:

```
Student.displayStudentMotto()
```

In other words, no object is necessary with a static method.

In some languages, notably C++, besides using a static method with the class name, you also can use a static method with any object of the class, as in oneSophomore.displayStudentMotto().

When you write an application program with a main() method and other methods it calls, they are static methods—you do not create objects to use them. Now that you understand the meaning of *static*, this book will use it in method headers as needed, including all main() methods in application programs.

Using Objects

A class is a complex data type defined by a programmer, but in many ways you can use its instances like you use items of simpler data types. For example, you can create an array of objects, pass an object to a method, or return an object from a method.

Consider the InventoryItem class in Figure 7-19. The class represents items that a company manufactures and holds in inventory. Each item has a number, description, and price. The class contains a get and set method for each of the three fields.

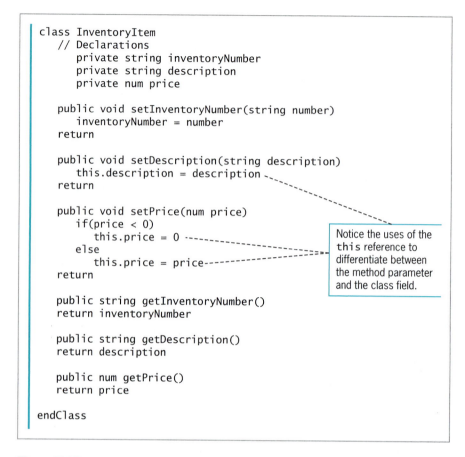

```
class InventoryItem
    // Declarations
        private string inventoryNumber
        private string description
        private num price

    public void setInventoryNumber(string number)
        inventoryNumber = number
    return

    public void setDescription(string description)
        this.description = description
    return

    public void setPrice(num price)
        if(price < 0)
            this.price = 0
        else
            this.price = price
    return

    public string getInventoryNumber()
    return inventoryNumber

    public string getDescription()
    return description

    public num getPrice()
    return price

endClass
```

Notice the uses of the this reference to differentiate between the method parameter and the class field.

Figure 7-19 InventoryItem class

Once you declare an InventoryItem object, you can use it in many of the ways you would use a simple numeric or string variable. For example, you could pass an InventoryItem object to a method or return one from a method. Figure 7-20 shows a program that declares an InventoryItem object and passes it to a method for display. The InventoryItem is declared in the main() method and assigned values. Then the completed item is passed to a method, where it is displayed. Figure 7-21 shows the execution of the program.

The InventoryItem declared in the main() method in Figure 7-20 is passed to the displayItem() method in much the same way a numeric or string variable would be. The method receives a copy of the InventoryItem that is known locally by the identifier item. Within the method, the field values of the local item can be retrieved, displayed, and used in arithmetic statements in the same way they could have been in the main() method where the InventoryItem was originally declared.

```
class InventoryDemo
    public static void main()
        // Declarations
            InventoryItem oneItem
        oneItem.setInventoryNumber("1276")
        oneItem.setDescription("Mahogany chest")
        oneItem.setPrice(450.00)
        displayItem(oneItem)
      return

    public static void displayItem(InventoryItem item)
        // Declarations
            num TAX_RATE = 0.06
            num tax
            num pr
            num total
        output "Item #", item.getInventoryNumber()
        output item.getDescription()
        pr = item.getPrice()
        tax = pr * TAX_RATE
        total = pr + tax
        output "Price is $", pr, " plus $", tax, " tax"
        output "Total is $", total
      return
endClass
```

Figure 7-20   Application program that declares and uses an `InventoryItem` object

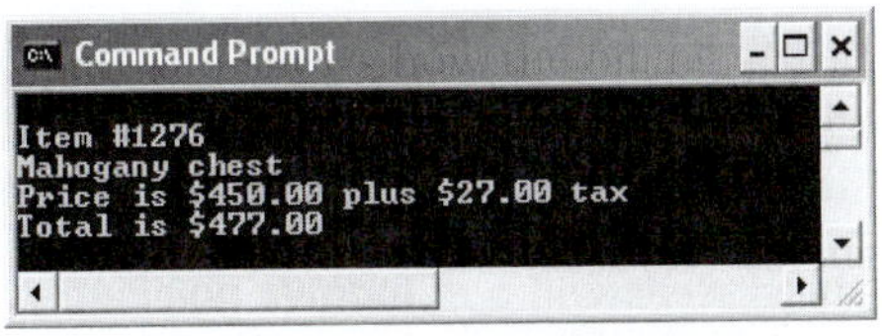

Figure 7-21   Typical execution of application in Figure 7-20

Figure 7-22 shows a more realistic application that uses `InventoryItem` objects. In the `main()` method of this program, an `InventoryItem` is declared and the user is prompted for a number. As long as the user does not enter the `QUIT` value, a loop is executed in which the entered inventory item number is passed to the `getItemValues()` method. Within that method, a local `InventoryItem` object is declared. This local object gathers and holds the user's input values. The user is prompted for a description and price, then the passed item number and its newly obtained description and price are assigned to the local `InventoryItem` object via its set methods. The completed object is returned to the `main()` method, where it is assigned to `main()`'s `InventoryItem` object. That item is then passed to the `displayItem()` method. As in the previous example, the method calculates tax and displays results. Figure 7-23 shows a typical execution.

```
class InventoryApplication
   public static void main()
      // Declarations
         InventoryItem oneItem
         string itemNum
         string QUIT = "0"
      output "Enter item number or ", QUIT, " to quit… "
      input itemNum
      while itemNum <> QUIT
         oneItem = getItemValues(itemNum)
         displayItem(oneItem)
         output "Enter next item number or ", QUIT, " to quit… "
         input itemNum
      endwhile
    return

   public static InventoryItem getItemValues(string number)
      // Declarations
         InventoryItem inItem
         string desc
         num price
      output "Enter description… "
      input desc
      output "Enter price… "
      input price
      inItem.setInventoryNumber(number)
      inItem.setDescription(desc)
      inItem.setPrice(price)
    return inItem

   public static void displayItem(InventoryItem item)
      // Declarations
         num TAX_RATE = 0.06
         num tax
         num pr
         num total
      output "Item #", item.getInventoryNumber()
      output item.getDescription()
      pr = item.getPrice()
      tax = pr * TAX_RATE
      total = pr + tax
      output "Price is $", pr, " plus $", tax, " tax"
      output "Total is $", total
    return
endClass
```

Figure 7-22 Application that uses `InventoryItem` objects

In Figure 7-22, notice that the return type for the `getItemValues()` method is `InventoryItem`. A method can return only a single value. Therefore, it is convenient that the `getItemValues()` method can encapsulate two strings and a number in a single `InventoryItem` object that it returns to the main program.

```
Command Prompt                                    _ □ X
Enter item number or 0 to quit... 1276
Enter description... Mahogany chest
Enter price... 450.00

Item #1276
Mahogany chest
Price is $450.00 plus $27.00 tax
Total is $477.00

Enter next item number or 0 to quit... 1488
Enter description... Wicker chair
Enter price... 129.98

Item #1488
Wicker chair
Price is $129.98 plus $7.80 tax
Total is $137.78

Enter next item number or 0 to quit... 2215
Enter description... Decorator pillow
Enter price... 40.00

Item #2215
Decorator pillow
Price is $40.00 plus $2.40 tax
Total is $42.40

Enter next item number or 0 to quit... 0
```

Figure 7-23   Typical execution of program in Figure 7-22

Understanding Composition

A class can contain the objects of another class as data members. For example, you might create a class named `Date` that contains a month, day, and year, and add two `Date` fields to an `Employee` class to hold the `Employee`'s birth date and hire date. Then you might create a class named `Department` that represents every department in a company, and create each `Department` class member to contain an array of 50 `Employee` objects. Using one class's object as an attribute within another class is known as **composition**. The resulting relationship is also called a **has-a relationship** because one class "has an" instance of another.

When your classes contain objects that are members of other classes, your programming job becomes increasingly complex. For example, you sometimes must refer to a method by a very long name. Suppose you create a `Department` class that contains a method named `getHighestPaidEmployee()`. This method returns an `Employee` object. Suppose the `Employee` class contains a method that returns a `Date` object that is an `Employee`'s hire date.

Further suppose that the Date class contains a method that returns the year portion of the Date. In that case, an application might contain a statement such as the following:

```
salesDepartment.getHighestPaidEmployee().getHireDate().getYear()
```

An Example of Using Predefined Classes: Creating GUI Objects

When you purchase or download a compiler for an object-oriented programming language, it comes packaged with many predefined, built-in classes. The classes are stored in **libraries**— collections of classes that serve related purposes. (In some languages, such as Java, libraries are also called **packages**.) Some of the most helpful are the classes you can use to create GUI objects such as frames, buttons, labels, and text boxes. You place these GUI components within interactive programs so that users can manipulate them using input devices—most frequently a keyboard and a mouse. For example, if you want to place a clickable button on the screen using a language that supports GUI applications, you instantiate an object that belongs to the existing class named Button. In many object-oriented languages, a class with a name similar to Button is already created. It contains private data fields such as text and height and public methods such as setText() and setHeight(), which allow you to place instructions on your Button object and to change its vertical size, respectively.

If no predefined GUI object classes existed, you could create your own. However, there would be several disadvantages:

- It would require extensive work. Creating graphical objects requires a lot of code and at least a modicum of artistic talent.

- It would be repetitious work. Almost all GUI programs require standard components such as buttons and labels. If each programmer created the classes for these components from scratch, a lot of work would be repeated unnecessarily.

- The components would look different in various applications. If each programmer created his or her own component classes, objects like buttons would not have a consistent appearance and would work in slightly different ways in different applications. Users prefer standardization in their components—title bars on windows that are a uniform height, buttons that appear to be pressed when clicked, frames and windows that contain maximize and minimize buttons in predictable locations, and so on. By using standard component classes, programmers are assured that the GUI components in their programs have the same look and feel as those in other programs.

Programming languages that supply existing GUI classes often provide a **visual development environment** in which you can create programs by dragging components such as buttons and labels onto a screen and arranging them visually. Then you write programming statements to control the actions that take place when a user manipulates the controls by clicking them using a mouse, for example. Many programmers never create classes of their own from which they will instantiate objects, but only write application classes that use built-in GUI component classes. Some languages—for example, Visual Basic and C#—lend themselves very well to this type of programming.

 In Chapter 1, you learned that the visual development environment is known by the acronym IDE in several languages. IDE stands for *integrated development environment*.

In Chapter 9, you will learn more about creating programs that use GUI objects.

Reviewing the Advantages of Object-Oriented Programming

Using the features of object-oriented programming languages provides many benefits as you develop programs. Whether you instantiate objects from classes you have created or from those created by others, you save development time because each object automatically includes appropriate, reliable methods and attributes. When using inheritance, you can develop new classes more quickly by extending existing classes that already work; you need to concentrate only on new features added by the new class. When using existing objects, you need to concentrate only on the interface to those objects, not on the internal instructions that make them work. By using polymorphism, you can use reasonable, easy-to-remember names for methods and concentrate on their purpose rather than on memorizing different method names.

Chapter Summary

- Classes are the basic building blocks of object-oriented programming. A class describes objects; each object is an instance of a class. A class's fields, or instance variables, hold its data, and every object that is an instance of a class possesses the same methods. A program or class that instantiates objects of another prewritten class is a class client or class user. In addition to classes and objects, three important features of object-oriented languages are polymorphism, inheritance, and encapsulation.

- A class definition is a set of program statements that lists the characteristics of each object and the methods that each object can use. A class definition can contain a name, data, and methods. Programmers often use a class diagram to illustrate class features. The purposes of many methods contained in a class can be divided into three categories: set methods, get methods, and work methods.

- Object-oriented programmers usually specify that their data fields will have private access —that is, the data cannot be accessed by any method that is not part of the class. The methods frequently support public access, which means that other programs and methods may use the methods that control access to the private data. In a class diagram, a minus sign (−) precedes the items that are private; a plus sign (+) precedes those that are public.

- As classes grow in complexity, deciding how to organize them becomes increasingly important. Depending on the class, you might choose to store the data fields by listing a key field first. You also might list fields alphabetically, by data type, or by accessibility. Methods might be stored in alphabetical order or in pairs of get and set methods.

- An instance method operates correctly yet differently for every object instantiated from a class. When an instance method is called, a this reference that holds the object's memory address is automatically passed to the method.

- Some methods do not require a this reference. When you write a class, you can indicate two types of methods: static methods, which are also known as class methods and do not receive a this reference as an implicit parameter; and nonstatic methods, which are instance methods and do receive a this reference.

- You can use objects in many of the same ways you use simpler data types.

- A class can contain the objects of another class as data members. Using a class's object as an attribute within another class is known as composition.

- Some of the most useful classes packaged in language libraries are classes you can use to create GUI objects such as frames, buttons, labels, and text boxes. Programming languages that supply existing GUI classes often provide a visual development environment in which you can create programs by dragging components such as buttons and labels onto a screen and arranging them visually.

- When you instantiate objects in programs, you save development time because each object automatically includes appropriate, reliable methods and attributes. You can develop new classes more quickly by extending existing classes that already work, and you can use reasonable, easy-to-remember names for methods.

Key Terms

Object-oriented programming (OOP) is a style of programming in which you create classes that encapsulate the data and methods of objects.

A **class** is the definition of the attributes and methods of a category of objects.

An **object** is one tangible example of a class; it is an instance of a class.

An **instance** is one existing object or tangible example of a class; it is an object.

An **instantiation** of a class is an instance.

To **instantiate** a class is to create an object from it.

Attributes are the characteristics that define an object as part of a class.

A class's **instance variables** are the data components that belong to every instantiated object.

Fields are object attributes or data held in an object's instance variables.

The **state** of an object is the set of all the values or contents of its instance variables.

A **class client** or **class user** is a program or class that instantiates objects of another prewritten class.

Pure polymorphism describes the situation in which one method implementation can be used with a variety of arguments.

Inheritance is the process of acquiring the traits of one's predecessors.

Encapsulation is the process of combining all of an object's attributes and methods into a single package.

Information hiding (or **data hiding**) is the concept that other classes should not alter an object's attributes—only the methods of an object's own class should have that privilege.

A **class definition** is a set of program statements that list the characteristics of each object and the methods that each object can use.

A **user-defined type**, or **programmer-defined type**, is a type that is not built into a language but is created by the programmer.

An **abstract data type (ADT)** is a programmer-defined type such as a class.

Primitive data types are simple numbers and characters that are not class types.

A **class diagram** consists of a rectangle divided into three sections that show the name, data, and methods of a class.

A **set method** is an instance method that sets the values of a data field within a class.

Mutator methods are instance methods that can modify an object's attributes.

A **property** provides methods that allow you to get and set a class field value using a simple syntax.

A **get method** is an instance method that returns a value from a class.

Accessor methods are instance methods that get values from class fields.

Work methods perform tasks within a class.

Help methods and **facilitators** are other names for work methods.

Private access specifies that data or methods within a class cannot be used by any method that is not part of the same class.

Public access specifies that data or methods within a class can be used by other programs and methods.

An **access specifier** is the adjective that defines the type of access outside classes will have to the attribute or method.

An **instance method** operates correctly yet differently for each instance of a class. An instance method is nonstatic and receives a `this` reference.

A **`this` reference** is an automatically created variable that holds the address of an object and passes it to an instance method whenever the method is called.

Static methods are those for which no object needs to exist; they are not instance methods and they do not receive a `this` reference.

A **class method** is a static method; it is not an instance method and it does not receive a `this` reference.

Nonstatic methods are methods that exist to be used with an object; they are instance methods and they receive a `this` reference.

Composition is the technique of using an object of one class as an attribute within another class.

A **has-a relationship** is the type that exists when using composition.

Libraries are stored collections of classes that serve related purposes.

Packages are another name for libraries in some languages.

A **visual development environment** is one in which you can create programs by dragging components such as buttons and labels onto a screen and arranging them visually.

Review Questions

1. Which of the following means the same as *object*?

   a. class   c. instance

   b. field   d. category

2. Which of the following means the same as *instance variable*?

   a. field   c. category

   b. instance   d. class

3. A program that instantiates objects of another prewritten class is a(n) _____ .

   a. object   c. instance

   b. client   d. GUI

4. The process of acquiring the traits of one's predecessors is ──────── .

   a. inheritance
   b. encapsulation
   c. polymorphism
   d. orientation

5. Every class definition must contain ──────── .

   a. a name
   b. data
   c. methods
   d. all of the above

6. Assume that a working program contains the following statements:

   ```
   Cat myCat
   myCat.setName("Socks")
   ```

   Which of the following do you know?

   a. myCat is an object of a class named Cat.
   b. setName() is a static method.
   c. both of the above
   d. none of the above

7. Assume that a working program contains the following statements:

   ```
   Dog myDog
   myDog.setName("Bowser")
   ```

   Which of the following do you know?

   a. setName() is a public method in the Dog class.
   b. setName() accepts a string parameter.
   c. both of the above
   d. none of the above

8. Which of the following is the most likely scenario for a specific class?

   a. Its data is private and its methods are public.
   b. Its data is public and its methods are private.
   c. Its data and methods are both public.
   d. Its data and methods are both private.

9. Which of the following is true?

   a. Methods can be private.
   b. Methods can be public.
   c. both of the above
   d. none of the above

10. Assume that a working program contains the following statement:

    `name = myDog.getName()`

    Which of the following do you know?

    a. `getName()` returns a string.
    b. `getName()` returns a value that is the same data type as `name`.
    c. both of the above
    d. none of the above

11. A class diagram _____.

    a. provides an overview of a class's data and methods
    b. provides method implementation details
    c. is never used by nonprogrammers because it is too technical
    d. all of the above

12. An instance method _____.

    a. is static
    b. receives a `this` reference
    c. both of the above
    d. none of the above

13. Assume that a working program contains the following statement:

    `myHorse.setAge(4)`

    Which of the following must be true about the `setAge()` method?

    a. The method is static.
    b. The method returns a number.
    c. both of the above
    d. none of the above

14. Assume that you have created a class named `Dog` that contains a data field named `weight` and an instance method named `setWeight()`. Further assume that the `setWeight()` method accepts a numeric parameter named `weight`. Which of the following statements correctly sets a `Dog`'s weight within the `setWeight()` method?

    a. `weight = weight`
    b. `this.weight = this.weight`
    c. `weight = this.weight`
    d. `this.weight = weight`

15. A static method is also known as a(n) _____ method.

    a. instance
    b. public
    c. private
    d. class

16. By default, methods contained in a class are _____ methods.

    a. static
    b. nonstatic
    c. class
    d. public

17. Assume that you have created a class named MyClass, and that a working program contains the following statement:

output MyClass.number

Which of the following do you know?

a. number is a numeric field.

b. number is a static field.

c. number is an instance variable.

d. all of the above

18. Assume that you have created an object named myObject, and that a working program contains the following statement:

output myObject.getSize()

Which of the following do you know?

a. getSize() is a static method.

b. getSize() returns a number.

c. getSize() receives a this reference.

d. all of the above

19. Assume that you have created a class that contains a private field named myField and a nonstatic public method named myMethod(). Which of the following is true?

a. myMethod() has access to myField and can use it.

b. myMethod() does not have access to myField and cannot use it.

c. myMethod() can use myField but cannot pass it to other methods.

d. myMethod() can use myField only if it is passed to myMethod() as a parameter.

20. An object can be _____.

a. stored in an array

b. passed to a method

c. returned from a method

d. all of the above

Exercises

1. Identify three objects that might belong to each of the following classes:

   a. Building

   b. Artist

   c. BankLoan

2. Identify three different classes that might contain each of these objects:

   a. William Shakespeare

   b. My favorite red sweater

   c. Public School 23 in New York City

3. Design a class named TermPaper that holds an author's name, the subject of the paper, and an assigned letter grade. Include methods to set the values for each data field and output the values for each data field. Create the class diagram and write the pseudocode that defines the class.

4. Design a class named Automobile that holds the vehicle identification number, make, model, and color of an automobile. Include methods to set the values for each data field, and include a method that displays all the values for each field. Create the class diagram and write the pseudocode that defines the class.

5. Design a class named CheckingAccount that holds a checking account number, name of account holder, and balance. Include methods to set values for each data field and a method that displays all the account information. Create the class diagram and write the pseudocode that defines the class.

6. Complete the following tasks:

   a. Design a class named StockTransaction that holds a stock symbol (typically one to four characters), stock name, number of shares bought or sold, and price per share. Include methods to set and get the values for each data field. Create the class diagram and write the pseudocode that defines the class.

   b. Design an application that declares two StockTransaction objects and sets and displays their values.

   c. Design an application that declares an array of 10 StockTransactions. Prompt the user for data for each of the objects, and then display all the values.

7. Complete the following tasks:

   a. Design a class named MagazineSubscription that has fields for a subscriber name, magazine name, and number of months remaining for the subscription. Include methods to set and get the values for each data field. Create the class diagram and write the pseudocode that defines the class.

   b. Design an application that declares two MagazineSubscription objects and sets and displays their values.

   c. Design an application that declares an array of six MagazineSubscriptions. Prompt the user for data for each object, and then display all the values. Then subtract 1 from each "months remaining" field and display the objects again.

8. a. Design a class named Pizza. Data fields include a string field for toppings (such as pepperoni) and numeric fields for diameter in inches (such as 12) and price (such as 13.99). Include methods to get and set values for each of these fields. Create the class diagram and write the pseudocode that defines the class.

   b. Design an application program that declares two Pizza objects and sets and displays their values.

9. a. Design a class named `Circle` with fields named `radius`, `area`, and `diameter`. Include get methods for each field, but include a set method only for the radius. When the radius is set, do not allow it to be zero or a negative number. When the radius is set, calculate the diameter (twice the radius) and the area (the radius squared times pi, which is approximately 3.14). Create the class diagram and write the pseudocode that defines the class.

   b. Design an application program that declares two `Circles` and sets their radii to different values. Then, display each `Circle`'s values.

10. a. Design a class named `Square` with fields that hold the length of a side, the length of the perimeter, and the area. Include get methods for each field, but include a set method only for the length of a side, and do not allow a side to be zero or negative. When the side is set, calculate the perimeter length (four times the side length) and the area (a side squared). Create the class diagram and write the pseudocode that defines the class.

    b. Design an application program that declares two `Squares` and sets their lengths to different values. Then, display each `Square`'s values.

11. a. Playing cards are used in many computer games, including versions of such classics as Solitaire, Hearts, and Poker. Design a `Card` class that contains a string data field to hold a suit (spades, hearts, diamonds, or clubs) and an integer data field for a value from 1 to 13. Include get and set methods for each field. Write an application that randomly selects two playing cards and displays their values.

    b. Using two `Card` objects, design an application that plays a simple version of the card game War. Deal two `Cards`—one for the computer and one for the player. Determine the higher card, then display a message indicating whether the cards are equal, the computer won, or the player won. (Playing cards are considered equal when they have the same value, no matter what their suit is.) For this game, assume that the Ace (value 1) is low. Make sure that the two `Cards` dealt are not the same `Card`. For example, a deck cannot contain more than one Queen of Spades.

Case Projects

Case: *Cost Is No Object*

1. You have been developing programs for Cost Is No Object—a car rental service that specializes in lending antique and luxury cars to clients on a short-term basis. Assume that you will need the following classes: `Name`, `Address`, `Date`, `Employee`, `Customer`, `Automobile`, and `RentalAgreement`.

The `Name` class contains two fields and get and set methods for each field:

- `string firstName`
- `string lastName`

The `Address` class contains the following fields and get and set methods for each field:

- `string streetAddress`
- `string city`
- `string state`
- `string zipCode`

The `Date` class contains the following fields and get and set methods for each field:

- `num month`
- `num day`
- `num year`

The set method for the `month` field prohibits any value of less than 1 or more than 12. The set method for the `day` field prohibits any day that is out of range for the given month.

The `Employee` class contains the following fields and get and set methods for each field:

- `string idNumber`
- `Name name`
- `Address address`
- `Date hireDate`
- `num hourlyPayRate`

The `Customer` class contains the following fields and get and set methods for each field:

- `string idNumber`
- `Name name`
- `Address address`

The `Automobile` class contains the following fields and get and set methods for each field:

- `string carId`
- `string make`
- `num year`

The `RentalAgreement` class contains the following fields and get and set methods for each field:

- string rentalAgreementNumber
- Customer renter
- Employee rentalAgent
- Date rentalStartDate
- Automobile carRented
- num dailyFee
- num numberOfDaysRented

a. Create a class diagram that could be used to describe data and methods needed for each of these classes.

b. Write pseudocode for each class.

c. Design an application program that declares a `RentalAgreement` object, prompts the user for all necessary values, and displays them.

 Case: Classic Reunions

2. You have been developing programs for Classic Reunions—a service that manages the details of planning reunion parties. Assume that you will need the following classes: `Name`, `School`, `Address`, `Date`, `ContactPerson`, `Employee`, `Party`, and `PartyAgreement`.

The `Name` class contains two fields and get and set methods for each field:

- string firstName
- string lastName

The `School` class contains two fields and get and set methods for each field:

- string schoolName
- Address schoolAddress

The `Address` class contains the following fields and get and set methods for each field:

- string streetAddress
- string city
- string state
- string zipCode

The `Date` class contains the following fields and get and set methods for each field:

- `num month`
- `num day`
- `num year`

The set method for the `month` field prohibits any value of less than 1 or more than 12. The set method for the `day` field prohibits any day that is out of range for the given month.

The `ContactPerson` class contains the following fields and get and set methods for each field:

- `Name name`
- `Address address`
- `string phoneNumber`

The `Employee` class contains the following fields and get and set methods for each field:

- `string idNumber`
- `Name name`
- `Address address`
- `Date hireDate`
- `num hourlyPayRate`

The `Party` class contains the following fields and get and set methods for each field:

- `string idNumber`
- `School school`
- `Date partyDate`
- `num numberOfGuests`
- `ContactPerson contactPerson`

The `PartyAgreement` class contains the following fields and get and set methods for each field:

- `string partyAgreementNumber`
- `Party party`
- `Employee partyCoordinator`
- `Date agreementDate`
- `num contractPrice`

a. Create a class diagram that could be used to describe data and methods needed for each of these classes.

b. Write pseudocode for each class.

c. Design an application program that declares a `PartyAgreement` object, prompts the user for all necessary values, and displays them.

Case: The Barking Lot

3. You have been developing programs for The Barking Lot—a dog-boarding facility. Assume that you will need the following classes: `Name`, `Address`, `Date`, `Employee`, `Owner`, `Dog`, and `BoardingContract`.

The `Name` class contains the following fields and get and set methods for each field:

- `string firstName`
- `string lastName`

The `Address` class contains the following fields and get and set methods for each field:

- `string streetAddress`
- `string city`
- `string state`
- `string zipCode`

The `Date` class contains the following fields and get and set methods for each field:

- `num month`
- `num day`
- `num year`

The set method for the `month` field prohibits any value of less than 1 or more than 12. The set method for the `day` field prohibits any day that is out of range for the given month.

The `Employee` class contains the following fields and get and set methods for each field:

- `string idNumber`
- `Name name`
- `Address address`
- `Date hireDate`
- `num hourlyPayRate`

The Owner class contains the following fields and get and set methods for each field:

- Name name
- Address address
- string phoneNumber

The Dog class contains the following fields and get and set methods for each field:

- string idNumber
- string name
- Owner owner
- Date birthDate
- num weight

The BoardingContract class contains the following fields and get and set methods for each field:

- Dog dog
- Date boardingStartDate
- num daysToBeBoarded
- Employee caretakerForThisContract
- num totalPriceForBoardingSession

a. Create a class diagram that could be used to describe data and methods needed for each of these classes.

b. Write pseudocode for each class.

c. Design an application program that declares a BoardingContract object, prompts the user for all necessary values, and displays them.

Up for Discussion

1. In this chapter, you learned that instance data and methods belong to objects (which are class members), but that static data and methods belong to a class as a whole. Consider the real-life class named StateInTheUnitedStates. Name some real-life attributes of this class that are static attributes and instance attributes. Create another example of a real-life class and discuss what its static and instance members might be.

2. Some programmers use a system called Hungarian notation when naming their variables and class fields. What is Hungarian notation, and why do many object-oriented programmers feel it is not a valuable style to use?

3. If you are completing all the programming exercises in this book, you can see how much work goes into planning a full-blown professional program. How would you feel if someone copied your work without compensating you? Investigate the magnitude of software piracy in our society. What are the penalties for illegally copying software? Are there circumstances under which it is acceptable to copy a program? If a friend asked you to make a copy of a program for him, would you? What do you suggest we do about this problem, if anything?

CHAPTER 8

More Object Concepts

In this chapter, you will learn about:

- ◎ Constructors
- ◎ Destructors
- ◎ The concept of inheritance
- ◎ Inheritance terminology
- ◎ Accessing private members of a parent class
- ◎ Overriding base class methods
- ◎ How constructors are called during inheritance
- ◎ The concept that a derived class object "is an" instance of the base class
- ◎ Using inheritance to achieve good software design

An Introduction to Constructors

In Chapter 7, you learned that you can create classes to encapsulate data and methods, and that you can instantiate objects from the classes you define. For example, you can create an `Employee` class that contains fields such as `lastName` and `hourlyWage` and methods that set and return values for those fields, as shown in Figure 8-1.

```
class Employee
    // Declarations
        private string lastName
        private num hourlyWage

    public void setLastName(string name)
        lastName = name
    return

    public void setHourlyWage(num wage)
        hourlyWage = wage
    return

    public string getLastName()
    return lastName

    public num getHourlyWage()
    return hourlyWage

endClass
```

Figure 8-1   The `Employee` class

In Chapter 7, you also learned that you can use a class such as `Employee` to instantiate an object with a statement such as the following:

`Employee chauffeur`

When you instantiate an `Employee` object, you are actually calling a method named `Employee()` that is provided automatically by the compiler of the object-oriented language you are using. A **constructor** is a method that establishes an object, reserving enough memory space for it and providing its name. In OO languages, a constructor is created automatically by the compiler for every class you write.

When you declare an `Employee` object, the prewritten constructor is called for the `Employee` class, and it establishes one `Employee` instance. Depending on the programming language, a constructor might provide initial values for the object's data fields; for example, a language might set all numeric fields to zero by default. If you do not want an object's fields to hold these default values, or if you want to perform additional tasks when you create an instance of a class, you can write your own constructor. In most programming languages, every constructor must have the same name as the class for which it constructs, and cannot have a return type. Normally, you declare constructors to be public so that other classes can instantiate objects that belong to the class. When you create a class without writing a constructor, an automatically supplied one is used every time you instantiate an object. However, if you write a constructor for a class, you lose the automatically created version.

For example, if you wanted every Employee object to have a starting hourly wage of $10.00, you could write the constructor that is shaded in the version of the Employee class in Figure 8-2. Any Employee object instantiated using this class will have an hourlyWage field value equal to 10.00. Because the lastName field is not used in the constructor, lastName is assigned the default value for strings in the programming language in which this class is implemented.

```
class Employee
    // Declarations
        private string lastName
        private num hourlyWage

    public Employee()
        setHourlyWage(10.00)
    return

    public void setLastName(string name)
        lastName = name
    return

    public void setHourlyWage(num wage)
        hourlyWage = wage
    return

    public string getLastName()
    return lastName

    public num getHourlyWage()
    return hourlyWage

endClass
```

Figure 8-2   Employee class with a default constructor that sets hourlyWage

In Figure 8-2, the constructor calls the setHourlyWage() method and passes it 10.00. Alternatively, you could set hourlyWage to 10.00 using the assignment operator.

If you use the class in Figure 8-2 to declare Employee objects, their hourlyWage values will be initialized to 10.00. You could change any Employee's hourlyWage later in a client program using the setHourlyWage() method. If you wanted no Employee object's hourlyWage ever to change after construction, you could either eliminate the setHourlyWage() method and assign 10.00 to hourlyWage directly in the constructor, or you could leave the constructor as is, but make setHourlyWage() a private method.

The constructor in Figure 8-2 is a default constructor. In object-oriented terminology, a **default constructor** is one with no parameters. In other words, a default constructor executes when an object is instantiated without using any arguments. A class's automatically supplied constructor is a default constructor because it has no parameters, but not all default constructors are automatically supplied. When you write a constructor that takes no parameters, like the one in Figure 8-2, it becomes the default constructor.

You can write any statement you want in a constructor; it is just a method. Although you usually have no reason to do so, you could display a message within a constructor, declare local variables, or perform any other task. You can place the constructor anywhere inside the class, outside of any other method. Typically, programmers place a class's constructor first in the list of methods because it is the first method that executes when an object is created.

Figure 8-3 shows a program in which two Employee objects are declared and their hourlyWage values are displayed. In the output in Figure 8-4, you can see that even though the setHourlyWage() method is never used in the program, the Employees possess valid hourly wages as set by their constructors.

```
public class DeclareTwoEmployees
    public static void main()
        // Declarations
            Employee myPersonalTrainer
            Employee myInteriorDecorator
        output "Trainer's wage: ",
            myPersonalTrainer.getHourlyWage()
        output "Decorator's wage: ",
            myInteriorDecorator.getHourlyWage()
    return
endClass
```

Figure 8-3   Program that declares Employee objects using class in Figure 8-2

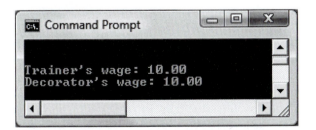

Figure 8-4   Output of program in Figure 8-3

Constructors with Parameters

Instead of forcing every Employee to be constructed with the same initial values, you might choose to create Employee objects with different values for each employee. For example, to initialize each Employee with a unique hourlyWage, you can pass a numeric value to the constructor; in other words, you can write constructors that receive parameters. Figure 8-5 shows an Employee class constructor that receives an argument. With this constructor, an argument is passed using a statement similar to one of the following:

```
Employee partTimeWorker(8.81)
Employee partTimeWorker(valueEnteredByUser)
```

When the constructor executes, the numeric value used as an argument in the constructor call is passed to Employee() as the parameter rate, which is passed to the setHourlyWage() method within the constructor.

```
class Employee
    // Declarations
        private string lastName
        private num hourlyWage

    public Employee(num rate)
        setHourlyWage(rate)
    return

    public void setLastName(string name)
        lastName = name
    return

    public void setHourlyWage(num wage)
        hourlyWage = wage
    return

    public string getLastName()
    return lastName

    public num getHourlyWage()
    return hourlyWage

endClass
```

Figure 8-5   Employee class with a constructor that accepts a parameter

When you create an Employee class with a constructor, such as the one shown in Figure 8-5, every Employee object you create must use a numeric argument. In other words, with this new version of the class, the declaration statement Employee partTimeWorker no longer works because it doesn't contain an argument that is required by the constructor. Once you write a constructor for a class, you no longer receive the automatically written parameterless constructor. If a class's only constructor requires an argument, you must provide an argument for every object of that class you create.

Overloading Instance Methods and Constructors

In Chapter 6, you learned that you can overload methods by writing multiple versions of a method with the same name but different argument lists. In the same way, you can overload instance methods and constructors. For example, Figure 8-6 shows two constructors that can coexist in an `Employee` class. One version requires no argument (so it is the class's default constructor), and the other requires a numeric argument.

```
public Employee(num rate)
    setHourlyWage(rate)
return

public Employee()
    setHourlyWage(10.00)
return
```

Figure 8-6 Overloaded `Employee` class constructors

When you use an `Employee` class that contains both of the constructors in Figure 8-6, you can make statements like the following:

```
Employee deliveryPerson
Employee myButler(25.85)
```

When you declare an `Employee` using the first of these statements, an `hourlyWage` of 10.00 is automatically set because the statement uses the parameterless version of the constructor. When you declare an `Employee` using the second statement, the `hourlyWage` is set to the passed value. Any method or constructor in a class can be overloaded, and you can provide as many versions as you want. You might create an `Employee` class with several constructor versions to provide flexibility for client programs. A particular client program might use only one version, and a different client might use another. Of course, as with all methods, you cannot create ambiguous constructors. In other words, the parameter lists for constructors must differ. For example, a class cannot contain two constructors if each requires a single numeric parameter.

If the language you are using allows it, you might have one constructor call another. For example, Figure 8-7 shows overloaded constructors in which the parameterless one calls the constructor that requires a parameter. The parameterless constructor uses a `this` reference to access the nondefault constructor for the currently constructed object. The advantage to using this technique is that if more constructor statements are required in the future, you can add them in one place. For example, if all employees should

```
public Employee(num rate)
    setHourlyWage(rate)
return

public Employee()
    this(10.00)
return
```

Figure 8-7 Overloaded constructors in which one calls the other

have a default name of *ZZZ*, you can add that assignment to the nondefault constructor, and when the default constructor executes, it will call the nondefault version.

 Watch the video *Constructors.*

Understanding Destructors

A **destructor** contains the actions you require when an instance of a class is destroyed. Most often, an instance of a class is destroyed when it goes out of scope. As with constructors, if you do not explicitly create a destructor for a class, one is automatically provided.

In some commonly used languages, you declare a destructor explicitly by using an identifier that consists of a tilde (~) followed by the class name. You cannot provide arguments to a destructor; it must have an empty parameter list. As a consequence, destructors cannot be overloaded; a class can have one destructor at most. Like a constructor, a destructor has no return type.

 The rules for creating and naming destructors vary among programming languages. For example, in Visual Basic.NET classes, the destructor is called `Finalize`.

Figure 8-8 shows a `Student` class that contains only one field (`idNumber`), a constructor, and a shaded destructor. Although it is unusual for a constructor or destructor to display anything, these output messages so that you can see when the objects are created and destroyed. When you execute the `main()` method in the `DemoStudentDestructor` class in Figure 8-9, you instantiate two `Student` objects, each with its own `idNumber` value. When the `main()` method ends, the two `Student` objects go out of scope, and the destructor for each object is called automatically. Figure 8-10 shows the program's execution.

```
class Student
    // Declarations
        private string idNumber

    public Student(string id)
        idNumber = id
        output "Student ", idNumber, " is created"
    return

    public ~Student()
        output "Student ", idNumber, " is destroyed"
    return
endClass
```

Figure 8-8   `Student` class with destructor

```
class DemoStudentDestructor
    public static void main()
        // Declarations
            Student aStudent("101")
            Student anotherStudent("102")
    return
endClass
```

Figure 8-9   DemoStudentDestructor program

Figure 8-10   Output of DemoStudentDestructor program

The program in Figure 8-9 never explicitly calls the Student class destructor, yet you can see from the output that the destructor executes twice. Destructors are invoked automatically, and in many programming languages you cannot explicitly call one. Interestingly, the last object created is the first object destroyed; the same relationship would hold true no matter how many objects the program instantiated.

 An instance of a class becomes eligible for destruction when it is no longer possible for code to use it—that is, when it goes out of scope. In many languages, the actual execution of an object's destructor might occur at any time after the object becomes eligible for destruction.

For now, you have little reason to create a destructor except to demonstrate how it is called automatically. Later, when you write more sophisticated programs that work with files, databases, or large quantities of computer memory, you might want to perform specific clean-up or close-down tasks when an object goes out of scope. For example, you might want to issue instructions to copy and then close files that were used by the program. Such instructions could be placed within a destructor.

Understanding Inheritance

Chapter 7 introduced you to the concept of inheritance—the principle that you can apply your knowledge of a general category to more specific objects. Understanding classes helps you organize objects in real life. Understanding inheritance helps you organize them more precisely. If you have never heard of a *Braford*, for example, you would have a hard time picturing one in your mind. When you learn that a Braford is an animal, you gain some understanding of what it must be like. That understanding grows when you learn it is a mammal, and the understanding is almost complete when you learn it is a cow. When you learn what a Braford is, you understand it has many characteristics that are common to all cows. To identify a Braford, you must learn only relatively minor details—its color or markings, for example. Most of a Braford's characteristics, however, derive from its membership in a particular hierarchy of classes: animal, mammal, and cow. All object-oriented programming languages make use of inheritance for the same reasons—to organize the objects that programs use, and to make new objects easier to understand based on your knowledge of their inherited traits.

When you drive a new car for the first time, you understand most of its characteristics, like how to steer and brake, because the car has inherited many of its features from older models. When you get a new coffee maker, the model might have some new features, but you understand most of its attributes because it has inherited attributes from its predecessors. Similarly, the classes you create in object-oriented programming languages can inherit data and methods from existing classes. When you create a class by making it inherit from another class, you are provided with data fields and methods automatically; you can reuse fields and methods that are already written and tested. For example, if you are already familiar with an `Employee` class and how its methods work, and then you learn that a programmer has created a `PartTimeEmployee` class that inherits from `Employee`, you feel confident that you already know some features of the new class.

You know how to create classes and how to instantiate objects that are instances of those classes. For example, consider the `Customer` class in Figure 8-11. The class contains two data fields, `idNum` and `purchaseTotal`, as well as methods that get and set each field.

```
class Customer
    // Declarations
        private string idNum
        private num purchaseTotal

    public void setIdNum(string id)
        idNum = id
    return

    public string getIdNum()
    return idNum

    public void setPurchaseTotal(num purchases)
        purchaseTotal = purchases
    return

    public num getPurchaseTotal()
    return purchaseTotal

endClass
```

Figure 8-11 A Customer class

After you create the Customer class, you can create specific Customer objects, as in the following declarations:

```
Customer firstCustomer
Customer secondCustomer
```

These Customer objects can eventually possess different ID numbers and purchase totals, but because they are Customer objects, you know that each possesses *some* ID number and purchase total.

Suppose that your boss decides to designate a new type of Customer who receives a discount on all purchases. You can create a class with a name such as PreferredCustomer and provide this class with three fields (idNum, purchaseTotal, and discountRate) and six methods to get and set each of the three fields. However, this work would duplicate much of the work that you already have done for the Customer class. The wise and efficient alternative is to create the class PreferredCustomer so it inherits all the attributes and methods of Customer. Then, you can add just the single field and two methods (the get and set methods for the new field) that are additions within the new class. Figure 8-12 depicts these relationships. The complete PreferredCustomer class is shown in Figure 8-13.

CHAPTER 8

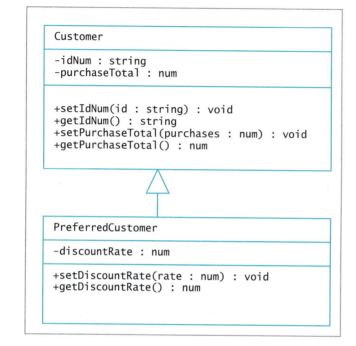

Figure 8-12   PreferredCustomer inherits from Customer

Recall from Chapter 7 that a plus sign in a class diagram indicates public access and a minus sign indicates private access. A class diagram is an example of a UML diagram. Chapter 11 describes UML diagrams in more detail.

```
class PreferredCustomer inheritsFrom Customer
    // Declarations
        private num discountRate

    public void setDiscountRate(num rate)
        discountRate = rate
    return

    public num getDiscountRate()
    return discountRate
endClass
```

Figure 8-13   PreferredCustomer class

The class in Figure 8-13 uses the phrase `inheritsFrom Customer` (see shading) to indicate inheritance. Each programming language uses its own syntax. For example, in Java you would write `extends`, in Visual Basic you would write `inherits`, and in C++ and C# you would use a colon between the new class name and the one from which it inherits.

When you use inheritance to create the `PreferredCustomer` class, you acquire the following benefits:

- You save time, because you need not re-create the `Customer` fields and methods.

- You reduce the chance of errors, because the `Customer` methods have already been used and tested.

- You make it easier for anyone who has used the `Customer` class to understand the `PreferredCustomer` class because such users can concentrate on the new features only.

- You reduce the chance for errors and inconsistencies in shared fields. For example, if your company decides to enforce a rule that customer ID numbers must be five digits, and you have code in the `Customer` class constructor that ensures valid ID numbers, then you can simply change the code in the `Customer` class; its descendents will automatically acquire the change. Without inheritance, not only would you make the change in many separate places, but the likelihood would increase that you would forget to make the change in one of the descendent classes.

The ability to use inheritance makes programs easier to write, easier to understand, and less prone to errors. Imagine that besides `PreferredCustomer`, you want to create several other more specific `Customer` classes (perhaps `DelinquentCustomer`, including a field for days past due, or `CommercialCustomer`, to hold data for customers that are businesses as opposed to individuals). By using inheritance, you can develop each new class correctly and more quickly.

In part, the concept of class inheritance is useful because it makes class code reusable. However, you do not use inheritance simply to save work. For example, just because two classes each require the same number of fields, you would not create one to inherit from the other if the classes weren't related. When properly used, inheritance always involves a general-to-specific relationship.

Understanding Inheritance Terminology

A class that is used as a basis for inheritance, like `Customer`, is a **base class**. When you create a class that inherits from a base class (such as `PreferredCustomer`), it is a **derived class** or **extended class**. When two classes have a base-derived relationship, you can distinguish the classes by using them in a sentence with the phrase *is a*. A derived class always *is a* case or instance of the more general base class. For example, a `Tree` class may be a base class to an `Evergreen` class. Every `Evergreen` *is a* `Tree`; however, not every `Tree` is an `Evergreen`. Thus, `Tree` is the base class and `Evergreen` is the derived class. Similarly, a `PreferredCustomer` *is a* `Customer`—not always the other way around—so `Customer` is the base class and `PreferredCustomer` is derived.

You can use the terms **superclass** and **subclass** as synonyms for base class and derived class. Thus, Evergreen can be called a subclass of the Tree superclass. You also can use the terms **parent class** and **child class**. A PreferredCustomer is a child to the Customer parent. Use the pair of terms you prefer; all of these terms will be used interchangeably in this book.

As an alternative way to differentiate a base class from a derived class, you can try saying the two class names together (although this technique might not work with every base-subclass pair). When people say their names in the English language, they state the more specific name before the all-encompassing family name, such as *Mary Johnson*. Similarly, with classes, the order that "makes more sense" is the child-parent order. Thus, because *Evergreen Tree* makes more sense than *Tree Evergreen*, you can deduce that Evergreen is the child class.

It also is convenient to think of a derived class as building upon its base class by providing the "adjectives" or additional descriptive terms for the "noun." Frequently, the names of derived classes are formed in this way, as in PreferredCustomer or EvergreenTree.

Finally, you usually can distinguish base classes from their derived classes by size. Although it is not required, a derived class is generally larger than its base class, in the sense that it usually has additional fields and methods. A subclass description may look small, but any subclass contains all the fields and methods of its base class as well as its own more specific fields and methods. Do not think of a subclass as a "subset" of another class—in other words, as possessing only parts of its base class. In fact, a derived class usually contains more than its parent.

A derived class can be further extended. In other words, a subclass can have a child of its own. For example, after you create a Tree class and derive Evergreen from it, you might derive a Spruce class from Evergreen. After you create the Spruce class, you might be ready to create Spruce objects. For example, you might create theTreeInMyBackYard, or you might create an array of 1000 Spruce objects for a tree farm. Similarly, myPoodlePierre might be a Poodle object. The Poodle class might derive from Dog, Dog from DomesticPet, and DomesticPet from Animal. In some programming languages, such as C#, Visual Basic, and Java, every class you create is a child of one ultimate base class, often called the Object class. The Object class usually provides basic functionality that is inherited by all the classes you create—for example, the ability to show its memory location and name. The entire list of parent classes from which a child class is derived constitutes the **ancestors** of the subclass. Figure 8-14 illustrates possible ancestors and descendents of a Dog class.

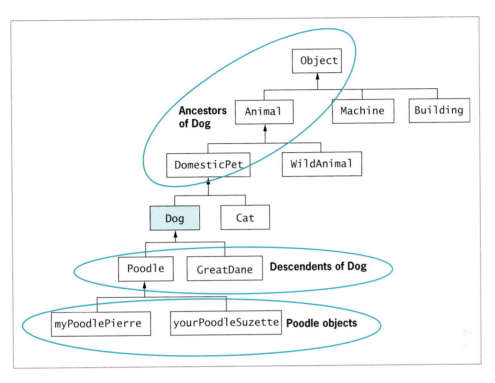

Figure 8-14 Ancestors and descendents of a Dog class

A child inherits all the members of all its ancestors. In other words, when you declare a Spruce object, it contains all the attributes and methods of both an Evergreen and a Tree; a PreferredCustomer contains all the attributes and methods of a Customer. The members of Customer and PreferredCustomer are as follows:

- Customer contains two fields and four methods, as shown in Figure 8-11.

- PreferredCustomer contains three fields and six methods, even though you do not see all of them in Figure 8-13.

Although a child class contains all the data fields and methods of its parent, a parent class does not gain any child class members. Therefore, when Customer and PreferredCustomer classes are defined as in Figures 8-11 and 8-13, all the statements in Figure 8-15 are valid. The customer2 object can use all the methods of its parent, plus it can use its own setDiscountRate() and getDiscountRate() methods. Figure 8-16 shows the output of the program as it would appear in a command-line environment.

```
class CustomerDemo
   public static void main()
      // Declarations
         Customer customer1
         PreferredCustomer customer2
      customer1.setIdNum("111")
      customer1.setPurchaseTotal(700.00)
      customer2.setIdNum("222")
      customer2.setPurchaseTotal(800.00)
      customer2.setDiscountRate(0.08)
      output "Customer 1  #", customer1.getIdNum(),
         customer1.getPurchaseTotal()
      output "Customer 2  #", customer2.getIdNum(),
         customer2.getPurchaseTotal(), customer2.getDiscountRate()
   return
endClass
```

Figure 8-15   The `CustomerDemo` application

```
Command Prompt

Customer 1  #111  700.00
Customer 2  #222  800.00   0.08
```

Figure 8-16   Output of `CustomerDemo` application

The following statements would not be allowed in the `CustomerDemo` application because `customer1`, as a `Customer`, does not have access to the methods of the `PreferredCustomer` child class:

```
customer1.setDiscountRate(0.08)
output customer1.getDiscountRate()
```

Don't Do It
This base class object cannot use methods that belong to its child.

When you create your own inheritance chains, you want to place fields and methods at their most general level. In other words, a method named **Grow()** rightfully belongs in a **Tree** class, whereas **LeavesTurnColor()** does not because the method applies only to some of the **Tree** child classes. Similarly, a **LeavesTurnColor()** method would be better located in a **Deciduous** class than separately within the **Oak** or **Maple** child class.

It makes sense that a parent class object does not have access to its child's data and methods. When you create the parent class, you do not know how many future child classes might be created, or what their data or methods might look like. In addition, derived classes are more specific. A HeartSurgeon class and an Obstetrician class are children of a Doctor class. You do not expect all members of the general parent class Doctor to have the HeartSurgeon's repairHeartValve() method or the Obstetrician's performCaesarianSection() method. However, HeartSurgeon and Obstetrician objects have access to the more general Doctor methods takeBloodPressure() and billPatients(). As with subclasses of doctors, it is convenient to think of derived classes as *specialists*. That is, their fields and methods are more specialized than those of the parent class.

 Watch the video *Inheritance*.

Accessing Private Members of a Parent Class

In Chapter 7, you learned that when you create classes, the most common scenario is for methods to be public but for data to be private. Making data private is an important object-oriented programming concept. By making data fields private and allowing access to them only through a class's methods, you protect the ways in which data can be altered and accessed. The likelihood of future errors increases when child classes are allowed direct access to a parent's fields. For example, suppose that a company uses a Customer class with a purchaseTotal field and a setPurchaseTotal() method in which a $1000 limit is placed on purchases. If a child class of Customer is allowed direct access to the Customer field purchaseTotal without using the setPurchaseTotal() method, then child class objects will not adhere to the new purchase limit. Classes that depend on field names from parent classes are said to be **fragile** because they are prone to errors—that is, they are easy to "break."

When a data field is private, no outside class can access it directly—including a child class. The principle of data hiding would be lost if you could access a class's private data merely by creating a child class. However, it can be inconvenient when a child class's methods cannot directly access its own inherited data.

For example, suppose that you want to modify the PreferredCustomer class so that when a discount rate is set, the purchase total is reduced appropriately. The new statement in the PreferredCustomer class is shaded in Figure 8-17.

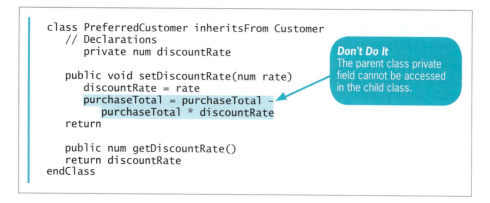

```
class PreferredCustomer inheritsFrom Customer
    // Declarations
        private num discountRate

    public void setDiscountRate(num rate)
        discountRate = rate
        purchaseTotal = purchaseTotal –
            purchaseTotal * discountRate
    return

    public num getDiscountRate()
        return discountRate
endClass
```

Don't Do It
The parent class private field cannot be accessed in the child class.

Figure 8-17   PreferredCustomer class that attempts to modify a parent class field

The logic in the setDiscountRate() method in Figure 8-17 makes sense, but the code does not compile. Although every PreferredCustomer *has* a purchaseTotal field by virtue of being a child of Customer, the PreferredCustomer methods do not have access to the purchaseTotal field because it is private within the Customer class. The private purchaseTotal field is inaccessible to any class other than the one in which it is defined.

One way to allow the setDiscountRate() method to access purchaseTotal would be to make the field public in the parent Customer class. Then any class, including the child class, could use it. However, that action would violate the important object-oriented principle of data hiding. Good OO design dictates that your data should be altered only by the properties and methods you choose and only in ways that you can control. If outside classes could alter a Customer's private fields, then the fields could be assigned values that the Customer class couldn't control. In such a case, the principle of data hiding would be destroyed, causing the behavior of the object to be unpredictable.

Therefore, object-oriented programming languages allow a medium-security access specifier that is more restrictive than public but less restrictive than private. The **protected access** specifier is used when you want no outside classes to be able to use a data field, except classes that are descendents of the original class. Figure 8-18 illustrates how a parent class's public, protected, and private fields can be used by other classes. Both outside classes and descendents of a class can use public data and methods from the parent class. Descendents of a class can use protected data and methods, but outside classes cannot. No classes, neither outside classes nor descendents, can use private class members directly.

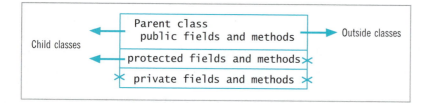

Figure 8-18   How data and methods are accessible by child and outside classes

Figure 8-19 shows a rewritten Customer class that uses the protected access specifier on its purchaseTotal field (see shading). When this modified class is extended (for example, to create a class such as PreferredCustomer), the child class methods will be able to access the parent's public and protected fields and methods. In other words, when the Customer class is written with a protected purchaseTotal field, as in Figure 8-19, the shaded statements that use it in the PreferredCustomer class in Figure 8-17 are legal.

```
class Customer
    // Declarations
        private string idNum
        protected num purchaseTotal

    public void setIdNum(string id)
        idNum = id
    return

    public string getIdNum()
    return idNum

    public void setPurchaseTotal(num purchases)
        purchaseTotal = purchases
    return

    public num getPurchaseTotal()
    return purchaseTotal

endClass
```

Figure 8-19 Customer class with a protected field

Although a child class's methods can access data fields originally defined in the parent class, a parent class's methods have no special privileges regarding any of its child class's data fields. That is, unless the child class's data fields are public, a parent cannot access them, just as any other unrelated class cannot.

In a class diagram, you use a pound sign (#) to precede items that are protected.

If purchaseTotal is defined as protected instead of private in the Customer class, then either the creator of the class anticipated that a child class would want to access the field or the Customer class was revised after it became known the child class would need access to the field. If the creator of the class did not foresee that a field would need to be accessible, or if it is preferable not to revise the class, then purchaseTotal will remain private. It is still possible to set a PreferredCustomer's purchase total—the PreferredCustomer is just required to use the same means as any other class would. That is, the PreferredCustomer class can use the public method setPurchaseTotal() that already exists in the parent class. Any class, including a child, can use a public member of the base class. So, assuming purchaseTotal remains private in Customer, Figure 8-20 shows how PreferredCustomer could be written to set purchaseTotal correctly.

```
class PreferredCustomer inheritsFrom Customer
    // Declarations
        private num discountRate

    public void setDiscountRate(num rate)
        // Declarations
            num purchases
        purchases = getPurchaseTotal()
        discountRate = rate
        purchases = purchases - purchases * discountRate
        setPurchaseTotal(purchases)
    return

    public num getDiscountRate()
    return discountRate
endClass
```

Figure 8-20   The PreferredCustomer class when purchaseTotal remains private

In the version of PreferredCustomer in Figure 8-20, the shaded statements within setDiscountRate() include the following:

- A local variable, purchases, is declared to hold the purchase total.

- The new purchases variable is assigned the purchaseTotal value from the parent class using the public method that returns it.

- The purchases value is reduced using the discount rate.

- The purchaseTotal variable from the parent class is assigned the modified value using the public method setPurchaseTotal().

In this example, no protected access specifiers are needed for any fields in the parent class, and the creators of the parent class did not have to foresee that a child class would eventually need to access any of its fields. Instead, any child classes of Customer simply follow the same access rules as any other outside class would. As an added benefit, if the parent class method setPurchaseTotal() contained additional code (for example, to enforce a maximum value), then that code would be enforced for PreferredCustomer objects as well as for Customer objects.

So, in summary, when a child class must access a private field of its parent's class, you can take one of several approaches:

- You can modify the parent class to make the field public. Usually, this is not advised because it violates the principle of data hiding.

- You can modify the parent class to make the field protected so that child classes have access to it, but other outside classes do not. This approach is necessary if you do not want outside classes to be able to access the parent class field. Be aware that some programmers oppose making any data fields nonprivate. They feel that public methods should always control data access, even by a class's children.

- You can keep the field private in the parent class and include a public or protected method that can access the field. A child class can use a protected method, but outside classes cannot. Either child classes or outside classes can use a public method; this is frequently the best option.

Using the `protected` access specifier for a field can be convenient, and it improves program performance a little by using a field directly instead of "going through" another method. Also, using the `protected` access specifier is occasionally necessary when no existing public method accesses a field in a way required by the child class. However, protected data members should be used sparingly. Whenever possible, the principle of data hiding should be observed, and even child classes should have to go through public methods to "get to" their parent's private data.

Some OOP languages, such as C++, allow a subclass to inherit from more than one parent class. For example, you might create an `InsuredItem` class that contains data fields such as value and purchase date for each insured possession, and an `Automobile` class with appropriate data fields (for example, vehicle identification number, make, model, and year). When you create an `InsuredAutomobile` class for a car rental agency, you might want to include information and methods both for `Automobile`s and `InsuredItem`s, so you might want to inherit from both. The capability to inherit from more than one class is called **multiple inheritance**.

Sometimes, a parent class is so general that you never intend to create any specific instances of the class. For example, you might never create an object that is "just" an `Employee`; each `Employee` is more specifically a `SalariedEmployee`, `HourlyEmployee`, or `ContractEmployee`. A class such as `Employee` that you create only to extend from, but not to instantiate objects from, is an abstract class. An **abstract class** is one from which you cannot create any concrete objects, but from which you can inherit.

Overriding Base Class Methods

When you create a subclass by extending an existing class, the new subclass contains all the data and methods that were defined in the original superclass, and any child class object can use all the nonprivate members of its parent. Sometimes, however, superclass methods are not entirely appropriate for the subclass objects; in those cases, you want to override the parent class methods. When you **override a method** in a child class, you create a method with the same signature (name and parameter list) as the parent's version; the parent's version then becomes hidden from objects of the child class. (Parent class methods that are not hidden are said to be **visible**.) When you use the method name with a child class object, the child class's version is used, but when you use the method name with a parent class object, the parent class's version is used.

When you use the English language, you often use the same method name to indicate diverse meanings. For example, if MusicalInstrument were a class, you could think of play() as a method of that class. If you think of various subclasses such as Guitar and Drum, you would carry out the play() method quite differently for each subclass. Using the same method name to indicate different implementations is called polymorphism, a term that means *many forms*. In other words, many forms of an action take place, depending on the object associated with the method name. You first learned the term *polymorphism* in Chapter 6, and it is a basic principle of OOP. If a programming language does not support polymorphism, the language is not considered object oriented.

For example, suppose that you create a Student class as shown in Figure 8-21. The class contains three fields: idNum, billableCredits, and tuition. The class also contains a get method for each field. Set methods are in place only for idNum and billableCredits because clients are not allowed to set tuition directly; instead, tuition is calculated based on billableCredits at a rate of $100.00 per credit hour. Figure 8-22 shows how the Student class is implemented. Whenever a Student's billableCredits field is set, tuition also is set.

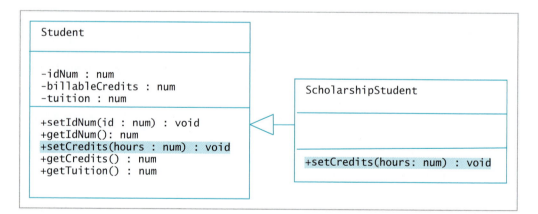

Figure 8-21　The Student class

```
class Student
    // Declarations
        private num idNum
        private num billableCredits
        private num tuition

    public void setIdNum(num id)
        idNum = id
    return

    public num getIdNum()
    return idNum

    public void setCredits(num hours)
        // Declarations
            num RATE_PER_CREDIT_HOUR = 100.00
        billableCredits = hours
        tuition = billableCredits * RATE_PER_CREDIT_HOUR
    return

    public num getCredits()
    return billableCredits

    public num getTuition()
    return tuition
endClass
```

Figure 8-22 Implementation of Student class

Suppose that you want to create a class named ScholarshipStudent that descends from Student. A ScholarshipStudent has an ID number and number of billable credit hours just like a Student, but a ScholarshipStudent's billableCredits and tuition are both 0, no matter how many actual credits the student carries. You could handle this situation in one of three ways:

1. You could create a special method in the ScholarshipStudent class with a name such as setScholarshipStudentCredits() and assign 0 to both billableCredits and tuition in this method. This method would not conflict with the parent class method because it has a different identifier, so you could use it with any ScholarshipStudent object. However, the parent method would still exist for child class objects, and if a client wrote a program and mistakenly used the setCredits() method with a ScholarshipStudent object instead of using setScholarshipStudentCredits(), then the original method would execute and the ScholarshipStudent would be assigned too much tuition.

2. You could create a method in the ScholarshipStudent class with the same name as the parent class method but a different parameter list. For example, you could

create a method with the header `setCredits(num hours, num x)`. To set a
`ScholarshipStudent`'s `billableCredits` and `tuition`, the client could use this new
method, passing the hours and any other numeric value to it; the second argument
would exist simply to distinguish this method from the one in the parent class.
In other words, this method would not override the parent class method. Instead,
it would be an *overloaded* version of the parent class method. (Overloading occurs
when multiple accessible methods have the same name but different parameter
lists.) The client would have to use the correct version of the method, but when
a programmer works with `ScholarshipStudent` objects, he could mistakenly use
the original version that requires one argument instead of the appropriate version.
That action would assign incorrect `tuition` to `ScholarshipStudent` objects.

3. The superior solution is to *override* the `setCredits()` method. To do so, you create
    a new method in the child class with the same signature as the parent class method.
    This action causes the child class version of the method to be the only one used
    with child class objects. When the parent class method is overridden, a client
    cannot possibly use the wrong version. The client simply uses the logical identifier
    `setCredits()` when credit hours and tuition need to be set, whether the client is
    working with base or derived class objects.

Figure 8-23 shows the `ScholarshipStudent` class that contains a single method named
`setCredits()`. The child class contains a field called `actualCredits`. When a program uses
the `setCredits()` method with a child class object, the number of credits for which the
student is enrolled is stored in the `actualCredits` field. The child class method then calls
the parent class method with the same name, passing a 0 so that `billableCredits` and
`tuition` both become 0. In the child class `setCredits()` method in Figure 8-23, the
shaded call to `super.setCredits()` means the program calls the superclass version of this
method. Figure 8-24 shows a program that declares a full-time `Student` and a full-time
`ScholarshipStudent` and displays their `tuition` values. In the execution in Figure 8-25,
you can see that even though both objects use a method named `setCredits()`, and both
use the same value for the number of enrolled credits, the `tuition` values are different
and correct for each object type.

The type of polymorphism that applies specifically to objects of the same parent class is sometimes
called **subtype polymorphism**.

Different programming languages use different syntax to call a parent class method from a child class
method. For example, Java uses the keyword `super`, as shown in Figure 8-23. C# uses the keyword `base`.
Visual Basic uses the keyword `MyBase`.

```
class ScholarshipStudent inheritsFrom Student
    // Declarations
        private num actualCredits
    public void setCredits(num hours)
        actualCredits = hours
        super.setCredits(0)
    return
endClass
```

Figure 8-23   ScholarshipStudent class

```
class StudentDemo
    public static void main()
        // Declarations
            num FULLTIME = 15
            Student aRegularStudent
            ScholarshipStudent aScholar
        aRegularStudent.setIdNum(444)
        aRegularStudent.setCredits(FULLTIME)
        aScholar.setIdNum(555)
        aScholar.setCredits(FULLTIME)
        output "ID #", aRegularStudent.getIdNum(),
            " Tuition $", aRegularStudent.getTuition()
        output "ID #", aScholar.getIdNum(),
            " Tuition $", aScholar.getTuition()
    return
endClass
```

Figure 8-24   Application that declares a full-time **Student** and a full-time **ScholarshipStudent**

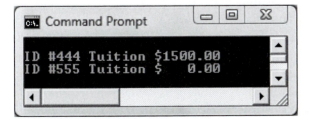

Figure 8-25   Execution of application in Figure 8-24

When you write polymorphic methods for subclasses, you must write each version of the method, which can entail extensive work. The benefits of polymorphism do not seem obvious while you are writing the methods, but the benefits are realized when you can use the methods in all sorts of applications. When you can use a single, easy-to-understand method name such as setCredits() with all sorts of objects, such as Students, ScholarshipStudents, GraduateStudents, and WorkStudyStudents, your objects behave more like their real-world counterparts and your programs are easier to understand.

 Watch the video *Overriding Base Class Methods.*

Understanding How Constructors are Called During Inheritance

When you create an object, as in SomeClass anObject, you are calling a class constructor that has the same name as the class itself. When you instantiate an object that is a member of a subclass, you are actually calling at least two constructors: the one for the base class and the one for the extended, derived class. When you create any subclass object, the superclass constructor must execute first, and then the subclass constructor executes.

 In languages that use a class named Object as the base for all objects (such as Visual Basic, Java, and C#), instantiating a child class object calls three constructors—one for the Object class, one for the parent class, and one for the child class.

If a superclass contains a default constructor, the execution of the superclass constructor often is transparent when a subclass object is instantiated. However, you should realize that when you create a subclass, both the superclass and subclass constructors execute.

When you create a class and do not provide a constructor, object-oriented languages automatically supply a default constructor—one that requires no arguments. When you write your own constructor, whether it requires arguments or not, you replace the automatically supplied version. You can write as many constructors for a class as you want, as long as they all have different parameter lists. When you use a class as a superclass and the class has only constructors that require arguments (that is, the class has no default constructor), you must be certain that any subclasses provide the superclass constructor with the arguments it needs.

When a superclass has a default constructor, you can create a subclass with or without its own constructor. This is true whether the superclass default constructor is automatically supplied or one you have written. However, when a superclass contains only constructors that require arguments, you must include at least one constructor for each subclass you create. Your subclass constructors can contain any number of statements, but each subclass constructor must call the superclass constructor and pass the required arguments to it. This is accomplished in slightly different ways depending on the programming language, but the principle is the same—a parent constructor must be fully executed before the child class constructor can operate. When a superclass requires parameters upon instantiation, even if you have no other reason to create a subclass constructor, you must write the subclass constructor so it can call its superclass's constructor.

If a superclass has multiple constructors, but one is a default constructor, you do not have to create a subclass constructor. If the subclass contains no explicitly written constructor, all subclass objects must use the superclass default constructor when they are instantiated.

For example, Figure 8-26 shows an `Employee` class with a single constructor that requires two parameters. Because `CommissionEmployee` descends from `Employee`, `CommissionEmployee` must contain a constructor that sends arguments to the parent constructor. In the example in Figure 8-26, the call to the superclass constructor is `super("999", 0.0)`. The arguments sent to the superclass constructor in this example are constants—the string "999" that becomes every `CommissionEmployee` object's employee number, and 0, which becomes every `CommissionEmployee`'s default weekly salary. In this example, 0 is assigned to each `CommissionEmployee`'s `commissionRate`.

```
class Employee
    // Declarations
        private string empNum
        private num weeklySalary

    public Employee(string idNum, num salary)
        empNum = idNum
        weeklySalary = salary
    return

    public string getEmpNum()
    return empNum

    public num getWeeklySalary()
    return weeklySalary
endClass

class CommissionEmployee inheritsFrom Employee
    // Declarations
        private num commissionRate

    public CommissionEmployee()
        super("999 ", 0.0)
        commissionRate = 0
    return

    public num getCommissionRate()
    return commissionRate
endClass
```

Figure 8-26 Child class constructor calling base class constructor with constant arguments

The method used to send parameters to a parent's constructor differs widely among programming languages. For example, in C++ you must call the parent class constructor by name (for example, `Employee()`) from the child class constructor header. In C# you also call the parent constructor from the child constructor header, but you use the keyword `base`. In Visual Basic, a base class constructor is called `New`, and a child calls `myBase.New()`. In Java you use the keyword `super`. Because Java's format is simple, it is used in Figures 8-26 and 8-27.

A subclass constructor does not have to pass constants to its parent constructor. For example, it might pass its own required parameters. Figure 8-27 shows how the CommissionEmployee constructor might be rewritten to receive three parameters for the employee number, salary, and commission rate. It passes two of these parameters to the base class constructor. The child class constructor is required to "take care" of the parent class's requirements before performing any other actions; it does not matter whether the child class constructor uses constants or variables.

```
class Employee
    // Declarations
        private string empNum
        private num weeklySalary

    public Employee(string idNum, num salary)
        empNum = idNum
        weeklySalary = salary
    return

    public string getEmpNum()
    return empNum

    public num getWeeklySalary()
    return weeklySalary
endClass

class CommissionEmployee inheritsFrom Employee
    // Declarations
        private num commissionRate

    public CommissionEmployee(string idNum, num wages, num rate)
        super(idNum, wages)
        commissionRate = rate
    return

    public num getCommissionRate()
    return commissionRate
endClass
```

Figure 8-27   Child class constructor calling base class constructor with variable arguments

The statement that instantiates a CommissionEmployee class, as defined in Figure 8-27, requires three arguments. For example, assuming all the variables have been assigned correct values, any of the following statements would work:

```
CommissionEmployee aSalesperson("123", 400.00, 0.12)
CommissionEmployee anAgent(idNumber, salary, rate)
CommissionEmployee aTrader(number, 500.00, percentage)
```

Understanding How a Derived Class Object "is an" Instance of the Base Class

Every derived class object "is a" specific instance of both the derived class and the base class. In other words, myCar "is a" Car as well as a Vehicle, and myDog "is a" Dog as well as a Mammal. You can assign a derived class object to an object of any types that are ancestors. When you do, an **implicit conversion** is made from derived class type to superclass type in many programming languages.

For example, when a ScholarshipStudent class inherits from Student, an object of either type can be passed to a method that accepts a Student parameter. In Figure 8-28, the application passes both a Student and a ScholarshipStudent to a method named display(). Each is referred to as stu within the method, and each is used correctly. The output is the same as shown in Figure 8-25.

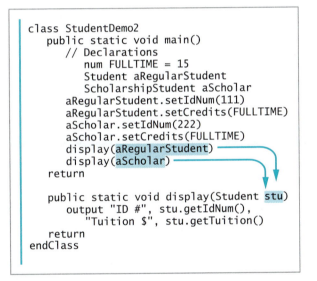

```
class StudentDemo2
    public static void main()
        // Declarations
            num FULLTIME = 15
            Student aRegularStudent
            ScholarshipStudent aScholar
        aRegularStudent.setIdNum(111)
        aRegularStudent.setCredits(FULLTIME)
        aScholar.setIdNum(222)
        aScholar.setCredits(FULLTIME)
        display(aRegularStudent)
        display(aScholar)
    return

    public static void display(Student stu)
        output "ID #", stu.getIdNum(),
            "Tuition $", stu.getTuition()
    return
endClass
```

Figure 8-28 Application that passes Student and ScholarshipStudent to the same method

Using Inheritance to Achieve Good Software Design

When an automobile maker designs a new car model, the company does not completely redesign every component. The company might design a new feature completely from scratch; for example, at some point a carmaker designed the first air bag. However, many of a new car's features are simply modifications of existing features. The manufacturer might create a larger gas tank or more comfortable seats, but even these new features still possess many properties of their predecessors in the older models. Most features of new car models are not even modified; instead, existing components such as air filters and windshield wipers are included in the new model without changes.

Similarly, you can create powerful computer programs more easily if many of their components are used either "as is" or with slight modifications. Inheritance makes your job easier because you don't have to create every part of a new class from scratch. Professional programmers constantly create new class libraries for use with OOP languages. Having these classes available to use and extend makes programming large systems more manageable. When you create a useful, extendable superclass, you and other future programmers gain several advantages:

- Subclass creators save development time because much of the code needed for the class has already been written.

- Subclass creators save testing time because the superclass code has already been tested and probably used in a variety of situations. In other words, the superclass code is **reliable**.

- Programmers who create or use new subclasses already understand how the superclass works, so the time it takes to learn the new class features is reduced.

- When you create a new subclass, neither the superclass source code nor the translated superclass object code is changed. The superclass maintains its integrity.

When you consider classes, you must think about their commonalities, and then you can create superclasses from which to inherit. You might be rewarded professionally when you see your own superclasses extended by others in the future.

Chapter Summary

- A constructor is a method that establishes an object. For every class you write, a default constructor is created automatically by the compiler. If you want to perform specific tasks when you create an instance of a class, you can write your own constructor. Any constructor you write must have the same name as the class it constructs, and cannot have a return type. Once you write a constructor for a class, the class no longer contains the automatically written default constructor. If a class's only constructor requires arguments, you must provide them for every object that you create.

- A destructor contains the actions you require when an instance of a class is destroyed. If you do not explicitly create a destructor for a class, one is automatically provided. The most common way to declare a destructor explicitly is to use an identifier that consists of a tilde (~) followed by the class name. You cannot provide arguments to a destructor; it must have an empty parameter list. As a consequence, destructors cannot be overloaded; a class can have one destructor at most.

- Inheritance is the principle that you can apply your knowledge of a general category to more specific objects. With inheritance you create new classes that contain all the fields and methods of an existing class, plus any new members you add. The ability to use inheritance makes programs easier to write, easier to understand, and less prone to errors.

- A class that is used as a basis for inheritance is a base class. A class that inherits from a base class is a derived class or extended class. You can use the terms *superclass* and *subclass* as synonyms for base class and derived class. You also can use the terms *parent class* and *child class*. A derived class is generally larger than a base class, in the sense that it usually has additional fields and methods. The entire list of parent classes from which a child class is derived constitutes the ancestors of the subclass.

- When a data field within a class is private, no outside class can access it directly— including a child class. However, it can be inconvenient when a child class's methods cannot directly access its own inherited data. Therefore, object-oriented programming languages allow a medium-security `protected` access specifier when you want no outside classes to be able to use a data field, except classes that are descendents of the original class. However, the likelihood of future errors increases when child classes are allowed direct access to a parent's fields.

- When a child class method overrides a parent class method, the child class method has the same signature as the parent's version and the parent's version then becomes hidden from child class objects. When you use the method name with a child class object, the child class's version is used, but when you use the method name with a parent class object, the parent class's version is used.

- When you instantiate an object that is a member of a subclass, you are actually calling at least two constructors: one for the base class and one for the extended, derived class. When you create a subclass object, the superclass constructor must execute first, and then the subclass constructor executes. When a superclass has a default constructor, you can create a subclass with or without its own constructor. However, when a superclass contains only nondefault constructors, you must include at least one constructor for each subclass because the subclass constructor must send needed arguments to the superclass constructor.

- Every derived class object "is a" specific instance of both the derived class and the base class. You can assign a derived class object to an object of any types that are ancestors. When you do, an implicit conversion is made from derived class to base class.

- You can create powerful computer programs more easily if many of their components are used either "as is" or with slight modifications. Inheritance makes your job easier, saves development time, provides reliable code, and makes it easier for clients to learn to use the new class.

Key Terms

A **constructor** is an automatically called method that establishes an object.

A **default constructor** is one that requires no arguments and that executes when an object is instantiated without using any arguments.

A **destructor** is an automatically called method that contains the actions you require when an instance of a class is destroyed.

A **base class** is a class that is used as a basis for inheritance.

A **derived class** or **extended class** is one that inherits from a base class.

A **superclass** or **parent class** is a base class.

A **subclass** or **child class** is a derived class.

The **ancestors** of a subclass are the entire list of parent classes from which the subclass is derived.

Fragile classes are those that depend on field names from parent classes.

The **protected access** specifier is used when you want no outside classes to be able to use a data field, except classes that are descendents of the original class.

Multiple inheritance is the capability to inherit from more than one class.

An **abstract class** is one from which you cannot create any concrete objects, but from which you can inherit.

To **override a method** in a child class is to create a method with the same signature as the parent's version so that the parent's version becomes hidden from objects of the child class.

Visible describes a superclass member that is not hidden by the derived class.

Subtype polymorphism is the ability of one method name to work appropriately for different subclass objects of the same parent class.

An **implicit conversion** is an automatic transformation from one type to another.

Reliable code has been tested and is trusted to work correctly.

Review Questions

1. When you instantiate an object, the automatically created method that is called is a _____ .

   a. creator

   b. initiator

   c. constructor

   d. architect

2. Which of the following can be overloaded?

   a. constructors

   b. destructors

   c. both of the above

   d. none of the above

3. A default constructor is _____.

   a. another name for a class's automatically created constructor

   b. a constructor that requires no arguments

   c. a constructor that sets a value for every field in a class

   d. the only constructor that is explicitly written in a class

4. When you write a constructor that receives a parameter, _____.

   a. the parameter must be numeric

   b. the parameter must be used to set a data field

   c. the default constructor no longer exists

   d. the constructor body must be empty

5. The principle that allows you to apply your knowledge of a general category to more specific objects is _____.

   a. polymorphism   c. object orientation

   b. inheritance   d. encapsulation

6. Which of the following is *not* an advantage of creating a class that inherits from another?

   a. You save time because subclasses are created automatically from those that come built in as part of a programming language.

   b. You save time because you need not re-create the fields and methods in the original class.

   c. You reduce the chance of errors because the original class's methods have already been used and tested.

   d. You make it easier for anyone who has used the original class to understand the new class.

7. Employing inheritance reduces errors because _____.

   a. the new classes have access to fewer data fields

   b. the new classes have access to fewer methods

   c. you can copy and paste methods that you already created

   d. many of the methods you need have already been used and tested

8. A class that is used as a basis for inheritance is called a _____.

   a. derived class   c. child class

   b. subclass   d. base class

9. A subclass is also called a _____.

   a. child class

   b. base class

   c. superclass

   d. parent class

10. Which of the following statements is true?

   a. A child class inherits from a parent class.

   b. A parent class inherits from a child class.

   c. Both of the preceding statements are true.

   d. Neither of the preceding statements is true.

11. When you use inheritance, _____.

   a. the parent class has access to its child's methods

   b. it is temporary

   c. a child inherits all the members of all its ancestors

   d. it changes your view of a class

12. When a data field within a class is private, _____.

   a. no outside class can use it

   b. no outside class can use it except a child of the class

   c. no outside class can use it except an ancestor of the class

   d. any class can use it

13. Object-oriented programming languages allow a medium-security access level that is more restrictive than public but less restrictive than private. This level is _____.

   a. intermediate

   b. sheltered

   c. accessible

   d. protected

14. Assume that a child class must access a private field of its parent's class. Of the following, the best course of action is to have the child class _____.

   a. use the field name directly

   b. use a public parent class method that accesses the field

   c. use a private parent class method that accesses the field

   d. define its own version of the same field

15. Classes that depend on field names from parent classes are _____.

   a. broken

   b. polymorphic

   c. fragile

   d. sturdy

16. When you override a method in a child class, you create a method with _____ .

    a. the same identifier as the parent's version
    b. the same parameter list as the parent's version
    c. both of the above
    d. none of the above

17. If a child class method has the same name but a different parameter list than a method in the parent class, the subclass method _____ the parent class version.

    a. oversees   c. overloads
    b. hides   d. overrides

18. When you instantiate an object that is a member of a subclass, the _____ constructor executes first.

    a. subclass   c. extended class
    b. child class   d. parent class

19. If a superclass constructor requires arguments, its subclass _____ .

    a. must contain a constructor
    b. must not contain a constructor
    c. must contain a constructor that requires arguments
    d. must not contain a constructor that requires arguments

20. Inheritance gives a programmer the ability to _____ .

    a. write programs that otherwise could not be written
    b. develop programs more quickly
    c. both of the above
    d. none of the above

Exercises

1. a. In the Exercises in Chapter 7, you designed a class named Automobile that holds a vehicle identification number, make, model, and color of an automobile. Design a class named Convertible that is a child class of Automobile. Include a new data field that holds a value indicating whether the top is currently up, and include get and set methods for the new field.

   b. Design an application that instantiates an object of each class and demonstrates all the methods.

2. a. In the Exercises in Chapter 7, you designed a class named CheckingAccount that holds a checking account number, name of account holder, and balance. Design a class named InterestBearingCheckingAccount that descends from CheckingAccount and includes a field that holds an annual interest rate. The InterestBearingCheckingAccount class contains a method that sets the new field value and a method that overrides the display method in the CheckingAccount class.

   b. Design an application that instantiates an InterestBearingCheckingAccount object and demonstrates all its methods.

3. a. In the Exercises in Chapter 7, you designed a class named StockTransaction that holds a stock symbol, stock name, number of shares bought or sold, and price per share. Design a class named FeeBearingStockTransaction that descends from StockTransaction and includes fields that hold the commission rate charged for the transaction and the dollar amount of the fee. The FeeBearingStockTransaction class contains a method that sets the commission rate and computes the fee by multiplying the rate by transaction price, which is the number of shares times the price per share. The class also contains get methods for each field.

   b. Design an application that instantiates a FeeBearingStockTransaction object and demonstrates all its methods.

4. a. Design a class named Player that holds a player number and name for a sports team participant. Include methods to get and set the values for each data field.

   b. Design two classes named BaseballPlayer and BasketballPlayer that are child classes of Player. Include a new data field in each class for the player's position. Include an additional field in the BaseballPlayer class for batting average. Include a new field in the BasketballPlayer class for free-throw percentage. Add appropriate methods in the child classes to get and set the new fields.

   c. Design an application that instantiates an object of each class and demonstrates all the methods.

5. a. Create a class named Rectangle that contains data fields for height, width, and surfaceArea, and a method named computeSurfaceArea().

   b. Create a child class named Box, which contains an additional data field named depth and a computeSurfaceArea() method that overrides the parent method appropriately for a three-dimensional box.

   c. Create the logic for an application that instantiates a Rectangle object and a Box object and displays the surface areas of both objects.

6. a. Create a class named `Order` that performs order processing of a single item. The class has four fields: customer name, customer number, quantity ordered, and unit price. Include set and get methods for each field. The set methods prompt the user for values for each field. This class also needs a `computePrice()` method to compute the total price (quantity multiplied by unit price) and a method to display the field values.

    b. Create a subclass named `ShippedOrder` that overrides `computePrice()` by adding a shipping and handling charge of $4.00.

    c. Create the logic for an application that instantiates an object of each of the `Order` and `ShippedOrder` classes. Prompt the user for data for the `Order` object and display the results; then prompt the user for data for the `ShippedOrder` object and display the results.

    d. Create the logic for an application that continuously prompts a user for order information until the user enters *ZZZ* for the customer name or until 10 orders have been taken, whichever comes first. Ask the user whether each order will be shipped, and create an `Order` or a `ShippedOrder` appropriately. Store each order in an array. When the user is finished entering data, display all the order information taken as well as the total price computed for each order.

7. a. Create a class named `Year` that contains data fields to hold the number of months in a year and the number of days in a year. Include a constructor that sets the number of months to 12 and the number of days to 365, and get and set methods for each field.

    b. Create a subclass named `LeapYear`. `LeapYear`'s constructor overrides `Year`'s constructor and sets the number of days to 366.

    c. Design an application that instantiates one object of each class and displays all the data.

    d. Add a method named `daysElapsed()` to the `Year` class. The `daysElapsed()` method accepts two arguments representing a month and a day; the method returns a value indicating the number of days that have elapsed since January 1 of that year. For example, on March 3, 61 days have elapsed (31 in January, 28 in February, and 2 in March). Create a `daysElapsed()` method for the `LeapYear` class that overrides the method in the `Year` class. For example, on March 3 in a `LeapYear`, 62 days have elapsed (31 in January, 29 in February, and 2 in March).

    e. Design an application that prompts the user for a month and day and then calculates the days elapsed in a `Year` and a `LeapYear`.

Case Projects

Case: Cost Is No Object

1. In Chapter 7, you developed classes needed for Cost Is No Object—a car rental service that specializes in lending antique and luxury cars to clients on a short-term basis. You created the logic for the following classes: Name, Address, Date, Employee, Customer, Automobile, and RentalAgreement.

   Now create the following:

   • Create a superclass named Person from which both Employee and Customer can descend. Include attributes and methods that any Person should possess— for example, a name and address. Then rewrite the Employee and Customer classes to descend from Person, including only attributes and methods appropriate for each subclass.

   • Create at least two subclasses that descend from Employee (for example, PartTimeEmployee), adding new fields and methods as appropriate. Override at least one parent method.

   • Create at least two subclasses that descend from Customer (for example, PreferredCustomer), adding new fields and methods as appropriate. Override at least one parent method.

   • Create at least two subclasses that descend from Automobile (for example, LuxuryCar), adding new fields and methods as appropriate. Override at least one parent method.

   • Create a program that demonstrates each of the classes' methods.

Case: Classic Reunions

2. In Chapter 7, you developed classes needed for Classic Reunions—a service that plans reunion parties. You created the logic for the following classes: Name, School, Address, Date, ContactPerson, Employee, Party, and PartyAgreement.

   Now create the following:

   • Create a superclass named Person from which both Employee and ContactPerson can descend. Include attributes and methods that any Person should possess—for example, a name and address. Then rewrite the Employee and ContactPerson classes to descend from Person. Besides the fields it inherits from Person, the Employee class should contain an ID number, hire date, and hourly pay rate. The ContactPerson class also inherits the fields from `Person`, and contains a phone number and get and set methods for it.

- Create at least two subclasses that descend from `Employee` (for example, `PartTimeEmployee`), adding new fields and methods as appropriate. Override at least one parent method.

- Create at least two subclasses that descend from `School` (for example, `HighSchool`), adding new fields and methods as appropriate. Override at least one parent method.

- Create at least two subclasses that descend from `Party` (for example, `DinnerParty`), adding new fields and methods as appropriate. Override at least one parent method.

- Create a program that demonstrates each of the classes' methods.

Case: The Barking Lot

3. In Chapter 7, you developed classes needed for The Barking Lot—a dog-boarding facility. You created the logic for the following classes: `Name`, `Address`, `Date`, `Employee`, `Owner`, `Dog`, and `BoardingContract`.

Now create the following:

- Create a superclass named `Person` from which both `Employee` and `Owner` can descend. Include attributes and methods that any `Person` should possess—for example, a name and address. Then rewrite the `Employee` and `Owner` classes to descend from `Person`. Besides the fields it inherits from `Person`, the `Employee` class should contain an ID number, hire date, and hourly pay rate. The `Owner` class also inherits the fields from `Person`, and contains a phone number and get and set methods for it.

- Create at least two subclasses that descend from `Employee` (for example, `PartTimeEmployee`), adding new fields and methods as appropriate. Override at least one parent method.

- Create at least two subclasses that descend from `Dog` (for example, `ServiceDog`), adding new fields and methods as appropriate. Override at least one parent method.

- Create a program that demonstrates each of the classes' methods.

Up for Discussion

1. Suppose that your organization asks you to develop a code of ethics for the Information Technology Department. What would you include?

2. When you create an `Employee` class, you might decide to store each employee's Social Security number. Besides using it for tax purposes, many organizations also use this number as an identification number. Is this a good idea? Is a Social Security number unique?

CHAPTER 9

Event-Driven Programming with Graphical User Interfaces

In this chapter, you will learn about:

- ◎ Event-driven programming
- ◎ The actions that GUI components can initiate
- ◎ Designing graphical user interfaces
- ◎ The steps to developing an event-driven application
- ◎ Threads and multithreading
- ◎ Creating animation

Understanding Event-Driven Programming

From the 1950s, when businesses began to use computers, through the 1980s, almost all interactive dialogues between people and computers took place at the command prompt (or on the command line). In Chapter 1, you learned that the command line is used to type entries to communicate with the computer's **operating system**—the software that you use to run a computer and manage its resources. In the early days of computing, interacting with an operating system was difficult because users had to know the exact syntax to use when typing commands, and they had to spell and type those commands accurately. People who use the Disk Operating System (DOS) also call the command line the **DOS prompt**. Figure 9-1 shows a command in the Windows operating system.

Figure 9-1   Command prompt screen

DOS was considered so difficult that a book titled *DOS for Dummies* was written in the early 1990s to explain the operating system in everyday language. The book's success spawned more than 1600 other titles in the *For Dummies* series.

If you use the Windows Vista operating system on a PC, you can locate the command prompt by clicking Start, All Programs, Accessories, and Command Prompt.

Fortunately for today's computer users, operating system software allows them to use a mouse or other pointing device to select pictures, or **icons**, on the screen. As you learned in Chapter 1, this type of environment is a graphical user interface, or GUI. Computer users can expect to see a standard interface in GUI programs. Rather than memorizing difficult commands that must be typed at a command line, GUI users can select options from menus and click buttons to make their preferences known to a program. Users can select objects that look like their real-world counterparts and get the expected results. For example, users may select an icon that looks like a pencil when they want to write a memo, or they may drag an icon shaped like a folder to a recycling bin icon to delete the files in the folder. Figure 9-2 shows a Windows program named Paint in which icons representing pencils, paint cans, and other objects appear on clickable buttons. Performing an operation on an icon (for example, clicking or dragging it) causes an **event**—an occurrence that generates a message sent to an object.

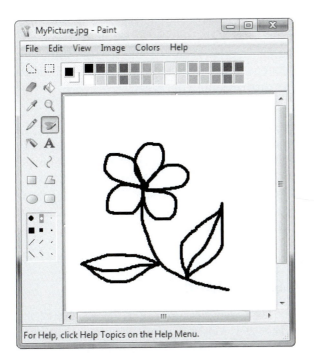

Figure 9-2 A GUI application that contains buttons and icons

GUI programs are called **event-driven** or **event-based** because actions occur in response to user-initiated events such as clicking a mouse button. When you program with event-driven languages, the emphasis is on objects that users can manipulate, such as buttons and menus, and on events that users can initiate with those objects, such as clicking or double-clicking. The programmer writes methods that execute in response to each type of event.

For the programmer, event-driven programs require unique considerations. The program logic you developed earlier for many methods in this book is procedural; each step occurs in the order the programmer determines. In a procedural application, if you issue a prompt and a statement to accept the user's response, the processing goes no further until the input is completed. In contrast, with event-driven programs, a user might initiate any number of events in any order. For example, with an event-driven word-processing program, a user might type words, select text with the mouse, click a button to change text to bold or italics, choose a menu item, and so on. With each word-processing document created, each user chooses options in the order that seems appropriate at the time, and the word-processing program must be ready to respond to any initiated event.

Within an event-driven program, a component from which an event is generated is the **source of the event**. A button that users can click to cause an action is an example of a source; a text box in which users enter typed characters is another source. An object that is "interested in" an event to which you want it to respond is a **listener**. It "listens for" events so it knows when to respond. Not all objects listen for all events—you probably have used programs in which clicking many areas of the screen has no effect. If you want an object such as a button to be a listener for an event such as a mouse click, you must write two types of appropriate program statements. You write the statements that define the object as a listener and the statements that constitute the event.

Although event-driven programming is newer than procedural programming, the instructions that programmers write to respond to events are still simply sequences, selections, and loops. Event-driven programs still declare variables, use arrays, and contain all the attributes of their procedural-program ancestors. An event-driven program might contain components with labels like "Compute Paycheck" or "Sort Records." The programming logic you use when writing code for these processes is the same logic you have learned throughout this book. Writing event-driven programs involves thinking of possible events as the methods that constitute the program.

User-Initiated Actions and GUI Components

To understand GUI programming, you need to have a clear picture of the possible events a user can initiate. A partial list is shown in Table 9-1. Most languages allow you to distinguish between many additional events. For example, you might be able to initiate different events when a key is pressed, when a mouse button is pressed, and when it is released.

Event	Description of User's Action
Key press	Pressing a key on the keyboard
Mouse point or mouse over	Placing the mouse pointer over an area on the screen
Mouse click or left mouse click	Pressing the left mouse button
Right mouse click	Pressing the right mouse button
Mouse double-click	Pressing the left mouse button two times in rapid sequence
Mouse drag	Holding down the left mouse button while moving the mouse over the desk surface

Table 9-1   Common user-initiated events

You also need to be able to picture common GUI components. Some are listed in Table 9-2. Figure 9-3 illustrates several common GUI components.

Component	Description
Label	A rectangular area that displays text
Text box	A rectangular area into which the user can type text
Check box	A label placed beside a small square; you can click the square to display or remove a check mark; this component allows the user to select or deselect an option
Option buttons	A group of options that are similar to check boxes. When the options are square, users typically can select any number of them; such options are called a *check box group*. When the options are round, they are often mutually exclusive and are called *radio buttons*.
List box	A window that displays a list of items. Depending on the options the programmer sets, you might be able to make only one selection, or you might be able to make multiple selections.
Button	A rectangular object you can click; when you do, its appearance usually changes to look pressed

Table 9-2   Common GUI components

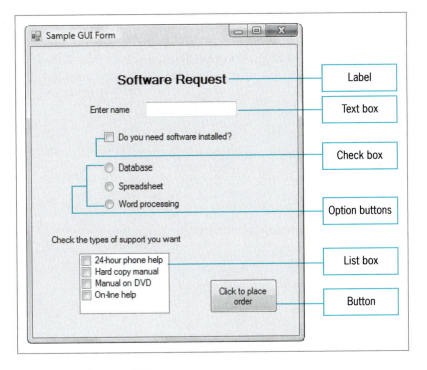

Figure 9-3   Common GUI components

When you program in a language that supports event-driven logic, you do not create the GUI components from scratch. Instead, you call prewritten methods that draw the components on the screen for you. The components are constructed using existing classes complete with names, attributes, and methods. In some programming language environments, you write statements that call the methods that create the GUI objects; in others, you can drag GUI objects onto your screen from a toolbox and arrange them appropriately for your application. Either way, you do not think about the details of constructing the components. Instead, you concentrate on the actions that should occur when a user initiates an event from one of the components. Thus, GUI components are excellent examples of the best principles of object-oriented programming (OOP)—they represent objects with attributes and methods that operate like black boxes, making them easy for you to use. They also exemplify one of the important principles of object-oriented design—reusability.

 GUI components are often referred to as *widgets*, which some sources claim is a combination of the terms *window* and *gadgets*. Originally, "widget" comes from the 1924 play "Beggar on Horseback," by George Kaufman and Marc Connelly. In the play, a young composer gets engaged to the daughter of a rich businessman, and foresees spending his life doing pointless work in a bureaucratic big business that manufactures widgets, items whose purpose is never explained.

When you use existing GUI components, you instantiate objects, each of which belongs to a prewritten class. For example, you might use a `Button` class object when you want the user to click a button to make a selection. Depending on the programming language, the `Button` class might contain attributes or properties such as the text on the `Button` and its position on the screen. The class might also contain methods such as `setText()` and `setPosition()`. For example, Figure 9-4 shows how a built-in `Button` class might be written.

```
class Button
    // Declarations
        private string text
        private num x_position
        private num y_position

    public void setText(string messageOnButton)
        text = messageOnButton
    return

    public void setPosition(num x, num y)
        x_position = x
        y_position = y
    return
endClass
```

Figure 9-4   `Button` class

The x_position and y_position of the Button object in Figure 9-4 refer to horizontal and vertical coordinates where the Button appears on an object, such as a window that appears on the screen during program execution. A **pixel** is one of the tiny dots of light that form a grid on your screen. The term *pixel* derives from combining the first syllables of *picture* and *element*. You will use x- and y-positions again when you learn about animation later in this chapter.

The Button class shown in Figure 9-4 is an abbreviated version, so you can easily see its similarity to classes such as Student and Employee, which you read about in Chapters 7 and 8. A working Button class in most programming languages would contain many more fields and methods. For example, you might need to set a Button's font, color, size, and so on.

To create a Button object using its default constructor, you would write a statement similar to the following:

```
Button myButton
```

Depending on the programming language, there might be one or more overloaded Button constructors. For example, many languages support a Button constructor that accepts the Button's text. To use that constructor, you could write a statement similar to the following:

```
Button myButton("Click here")
```

To use a Button's methods, you would write statements similar to the following:

```
myButton.setText("Click to place order")
myButton.setPosition(10, 30)
myButton.setColor(blue)
```

Different GUI classes support different attributes and methods. For example, a CheckBox class might contain a method named setChecked() that places a check mark in the CheckBox. A Button, however, would have no need for such a method.

In Chapter 1, you learned that integrated development environments (IDEs) provide programmer-friendly tools that make your programming job easier. When you write GUI programs in an IDE, you can drag components such as buttons and check boxes onto a screen without explicitly writing declarations. Similarly, in many environments, you can select attributes like color and position by using drop-down lists instead of writing set methods. In such environments, the coding statements are generated for you. For example, when you drag a Button onto a screen, its setPosition() method is called automatically and passed the values of the coordinates where you drop the Button with your mouse. If you move the Button, the setPosition() method is called again and the new coordinates are passed to it. In graphical languages, you also can set GUI object properties by writing the code statements yourself instead of allowing them to be automatically generated. In other words, you can design the screen "the hard way" by writing code. The drag-and-drop options and property list features are available to you as a convenience.

Watch the video *Event-Driven Programming*.

Designing Graphical User Interfaces

You should consider several general design principles when creating a program that will use a GUI:

- The interface should be natural and predictable.

- The interface should be attractive, easy to read, and nondistracting.

- To some extent, it's helpful if the user can customize your applications.

- The program should be forgiving.

- The GUI is only a means to an end.

The Interface Should Be Natural and Predictable

The GUI program interface should represent objects like their real-world counterparts. In other words, it makes sense to use an icon that looks like a recycling bin to let a user drag files or other components to the bin and delete them. Using a recycling bin icon is "natural" in that people use one in real life when they want to discard actual items; dragging files to the bin is also "natural" because that's what people do with real items they discard. Using a recycling bin for discarded items is also predictable, because users are already familiar with the icon in other programs. Some icons may be natural, but if they are not predictable as well, then they are not as effective. An icon that depicts a recycling truck seems natural, but because other programs do not use such imagery, it is not as predictable.

GUIs should also be predictable in their layout. For example, a menu bar appears at the top of the screen in most GUI programs, and the first menu item is almost always *File*. If you design a program interface in which the menu runs vertically down the right side of the screen, or in which *File* is the last menu option instead of the first, you will confuse users. Either they will make mistakes when using your program or they may give up using it entirely. It doesn't matter if you can prove that your layout plan is more efficient than the standard one—if you do not use a predictable layout, your program will be rejected in the marketplace.

Many studies have proven that the Dvorak keyboard layout is more efficient for typists than the QWERTY keyboard layout that most of us use. The QWERTY keyboard layout gets its name from the first six letter keys in the top row. With the Dvorak layout, which is named for its inventor, the most frequently used keys are in the home row, allowing typists to complete many more keystrokes per minute. However, the Dvorak keyboard has not caught on because it is not predictable to users who know the QWERTY keyboard.

Some real-world objects have unnatural interfaces, making them more difficult to use. For example, most stovetops have four burners arranged in two rows, but the knobs that control the burners frequently are placed in a single horizontal row. Because there is not a natural correlation between the placement of a burner and its control, you are likely to select the wrong knob when adjusting the burner's flame or heating element.

The Interface Should Be Attractive, Easy to Read, and Nondistracting

If your interface is attractive, people are more likely to use it. If it is easy to read, they are less likely to make mistakes. When it comes to GUI design, fancy fonts and weird color combinations are the signs of amateur designers. In addition, you should make sure that unavailable screen options are either sufficiently dimmed or removed, so the user does not waste time clicking components that aren't functional. Dimming or *graying* a component provides another example of predictability—experienced users do not expect to be able to use a dimmed component.

Screen designs should not be distracting. When a screen has too many components, users can't find what they're looking for. When a component is no longer needed, it should be removed from the interface. GUI programmers sometimes refer to screen space as *real estate*. Just as a plot of land becomes unattractive when it supports no open space, your screen becomes unattractive when you fill the limited space with too many components. You also want to avoid distracting users with overly creative design elements. When users click a button to open a file, they might be amused the first time a filename dances across the screen or the speakers play a tune. However, after one or two experiences with your creative additions, users find that intruding design elements hamper the actual work of the program. Also, creative additions might consume a lot of memory and CPU time, slowing an application's performance.

An excellent way to learn about effective GUI design is to pay attention to the design features used in popular applications and in Web sites you visit.

To Some Extent, It's Helpful If the User Can Customize Your Applications

All users work in their own ways. If you are designing an application that will use numerous menus and toolbars, it's helpful if users can position components in the order that's easiest for them. Users appreciate being able to change features like color schemes. Allowing a user to change the background color in your application may seem frivolous to you, but to users who are color blind or visually impaired, it might make the difference in whether they use your application at all. The screen design issues that make programs easier to use for people with physical limitations are known as **accessibility** issues. You might also want to consider cultural aspects of your designs. For example, many programs are used internationally. If you can allow the user to work in a choice of languages, you might be able to market your program more successfully in other countries.

The Program Should Be Forgiving

Perhaps you have had the inconvenience of accessing a voice mail system in which you selected several sequential options, only to find yourself at a dead end with no recourse but to hang up and redial the number. Good program design avoids similar problems. You should always provide an escape route to accommodate users who make bad choices or change their minds. By providing a Back button or a working Escape key, you provide more functionality to your users.

It also can be helpful to include an option for the user to revert to the default settings after making changes. Some users might be afraid to alter an application's features if they are not sure they can easily return to the original settings.

Users also appreciate being able to perform tasks in a variety of ways. For example, you might allow a user to select a word on a screen by highlighting it using a mouse or by holding down the Ctrl and Shift keys while pressing the right arrow key. A particular technique might be easier for people with disabilities, and it might be the only one available after the mouse batteries fail or the user accidentally disables the keyboard by spilling coffee on it.

The GUI Is Only a Means to an End

The most important principle of GUI design is to remember that a GUI is only an interface. Using a mouse to click items and drag them around is not the point of any business programs except those that train people how to use a mouse. Instead, the point of a graphical interface is to help people be more productive. To that end, the design should help the user see what options are available, allow the use of components in the ordinary way, and not force the user to concentrate on how to interact with your application. The real work of a GUI program is done after the user clicks a button or makes a list box selection. Actual program tasks then take place.

The Steps to Developing an Event-Driven Application

In Chapter 1, you first learned about the steps to developing a computer program. When you develop an event-driven application, you expand on the planning and design steps to include three new tasks as follows:

- Create storyboards.
- Define the objects.
- Define the connections between the screens the user will see.

For example, suppose that you want to create a simple, interactive program that determines premiums for prospective insurance customers. A graphical interface will allow users to select a policy type—health or auto. Next, the users answer pertinent questions about their age, driving record, and whether they smoke. Although most insurance premiums would be based on more characteristics than these, assume that policy rates are determined using the factors shown in Table 9-3. The final output of the program is a second screen that shows the semiannual premium amount for the chosen policy.

Health Policy Premiums	Auto Policy Premiums
Base rate: $500	Base rate: $750
Add $100 if over age 50	Add $400 if more than 2 tickets
Add $250 if smoker	Subtract $200 if over age 50

Table 9-3   Insurance premiums based on customer characteristics

Creating Storyboards

A **storyboard** represents a picture or sketch of a screen the user will see when running a program. Filmmakers have long used storyboards to illustrate key moments in the plots they are developing; similarly, GUI storyboards represent "snapshot" views of the screens the user will encounter during the run of a program. If the user could view up to four screens during the insurance premium program, then you would draw four storyboard cells, or frames.

Figure 9-5 shows two storyboard sketches for the insurance program. They represent the introductory screen at which the user selects a premium type and answers questions, and the final screen, which displays the semiannual premium.

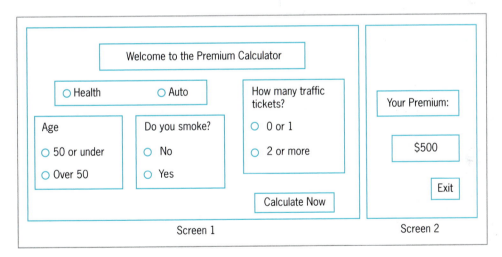

Figure 9-5   Storyboard for insurance program

Defining the Storyboard Objects in an Object Dictionary

An event-driven program may contain dozens or even hundreds of objects. To keep track of them, programmers often use an object dictionary. An **object dictionary** is a list of the objects used in a program, including which screens they are used on and whether any code, or script, is associated with them. Some organizations also include the disk location where an object is stored as part of the object dictionary.

Figure 9-6 shows an object dictionary for the insurance premium program. The type and name of each object to be placed on a screen are listed in the two columns on the left side. The third column shows the screen number on which the object appears. The next column names any variables that are affected by an action on the object. The right column indicates whether any code or script is associated with the object. For example, the label named welcomeLabel appears on the first screen. It has no associated actions—it does not call any methods or change any variables; it is just a label. The calcButton, however, does cause execution of a method named computePremium(). This method calculates the semiannual premium amount and stores it in the premiumAmount variable. Depending on the programming language, you might need to name computePremium() something similar to calcButton.click(). In languages that use this format, a standard method named click() holds the statements that execute when the user clicks the calcButton.

Object Type	Name	Screen Number	Variables Affected	Script?
Label	welcomeLabel	1	none	none
RadioButton	healthRadioButton	1	premiumAmount	none
RadioButton	autoRadioButton	1	premiumAmount	none
Label	ageLabel	1	none	none
RadioButton	lowAgeRadioButton	1	premiumAmount	none
RadioButton	highAgeRadioButton	1	premiumAmount	none
Label	smokeLabel	1	none	none
RadioButton	smokeNoRadioButton	1	premiumAmount	none
RadioButton	smokeYesRadioButton	1	premiumAmount	none
Label	ticketsLabel	1	none	none
RadioButton	lowTicketsRadioButton	1	premiumAmount	none
RadioButton	highTicketsRadioButton	1	premiumAmount	none
Button	calcButton	1	premiumAmount	computePremium()
Label	premiumLabel	2	none	none
Label	premAmtLabel	2	none	none
Button	exitButton	2	none	exitRoutine()

Figure 9-6   Object dictionary for insurance premium program

Defining Connections Between the User Screens

The insurance premium program is small, but with larger programs you may need to draw the connections between the screens to show how they interact. Figure 9-7 shows an interactivity diagram for the screens used in the insurance premium program. An **interactivity diagram** shows the relationship between screens in an interactive GUI program. Figure 9-7 shows that the first screen calls the second screen, and the program ends.

Figure 9-7   Interactivity diagram for insurance premium program

Figure 9-8 shows how a diagram might look for a more complicated program in which the user has several options available at Screens 1, 2, and 3. Notice how each of these three screens may lead to different screens, depending on the options the user selects at a previous screen.

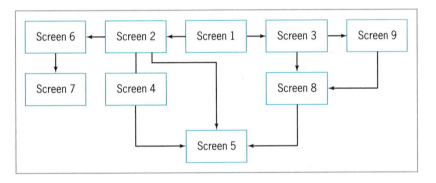

Figure 9-8   Interactivity diagram for a complicated program

Planning the Logic

In an event-driven program, you design the screens, define the objects, and define how the screens will connect. Then you can start to plan the insurance program class. For example, following the storyboard plan for the insurance program (see Figure 9-5), you need to create the first screen, which contains four labels, four sets of radio buttons, and a button. Figure 9-9 shows the pseudocode that creates these components.

```
// Declarations
    Label welcomeLabel
    RadioButton healthRadioButton
    RadioButton autoRadioButton
    Label ageLabel
    RadioButton lowAgeRadioButton
    RadioButton highAgeRadioButton
    Label smokeLabel
    RadioButton smokeNoRadioButton
    RadioButton smokeYesRadioButton
    Label ticketsLabel
    RadioButton lowTicketsRadioButton
    RadioButton highTicketsRadioButton
    Button calcButton
```

Figure 9-9   Component definitions for first screen of insurance program

You also need to create the component that holds all the GUI elements in Figure 9-9. Depending on the programming language, you might use a class with a name such as Screen, Form, or Window. Each of these generically is a **container**, or a class of objects whose main purpose is to hold other elements. The container class contains methods that allow you to set physical properties such as height and width, as well as methods that allow you to add the appropriate components to a container. Figure 9-10 shows how you would define a Screen class, set its size, and add the necessary components.

```
// Declarations
   Screen screen1

screen1.setSize(150, 150)
welcomeLabel.setText("Welcome to the Premium Calculator")
screen1.add(welcomeLabel)
healthRadioButton.setText("Health")
screen1.add(healthRadioButton)
autoRadioButton.setText("Auto")
screen1.add(autoRadioButton)
ageLabel.setText("Age")
screen1.add(ageLabel)
lowAgeRadioButton.setText("50 or under")
screen1.add(lowAgeRadioButton)
highAgeRadioButton.setText("Over 50")
screen1.add(highAgeRadioButton)
smokeLabel.setText("Do you smoke?")
screen1.add(smokeLabel)
smokeNoRadioButton.setText("No")
screen1.add(smokeNoRadioButton)
smokeYesRadioButton.setText("Yes")
screen1.add(smokeYesRadioButton)
ticketsLabel.setText("How many traffic tickets?")
screen1.add(ticketsLabel)
lowTicketsRadioButton.setText("0 or 1")
screen1.add(lowTicketsRadioButton)
highTicketsRadioButton.setText("2 or more")
screen1.add(highTicketsRadioButton)
calcButton.setText("Calculate Now")
screen1.add(calcButton)
calcButton.registerListener(computePremium())
```

Figure 9-10   Statements that create `screen1`

In Figure 9-10, the last statement, `calcButton.registerListener(computePremium())`, specifies that `computePremium()` executes when a user clicks the `calcButton`. The syntax of this statement varies among programming languages.

In reality, you might generate more code than that shown in Figure 9-10 when you create the insurance program components. For example, each component might require a color and font. You also might want to initialize some components with default values to indicate they are selected. For example, you might want one radio button in a group to be selected already, which allows the user to click a different option only if he does not want the default value.

Similarly, Figure 9-11 shows how you can create and define the components for the second screen in the insurance program and how to add the components to the container. Notice the label that holds the user's insurance premium (premAmtLabel) is not filled with text, because the amount is not known until the user makes all the selections on the first screen.

```
// Declarations
    Screen screen2
    Label premiumLabel
    Label premAmtLabel
    Button exitButton

screen2.setSize(100, 100)

premiumLabel.setText("Your Premium:")
premiumLabel.setPosition(5, 30)

premAmtLabel.setPosition(20, 50)

exitButton.setText("Exit")
exitButton.setPosition(60, 80)
exitButton.registerListener(exitRoutine())

screen2.add(premiumLabel)
screen2.add(premAmtLabel)
screen2.add(exitButton)
```

Figure 9-11   Statements that define and create screen2 and its components

After the GUI components are designed and arranged, you can plan the logic for each of the methods that the program will use. For example, given the program requirements shown in Table 9-3, you can write the pseudocode for the computePremium() method of the insurance premium program, as shown in Figure 9-12. The computePremium() method does not execute until the user clicks the calcButton. At that point, the user's choices are sent to the method and used to calculate the premium amount.

```
public static void computePremium()
   // Declarations
      num HEALTH_AMT = 500
      num HIGH_AGE = 100
      num SMOKER = 250
      num AUTO_AMT = 750
      num HIGH_TICKETS = 400
      num HIGH_AGE_DRIVER_DISCOUNT = 200
      num premiumAmount
   if healthRadioButton.getChecked() then
      premiumAmount = HEALTH_AMT
      if highAgeRadioButton.getChecked() then
         premiumAmount = premiumAmount + HIGH_AGE
      endif
      if smokeYesRadioButton.getChecked() then
         premiumAmount = premiumAmount + SMOKER
      endif
   else
      premiumAmount = AUTO_AMT
      if highTicketsRadioButton.getChecked() then
         premiumAmount = premiumAmount + HIGH_TICKETS
      endif
      if highAgeRadioButton.getChecked() then
         premiumAmount = premiumAmount - HIGH_AGE_DRIVER_DISCOUNT
      endif
   endif
   premAmtLabel.setText(premiumAmount)
   screen1.remove()
   screen2.display()
return
```

Figure 9-12 Pseudocode for `computePremium()` method for insurance premium program

The pseudocode in Figure 9-12 should look very familiar to you—it declares numeric constants and a variable and uses decision-making logic you have used since the early chapters of this book. After the premium is calculated based on the user's choices, it is placed in the label that appears on the second screen. The basic structures of sequence, selection, and looping will continue to serve you well, whether you are programming in a procedural or event-driven environment.

The last two statements in the `computePremium()` method indicate that after the insurance premium is calculated and placed in its label, the first screen is removed and the second screen is displayed. Screen removal and display are accomplished differently in different languages; this example assumes that the appropriate methods are named `remove()` and `display()`.

Two more methods are needed to complete the insurance premium program. These methods include the first method that executes when the program starts and the last method that executes when the program ends. For this example, the first method is called main(). In many GUI languages, the process is slightly more complicated, but the general logic appears in Figure 9-13. The final method in the program is associated with the exitButton on screen2. In Figure 9-13, this method is called exitRoutine(). In this program, the initialization method sets up the first screen and the last method removes the last screen.

```
public static void main()
    screen1.display()
return

public static void exitRoutine()
    screen2.remove()
return
```

Figure 9-13   The main() and exitRoutine() methods for the insurance program

With most OOP languages, you must **register**, or sign up, methods that will react to user-initiated events. The details vary among languages, but the basic process is to write a statement that links the appropriate method (such as the computePremium() or exitRoutine() method) with an event such as a user's button click. In many development environments, the statement that registers a method to react to a user-initiated event is written for you automatically when you click components while designing your screen.

Understanding Threads and Multithreading

A **thread** is the flow of execution of one set of program statements. When you execute a program statement by statement, from beginning to end, you are following a thread. Many applications follow a single thread; this means that the application executes only a single program statement at a time. If a computer has more than one central processing unit (CPU), then each can execute a thread at the same time. However, if a computer has a single CPU and the system supports only single threading, then tasks must occur one at a time. For example, Figure 9-14 shows how three tasks might execute in a single thread in a computer with a single CPU. Each task must end before the next task starts.

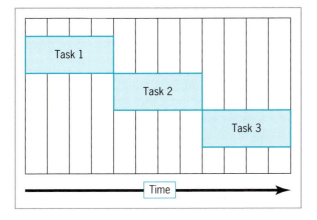

Figure 9-14 Executing multiple tasks as single threads in a single-processor system

Even if the computer has only one CPU, all major OOP languages allow you to launch, or start, multiple threads of execution by using a technique known as **multithreading**. With multithreading, threads share the CPU's time, as shown in Figure 9-15. The CPU devotes a small amount of time to one task, and then devotes a small amount of time to another. The CPU never actually performs two tasks at the same instant. Instead, it performs a piece of one task and then part of another. The CPU performs so quickly that each task seems to execute without interruption.

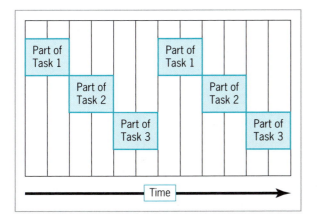

Figure 9-15 Executing multiple threads in a single-processor system

Perhaps you have seen an expert chess player participate in games with several opponents at once. The expert makes a move on the first chess board, and then moves to the second board against a second opponent while the first opponent analyzes his next move. The master can move to the third board, make a move, and return to the first board before the first opponent is even ready to respond. To the first opponent, it might seem as though the expert is devoting all of his time to the first game. Because the expert is so fast, he can play other opponents while the first opponent contemplates his next move. Executing multiple threads on a single CPU is a similar process. The CPU transfers its attention from thread to thread so quickly that the tasks don't even "miss" the CPU's attention.

You use multithreading to improve the performance of your programs. Multithreaded programs often run faster, but more importantly, they are more user-friendly. With a multithreaded program, a user can continue to make choices by clicking buttons while the program is reading a data file. An animated figure can appear on one part of the screen while the user makes menu selections elsewhere on the screen. When you use the Internet, the benefits of multithreading increase. For example, you can begin to read a long text file, watch a video, or listen to an audio file while the file is still downloading. Web users are likely to abandon a site if they cannot use it before a lengthy downloading process completes. When you use multithreading to perform concurrent tasks, you are more likely to retain visitors to your Web site—this is particularly important if your site sells a product or service.

Programmers sometimes describe thread execution as a *lightweight process* because it is not a full-blown program. Rather, a thread must run within the context of a full, heavyweight program.

Writing good code to execute multithreading requires skill. Without careful coding, problems can arise such as **deadlock**, in which two or more threads wait for each other to execute, and **starvation**, in which a thread is abandoned because other threads occupy all the computer's resources.

When threads share an object, special care is needed to avoid unwanted results. For example, consider a customer order program in which two clerks are allowed to fill orders concurrently. Imagine the following scenario:

- The first clerk accesses an inventory file and tells a customer that one item is left.

- A second clerk accesses the file and tells a different customer that one item is left.

- The first customer places an order, and inventory is reduced to 0.

- The second customer places an order, and inventory is reduced to −1.

Two items have been ordered, but only one exists, and the inventory file is now incorrect. There will be confusion in the warehouse, problems in the Accounting Department, and one unsatisfied customer. Similar problems can occur in programs that reserve airline seats or concert tickets. OOP languages provide sophisticated techniques, known as **thread synchronization**, that help avoid these potential problems.

Object-oriented languages often contain a built-in `Thread` class that contains methods to help handle and synchronize multiple threads. For example, a `sleep()` method is frequently used to pause program execution for a specified amount of time. Computer processing speed is so rapid that sometimes you have to slow down processing for human consumption. The next section describes one application that frequently requires a `sleep()` method—computer animation.

Watch the video *Threads and Multithreading*.

Creating Animation

Animation is the rapid sequence of still images, each slightly different from the previous one, that produces the illusion of movement. Many object-oriented languages offer built-in classes that contain methods you can use to draw geometric figures. The methods typically have names like `drawLine()`, `drawCircle()`, `drawRectangle()`, and so on. You place figures on the screen based on a graphing coordinate system. Each component has a horizontal, or **x-axis**, position as well as a vertical, or **y-axis**, position on the screen. The upper-left corner of a display is position 0, 0. The first, or **x-coordinate**, value increases as you travel from left to right across the window. The second, or **y-coordinate**, value increases as you travel from top to bottom. Figure 9-16 shows four screen coordinate positions.

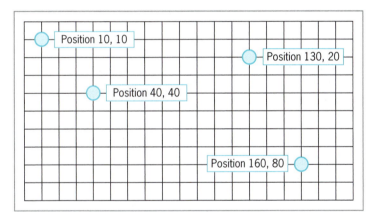

Figure 9-16 Selected screen coordinate positions

Cartoonists create animated films by drawing a sequence of frames or cells. These individual drawings are shown to the audience in rapid succession to give the illusion of natural movement. You create computer animation using the same techniques. However, modern computers are so fast that if you display computer images as quickly as your CPU can process them, you might not be able to see anything. Most computer animation employs a `Thread` class `sleep()` method to pause for short intervals between animation cells, so the human brain has time to absorb each image's content.

As a simple example, Figure 9-17 shows pseudocode for a `MovingCircle` class. As its name implies, the class moves a circle across the screen. The class contains data fields to hold x- and y-coordinates that identify the location at which a circle appears. The constants `SIZE` and `INCREASE` define the size of the first circle drawn and the relative increase in size and position of each subsequent circle. The `MovingCircle` class assumes you are working with a language that provides a `drawCircle()` method, which creates the circle when given parameters for horizontal and vertical positions and radius. Assuming you are working with a language that provides a `sleep()` method to accept a pause time in milliseconds, the SLEEP_TIME constant provides a 100-millisecond gap before the production of each new circle.

```
class MovingCircle
    // Declarations
        private num x = 20
        private num y = 20
        private num SIZE = 40
        private num INCREASE = SIZE / 10
        private num SLEEP_TIME = 100

    public static void main()
        while true
            repaintScreen()
        endwhile
    return

    public static void repaintScreen()
        drawCircle(x, y, x + SIZE)
        x = x + INCREASE
        y = y + INCREASE
        sleep(SLEEP_TIME)
    return
endClass
```

Figure 9-17 The `MovingCircle` class

The `main()` method in the `MovingCircle` class executes a continuous loop. A similar technique is used in many languages that support GUI interfaces. Program execution will cease only when the user quits the application—by clicking a window's Close button, for example. In the `repaintScreen()` method of the `MovingCircle` class, a circle is drawn at the x, y position, then x and y are both increased. The application sleeps for one-tenth of a second (the SLEEP_TIME value), and then the `repaintScreen()` method draws a new circle more to the right, further down, and a little larger. The effect is a moving circle that leaves a trail of smaller circles behind as it moves diagonally across the screen. Figure 9-18 shows the output as a Java version of the application executes.

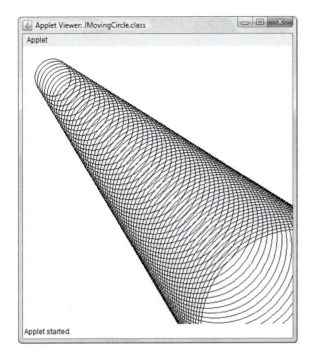

Figure 9-18 Output of the `MovingCircle` application

Although an object-oriented language might make it easy to draw geometric shapes, you also can substitute a variety of more sophisticated, predrawn animated images to achieve the graphic effects you want within your programs. An image is loaded in a separate thread of execution, which allows program execution to continue while the image loads. This is a significant advantage because loading a large image can be time-consuming.

 Many animated images are available on the Web for you to use freely. Use your search engine and keywords such as *gif files*, *jpeg files*, and *animation* to find sources for shareware and freeware files.

 Watch the video *Animation*.

Chapter Summary

- Interacting with a computer operating system from the command line is difficult; it is easier to use an event-driven graphical user interface (GUI), in which users manipulate objects such as buttons and menus. Within an event-driven program, a component from which an event is generated is the source of the event. A listener is an object that is "interested in" an event to which you want it to respond.

- Possible events that a user can initiate include a key press, mouse point, click, right-click, double-click, and drag. Common GUI components include labels, text boxes, check boxes, option buttons, list boxes, and buttons. GUI components are excellent examples of the best principles of OOP; they represent objects with attributes and methods that operate like black boxes.

- When you create a program that uses a GUI, the interface should be natural, predictable, attractive, easy to read, and nondistracting. It's helpful if the user can customize your applications. The program should be forgiving, and you should not forget that the GUI is only a means to an end.

- Developing an event-driven application requires more steps than developing other programs, including creating storyboards, defining objects, and defining the connections between the screens the user will see.

- A thread is the flow of execution of one set of program statements. Many applications follow a single thread; using multiple threads of execution is known as multithreading.

- You create computer animation by drawing a sequence of images that are shown in rapid succession. Many object-oriented languages contain built-in classes that contain methods you can use to draw geometric figures on the screen. Each component has a horizontal, or x-axis, position as well as a vertical, or y-axis, position on the screen.

Key Terms

An **operating system** is the software that you use to run a computer and manage its resources.

The **DOS prompt** is the command line in the DOS operating system.

Icons are small pictures on the screen that the user can select with a mouse.

An **event** is an occurrence that generates a message sent to an object.

GUI programs are called **event-driven** or **event-based** because actions occur in response to user-initiated events such as clicking a mouse button.

The **source of an event** is the component from which the event is generated.

A **listener** is an object that is "interested in" an event to which you want it to respond.

A **pixel** is a picture element, or one of the tiny dots of light that form a grid on your screen.

Accessibility issues are the screen design concerns that make programs easier to use for people with physical limitations.

A **storyboard** represents a picture or sketch of a screen the user will see when running a program.

An **object dictionary** is a list of the objects used in a program, including which screens they are used on and whether any code, or script, is associated with them.

An **interactivity diagram** shows the relationship between screens in an interactive GUI program.

A **container** is a class of objects whose main purpose is to hold other elements—for example, a window.

To **register** a method is to sign it up so that it will react to user-initiated events.

A **thread** is the flow of execution of one set of program statements.

Multithreading is using multiple threads of execution.

Deadlock is a flaw in multithreaded programs in which two or more threads wait for each other to execute.

Starvation is a flaw in multithreaded programs in which a thread is abandoned because other threads occupy all the computer's resources.

Thread synchronization is a set of techniques that coordinates threads of execution to help avoid potential multithreading problems.

Animation is the rapid sequence of still images, each slightly different from the previous one, that produces the illusion of movement.

The **x-axis** represents horizontal positions in a screen window.

The **y-axis** represents vertical positions in a screen window.

The **x-coordinate** value increases as you travel from left to right across a window.

The **y-coordinate** value increases as you travel from top to bottom across a window.

Review Questions

1. Compared to using a command line, an advantage to using an operating system that employs a GUI is _____.

   a. you can interact directly with the operating system
   b. you do not have to deal with confusing icons
   c. you do not have to memorize complicated commands
   d. all of the above

2. When users can initiate actions by clicking the mouse on an icon, the program is _____ -driven.

   a. event   c. command
   b. prompt   d. incident

3. A component from which an event is generated is the _____ of the event.

   a. base   c. listener
   b. icon   d. source

4. An object that responds to an event is a _____.

   a. source   c. transponder
   b. listener   d. snooper

5. All of the following are user-initiated events except a _____.

   a. key press   c. right-mouse click
   b. key drag   d. mouse drag

6. All of the following are typical GUI components except a _____.

   a. label   c. list box
   b. text box   d. button box

7. GUI components operate like _____.

   a. black boxes   c. looping structures
   b. procedural functions   d. command lines

8. Which of the following is *not* a principle of good GUI design?

   a. The interface should be predictable.
   b. The fancier the screen design, the better.
   c. The program should be forgiving.
   d. The user should be able to customize your applications.

9. Which of the following aspects of a GUI layout is most predictable and natural for the user?

    a. A menu bar runs down the right side of the screen.
    b. *Help* is the first option on a menu.
    c. A dollar sign icon represents saving a file.
    d. Pressing *Esc* allows the user to cancel a selection.

10. In most GUI programming environments, you can change all of the following attributes of most components except their _____ .

    a. color
    b. screen location
    c. size
    d. You can change all of these attributes.

11. Depending on the programming language, you might _____ to change a screen component's attributes.

    a. use an assignment statement
    b. call a method
    c. enter a value into a list of properties
    d. all of the above

12. When you create an event-driven application, which of the following must be done before defining objects?

    a. Plan the logic.   c. Test the program.
    b. Create storyboards.   d. Code the program.

13. A _____ is a sketch of a screen the user will see when running a program.

    a. flowchart   c. storyboard
    b. hierarchy chart   d. tale timber

14. A list of objects used in a program is an object _____ .

    a. thesaurus   c. index
    b. glossary   d. dictionary

15. A(n) _____ diagram shows the connections between the various screens a user might see during a program's execution.

    a. interactivity   c. cooperation
    b. help   d. communication

16. The flow of execution of one set of program statements is a ——————— .

   a. thread   c. path
   b. string   d. route

17. When a computer contains a single CPU, it can execute ——————— computer instruction(s) at a time.

   a. one   c. an unlimited number of
   b. several   d. from several to thousands of

18. Each component on a screen has a horizontal, or ——————— , position as well as a vertical position.

   a. x-axis   c. v-axis
   b. y-axis   d. h-axis

19. You create computer animation by ——————— .

   a. drawing an image and setting its animation property to true
   b. drawing a single image and executing it on a multiprocessor system
   c. drawing a sequence of frames that is shown in rapid succession
   d. Animation is not used in computer applications.

20. You can use sophisticated, predrawn animated images to achieve graphic effects within your programs ——————— .

   a. by loading them in a separate thread of execution
   b. only by subscribing to expensive imaging services
   c. with multiprocessing systems, but not on a computer with a single processor
   d. two of the above

Exercises

1. Take a critical look at three GUI applications you have used—for example, a spreadsheet, a word-processing program, and a game. Describe how well each conforms to the GUI design guidelines listed in this chapter.

2. Select one element of poor GUI design in a program you have used. Describe how you would improve the design.

3. Select a GUI program that you have never used before. Describe how well it conforms to the GUI design guidelines listed in this chapter.

4. Design the storyboards, interactivity diagram, object dictionary, and any necessary scripts for an interactive program for customers of Wall-to-Wall Floor Solutions.

Allow customers the option of choosing carpeting ($12 per square foot), ceramic tile ($15 per square foot), or hardwood ($18 per square foot). Let the customer use text boxes to enter the length and width of the room in feet. After the customer clicks an Order Now button, display the price of the order.

5. Design the storyboards, interactivity diagram, object dictionary, and any necessary scripts for an interactive program for customers of Flicks Online, a service that delivers movies to cable subscribers.

Allow customers the option of five featured movie titles, each with a unique price. For an extra $1, the customer can have Flicks Online select a movie from a chosen genre (Drama, Comedy, or Action). After the customer clicks the Order Now button, display the price of the movie rental.

6. Design the storyboards, interactivity diagram, object dictionary, and any necessary scripts for an interactive program for customers of The Complete Dinner Experience.

Allow customers to choose an appetizer, entree, and dessert. Customers choose from three options to select each course; each option has a unique price. After the customer clicks a Select button, display the price of the meal.

Case Projects

Case: Cost Is No Object

1. In earlier chapters, you developed classes needed for Cost Is No Object—a car rental service. You created the logic for the following classes: Name, Address, Date, Employee, Customer, Automobile, and RentalAgreement.

Design an interactive application that displays the following:

- A main screen containing at least the company name, an animated image, and two buttons. One button allows the rental agent to proceed to a data entry screen and enter customer data (name, address, and so on). The other button allows the agent to enter rental agreement data.

- A customer data entry screen

- A rental agreement data entry screen

Create storyboards, define the objects you need, and define the connections between the screens.

Case: Classic Reunions

2. In earlier chapters, you developed classes needed for Classic Reunions—a reunion planning service. You created the logic for the following classes: Name, School, Address, Date, ContactPerson, Employee, Party, and PartyAgreement.

    Design an interactive application that displays the following:

    - A main screen containing at least the company name, an animated image, and two buttons. One button allows a party consultant to proceed to a data entry screen and enter contact person data (name, address, and so on). The other button allows the party consultant to enter party data.

    - A contact person data entry screen

    - A party data entry screen

    Create storyboards, define the objects you need, and define the connections between the screens.

Case: The Barking Lot

3. In earlier chapters, you developed classes needed for The Barking Lot—a dog-boarding facility. You created the logic for the following classes: Dog, Name, Address, Employee, Owner, Date, and BoardingContract.

    Design an interactive application that displays the following:

    - A main screen containing at least the company name, an animated image, and two buttons. One button allows a kennel employee to proceed to a data entry screen and enter dog data. The other button allows the employee to enter boarding contract data.

    - A dog data entry screen

    - A boarding contract data entry screen

    Create storyboards, define the objects you need, and define the connections between the screens.

Up for Discussion

1. Making exciting, entertaining, professional-looking GUI applications becomes easier once you learn to include graphics images. You can copy these images from many locations on the Web. Should there be any restrictions on their use? Does it make a difference if you are writing programs for your own enjoyment as opposed to putting them on the Web where others can see them? Is using photographs different from using drawings? Does it matter if the photographs contain recognizable people? Would you impose any restrictions on images posted to your organization's Web site?

2. Playing computer games has been shown to increase the level of dopamine in the human brain. High levels of this substance are associated with addiction to drugs. Suppose that you work for a computer game company that decides to research how its products can produce more dopamine in the brains of players. Would you support the company's decision?

3. When people use interactive programs on the Web, do you feel it is appropriate to track which buttons they click or to record the data they enter? When is it appropriate, and when is it not? Does it matter how long the data is stored? Does it matter if a profit is made from using the data?

4. Should there be limits on Web content? Consider sites that might display pornography, child abuse, suicide, or the assassination of a political leader. Does it make a difference if the offensive images are shown as animation?

Exception Handling

In this chapter, you will learn about:

◎ Exceptions

◎ The limitations of traditional error handling

◎ Trying code and catching exceptions

◎ Throwing and catching multiple exceptions

◎ Using the `finally` block

◎ The advantages of exception handling

◎ Tracing exceptions through the call stack

◎ Creating your own exceptions

Learning About Exceptions

An **exception** is an unexpected or error condition that occurs while a program is running. The programs you write can generate many types of potential exceptions, including the following:

- The program issues a command to read a file from a disk, but the file does not exist there.

- The program attempts to write data to a disk, but the disk is full.

- The program asks for user input, but the user enters invalid data.

- The program attempts to divide a value by 0.

- The program tries to access an array using a subscript that is too large.

- The program calculates a value that exceeds the limit of its variable type.

These errors are called exceptions because they are not usual occurrences; they are "exceptional." The object-oriented techniques to manage such errors comprise the group of techniques known as **exception handling**. Sometimes, computer programs generate errors from which the programmer cannot write code to recover. For example, a power failure might interrupt production of your paycheck. Exception handling does not deal with these kinds of errors; its concern is predictable errors. Providing for exceptions involves an oxymoron; you must expect the unexpected.

For example, Figure 10-1 contains a `dividingMethod()` method that displays the result of dividing two parameters. When this method executes, it's possible that an attempt will be made to divide by 0. Dividing by 0 is an error in every programming language because the operation is not defined mathematically. Of course, you never should write a method that purposely divides a value by 0. However, this situation certainly could occur by accident—for example, if the variable used as a divisor gets its value as the result of user input.

```
public static void dividingMethod(num dividend, num divisor)
   // Declarations
      num result
   result = dividend / divisor
   output "Result is ", result
return
```

Figure 10-1   Method that might divide by 0

In Figure 10-1, the method fails to execute if the `divisor` value is 0. When this error occurs, the application that calls the method typically terminates, control returns to the operating system, and an error message is generated. The method has generated an exception object and the operating system describes it for you. For example, Figure 10-2 shows a message generated when the program that divides by 0 is implemented in Java. The message explains that an `ArithmeticException` object has been created, and it cites the reason as / *by zero*. In Java, an `ArithmeticException` is an object that is a member of the `RuntimeException` class, which in turn is a child class of a built-in class named `Exception`. Like all objects, exceptions encapsulate data and methods.

```
Command Prompt

C:\Java>java DivisionDemo
Exception in thread "main" java.lang.ArithmeticException: / by zero
        at DivisionDemo.dividingMethod(DivisionDemo.java:10)
        at DivisionDemo.main(DivisionDemo.java:5)

C:\Java>_
```

Figure 10-2 Exception message generated in Java when program attempts to divide by 0

When a method in an object-oriented program causes an exception such as dividing by 0, the method **throws the exception**; you can picture the program tossing out an `Exception` object that "someone else" (another method or the operating system) might handle. Just because a program throws an exception, you don't necessarily have to deal with it. In the `dividingMethod()` method, you can simply let the offending program terminate, as shown in Figure 10-2.

However, program termination is abrupt and unforgiving. When a program divides two numbers (or performs a less trivial task such as balancing a checkbook), the user might be annoyed if the program ends abruptly. However, if the program is used for air-traffic control or to monitor a patient's vital statistics during surgery, an abrupt conclusion could be disastrous. You can handle exceptions either in a traditional or object-oriented manner, but object-oriented exception handling provides safer, more elegant solutions.

The exceptions automatically created and thrown differ by programming language, but some typical examples are:

- `ArithmeticException` or `DivideByZeroException`, thrown when an attempt to divide by 0 occurs

- `ArrayTypeMismatchException`, thrown when you attempt to store an object of the wrong data type in an array

- `IndexOutOfRangeException`, thrown when you attempt to access an array with an invalid subscript

- `NullReferenceException`, thrown when an object reference does not correctly refer to a created object

- `OverflowException`, thrown when an arithmetic operation produces a value greater than the assigned memory location can accommodate

Even though a method might throw exceptions, they are created and thrown only occasionally, when something goes wrong. Programmers sometimes call a situation in which nothing goes wrong the **sunny day case**.

Until you have significant programming experience, it can be difficult to predict all the possible exceptions that might be thrown by a segment of code. The documentation that supports each language describes possible exceptions for the language's built-in methods. Additionally, some integrated development environments assist you as you write a program by displaying messages that describe possible exceptions your code might generate.

Understanding the Limitations of Traditional Error Handling

Programmers had to deal with error conditions long before object-oriented methods were conceived. Probably the most common error-handling solution has been to require a decision before working with a value that might cause an error. For example, you can change the dividingMethod() method to avoid division if the divisor is 0, as shown in Figure 10-3.

```
public static void dividingMethod(num dividend, num divisor)
   // Declarations
      num result
   if divisor = 0 then
      output "Cannot divide by 0"
   else
      result = dividend / divisor
      output "result is ", result
   endif
return
```

Figure 10-3 The dividingMethod() method using a traditional error-handling technique

In the method in Figure 10-3, the division operation only occurs when the divisor value is not 0. An error message is displayed if the divisor is 0. Alternatively, you could force the divisor to 1 or some other acceptable value before dividing, avoiding the error. Another possibility would be to insert a loop into the method and continuously prompt the user to enter a divisor value; the loop would execute until the user entered a value other than 0. In short, you have several options for avoiding the abrupt termination of the dividingMethod() method.

A drawback to using these alternative approaches is that a client must accept the dividingMethod() method's chosen way of handling the error. A method that prompts for a new value is not useful in an application that gets its values from a file instead of a user, so the client might prefer to force the divisor to 1. However, a method that forces the divisor to

1 might be wrong for other applications. In short, using a traditional error-handling method to avoid dividing by 0 prevents the error, but it can make the method inflexible. Programmers might have to write multiple versions of the method to fit different client needs, wasting time and money.

Exception handling provides a more elegant solution for handling error conditions. In object-oriented methods, you detect errors but allow the client to handle them appropriately. In object-oriented terminology, a client *tries* some code that might cause an error. The code that detects an error condition *throws an exception*, and you can create a block of code that *catches the exception* and takes appropriate action.

Trying Code and Catching Exceptions

When you create a segment of code in which something might go wrong, you place the code in a **try block**, which is a block of code you attempt to execute while acknowledging that an exception might occur. A try block consists of the keyword try followed by any number of statements, some of which might cause exceptions. (Some of the statements might be method calls, and the methods might throw exceptions.) If a statement in the block causes an exception, the remaining statements in the try block do not execute and the try block is abandoned. For pseudocode purposes, you can end a try block with a sentinel such as endtry.

You almost always code at least one catch block immediately following a try block. A **catch block** is a segment of code written to handle an exception that might be thrown by the try block that precedes it. A **throw statement** sends an exception object out of a method so it can be handled elsewhere. Each catch block can "catch" one type of exception—that is, one object of the type Exception or one of its child classes. You create a catch block using the following elements:

- The keyword catch followed by parentheses that contain an Exception type and an identifier
- Statements that take the action to handle the error condition
- An endcatch statement that indicates the end of the catch block in the pseudocode

In some object-oriented programming languages, notably C++, you can throw a number or string as well as an exception.

Figure 10-4 shows the general format of a method that includes a shaded try...catch pair. In the figure, theExceptionThatWasThrown represents an object of the Exception class or any of its subclasses. If an exception occurs during the execution of the try block, an Exception object is generated and sent to the catch block, where it becomes known by the identifier in the catch statement. The statements in the catch block then execute. If no exception occurs within the try block (in other words, if the logic reaches endtry), the catch block does not execute. Either way, the statements following the catch block execute normally.

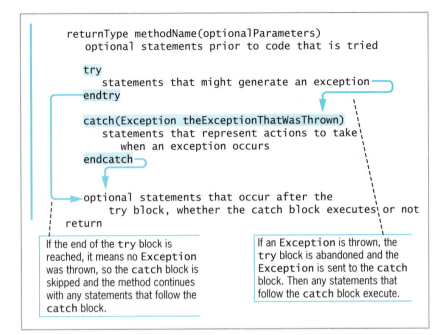

```
returnType methodName(optionalParameters)
    optional statements prior to code that is tried

    try
        statements that might generate an exception
    endtry

    catch(Exception theExceptionThatWasThrown)
        statements that represent actions to take
            when an exception occurs
    endcatch

    optional statements that occur after the
        try block, whether the catch block executes or not
    return
```

If the end of the try block is reached, it means no Exception was thrown, so the catch block is skipped and the method continues with any statements that follow the catch block.

If an Exception is thrown, the try block is abandoned and the Exception is sent to the catch block. Then any statements that follow the catch block execute.

Figure 10-4   General format of a try...catch pair

A catch block looks like a method named catch() that takes an argument that is some type of exception. However, it is not a method; it has no return type and you can't call it directly.

Figure 10-5 shows a rewritten dividingMethod() method with a try block that attempts division. When illegal division by 0 takes place, an Exception object that contains information about the error is created automatically. When the exception is created and thrown, the catch block executes; it follows the try block and contains an Exception parameter.

```
public static void dividingMethod(num dividend, num divisor)
    // Declarations
        num result

    try
        result = dividend / divisor
        output "result is ", result
    endtry

    catch(Exception mistake)
        output "Cannot divide by 0"
    endcatch
return
```

Figure 10-5   The dividingMethod() method with a try...catch pair

When you learn a programming language, you will learn about subclasses of Exception that you might want to use in your code. For example, you saw in Figure 10-2 that in Java, an ArithmeticException is created automatically. Therefore, in the code in Figure 10-5, you could catch a more specific ArithmeticException instead of the more general Exception.

If the division-by-0 error occurs in Figure 10-5, an Exception object is created automatically and thrown to the catch block. The programmer did not have to write a throw statement; the throw operation occurred implicitly. Later in this chapter, you will see methods in which the programmer explicitly throws an exception. In this application, the try block and its throw operation reside in the same method as the catch block. This is not much different from including an if...else pair to handle the mistake. Later in this chapter, you will learn that try blocks, throw statements, and their corresponding catch blocks frequently reside in separate methods, which increases the client's flexibility in error handling.

In the method in Figure 10-5, the parameter mistake in the catch block is an object of type Exception. The object is not used within this catch block, but it could be. For example, depending on the language, the Exception class might contain a method named getMessage() that returns a string with details about the cause of the error. In that case, you could place a statement such as the following in the catch block:

```
output mistake.getMessage()
```

The message generated by this built-in method would be similar to / by zero. As you will recall from the Java example in Figure 10-2, this message is generated when exception handling occurs automatically.

Watch the video *Throwing and Catching an Exception.*

Throwing and Catching Multiple Exceptions

You can place as many statements as you need within a try block, and you can catch as many exceptions as you want. If you try more than one statement, only the first error-generating statement throws an exception. As soon as the exception occurs, logical control is transferred to the catch block, and the remaining statements in the try block are not executed.

When a program contains multiple catch blocks, they are examined in sequence until a match is found for the type of exception that occurred. Then, the matching catch block executes and each remaining catch block is bypassed.

For example, consider the application in Figure 10-6. The main() method in the TwoMistakes class throws two types of exceptions: ArithmeticExceptions and IndexOutOfBoundsExceptions. (An IndexOutOfBoundsException occurs when an array subscript is not within the allowed range.)

In some programming languages, notably C++, exceeding an array's bounds is not an exception. That is, the programmer can access memory outside of the array, even though it is a logical error. However, in newer object-oriented languages such as Visual Basic, Java, and C#, exceeding an array's bounds generates an exception.

The TwoMistakes class declares a numeric array with three elements. In the main() method, the try block executes. At the first statement within the try block (shaded), an exception occurs because the divisor in the division problem, values[1], is 0. The try block is abandoned and logical control is transferred to the first catch block (shaded). Division by 0 causes an ArithmeticException; because the first catch block receives an ArithmeticException, which has the local name mistake1, the message *Arithmetic mistake* is displayed. In this example, the second statement in the try block is never attempted, and the second catch block is skipped.

```
public class TwoMistakes
    public static void main()
        // Declarations
            num values[3] = 4, 0, 0

        try
            values[2] = values[0] / values[1]
            values[2] = values[3] / values[0]
        endtry

        catch(ArithmeticException mistake1)
            output "Arithmetic mistake"
        endcatch

        catch(IndexOutOfBoundsException mistake2)
            output "Index mistake"
        endcatch

    return
endclass
```

Figure 10-6 The TwoMistakes class

By making a minor change, you can force execution of the second catch block, the one with the IndexOutOfBoundsException argument. For example, you can force the division in the try block to succeed by substituting a nonzero value for the divisor in the first shaded arithmetic statement in the try block, as shown in Figure 10-7. Alternatively, you could reverse the positions of the two arithmetic statements or comment out the first statement. With any of these changes, division by 0 does not take place. In the code in Figure 10-7, the first statement in the try block succeeds, and the logic proceeds to the second statement in the `try` block. This shaded statement attempts to access the fourth element of a three-element array, so it throws an `IndexOutOfBoundsException`. The `try` block is abandoned, and the first `catch` block is examined and found unsuitable because it does not catch an `IndexOutOfBoundsException`. The program logic proceeds to the second `catch` block (shaded), whose `Exception` argument type is a match for the thrown exception, so the message *Index mistake* appears.

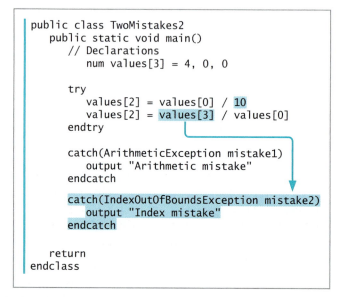

```
public class TwoMistakes2
   public static void main()
      // Declarations
         num values[3] = 4, 0, 0

      try
         values[2] = values[0] / 10
         values[2] = values[3] / values[0]
      endtry

      catch(ArithmeticException mistake1)
         output "Arithmetic mistake"
      endcatch

      catch(IndexOutOfBoundsException mistake2)
         output "Index mistake"
      endcatch

      return
endclass
```

Figure 10-7 The `TwoMistakes2` class

Sometimes, you want to execute the same code no matter which `Exception` type occurs. For example, in the `TwoMistakes2` application in Figure 10-7, each of the two `catch` blocks displays a unique message. If the `ArithmeticException` and `IndexOutOfBoundsException` classes both descend from the same base class, `Exception`, then you can use a single `catch` block to accept both types of objects. Figure 10-8 shows a rewritten `TwoMistakes3` class that uses a single generic `catch` block (shaded) to catch any type of exception.

```
public class TwoMistakes3
    public static void main()
        // Declarations
            num values[3] = 4, 0, 0

        try
            values[2] = values[0] / 10
            values[2] = values[3] / values[0]
        endtry

        catch(Exception mistake)-----------  Any type of
            output "Something went wrong!"    Exception
        endcatch                             ends up here.

    return
endclass
```

Figure 10-8   The TwoMistakes3 class

The catch block in Figure 10-8 accepts a more generic Exception argument type than that thrown by either of the potentially error-causing try statements, so the generic catch block can act as a "catch-all" block. When either an arithmetic or array error occurs, the thrown exception is "promoted" to an Exception error in the catch block. Through inheritance, ArithmeticExceptions and IndexOutOfBoundsExceptions are Exceptions.

When you list multiple catch blocks following a try block, you must be careful that some catch blocks don't become unreachable. **Unreachable code** describes program statements that can never execute under any circumstances. (Unreachable code is also called **dead code**.) For example, if two successive catch blocks catch an IndexOutOfBoundsException and an ordinary exception, the IndexOutOfBoundsException errors will cause the first catch to execute and other exceptions will "fall through" to the more general Exception catch block. However, if you reverse the sequence of the catch blocks so that the code that catches general Exception objects is first, as shown in Figure 10-9, even IndexOutOfBoundsExceptions will be caught by the Exception catch block. In this case, the IndexOutOfBoundsException catch block is unreachable because the Exception catch block is in its way and the class will not compile.

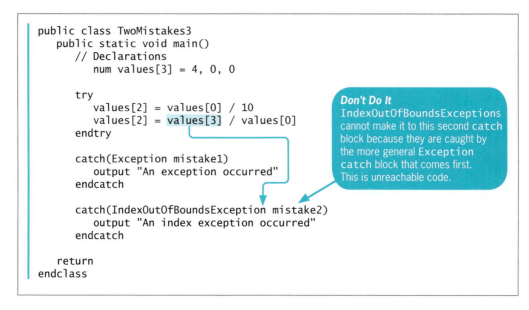

```
public class TwoMistakes3
    public static void main()
        // Declarations
            num values[3] = 4, 0, 0

        try
            values[2] = values[0] / 10
            values[2] = values[3] / values[0]
        endtry

        catch(Exception mistake1)
            output "An exception occurred"
        endcatch

        catch(IndexOutOfBoundsException mistake2)
            output "An index exception occurred"
        endcatch

        return
endclass
```

Don't Do It
IndexOutOfBoundsExceptions cannot make it to this second catch block because they are caught by the more general Exception catch block that comes first. This is unreachable code.

Figure 10-9   The TwoMistakes3 application with unreachable code

Watch the video *Throwing and Catching Multiple Exceptions*.

Using the `finally` Block

When specific actions are needed at the end of a `try…catch` sequence whether an exception was thrown or not, some languages allow you to use a **finally block**. The code within a `finally` block always executes; it does not matter whether the preceding `try` block identified an exception or whether any exceptions were caught. Figure 10-10 shows the format of a `try…catch` sequence that uses a `finally` block.

```
statements before try-catch-finally block starts
try
    statements to try
endtry

catch (Exception e)
    actions that occur if exception was thrown
endcatch

finally
    actions that occur whether catch block executed or not
endfinally

statements after try-catch-finally block is complete
```

Figure 10-10 Format of `try..catch..finally` sequence

Compare Figure 10-10 to Figure 10-4 shown earlier in this chapter. When the `try` code works without error in Figure 10-4, control passes to the statements at the end of the method. Also, when the `try` code fails and throws an exception, and the exception is caught, the `catch` block executes and control again passes to the statements at the end of the method. At first glance, it seems as though the statements at the end of the method always execute. However, the last set of statements in Figure 10-4 might not execute for at least two reasons:

- An unplanned exception might occur, throwing an `Exception` type that no `catch` block is prepared to accept. In this case, the exception would be thrown to the operating system, and program execution would stop immediately.

- The `try` or `catch` block might contain a statement that terminates the program.

A `try` block might throw an exception for which you did not provide a `catch` block. After all, exceptions occur all the time without your involvement, as one would if you attempted division by 0 without `try` and `catch` blocks. In the case of an unhandled exception, program execution stops immediately, the exception is sent to the operating system for handling, and the current method is abandoned. Likewise, the `try` block might contain a statement that stops program execution immediately in the programming language you are using. Additionally, the `try` block might correctly throw an exception to the `catch` block, but the `catch` block might contain a program-ending statement or throw an unhandled exception; either way, the program would end abruptly.

 In several languages, the statement that stops program execution is `exit` or `exit()`.

When you include a `finally` block, you are assured that the `finally` statements will execute before the method is abandoned, even if the method concludes prematurely. For example, programmers often use a `finally` block when the program uses data files that must be closed. Consider the pseudocode in Figure 10-11, which represents part of the logic for a typical file-handling program.

```
try
    Open the input file
    Read the file
    Place the file data in an array
    Calculate an average from the data
    Display the average
endtry

catch (FileException mistake)
    Issue an error message
    Exit
endcatch

finally
    If the file is open, close it
endfinally
```

Figure 10-11   Pseudocode that tries reading a file and handles an exception

 You can avoid using a `finally` block, but you would need repetitious code. For example, instead of using the `finally` block in the pseudocode in Figure 10-11, you could insert *If the file is open, close it* as both the last statement in the `try` block and the second-to-last statement in the `catch` block, just before the `Exit` statement. However, writing code just once in a `finally` block is clearer and less prone to error.

The pseudocode in Figure 10-11 represents an application that opens an input file; if an input file does not exist when you try to open it, most object-oriented languages automatically throw an exception. (This pseudocode assumes that the class that contains file-processing error information is called `FileException`.) However, other exceptions might be generated. For example, you can see in the figure that the application uses an array; therefore, even though the file opened successfully, an uncaught `IndexOutOfBoundsException` might occur. Also, because the application performs division (see the statement *Calculate an average from the data*), an uncaught `ArithmeticException` might occur. In such events, you should close the file before proceeding. By using the `finally` block, you ensure that the file is closed because the code in the `finally` block executes before control returns to the operating system. The code in the `finally` block executes no matter which of the following outcomes occurs in the `try` block:

- The `try` ends normally with no exceptions.

- The `try` throws a `FileException` to the `catch` block, which executes and ends the program.

- Another exception causes the `try` block to be abandoned prematurely. An unanticipated exception would not allow the `try` block to finish, and it might not have a usable `catch` block.

 C#, Java, and Visual Basic all support a `finally` block. C++ does not provide a `finally` block, but it does provide a default "catch all" block that can catch any previously uncaught exceptions.

Many well-designed programs that try code do not include `catch` blocks; instead, they contain only `try-finally` pairs. The `finally` block is used to release resources that other applications might be waiting for, such as database connections.

Understanding the Advantages of Exception Handling

Before the inception of OOP languages, many program errors were handled using somewhat confusing, error-prone techniques. For example, a traditional procedural program might perform three methods that depend on each other using error-checking statements similar to the pseudocode in Figure 10-12.

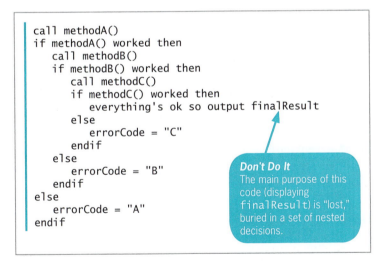

```
call methodA()
if methodA() worked then
    call methodB()
    if methodB() worked then
        call methodC()
        if methodC() worked then
            everything's ok so output finalResult
        else
            errorCode = "C"
        endif
    else
        errorCode = "B"
    endif
else
    errorCode = "A"
endif
```

> **Don't Do It**
> The main purpose of this code (displaying `finalResult`) is "lost," buried in a set of nested decisions.

Figure 10-12 Pseudocode representing traditional error checking—not recommended in OO languages

The pseudocode in Figure 10-12 represents an application in which the logic must pass three tests before a final result can be displayed. The application performs `methodA()`; it then performs `methodB()` only if `methodA()` is successful. Similarly, `methodC()` executes only when `methodA()` and `methodB()` are both successful. When any method fails, the program sets an appropriate errorCode to "A", "B", or "C". (Presumably, the errorCode is used later in the application.) The logic in Figure 10-12 is difficult to follow, and the application's purpose and intended outcome—to display the finalResult—is lost in the maze of if statements. Also, you can easily make coding mistakes because of the complicated nesting and indenting.

Compare the same program logic using the object-oriented, error-handling technique shown in Figure 10-13. Each of the methods, methodA(), methodB(), and methodC(), throws a different type of error that is caught by the appropriate catch block. Using the try...catch object-oriented technique provides the same results as the traditional method, but the statements that do the "real" work (calling methods A, B, and C, and outputting finalResult) are placed together where their logic is easy to follow. The try steps should usually work without generating errors; after all, the errors are "exceptions." It is convenient to see these business-as-usual steps in one location. The unusual, exceptional events are grouped and moved out of the way of the primary action. This makes the program easier to understand and reduces maintenance costs over the life of the program.

```
try
    call methodA()                          Concise list of four
    call methodB()                          major tasks
    call methodC()
    everything's ok so output finalResult
endtry

catch (methodA()'s type of exception)
    errorCode = "A"
endcatch

catch (methodB()'s type of exception)
    errorCode = "B"
endcatch

catch(methodC()'s type of exception)
    errorCode = "C"
endcatch
```

Figure 10-13   Pseudocode representing object-oriented approach to code in Figure 10-12

Besides clarity, an advantage to object-oriented exception handling is the flexibility it allows in handling errors. When a method throws an exception, the same method can catch the exception, although it is not required to do so, and in most object-oriented programs it will not. Often, you won't want a method to handle its own exceptions. In many cases, you want a client to be able to handle the exception in the most appropriate way for its application. Just as a police officer can deal with a speeding driver differently depending on circumstances, your client programs can react to exceptions specifically to suit the current purposes.

Methods are flexible partly because they are reusable—a well-written method might be used by any number of applications. Each calling application might need to handle the same error differently, depending on its purpose. For example, an application that uses a method that divides values might need to terminate if division by 0 occurs. A different program simply might prompt the user to reenter the data, and a third program might force division by 1. The method that contains the division statement can throw the error, but each calling program can assume responsibility for handling the error in an appropriate way.

For example, Figure 10-14 shows a PriceList class used by a company to hold a list of prices for items it sells. For simplicity, the class includes only four prices and a single method that displays the price of a single item. The displayPrice() method accepts an argument to use as the array subscript, and because the subscript could be out of bounds, the method might throw an exception.

```
class PriceList
    // Declarations
        private num price[4] = 15.99, 27.88, 34.56, 45.89

    public static void displayPrice(num item)
        output "The price is $", price[item]
    return
endClass
```

Figure 10-14 The PriceList class

In some languages—for example, Java—if an exception is thrown from one method and caught by another, you must write an **exception specification clause**, which is a statement in the method header that indicates exception types that might be thrown. In C++ you may write an exception specification, but it is not required. C# and Visual Basic do not allow exception specifications.

Figures 10-15 and 10-16 show two applications in which programmers have handled the exception differently. In the first class, PriceListApplication1, the programmer has handled the exception in the shaded catch block by displaying a price of $0. In the second class, PriceListApplication2, the programmer has continued using an input dialog box in the shaded catch block to prompt the user for a new item number until it is within the correct range. Other programmers could choose different actions, but they all can use the flexible displayPrice() method because it throws the error but doesn't limit the calling method's choice of recourse.

```
class PriceListApplication1
    public static void main()
        // Declarations
            num item = 4
        try
            PriceList.displayPrice(item)
        endtry
        catch(IndexOutOfBoundsException mistake)
            output "Price is $0"
        endcatch
    return
endClass
```

Figure 10-15   The PriceListApplication1 class

```
class PriceListApplication2
    public static void main()
        // Declarations
            num item = 4
        try
            PriceList.displayPrice(item)
        endtry
        catch(IndexOutOfBoundsException mistake)
            while item < 0 OR item > 3
                output "Please reenter a value 0, 1, 2 or 3 "
                input item
            endwhile
            PriceList.displayPrice(item)
        endcatch
    return
endClass
```

Figure 10-16   The PriceListApplication2 class

Tracing Exceptions Through the Call Stack

When one method calls another, the computer's operating system must keep track of where the method call came from, and program control must return to the calling method when the called method is completed. For example, if methodA() calls methodB(), the operating system must "remember" to return to methodA() when methodB() ends. Likewise, if methodB() calls methodC() and causes it to execute, the computer must "remember" to return to methodB(), and eventually to methodA(). The memory location known as the **call stack** is where the computer stores the list of method locations to which the system must return.

When a method throws an exception and the same method does not catch it, the exception is thrown to the next method up the call stack—in other words, to the method that called the offending method. Figure 10-17 shows how the call stack works.

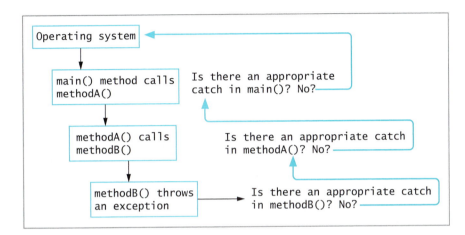

Figure 10-17 Cycling through the call stack

Consider this sequence of events:

1. The operating system starts the program.

2. main() calls methodA().

3. methodA() calls methodB().

4. methodB() throws an exception.

5. The program looks first for an appropriate catch block in methodB().

6. If none exists, the program looks for the same thing in methodA().

7. If methodA() does not have a catch block for the exception, then the program looks to the main() method.

8. If main() doesn't catch the exception, then the program terminates, control is returned to the operating system, and the operating system displays an error message.

This system of passing exceptions through the chain of calling methods has great advantages because it allows methods to handle exceptions where the programmer has decided it is most appropriate—including allowing the operating system to handle the error. However, when a program uses several classes, this system makes it difficult for the programmer to locate the original source of an exception. Many object-oriented languages contain an Exception class method with a name like printStackTrace() that allows you to display a list of methods in the call stack so you can determine the location of the exception. Often, you do not want to place a printStackTrace() method call in a finished program. The typical application user has no interest in the cryptic messages that are displayed. However, while you are developing an application, printing a list of the method calls in the stack can be a useful tool for diagnosing your application's problems.

At the beginning of this chapter, you read about modifying a dividingMethod() to contain a try...catch pair to handle a potential exception. Now that you understand how one method can throw an exception to another that calls it, you can see that instead of modifying dividingMethod() by placing a try...catch pair inside it, you could use the original version of the method but place the call to it within a try block and let the calling method catch any exception.

A Case Study: Tracing the Source of an Exception

To illustrate the usefulness of tracing exceptions through the stack, consider the Tax class in Figure 10-18. Suppose that your company has created or purchased this class to calculate tax rates on products sold. For simplicity, assume that only two tax rates are used—6 percent for sales of $20 or less and 7 percent for sales over $20. The Tax class would be useful for any program involving product sales, except for one flaw: In the shaded statement, the subscript is erroneously set to 2 instead of 1 for the higher tax rate. If this subscript is used with the taxRate array in the next statement, it will be out of bounds. However, assume that this class was purchased as a completed package—it was written and compiled by someone else and you do not even see the code. In other words, it is a black box to you.

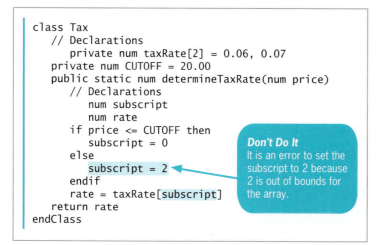

Figure 10-18 The Tax class that contains a mistake

Assume that your company has also created a Prices class, as shown in Figure 10-19. This class contains four prices of items sold by your company. The class contains a single method that accepts an item number (0 through 3 for convenience) and uses it to access one of the prices in the price array. Then, the price is sent to the determineTaxRate() method in the Tax class so the correct tax can be applied. The tax is 6 percent or 7 percent, depending on whether the price is over $20.

```
class Prices
    private num[4] price = 15.99, 27.88, 34.56, 45.89
    public static void displayPrice(num item)
        // Declarations
            num tax
            num total
            num pr
        pr = price[item]
        tax = pr * Tax.determineTaxRate(pr)
        total =  pr + tax
        output "The total price is ", total
    return
endClass
```

This statement uses a method in the Tax class.

Figure 10-19   The Prices class

Suppose that you write the application shown in Figure 10-20. This application asks the user to enter an item number and passes it to Prices.displayPrice(). The program tries the item entry and catches any exception. You created the try...catch pair because if an item number of less than 0 or more than 3 was passed to displayPrice(), the index would be out of range and an exception would be thrown.

```
class PricesApplication
    public static void main()
        // Declarations
            num item
        try
            output "Enter an item number from 0 through 3 >> "
            input item
            Prices.displayPrice(item)
        endtry
        catch(Exception mistake)
            output "Error!"
        endcatch
    return
endClass
```

Your intention is to catch bad item numbers.

Figure 10-20   The PricesApplication class

When you run the program using an out-of-range number such as 5, the shaded *Error!* message in the catch block is displayed. You consider that test to be correct. When you run the program using a valid item number—for example, 1—you might be surprised to see the *Error!* message. To attempt to discover what caused the message, you can replace the catch block statement with a stack trace call such as the following:

```
mistake.printStackTrace()
```

In this statement, mistake is the local name for the Exception object in the catch block and printStackTrace() is a method in the Exception class. For example, when this program is implemented in C#, the output looks like Figure 10-21. From the list of methods, you can see that the error did not come from the displayPrice() method. Rather, it came from the Tax.DetermineTaxRate() method, which was called by the Prices.DisplayPrice() method, which in turn was called by the PricesApplication.Main() method. You might not have considered that the Tax class was the source of the problem because it was provided to you as a working method. If you work in a small organization, you might be allowed to look at the code yourself and fix it. If you work in a larger organization or you purchased the class from an outside vendor, you might be able to contact the programmer or team that created the class for assistance.

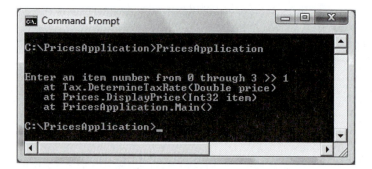

Figure 10-21   Execution of PricesApplication program in which the stack trace is displayed in the catch block

The stack trace in Figure 10-21 was generated by a C# program. The method names listed begin with uppercase letters because that is the convention in C#.

The classes in this example were small to help you follow the discussion. However, a full-blown application might have many more classes that contain many more methods, so displaying the trace of the stack would become increasingly beneficial.

Watch the video *Tracing the Source of an Exception.*

Creating Your Own Exceptions

Many OOP languages provide built-in exception types that inherit from a base Exception class. For example, Java, Visual Basic, and C# each provide dozens of categories of exceptions that you can use in your programs, such as ArithmeticException and IndexOutOfBoundsException. The built-in Exceptions in a programming language cannot account for every condition that might be an exception in your applications. For example, you might want to declare an exception when your bank balance is negative or when an outside party attempts to access your e-mail account. Most organizations have specific rules for exceptional data; for example, an employee number must not exceed three digits, or an hourly salary must not be less than the legal minimum wage. You can handle these potential error situations with if statements, but you also can create your own exceptions.

Even if you never create your own Exception classes, you should become familiar with your language's built-in exceptions so that you understand error messages you might receive during a program's execution.

To create your own throwable exception, you usually extend a built-in Exception class. Depending on the programming language, you might be able to extend from other throwable classes as well as Exception. When you create an exception, the convention is to end its name with Exception. For example, you might create a class named NegativeBankBalanceException or EmployeeNumberTooLargeException. Each would be a subclass of the more general Exception class. By inheriting from the Exception class, you gain access to methods in the parent class, such as those that display a default message describing the exception and that display the stack trace.

For example, Figure 10-22 shows a HighBalanceException class. This example assumes that the parent class contains a setMessage() method that assigns the passed string to a field in the parent class. Also assume that a parent class getMessage() method can retrieve the message. The HighBalanceException class constructor contains a single statement that sets the error message. This string would be retrieved if you called the getMessage() method using a HighBalanceException object.

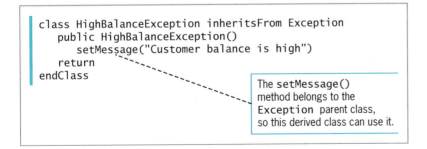

```
class HighBalanceException inheritsFrom Exception
    public HighBalanceException()
        setMessage("Customer balance is high")
    return
endClass
```

The setMessage() method belongs to the Exception parent class, so this derived class can use it.

Figure 10-22 The HighBalanceException class

Figure 10-23 shows a `CustomerAccount` class that uses a `HighBalanceException`. The `CustomerAccount` class contains an account number, a balance, and a constant that stores a limit for customer credit. If the account balance exceeds the limit, an instance of the `HighBalanceException` class is created and thrown (see the shaded statements in the figure).

```
class CustomerAccount
    // Declarations
        private num acctNum
        private num balance
        private num HIGH_CREDIT_LIMIT = 20000.00

    public CustomerAccount(num acct, num bal)
        // Declarations
            HighBalanceException anError
        acctNum = acct
        balance = bal
        if balance > HIGH_CREDIT_LIMIT then
            throw anError
        endif
    return
endClass
```

Figure 10-23   The `CustomerAccount` class

In Figure 10-23, the `HighBalanceException` object is created at the start of the method, following the convention that all declarations are made at the start of methods. If the programming language allows declarations throughout a method, many programmers would not create the object until they determined it was needed, after the `if` statement.

Figure 10-24 shows an application that instantiates a `CustomerAccount`. In this application, a user is prompted for an account number and balance. After those values are entered, an attempt is made to construct a `CustomerAccount` in a `try` block. If the attempt is successful— that is, if the `CustomerAccount` constructor does not throw an exception—the `CustomerAccount` information is displayed. However, if the `CustomerAccount` constructor does throw a `HighBalanceException`, the `catch` block receives it and displays two messages. This `catch` block demonstrates that you can create your own message or use the message that is part of every `HighBalanceException`—the one set in the constructor in Figure 10-22. A different application could take any number of different actions in its `catch` block; for example, it could display only one of the messages, display a different message, construct a new `CustomerAccount` object with a lower balance, or construct a different type of object—perhaps a child of `CustomerAccount` called `PreferredCustomerAccount` that allows a higher balance.

```
public class UseCustomerAccount
    public static void main()
        // Declarations
            num acct
            num balance

        output "Enter account number "
        input acct
        output "Enter balance "
        input balance

        try
            CustomerAccount newAccount(acct, balance)
            output "Customer created"
        endtry

        catch(HighBalanceException hbe)
            output "Customer #", num, "Has a balance that is too high"
            output hbe.getMessage()
        endcatch
    return
endClass
```

In a full-blown application, you might want to perform other tasks at this point. For example, you might want to save CustomerAccount objects to a data file.

Figure 10-24   The UseCustomerAccount class

In Figure 10-24, balance is a local variable in the main() method. When balance is passed to the CustomerAccount constructor, its value is assigned to the parameter bal as defined in the header of the CustomerAccount constructor class. Then, the parameter value is assigned to the balance field in the CustomerAccount class.

In the catch block of the main() method shown in Figure 10-24, the getMessage() method is used with the hbe object. Because the hbe object is a HighBalanceException, which is an Exception, and because the HighBalanceException class defined in Figure 10-22 contains no method named getMessage(), you know that HighBalanceException must inherit the getMessage() method from the more general Exception class (or some other class from which Exception is derived).

You should not create an excessive number of special Exception types for your classes, especially if the language already contains an appropriate exception type. Extra Exception types add complexity for other programmers who use your classes. However, when appropriate, specialized Exception classes provide an elegant way to handle error situations. They enable you to separate error code from the usual, nonexceptional sequence of events, they allow errors to be passed up the stack and traced, and they allow clients of your classes to handle exceptional situations in the manner most suitable for their application.

Exceptions can be particularly useful when you throw them from constructors. Constructors do not have a return type, so they have no other way to send information back to the calling method.

Chapter Summary

- An exception is an unexpected or error condition. Exception handling is the group of object-oriented techniques to manage such errors.

- Exception handling provides an elegant solution for handling error conditions. In object-oriented terminology, you *try* a procedure that might cause an error. A method that detects an error condition *throws an exception*, and the block of code that processes the error *catches the exception*.

- When you create a segment of code in which something might go wrong, you place the code in a try block, which is a block of code you attempt to execute while acknowledging that an exception might occur. You must code at least one catch block immediately following a try block. A catch block is a segment of code written to handle an exception that might be thrown by the try block that precedes it.

- You can place as many statements as you need within a try block, and you can catch as many exceptions as you want. If you try more than one statement, only the first error-generating statement throws an exception. As soon as the exception occurs, logical control is transferred to the catch block; the remaining statements in the try block are not executed. When a program contains multiple catch blocks, they are examined in sequence until a match is found for the type of exception that occurred. Then, the matching catch block executes and each remaining catch block is bypassed.

- When specific actions are needed at the end of a try...catch sequence whether an exception was thrown or not, some languages allow you to use a finally block. Typically, you use a finally block to perform clean-up tasks. The code within a finally block always executes; it does not matter whether the preceding try block identified an exception or whether any exceptions were caught.

- Besides clarity, an advantage to object-oriented exception handling is the flexibility it allows for each calling application to handle the same error appropriately.

- When one method calls another, the computer's operating system must keep track of where the method call came from, and program control must return to the calling method when the called method is completed. The memory location known as the call stack is where the computer stores the list of method locations to which the system must return.

- The built-in exceptions of a programming language cannot account for every condition that might be an exception in your applications, so you can create your own exceptions. Usually you accomplish this by creating a subclass based on a built-in Exception class.

Key Terms

An **exception** is an unexpected or error condition that occurs while a program is running.

Exception handling is an object-oriented technique for managing errors.

Throwing an exception is the process of tossing out an `Exception` object that might be handled by a `catch` block, another method, or the operating system.

A **sunny day case** is a program execution in which no exceptions are thrown.

A **try block** is a block of code you attempt to execute while acknowledging that an exception might occur.

A **catch block** is a segment of code written to handle an exception that might be thrown by the `try` block that precedes it.

A **throw statement** sends an exception out of a method so it can be handled elsewhere.

Unreachable code statements are program statements that can never execute under any circumstances.

Dead code is another term for unreachable code.

A **`finally` block** holds statements that execute at the end of a `try`…`catch` sequence.

An **exception specification clause** is a declaration of a method's possible `throw` types.

The **call stack** is the memory location where the computer stores the list of method locations to which the system must return.

Review Questions

1. In object-oriented programming, an unexpected or error condition is a(n) _____.

   a. anomaly

   b. aberration

   c. deviation

   d. exception

2. A programmer can recover from _____ errors.

   a. all

   b. some

   c. only unpredictable

   d. no

3. When a program might generate an exception, you _____.

   a. must write statements to handle it

   b. must write a class to handle it

   c. can choose to handle it or not

   d. cannot handle it; the operating system must do so

4. Which of the following is *not* typical of a situation in which an exception would be automatically created and thrown?

   a. You attempt to access an array element using an illegal subscript.

   b. You attempt to store an object in an array that is an incorrect data type.

   c. An arithmetic operation produces a value greater than the assigned memory location can accommodate.

   d. You store an employee's Social Security number that contains only eight digits instead of nine.

5. In object-oriented terminology, you _____ a series of steps or a procedure when you think it might throw an exception.

   a. try   c. handle

   b. catch   d. encapsulate

6. A catch block _____ an exception.

   a. tries   c. handles

   b. returns   d. encapsulates

7. If a try block is followed by a catch block and a statement in the try block throws an exception, _____ .

   a. the rest of the statements in the try block execute, and then the catch block executes

   b. the try block is abandoned and the statements in the catch block execute

   c. the catch block executes and then the rest of the statements in the try block execute

   d. the try block is abandoned and control returns to the operating system

8. The segment of code that handles an exception or takes appropriate action after an exception is thrown is a _____ block.

   a. try   c. throws

   b. catch   d. class

9. You _____ within a try block.

   a. must place only a single statement   c. must place at least two statements

   b. can place any number of statements   d. must place a catch block

10. If you try three statements and include three catch blocks, and the second statement throws an exception, _____ .

   a. the first catch block executes

   b. the first two catch blocks execute

   c. only the second catch block executes

   d. the first matching catch block executes

11. When a `try` block does not generate an exception and you have included multiple `catch` blocks, _____ .

   a. they all execute
   b. only the first one executes
   c. only the first matching one executes
   d. no `catch` blocks execute

12. In most languages, a `catch` block that begins `catch(Exception e)` probably can catch `Exceptions` of type _____ .

   a. `IndexOutOfBoundsException`
   b. `ArithmeticException`
   c. both of the above
   d. none of the above

13. The code within a `finally` block executes when the `try` block _____ .

   a. identifies one or more exceptions
   b. does not identify any exceptions
   c. either a or b
   d. neither a nor b

14. An advantage to using a `try...catch` block is that exceptional events are _____ .

   a. eliminated
   b. reduced
   c. integrated with regular events
   d. isolated from regular events

15. Which methods can throw an exception?

   a. only methods with a `throw` statement
   b. only methods with a `catch` block
   c. only methods with both a `throw` statement and a `catch` block
   d. any method

16. The most frequently used object-oriented technique is for a called method that might generate an exception to _____ .

   a. throw the exception to the calling method
   b. handle the exception
   c. either of the above
   d. neither of the above

17. If `method1()` calls `method2()` and `method2()` throws an exception, then _____ .

   a. `method1()` must catch the exception
   b. `method2()` must catch the exception
   c. `method2()` must catch the exception and then throw it to `method1()`
   d. None of the above is true.

18. The memory location where the computer stores the list of method locations to which the system must return is the _____ .

   a. registry   c. chronicle
   b. call stack   d. archive

19. You can get a list of the methods through which an exception has traveled by displaying the method's _____ .

   a. constructor   c. stack trace
   b. getMessage() value   d. path

20. To create your own Exception class, in most object-oriented languages you must create _____ .

   a. a subclass of an existing Exception class
   b. an overloaded constructor for the existing Exception class
   c. a new class that does not descend from any class
   d. additional methods for the class that will throw the new Exception type

Exercises

1. Design an application in which you declare an array of three strings and store three values in the array. Write a try block in which you loop to display each successive element of the array, increasing a subscript by one on each pass through the loop. Assume that an ArrayIndexOutOfBoundsException is created automatically when a subscript is not correct for an array. Create a catch block that catches any exception and displays the message *Now you've gone too far*.

2. Design a class that contains public methods named add(), subtract(), multiply(), and divide(). Each of the methods accepts two numeric arguments and returns a number that represents the result of the appropriate arithmetic operation. Design a main() method that prompts the user for two numbers and tries each of the methods. Assume that a NumberFormatException is automatically created and thrown when a method's argument is not numeric, and that an ArithmeticException is created and thrown if the user attempts to divide by 0. Display an appropriate message when an exception is caught.

3. Design an application that prompts the user to enter a number as an array size, and then attempt to declare an array using the entered size. If the array is created successfully, display an appropriate message. Assume that a NegativeArraySizeException is generated if you attempt to create an array with a negative size, and that a NumberFormatException is generated if you attempt to create an array using a nonnumeric value for the size. Use a catch block that

executes if the array size is nonnumeric or negative and displays a message that the array was not created.

4. Design an application that throws and catches an automatically generated `ArithmeticException` when you attempt to take the square root of a negative value. Prompt the user for an input value and try a `squareRoot()` method that accepts a numeric argument and returns its square root. (You do not need to design the implementation of the `squareRoot()` method.) The application either displays the square root or catches the thrown exception and displays an appropriate message.

5. a. Design an `InventoryException` class whose constructor receives a string that describes an inventory item. Include a `getMessage()` method that returns a string containing the inventory item's data.

   b. Create an `InventoryItem` class with two fields, `description` and `quantity`. The `InventoryItem` constructor requires values for both fields. Upon construction, throw an `InventoryException` if `quantity` is less than 0 or more than 9999.

   c. Write an application that establishes an array of 20 `InventoryItems`. Prompt the user for a description and quantity for each object. Display an appropriate message when an `InventoryItem` is successfully created and when one is not.

6. Write an application for the Carter Clothing Company that displays a series of five product numbers you store in an array: 1122, 2233, 3344, 4455, and 5566. Ask the user to enter a price for each product. Create a `PriceException` class and throw a `PriceException` if the user does not enter a valid price (greater than or equal to 0 and less than or equal to 99). Catch the `PriceException`, display an appropriate message, and store a 0 for the price. At the end of the application, display all the product numbers and their prices.

7. Write an application for the Littletown Real Estate Company that displays a series of 10 property ID numbers you have stored in an array. Ask the user to enter a category for each property: *S* for *Single-family*, *M* for *Multi-family*, or *L* for *Land*. Create an `Exception` class named `PropertyTypeException` that contains an array of valid property types. In your application, throw a `PropertyTypeException` if the user does not enter a valid type. Catch the `PropertyTypeException` and then display an appropriate message. In addition, store a *U* (for *Unknown*) for any property for which an exception is caught. At the end of the application, display all the property IDs and types.

Case Projects

Case: Cost Is No Object

1. In earlier chapters, you developed classes needed for Cost Is No Object—a car rental service that specializes in lending antique and luxury cars to clients on a short-term basis. In Chapter 7, you created the RentalAgreement class to contain all the attributes and methods associated with one rental contract. Specifically, a RentalAgreement contains the following:

- string rentalAgreementNumber
- Customer renter
- Employee rentalAgent
- Date rentalStartDate
- Automobile carRented
- num dailyFee
- num numberOfDaysRented

Now do the following:

- Design a DateException class. The class contains a string field that holds an error message. The constructor accepts a string message that it can return with a getMessage() method.
- Modify the Date class so that its set methods throw an exception when a month is not a valid value (1 through 12) or the day is out of range for the month.
- Design a RentalAgreementException class. The class contains a string field that holds an error message. The constructor accepts a string message that it can return with a getMessage() method.
- Modify the RentalAgreement class so that each set method throws a RentalAgreementException that contains an appropriate message if any of the method's arguments are out of range, according to the following guidelines:
  - The rental agreement number must be a string between "10000" and "99999" inclusive.
  - The customer ID number must be a string between "100" and "999" inclusive.
  - The car ID number must be a string between "100" and "999" inclusive.
  - The starting date for the rental agreement must be valid. In other words, if a DateException object is thrown when the starting date is set, then the starting-date set method should throw a RentalAgreementException.

- The starting date for the rental agreement must not be prior to today's date.

- The number of days rented must be between 1 and 30 days inclusive.

- Design an application that creates an array of 10 `RentalAgreement` objects. In a loop, prompt the user to enter the needed data for each object. If a `RentalAgreementException` is thrown, display the `RentalAgreementException` message and end the application.

- Design a second application that creates an array of 10 `RentalAgreement` objects. In a loop, prompt the user to enter the needed data for each object. If a `RentalAgreementException` is thrown after the user enters data for any field, display the `RentalAgreementException` message and continue to prompt until the user enters a valid value for the erroneous field. After all the objects are entered, display all 10 `RentalAgreement` objects.

- Design a third application that creates an array of 10 `RentalAgreement` objects. In a loop, prompt the user to enter the needed data for each object. If a `RentalAgreementException` is thrown after the user enters data for any field, force the user to reenter all the data for the object until there are 10 valid objects. After all the objects are entered, display all 10 `RentalAgreement` objects.

Case: Classic Reunions

2. In earlier chapters, you developed classes needed for Classic Reunions—a service that manages the details of planning reunion parties. In Chapter 7, you created the `PartyAgreement` class to contain all the attributes and methods associated with one reunion contract. Specifically, a `PartyAgreement` contains the following:

- `string partyAgreementNumber`

- `Party party`

- `Employee partyCoordinator`

- `Date agreementDate`

- `num contractPrice`

Now do the following:

- Design a `DateException` class. The class contains a string field that holds an error message. The constructor accepts a string message that it can return with a `getMessage()` method.

- Modify the `Date` class so that its set methods throw an exception when a month is not a valid value (1 through 12) or the day is out of range for the month.

- Design a `PartyAgreementException` class. The class contains a string field that holds an error message. The constructor accepts a string message that it can return with a `getMessage()` method.

- Modify the `PartyAgreement` class so that each set method throws a `PartyAgreementException` that contains an appropriate message if any of the method's arguments are out of range, according to the following guidelines:

  ◆ The party agreement number must be a string between "10000" and "99999" inclusive.

  ◆ The party ID number must be a string between "100" and "999" inclusive.

  ◆ The party date must be valid. In other words, if a `DateException` object is thrown when the date is set, then the party-date set method should throw a `PartyAgreementException`.

  ◆ The agreement date must be valid.

  ◆ The party date must not be prior to the agreement date.

  ◆ The party coordinator's ID number must be a string between "00" and "99" inclusive.

  ◆ The party coordinator's hire date must be valid.

  ◆ The party coordinator's hire date must not be prior to today's date.

  ◆ The contract price must not be negative.

- Design an application that creates an array of 10 `PartyAgreement` objects. In a loop, prompt the user to enter the needed data for each object. If a `PartyAgreementException` is thrown, display the `PartyAgreementException` message and end the application.

- Design a second application that creates an array of 10 `PartyAgreement` objects. In a loop, prompt the user to enter the needed data for each object. If a `PartyAgreementException` is thrown after the user enters data for any field, display the `PartyAgreementException` message and continue to prompt until the user enters a valid value for the erroneous field. After all the objects are entered, display all 10 `PartyAgreement` objects.

- Design a third application that creates an array of 10 `PartyAgreement` objects. In a loop, prompt the user to enter the needed data for each object. If a `PartyAgreementException` is thrown after the user enters data for any field, force the user to reenter all the data for the object until there are 10 valid objects. After all the objects are entered, display all 10 `PartyAgreement` objects.

Case: The Barking Lot

3. In earlier chapters, you developed classes needed for The Barking Lot—a dog-boarding facility. In Chapter 7, you created the BoardingContract class to contain all the attributes and methods associated with one boarding contract. Specifically, a BoardingContract contains the following:

- Dog dog
- Date boardingStartDate
- num daysToBeBoarded
- Employee caretakerForThisContract
- num totalPriceForBoardingSession

Now do the following:

- Design a DateException class. The class contains a string field that holds an error message. The constructor accepts a string message that it can return with a getMessage() method.

- Modify the Date class so that its set methods throw an exception when a month is not a valid value (1 through 12) or the day is out of range for the month.

- Design a BoardingContractException class. The class contains a string field that holds an error message. The constructor accepts a string message that it can return with a getMessage() method.

- Modify the BoardingContract class so that each set method throws a BoardingContractException that contains an appropriate message if any of the method's arguments are out of range, according to the following guidelines:

  ◆ The dog ID number must be a string between "10000" and "99999" inclusive.

  ◆ The boarding start date must be valid. In other words, if a DateException object is thrown when the date is set, then the start-date set method should throw a BoardingContractException.

  ◆ The boarding start date must not be prior to today's date.

  ◆ The number of days to be boarded must be between 1 and 28 days inclusive. If the number of days is a valid value, then compute the total price for a boarding session as $20 per day for the first 10 days, and $18 per day for additional days after 10.

- Design an application that creates an array of 10 BoardingContract objects. In a loop, prompt the user to enter the needed data for each object. If a BoardingContractException is thrown, display the BoardingContractException message and end the application.

- Design a second application that creates an array of 10 BoardingContract objects. In a loop, prompt the user to enter the needed data for each object. If a BoardingContractException is thrown after the user enters data for any field, display the BoardingContractException message and continue to prompt until the user enters a valid value for the erroneous field. After all the objects are entered, display all 10 BoardingContract objects.

- Design a third application that creates an array of 10 BoardingContract objects. In a loop, prompt the user to enter the needed data for each object. If a BoardingContractException is thrown after the user enters data for any field, force the user to reenter all the data for the object until there are 10 valid objects. After all the objects are entered, display all 10 BoardingContract objects.

Up for Discussion

1. Have you ever been victimized by a computer error? For example, were you ever denied credit incorrectly, billed for something you did not purchase, or assigned an incorrect grade in a course? How did you resolve the problem? On the Web, find an outrageous story involving a computer error.

2. Search the Web for information about educational video games in which historical simulations are presented in an effort to teach students about history. For example, Civilization IV is a game in which players control a society as it progresses through time. Do you believe such games are useful to history students? Does the knowledge gained warrant the hours it takes to master the games? Do the makers of the games have any obligations to present history factually? Do they have a right to penalize players who choose options of which the game writers disapprove (such as using nuclear weapons or allowing slavery)? Do game creators have the right to include characters who possess negative stereotypical traits—for example, a person of a specific nationality portrayed as being stupid, weak, or evil? Would you like to take a history course that uses similar games?

System Modeling with the UML

In this chapter, you will learn about:

- ◎ System modeling
- ◎ The Unified Modeling Language (UML)
- ◎ UML use case diagrams
- ◎ UML class and object diagrams
- ◎ Other UML diagrams
- ◎ Deciding when to use the UML and which UML diagrams to use

Understanding System Modeling

Computer programs often stand alone to solve a user's specific problem. For example, a program might exist only to print paychecks for the current week. Most computer programs, however, are part of a larger system. Your company's payroll system might consist of dozens of programs, including programs that produce employee paychecks, apply raises to employee salaries, alter employee deduction options, and create federal and state tax forms at the end of the year. Each program you write as part of a system might be related to several others. Some programs depend on input from other programs in the system or produce output to be fed into other programs. Similarly, an organization's accounting, inventory, and customer ordering systems all consist of many interrelated programs. Producing a set of programs that operates correctly as one unit requires careful planning. **System design** is the detailed specification of how all the parts of a system will be implemented and coordinated. Usually, system design refers to computer system design, but even a noncomputerized, manual system can benefit from good design techniques. Planning the parts of a system before creating them is also called **modeling**.

Many textbooks cover the theories and techniques of system design and modeling. If you continue to study in a Computer Information Systems program at a college or university, you probably will be required to take a semester-long course in system design. Explaining all the techniques of system design is beyond the scope of this book. However, some basic principles parallel those you have used throughout this book in designing individual programs:

- Large systems are easier to understand when you break them down into subsystems.

- Good modeling techniques are increasingly important as the size and complexity of systems increase.

- Good models promote communication among technical and nontechnical workers while ensuring professional and efficient business solutions.

In other words, developing a model for a single program or an entire business system requires organization and planning. In this chapter, you learn the basics of one popular design tool, the **Unified Modeling Language (UML)**, which is based on the preceding principles. The UML allows you to envision systems with an object-oriented perspective: breaking a system into subsystems, focusing on the big picture, and hiding the implementation details. In addition, the UML provides a means for programmers and businesspeople to communicate about system design. It also provides a way to divide responsibilities for large systems. Understanding the principles of the UML helps you design a variety of system types and talk about systems with the people who will use them.

In addition to modeling a system before creating it, system analysts sometimes model an existing system to get a better picture of its operation. Scrutinizing an existing system and creating an improved one is called **reverse engineering**.

What is the UML?

The UML is a standard way to specify, construct, and document systems that use object-oriented methods. The UML is a modeling language, not a programming language. The systems you develop using the UML probably will be implemented later in object-oriented programming languages such as Java, C++, C#, or Visual Basic. As with flowcharts, pseudocode, hierarchy charts, and class diagrams, the UML has its own notation that consists of a set of specialized shapes and conventions. You can use UML shapes to construct different kinds of software diagrams and model different kinds of systems. Just as you can use a flowchart or hierarchy chart to diagram real-life activities or organizational relationships as well as computer programs, you can also use the UML for many purposes, including modeling business activities, organizational processes, or software systems.

 You can purchase compilers for most programming languages from a variety of manufacturers, and you can purchase several different flowcharting programs. Similarly, you can purchase a variety of tools to help you create UML diagrams, but the UML itself is vendor-independent.

 The UML was created at Rational Software by Grady Booch, Ivar Jacobson, and Jim Rumbaugh. The Object Management Group (OMG) adopted the UML as a standard for software modeling in 1997. The OMG includes more than 800 software vendors, developers, and users who seek a common architectural framework for object-oriented programming. The UML is in its second major version; the current version is UML 2.4. You can view or download the entire UML specification and usage guidelines from the OMG at *www.uml.org*.

When you draw a flowchart or write pseudocode, your purpose is to illustrate the individual steps in a process. When you draw a hierarchy chart, you use more of a "big picture" approach. As with a hierarchy chart, you use the UML to create top-view diagrams of business processes that let you hide details and focus on functionality. This approach lets you start with a generic view of an application and introduce details and complexity later. UML diagrams are useful as you begin designing business systems, when customers who are not technically oriented must accurately communicate with the technical staff members who will create the actual systems. The UML was intentionally designed to be nontechnical so that developers, customers, and implementers (programmers) could all "speak the same language." If business and technical people can agree on what a system should do, the chances improve that the final product will be useful.

The UML is very large; its documentation is more than 800 pages, and new diagram types are added frequently. Currently, the UML provides 14 diagram types that you can use to model systems. Each of the diagram types lets you see a business process from a different angle, and each type appeals to a different type of user. Just as an architect, interior designer, electrician, and plumber use different diagram types to describe the same building, different computer users appreciate different perspectives. For example, a business user most values a system's use case diagrams because they illustrate who is doing what. On the other hand, programmers find class and object diagrams more useful because they help explain details of how to build classes and objects into applications.

The UML superstructure groups the diagram types into two broad categories—structure diagrams and behavior diagrams. A subcategory of behavior diagrams is interaction diagrams. The UML diagram types are listed below.

- **Structure diagrams** emphasize the "things" in a system, and include:
    - Class diagrams
    - Object diagrams
    - Component diagrams
    - Composite structure diagrams
    - Package diagrams
    - Deployment diagrams
    - Profile diagrams
- **Behavior diagrams** emphasize what happens in a system, and include:
    - Use case diagrams
    - Activity diagrams
    - State machine diagrams
- **Interaction diagrams** emphasize the flow of control and data among the system elements being modeled, and include:
    - Sequence diagrams
    - Communication diagrams
    - Timing diagrams
    - Interaction overview diagrams

An alternate way to categorize UML diagrams is to divide them into diagrams that illustrate the static, or steady, aspects of a system and those that illustrate the dynamic, or changing, aspects of a system. For example, the static elements of a restaurant system might include the menu and employees, and the dynamic elements would include how the restaurant reacts to a customer. Static diagrams include class, object, component, deployment, and profile diagrams. Dynamic diagrams include use case, sequence, communication, state machine, and activity diagrams.

Each UML diagram type supports multiple variations, and explaining them all would require an entire textbook. This chapter presents an overview and simple examples of several diagram types, which provides a good foundation for further study of the UML. You also can find several tutorials on the UML at *www.uml.org*.

Watch the video *The UML.*

Using UML Use Case Diagrams

The **use case diagram** shows how a business works from the perspective of those who actually interact with the business, such as employees, customers, and suppliers. Although users can also be governments, private organizations, machines, or other systems, it is easiest to think of them as people, so users are called actors and are represented by stick figures in use case diagrams. The actual use cases are represented by ovals.

Use cases do not necessarily represent all the functions of a system; they are the system functions or services that are visible to the system's actors. In other words, they represent the cases by which an actor uses and presumably benefits from the system. Determining all the cases for which users interact with systems helps you divide a system logically into functional parts.

Establishing use cases usually follows from analyzing the main events in a system. For example, from a librarian's point of view, two main events are `acquireNewBook()` and `checkOutBook()`. Figure 11-1 shows a use case diagram for these two events.

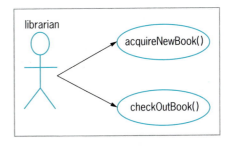

Figure 11-1   Use case diagram for librarian

Many system developers would use the standard English form to describe activities in their UML diagrams—for example, `check out book` instead of `checkOutBook()`, which looks like a programming method call. Because you are used to seeing method names in camel casing and with trailing parentheses throughout this book, this discussion of the UML continues with the same format.

Many systems have variations in use cases. The three possible types of variations are:

- Extend
- Include
- Generalization

An **extend variation** is a use case variation that shows functions beyond those found in a base case. In other words, an extend variation is usually an optional activity. For example, checking out a book for a new library patron who doesn't have a library card is slightly more complicated than checking out a book for an existing patron. Each variation in the sequence of actions required in a use case is a **scenario**. Each use case has at least one main scenario, but the case might have several more that are extensions or variations of the main one. Figure 11-2 shows how you would diagram the relationship between the use case `checkOutBook()` and the more specific scenario `checkOutBookForNewPatron()`. Extended use cases are shown in an oval with a dashed arrow pointing to the more general base case.

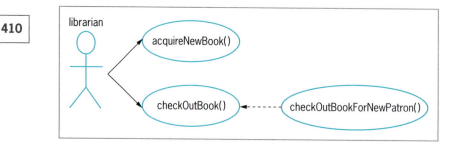

Figure 11-2 Use case diagram for librarian with scenario extension

For clarity, you can add <<extend>> near the line that shows a relationship extension. Such a feature, which adds to the UML vocabulary of shapes to make them more meaningful, is called a **stereotype**. Figure 11-3 includes a stereotype.

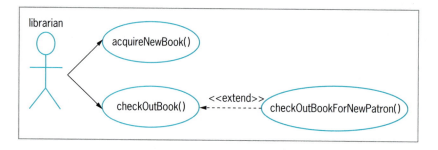

Figure 11-3 Use case diagram for librarian using stereotype

In addition to extend relationships, use case diagrams can also show include relationships. You use an **include variation** when a case can be part of multiple use cases. This concept is very much like that of a subroutine or submodule. You show an include use case in an oval with a dashed arrow pointing to the subroutine use case. For example, `issueLibraryCard()` might be a function of `checkOutBook()` used when a new patron checks out a book, but it might also be a function of `registerNewPatron()`, which occurs when a patron registers at the library but does not want to check out books yet. See Figure 11-4.

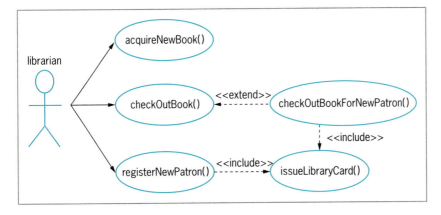

Figure 11-4 Use case diagram for librarian using include relationship

You use a **generalization variation** when a use case is less specific than others and you want to be able to substitute the more specific case for a general one. For example, a library has certain procedures for acquiring new materials, whether they are videos, tapes, CDs, hardcover books, or paperbacks. However, the procedures might become more specific during a particular acquisition—perhaps the librarian must procure plastic cases for circulating videos or assign locked storage locations for CDs. Figure 11-5 shows the generalization acquireNewItem() with two more specific situations: acquiring videos and acquiring CDs. The more specific scenarios are attached to the general scenario with open-headed dashed arrows.

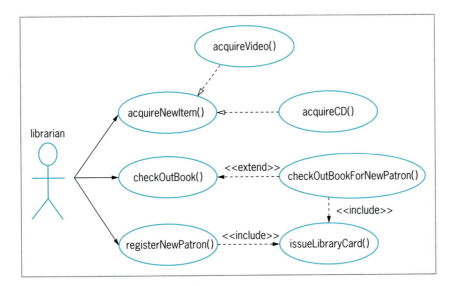

Figure 11-5 Use case diagram for librarian with generalizations

Many use case diagrams show multiple actors. For example, Figure 11-6 shows that a library clerk cannot perform as many functions as a librarian; the clerk can check out books and register new patrons but cannot acquire new materials.

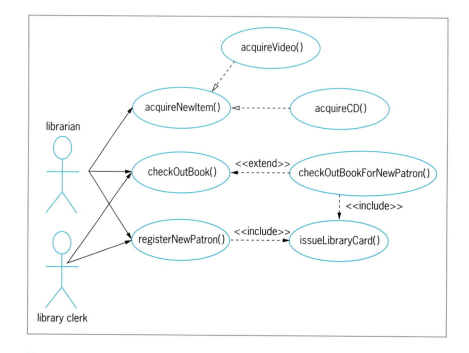

Figure 11-6   Use case diagram for librarian with multiple actors

While designing an actual library system, you could add many more use cases and actors to the use case diagram. The purpose of such a diagram is to encourage discussion between the system developer and the library staff. Library staff members do not need to know the technical details of the system that the analysts will eventually create, and they certainly do not need to understand computers or programming. However, by viewing the use cases, the library staff can visualize activities they perform while doing their jobs and correct the system developer if inaccuracies exist. The final software products developed for such a system are far more likely to satisfy users than those developed without this design step.

A use case diagram is only a tool to aid communication. No single "correct" use case diagram exists; you might correctly represent a system in several ways. For example, you might choose to emphasize the actors in the library system, as shown in Figure 11-7, or to emphasize system requirements, as shown in Figure 11-8. Diagrams that are too crowded are neither visually pleasing nor very useful. Therefore, the use case diagram in Figure 11-7 shows all the specific actors and their relationships, but purposely omits more specific system functions. By comparison, Figure 11-8 shows many actions that are often hidden from users, but purposely omits more specific actors. For example, the activities carried out to manageNetworkOutage(), if done properly, should be invisible to library patrons checking out books.

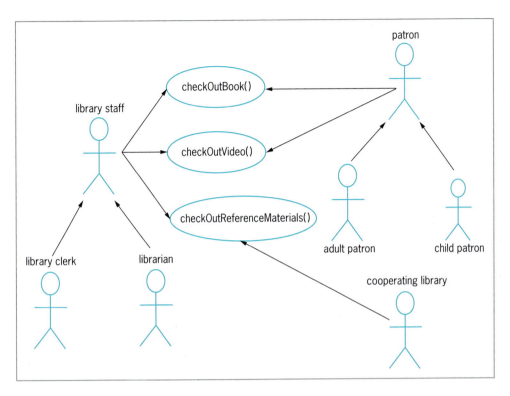

Figure 11-7 Use case diagram emphasizing actors

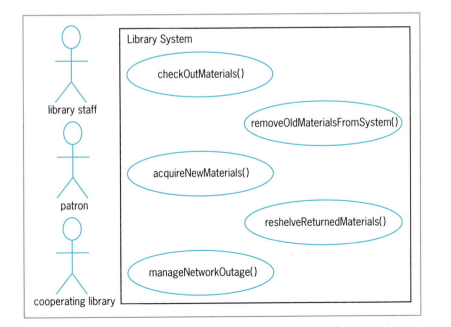

Figure 11-8 Use case diagram emphasizing system requirements

In Figure 11-8, the relationship lines between the actors and use cases have been removed because the emphasis is on the system requirements, and too many lines would make the diagram confusing. When system developers omit parts of diagrams for clarity, they refer to the missing parts as **elided**. For the sake of clarity, eliding extraneous information is perfectly acceptable. The main purpose of UML diagrams is to facilitate clear communication.

Using UML Class and Object Diagrams

You use a class diagram to illustrate the names, attributes, and methods of a class or set of classes. (You saw some examples in Chapter 7.) Class diagrams are more useful to a system's programmers than to its users because they closely resemble code the programmers will write. A class diagram illustrating a single class contains a rectangle divided into three sections: The top section contains the name of the class, the middle section contains the names of the attributes, and the bottom section contains the names of the methods. Figure 11-9 shows the class diagram for a Book class. Each Book object contains an idNum, title, and author. Each Book object also contains methods to create a Book when it is acquired, and to retrieve or get title and author information when the Book object's idNum is supplied.

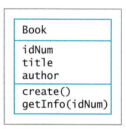

Figure 11-9   Book class diagram

In the preceding section, you learned how to use generalizations with use case diagrams to show general and more specific use cases. With use case diagrams, you drew an open-headed arrow from the more specific case to the more general one. Similarly, you can use generalizations with class diagrams to show more general (or parent) classes and more specific (or child) classes that inherit attributes from parents. (You learned about parent and child classes in Chapter 8.) For example, Figure 11-10 shows Book and Video classes that are more specific than the general LibraryItem class. All LibraryItem objects contain an idNum and title, but each Book item also contains an author, and each Video item also contains a runningTime. Child classes contain all the attributes of their parents and usually contain additional attributes not found in the parent.

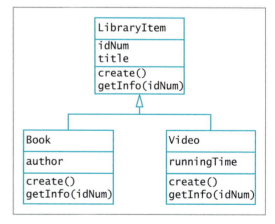

Figure 11-10   LibraryItem class diagram showing generalization

When a child class contains a method with the same signature as one in the parent class, the child class version **overrides** the version in the parent class. That is, by default, the child class version is used with any child class object. The `create()` and `getInfo()` methods in the `Book` and `Video` classes override the versions in the `LibraryItem` class.

Class diagrams can include symbols that show the relationships between objects. You can show two types of relationships:

- An association relationship

- A whole-part relationship

An **association relationship** describes the connection or link between objects. You represent an association relationship between classes with a straight line. Frequently, you include information about the arithmetical relationship or ratio (called **cardinality** or **multiplicity**) of the objects. For example, Figure 11-11 shows the association relationship between a `Library` and the `LibraryItems` it lends. Exactly one `Library` object exists, and it can be associated with any number of `LibraryItems` from 0 to infinity, which is represented by an asterisk. Figure 11-12 adds the `Patron` class to the diagram and shows how you indicate that any number of `Patrons` can be associated with the `Library`, but that each `Patron` can borrow only up to five `LibraryItems` at a time, or currently might not be borrowing any. In addition, each `LibraryItem` can be associated with one `Patron` at most, but at any given time might not be on loan.

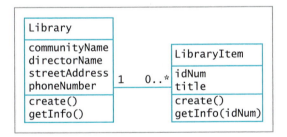

Figure 11-11 Class diagram with association relationship

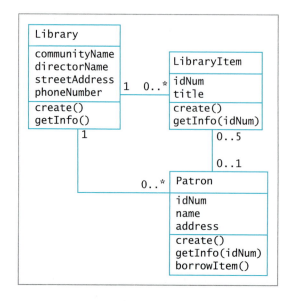

Figure 11-12   Class diagram with several association relationships

As you learned in Chapter 7, an association that uses composition is one in which one or more classes make up the parts of a larger whole class. Such a relationship is also called a **whole-part relationship**. For example, 50 states make up the United States, and 10 departments might make up a company. This type of relationship is represented by a filled diamond at the "whole part" end of the line that indicates the relationship. You can also call a whole-part relationship a *has-a relationship* because the phrase describes the association between the whole and one of its parts; for example, "The library has a Circulation Department." Figure 11-13 shows a whole-part relationship for a `Library`.

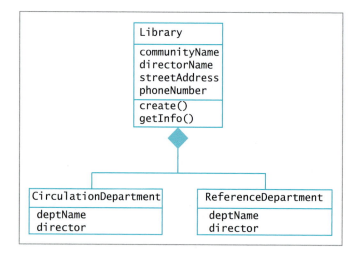

Figure 11-13   Class diagram with whole-part relationship

When a part is completely owned by a whole and ceases to exist without the whole, then the relationship is called composition, and the diamond in the UML diagram is filled as in Figure 11-13. For example, composition describes the relationship between a Hotel and its Lobby. When the part also exists without the whole or belongs to other wholes, then the relationship is called an **aggregation**, and the diamond is open. For example, aggregation describes the relationship between a Customer and a Hotel if the Customer is also part of a CarRental and Restaurant class.

Object diagrams are similar to class diagrams, but they model specific instances of classes. You use an object diagram to show a snapshot of an object at one point in time, so you can more easily understand its relationship to other objects. Imagine looking at the travelers in a major airport. If you try to watch them all at once, you see a flurry of activity, but it is hard to understand all the tasks a traveler must accomplish, such as buying a ticket and checking luggage. However, if you concentrate on one traveler and follow his or her actions through the airport from arrival to takeoff, you get a clearer picture of the required activities. An object diagram serves the same purpose; you concentrate on a specific instance of a class to better understand how a class works.

Figure 11-14 contains an object diagram showing the relationship between one Library, one LibraryItem, and one Patron. Notice the similarities between Figures 11-12 and 11-14. If you need to describe the relationships among three classes, you can use either model—a class diagram or an object diagram—interchangeably. You simply use the model that seems clearer to you and your intended audience.

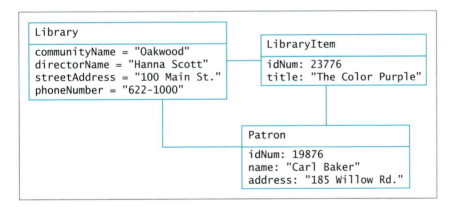

Figure 11-14   Object diagram for Library

   Watch the video *Class and Object Diagrams*.

Using Other UML Diagrams

The wide variety of UML diagrams allow you to illustrate systems from many perspectives. You have already read about use case diagrams, class diagrams, and object diagrams. This section provides a brief overview of other UML diagram types.

Sequence Diagrams

You use a **sequence diagram** to show the timing of events in a single use case. A sequence diagram makes it easier to see the order in which activities occur. The horizontal axis (x-axis) of a sequence diagram represents objects, and the vertical axis (y-axis) represents time. You create a sequence diagram by placing objects that are part of an activity across the top of the diagram along the x-axis, starting at the left with the object or actor that begins the action. Beneath each object on the x-axis, you place a vertical dashed line that represents the period of time the object exists. Then, you use horizontal arrows to show how the objects communicate with each other over time.

In a sequence diagram, time increases vertically down the diagram. A *timing diagram* is a type of sequence diagram in which the time axis is represented horizontally.

For example, Figure 11-15 shows a sequence diagram for a scenario that a librarian can use to create a book check-out record. The librarian begins a `create()` method with `Patron idNum` and `Book idNum` information. The `BookCheckOutRecord` object requests additional `Patron` information (such as `name` and `address`) from the `Patron` object with the correct `Patron idNum`, and additional `Book` information (such as `title` and `author`) from the `Book` object with the correct `Book idNum`. When `BookCheckOutRecord` contains all the data it needs, a completed record is returned to the librarian.

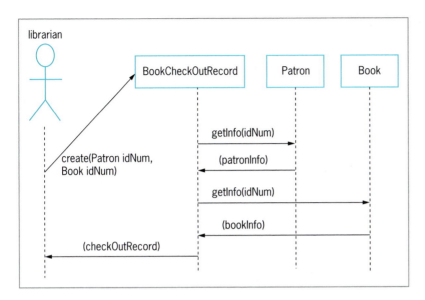

Figure 11-15 Sequence diagram for checking out a Book for a Patron

In Figures 11-15 and 11-16, patronInfo and bookInfo represent group items that contain all of a Patron's and Book's data. For example, patronInfo might contain idNum, lastName, firstName, address, and phoneNumber, all of which have been defined as attributes of that class.

Communication Diagrams

A **communication diagram** emphasizes the organization of objects that participate in a system. It is similar to a sequence diagram, except that it contains sequence numbers to represent the precise order in which activities occur. Communication diagrams focus on object roles instead of the times that messages are sent. Figure 11-16 shows the same sequence of events as Figure 11-15, but the steps to creating a BookCheckOutRecord are clearly numbered. Decimal numbered steps (1.1, 1.2, and so on) represent substeps of the main steps. Checking out a library book is a fairly straightforward event, so a sequence diagram sufficiently illustrates the process. Communication diagrams become more useful with more complicated systems.

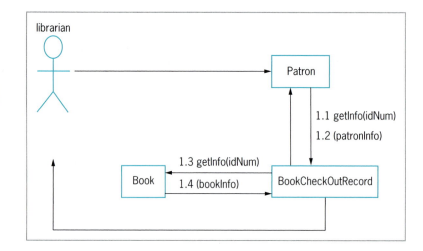

Figure 11-16   Communication diagram for checking out a Book for a Patron

State Machine Diagrams

Like use case diagrams, state machine and activity diagrams both illustrate the behavior of a system.

A **state machine diagram** shows the different statuses of a class or object at different points in time. You use a state machine diagram to illustrate aspects of a system that show interesting changes in behavior as time passes. Conventionally, you use rounded rectangles to represent each state and labeled arrows to show the sequence in which events affect the states. A solid dot indicates the start and stop states for the class or object. Figure 11-17 contains a state machine diagram that describes the states of a Book.

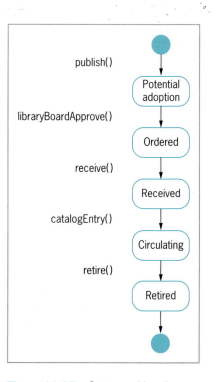

Figure 11-17   State machine diagram for states of a Book

To make sure that your diagrams are clear, you should use the correct symbol in each UML diagram you create, just as you should use the correct symbol in each program flowchart. However, if you create a flowchart and use a rectangle for an input or output statement where a parallelogram is conventional, others will still understand your meaning. Similarly, with UML diagrams, the exact shape you use is not nearly as important as the sequence of events and relationships between objects.

Activity Diagrams

The UML diagram that most closely resembles a conventional flowchart is an activity diagram. In an **activity diagram**, you show the flow of actions of a system, including branches that occur when decisions affect the outcome. Conventionally, activity diagrams use flowchart start and stop symbols (called lozenges) to describe actions and solid dots to represent start and stop states. Like flowcharts, activity diagrams use diamonds to describe decisions. Unlike the diamonds in flowcharts, the diamonds in UML activity diagrams usually are empty; the possible outcomes are documented along the branches emerging from the decision symbol. As an example, Figure 11-18 shows a simple activity diagram with a single branch.

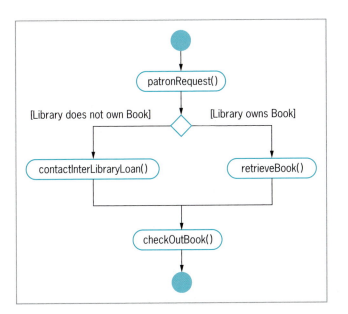

Figure 11-18   Activity diagram showing a branch

Many real-life systems contain actions that are meant to occur simultaneously. For example, when you apply for a home mortgage with a bank, a bank officer might perform a credit or background check while an appraiser determines the value of the house you are buying. When both actions are complete, the loan process continues. UML activity diagrams use forks and joins to show simultaneous activities. A **fork** is similar to a decision, but whereas the flow of control follows only one path after a decision, a fork defines a branch in which all paths are followed simultaneously or concurrently. A **join**, as its name implies, reunites the flow of control after a fork. You indicate forks and joins with thick straight lines. Figure 11-19 shows how you might model the way an interlibrary loan system processes book requests. When a request is received, simultaneous searches begin at three local libraries that are part of the library system.

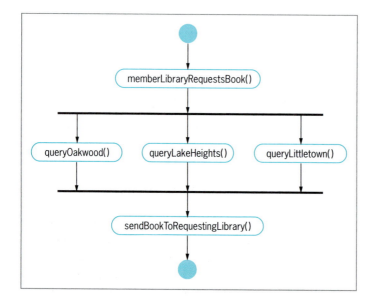

Figure 11-19   Activity diagram showing fork and join

An activity diagram can contain a time signal. A **time signal** indicates that a specific amount of time should pass before an action starts. The time signal looks like two stacked triangles (resembling the shape of an hourglass). Figure 11-20 shows a time signal indicating that if a patron requests a book checked out to another patron, then only if the book's due date has passed should a request be issued to return the book. In activity diagrams for other systems, you might see explanations at time signals, such as "10 hours have passed" or "at least January 1." If an action is time-dependent, whether by a fraction of a second or by years, using a time signal is appropriate.

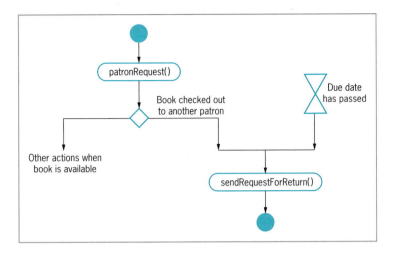

Figure 11-20   A time signal starting an action

Component and Deployment Diagrams

Component and deployment diagrams model the physical aspects of systems. You use a **component diagram** when you want to emphasize the files, database tables, documents, and other components used by a system's software. You use a **deployment diagram** when you want to focus on a system's hardware. You can use a variety of icons in each type of diagram, but each icon must convey meaning to the reader. Figures 11-21 and 11-22 show component and deployment diagrams, respectively, that illustrate aspects of a library system. Figure 11-21 contains icons that symbolize paper and Internet requests for library items, the library database, and two tables that constitute the database. Figure 11-22 shows some commonly used icons that represent hardware components.

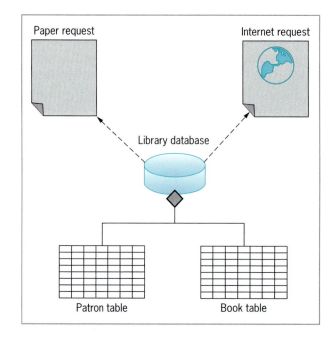

Figure 11-21   Component diagram

In Figure 11-21, notice the filled diamond connecting the two tables to the database. Just as it does in a class diagram, the diamond aggregation symbol shows the whole-part relationship of the tables to the database. You use an open diamond when a part might belong to several wholes; for example, **Door** and **Wall** objects belong to many **House** objects. You use a filled diamond when a part can belong to only one whole at a time (the **Patron** table can belong only to the **Library** database). You can use most UML symbols in multiple types of diagrams.

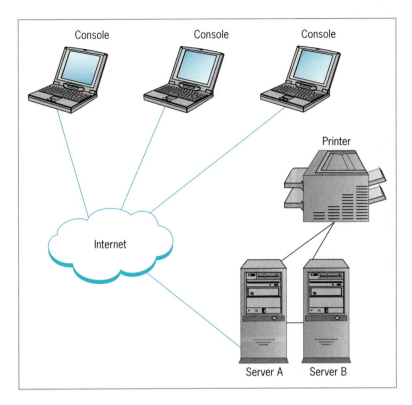

Figure 11-22 Deployment diagram

Profile Diagrams

The **profile diagram** is a newer UML diagram type. It is used to extend a UML model for a particular domain (such as financial or healthcare applications) or a particular platform (such as .NET or Java).

Diagramming Exception Handling

As you learned in Chapter 10, exception handling is a set of object-oriented techniques used to handle program errors. When a segment of code might cause an error, you can place that code in a try block. If the error occurs, an object called an exception is thrown, or sent, to a catch block where appropriate action can be taken. For example, depending on the application, a catch block might display a message, assign a default value to a field, or prompt the user for direction.

In the UML, a try block is called a **protected node** and a catch block is a **handler body node**. In a UML diagram, a protected node is enclosed in a rounded rectangle. Any exceptions that might be thrown are listed next to arrows shaped like lightning bolts, which extend to the appropriate handler body node.

Figure 11-23 shows an example of an activity that uses exception handling. When a library patron tries to check out a book, the patron's card is scanned and the book is scanned. These actions might cause three errors—the patron owes fines, and so cannot check out new books; the patron's card has expired, requiring a new card application; or the book might be on hold for another patron. If no exceptions occur, the activity proceeds to the checkOutBook() process.

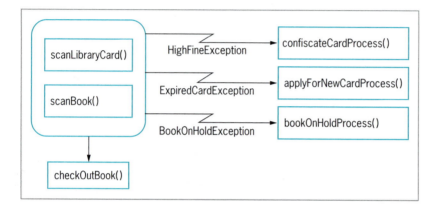

Figure 11-23   Exceptions in the **Book** check-out activity

Deciding When to Use the UML and Which UML Diagrams to Use

The UML is widely recognized as a modeling standard, but it is also frequently criticized. The criticisms include:

- *Size*—The UML is often criticized as being too large and complex. Many of the diagrams are infrequently used, and some critics claim several are redundant.

- *Imprecision*—The UML is a combination of rules and English. In particular, problems occur when the diagrams are applied to tasks other than those implemented in object-oriented programming languages.

- *Complexity*—Because of its size and imprecision, the UML is relatively difficult to learn.

Still, under the right circumstances, the UML can increase communication between developers and users of a system. Each UML diagram type provides a different view of a system. Just as a portrait artist, psychologist, and neurosurgeon each prefers a different conceptual view of your head, the users, managers, designers, and technicians of computer and business systems each prefer specific system views. Very few systems require diagrams of all UML types; you can illustrate the objects and activities of many systems by using a single diagram, or perhaps one that is a hybrid of two or more basic types. No view is superior to the others; you can achieve the most complete picture of any system by using several views.

Finally, don't be intimidated by the UML. Making a diagram that is clear to the audience but that does not follow specifications precisely is better than following the rules but creating a diagram that is difficult to understand. The most important reason to use any UML diagram is to communicate clearly and efficiently with the people for whom you are designing a system.

Chapter Summary

- System design is the detailed specification of how all the parts of a system will be implemented and coordinated. Good designs make systems easier to understand. The UML (Unified Modeling Language) provides a means for programmers and businesspeople to communicate about system design.

- The UML is a standard way to specify, construct, and document systems that use object-oriented methods. The UML has its own notation, with which you can construct software diagrams that model different kinds of systems. The UML provides 14 diagram types that you use at the beginning of the design process.

- A use case diagram shows how a business works from the perspective of those who actually interact with the business. The diagram often includes actors, represented by stick figures, and use cases, represented by ovals. Use cases can include variations such as extend relationships, include relationships, and generalizations.

- You use a class diagram to illustrate the names, attributes, and methods of a class or set of classes. A class diagram of a single class contains a rectangle divided into three sections: the name of the class, the names of the attributes, and the names of the methods. Class diagrams can show generalizations and the relationships between objects. Object diagrams are similar to class diagrams, but they model specific instances of classes at one point in time.

- You use a sequence diagram to show the timing of events in a single use case. A communication diagram emphasizes the organization of objects that participate in a system. It is similar to a sequence diagram, except that it contains sequence numbers to represent the precise order in which activities occur. A state machine diagram shows the different statuses of a class or object at different points in time. In an activity diagram, you show the flow of actions of a system, including branches that occur when decisions affect the outcome. UML activity diagrams use forks and joins to show simultaneous activities. You use a component diagram when you want to emphasize the files, database tables, documents, and other components used by a system's software. You use a deployment diagram when you want to focus on a system's hardware. A profile diagram is used to extend a UML model for a particular domain or platform. Exception handling is diagrammed in the UML using a rounded rectangle to represent a `try` block protected node. Any exceptions that might be thrown are listed next to arrows shaped like lightning bolts, which extend to the appropriate handler body node.

- Each UML diagram type provides a different view of a system. Very few systems require diagrams of all 14 types; the most important reason to use any UML diagram is to communicate clearly and efficiently with the people for whom you are designing a system.

Key Terms

System design is the detailed specification of how all the parts of a system will be implemented and coordinated.

Modeling is the designing of applications before writing code for them.

The **Unified Modeling Language (UML)** is a standard way to specify, construct, and document systems that use object-oriented methods.

Reverse engineering is the process of creating an improved model of an existing system.

Structure diagrams emphasize the "things" in a system.

Behavior diagrams emphasize what happens in a system.

Interaction diagrams emphasize the flow of control and data among the system elements being modeled.

The **use case diagram** is a UML diagram that shows how a business works from the perspective of those who actually interact with the business.

An **extend variation** is a use case variation that shows functions beyond those found in a base case.

A **scenario** is a variation in the sequence of actions required in a use case.

A **stereotype** is a feature that adds to the UML vocabulary of shapes to make them more meaningful for the reader.

An **include variation** is a use case variation in a case that can be part of multiple use cases in a UML diagram.

A **generalization variation** is used in a UML diagram when a use case is less specific than others and you want to be able to substitute the more specific case for a general one.

Elided describes the omitted parts of UML diagrams that are edited for clarity.

When a method **overrides** another, it is used by default in place of a method with the same signature.

An **association relationship** describes the connection or link between objects in a UML diagram.

Cardinality and **multiplicity** refer to the arithmetic relationships between objects.

A **whole-part relationship** is an association in which one or more classes make up the parts of a larger whole class.

An **aggregation** is a whole-part relationship in which the part or parts can exist without the whole.

Object diagrams are UML diagrams that are similar to class diagrams, but they model specific instances of classes.

A **sequence diagram** is a UML diagram that shows the timing of events in a single use case.

A **communication diagram** is a UML diagram that emphasizes the organization of objects that participate in a system.

A **state machine diagram** is a UML diagram that shows the different statuses of a class or object at different points in time.

An **activity diagram** is a UML diagram that shows the flow of actions of a system, including branches that occur when decisions affect the outcome.

A **fork** is a feature of a UML activity diagram; it is similar to a decision, but whereas the flow of control follows only one path after a decision, a fork defines a branch in which all paths are followed simultaneously or concurrently.

A **join** is a feature of a UML activity diagram; it reunites the flow of control after a fork.

A **time signal** is a UML diagram symbol indicating that a specific amount of time has passed before an action is started.

A **component diagram** is a UML diagram that emphasizes the files, database tables, documents, and other components used by a system's software.

A **deployment diagram** is a UML diagram that focuses on a system's hardware.

A **profile diagram** is used to extend a UML model for a particular domain or platform.

A **protected node** is the UML diagram name for an exception-throwing `try` block.

A **handler body node** is the UML diagram name for an exception-handling `catch` block.

Review Questions

1. The detailed specification of how all the parts of a system will be implemented and coordinated is called _____ .

   a. programming

   b. paraphrasing

   c. system design

   d. structuring

2. The primary purpose of good modeling techniques is to _____.

    a. promote communication
    b. increase functional cohesion
    c. reduce the need for structure
    d. reduce dependency between modules

3. The UML provides standard ways to do all of the following to business systems except _____ them.

    a. construct   c. describe
    b. document   d. destroy

4. The UML is commonly used to model all of the following except _____.

    a. computer programs   c. organizational processes
    b. business activities   d. software systems

5. The UML was intentionally designed to be _____.

    a. low-level, detail-oriented   c. nontechnical
    b. used with Visual Basic   d. inexpensive

6. The UML diagrams that show how a business works from the perspective of those who actually interact with the business, such as employees or customers, are _____ diagrams.

    a. communication   c. state machine
    b. use case   d. class

7. Which of the following would be portrayed as an extend relationship in a use case diagram for a hospital?

    a. the relationship between the head nurse and the floor nurses
    b. admitting a patient who has never been admitted before
    c. serving a meal
    d. scheduling the monitoring of patients' vital signs

8. The people shown in use case diagrams are called _____.

    a. workers   c. actors
    b. clowns   d. relatives

9. One aspect of use case diagrams that makes them difficult to learn is that _____.

    a. they require programming experience to understand
    b. they use a technical vocabulary
    c. there is no single right answer for any case
    d. all of the above

10. The arithmetic association relationship between a college student and college courses would be expressed as _____ .

   a. 1   0   c. 1   0..*
   b. 1   1   d. 0..* 0..*

11. In the UML, object diagrams are most similar to _____ diagrams.

   a. use case   c. class
   b. activity   d. sequence

12. In any given situation, you should choose the type of UML diagram that is _____ .

   a. shorter than others
   b. clearer than others
   c. more detailed than others
   d. closest to the programming language you will use to implement the system

13. A whole-part relationship can be described as a(n) _____ relationship.

   a. parent-child   c. is-a
   b. has-a   d. creates-a

14. The timing of events is best portrayed in a(n) _____ diagram.

   a. sequence   c. communication
   b. use case   d. association

15. A communication diagram is closest to a(n) _____ diagram.

   a. activity   c. deployment
   b. use case   d. sequence

16. A(n) _____ diagram shows the different statuses of a class or object at different points in time.

   a. activity   c. sequence
   b. state machine   d. deployment

17. The UML diagram that most closely resembles a conventional flowchart is a(n) _____ diagram.

   a. activity   c. sequence
   b. state machine   d. deployment

18. You use a _____ diagram when you want to emphasize the files, database tables, documents, and other components used by a system's software.

   a. state machine   c. deployment
   b. component   d. use case

19. The UML diagram that focuses on a system's hardware is a(n) _____ diagram.

   a. deployment   c. activity

   b. sequence   d. use case

20. When using the UML to describe a single system, most designers would use _____ .

   a. a single type of diagram

   b. at least three types of diagrams

   c. most of the available types of diagrams

   d. all the types of diagrams

Exercises

1. Complete the following tasks:

   a. Develop a use case diagram for a convenience food store. Include an actor representing the store manager and use cases for orderItem(), stockItem(), and sellItem().

   b. Add more use cases to the diagram you created in Exercise 1a. Include two generalizations for stockItem() called stockPerishable() and stockNonPerishable(). Also include an extension to sellItem() called checkCredit() for cases in which a customer purchases items using a credit card.

   c. Add a customer actor to the use case diagram you created in Exercise 1b. Show that the customer participates in sellItem(), but not in orderItem() or stockItem().

2. Develop a use case diagram for a department store credit card system. Include at least two actors and four use cases.

3. Develop a use case diagram for a college registration system. Include at least three actors and five use cases.

4. Develop a class diagram for a Yard class that describes objects serviced by a landscaping maintenance company. Include at least four attributes and three methods.

5. Develop a class diagram for a Shape class. Include generalizations for child classes Rectangle, Circle, and Triangle.

6. Develop a class diagram for a Message class for a cell phone company. Include generalizations for child classes TextMessage, VideoMessage, and VoiceMessage.

7. Develop a class diagram for a college registration system. Include at least three classes that cooperate to register students.

8. Develop a sequence diagram that shows how a clerk at a mail-order company places a customer Order. The Order accesses Inventory to check availability. Then, the Order accesses Invoice to produce a customer invoice that returns to the clerk.

9. Develop a state machine diagram that shows the states of an Employee from Applicant to Retiree.

10. Develop a state machine diagram that shows the states of a Movie from Concept to Production.

11. Develop an activity diagram that illustrates how to throw a party.

12. Develop an activity diagram that illustrates how to clean a room.

13. Develop the UML diagram of your choice that illustrates some aspect of your life.

14. Complete the following tasks:

   a. Develop the UML diagram of your choice that best illustrates some aspect of a place you have worked.

   b. Develop a different UML diagram type that illustrates the same functions as the diagram you created in Exercise 14a.

Case Projects

Case: Cost Is No Object

1. In earlier chapters, you developed classes needed for Cost Is No Object—a car rental service. Now complete the following tasks:

   a. Develop a use case diagram for renting a car. Include actors representing a fleet mechanic, a rental agent, and a customer. Include use cases for reportMechanicalProblems(), orderRepairs(), makeRepairs(), makeReservation(), rentCar(), and returnCar().

   b. Develop an activity diagram that illustrates how to rent a car.

   c. Develop a sequence diagram that illustrates how to rent a car.

Case: Classic Reunions

2. In earlier chapters, you developed classes needed for Classic Reunions—a reunion planning service. Now complete the following tasks:

    a. Develop a use case diagram for planning a reunion. Include actors representing an event coordinator, a client, a band manager, and a caterer. Include use cases for `initialConsultation()`, `reserveDate()`, `bookBand()`, and `bookCaterer()`.

    b. Develop an activity diagram that illustrates how to schedule a reunion.

    c. Develop a sequence diagram that illustrates how to plan a reunion.

Case: The Barking Lot

3. In earlier chapters, you developed classes needed for The Barking Lot—a dog-boarding facility. Now complete the following tasks:

    a. Develop a use case diagram for boarding a dog. Include actors representing the dog, its owner, and the boarding facility agent. Include use cases for `makeReservation()`, `checkDogIn()`, `boardDog()`, and `releaseDogToOwner()`.

    b. Develop an activity diagram that illustrates how to board a dog.

    c. Develop a sequence diagram that illustrates how to board a dog.

Up for Discussion

1. Which do you think you would enjoy more on the job—designing large systems that contain many programs, or writing the programs themselves? Why?

2. In earlier chapters, you considered ethical dilemmas in writing programs that select candidates for organ transplants. Are the ethical responsibilities of a system designer different from those of a programmer? If so, how?

Manipulating Larger Quantities of Data

In this chapter, you will learn about:

- ◎ The need for sorting data
- ◎ The bubble sort algorithm
- ◎ Sorting data in parallel arrays
- ◎ Sorting objects
- ◎ The insertion sort algorithm
- ◎ Multidimensional arrays
- ◎ Indexed files and linked lists

Throughout this book, you have learned many helpful techniques for manipulating data items, including storing them in arrays, passing them to methods, and encapsulating and hiding them in classes. Working with larger quantities of data provides several additional challenges, and this chapter introduces you to some useful techniques. You will learn how to sort data items so that they can be placed in a new physical order. You will learn to work with multidimensional arrays, which are structures that provide a new logical paradigm for data items. Finally, you will learn about indexed files and linked lists, which give you the ability to access data items in a logical order that differs from their physical order.

Understanding the Need for Sorting Records

When you store data records, they exist in some type of order; that is, one record is first, another second, and so on. When records are in **sequential order**, they are arranged one after another on the basis of the value in a particular field. Examples include employee records stored in numeric order by Social Security number or department number, or in alphabetical order by last name or department name. Even if the records are stored in a random order—for example, the order in which a clerk felt like entering them—they still are *in order*, although probably not the order desired for processing or viewing. Such data records need to be **sorted**, or placed in order based on the contents of one or more fields. You can sort either in **ascending order**, arranging records from lowest to highest value within a field, or in **descending order**, arranging records from highest to lowest value. Here are some examples of occasions when you would need to sort records:

- A college stores student records in ascending order by student ID number, but the registrar wants to view the data in descending order by credit hours earned so he can contact students who are close to graduation.

- A department store maintains customer records in ascending order by customer number, but at the end of a billing period, the credit manager wants to contact customers whose balances are 90 or more days overdue. The manager wants to list these overdue customers in descending order by the amount owed, so the customers with the largest debt can be contacted first.

- A sales manager keeps records for her salespeople in alphabetical order by last name, but she needs to list the annual sales figure for each salesperson so she can determine the median annual sale amount. (The **median** value in a list is the value of the middle item when the values are listed in order. The median is not the same as the arithmetic average, or **mean**. The median is often used as a statistic because it represents a more typical case—half the values are below it and half are above it. Unlike the median, the mean is skewed by a few very high or low values.)

 The sorting process usually is reserved for a relatively small number of data items. If thousands of customer records are stored, and they frequently need to be accessed in order based on different fields (alphabetical order by customer name one day, zip code order the next), the records would probably not be sorted at all, but would be indexed or linked. You learn about indexing and linking later in this chapter.

When computers sort data, they always use numeric values to make comparisons between values. This is clear when you sort records by fields such as a numeric customer ID or balance due. However, even alphabetic sorts are numeric, because computer data is stored as a number using a series of 0s and 1s. Ordinary computer users seldom think about the numeric codes behind the letters, numbers, and punctuation marks they enter from their keyboards or see on a monitor. However, they see the consequence of the values behind letters when they see data sorted in alphabetical order. In every popular computer coding scheme, B is numerically one greater than A, and y is numerically one less than z. Unfortunately, your system dictates whether A is represented by a number that is greater or smaller than the number representing a. Therefore, to obtain the most useful and accurate list of alphabetically sorted records, either a company's data-entry personnel should be consistent in the use of capitalization or the programmer should convert all the data to use consistent capitalization.

The most popular coding schemes include ASCII, Unicode, and EBCDIC. In each code, a number represents a specific computer character. Appendix C contains additional information about these codes.

As a professional programmer, you might never have to write a program that sorts data, because organizations can purchase prewritten, "canned" sorting programs. Additionally, many popular language compilers come with built-in methods that can sort data for you. However, it is beneficial to understand the sorting process so that you can write a special-purpose sort when needed. Understanding the sorting process also improves your array-manipulating skills.

Using the Bubble Sort Algorithm

One of the simplest sorting techniques to understand is a bubble sort. You can use a bubble sort to arrange data items in either ascending or descending order. In a **bubble sort**, items in a list are compared with each other in pairs. When an item is out of order, it swaps values with the item below it. With an ascending bubble sort, after each adjacent pair of items in a list has been compared once, the largest item in the list will have "sunk" to the bottom. After many passes through the list, the smallest items rise to the top like bubbles in a carbonated drink. A bubble sort is sometimes called a **sinking sort**.

When you learn a method like sorting, programmers say you are learning an algorithm. An **algorithm** is a list of instructions that accomplishes a task. In this section, you will learn about the bubble sort algorithm for sorting a list of simple values; later in this chapter you will learn how objects with multiple data fields are sorted. To understand the bubble sort algorithm, you first must learn about swapping values.

Understanding Swapping Values

A central concept of many sorting algorithms, including the bubble sort, is the idea of swapping values. When you **swap values** stored in two variables, you exchange their values; you set the first variable equal to the value of the second, and the second variable equal to the value of the first. However, there is a trick to swapping any two values. Assume that you have declared two variables as follows:

```
num score1 = 90
num score2 = 85
```

You want to swap the values so that score1 is 85 and score2 is 90. If you first assign score1 to score2 using a statement such as score2 = score1, both score1 and score2 hold 90 and the value 85 is lost. Similarly, if you first assign score2 to score1 using a statement such as score1 = score2, both variables hold 85 and the value 90 is lost.

To correctly swap two values, you create a temporary variable to hold a copy of one of the scores so that it doesn't get lost. Then, you can accomplish the swap as shown in Figure 12-1. First, the value in score2, 85, is assigned to a temporary holding variable named temp. Next, the score1 value, 90, is assigned to score2. At this point, both score1 and score2 hold 90. Then, the 85 in temp is assigned to score1. Therefore, after the swap process, score1 holds 85 and score2 holds 90.

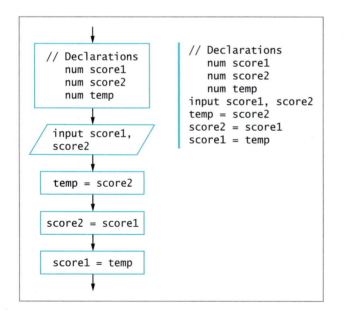

Figure 12-1   Program segment that swaps two values

In Figure 12-1, you can accomplish identical results by assigning score1 to temp, assigning score2 to score1, and finally assigning temp to score2.

Watch the video *Swapping Values*.

Understanding the Bubble Sort

Assume that you want to sort five student test scores in ascending order. Figure 12-2 shows an application in which a constant is declared to hold an array's size, and then the array is declared to hold five scores. The main() method calls three other methods—one to input the five scores, one to sort them, and the final one to display the sorted result.

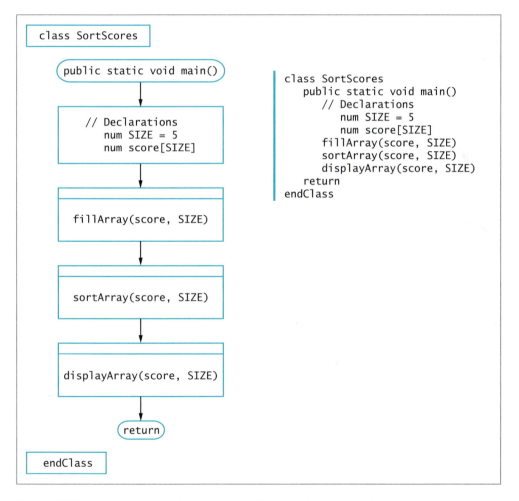

Figure 12-2   A main() method for a program that accepts, sorts, and displays scores

 In the application in Figure 12-2, each method receives the array and its size. Recall from Chapter 5 that many programming languages provide a built-in constant that represents the size of each declared array. If the program in Figure 12-2 was implemented in one of those languages, there would be no need to pass the array size to the methods because it would automatically "come with" the array.

Figure 12-3 shows the `fillArray()` method. The method accepts parameters for the array and its size. Within the method, a subscript, x, is declared locally and initialized to 0, and each array element is filled. After a user enters five scores, control returns to the `main()` method. Recall from Chapter 6 that when an array is passed to a method, its address is passed, so there is no need to return anything from the method in order for the `main()` method to have access to the newly entered array values.

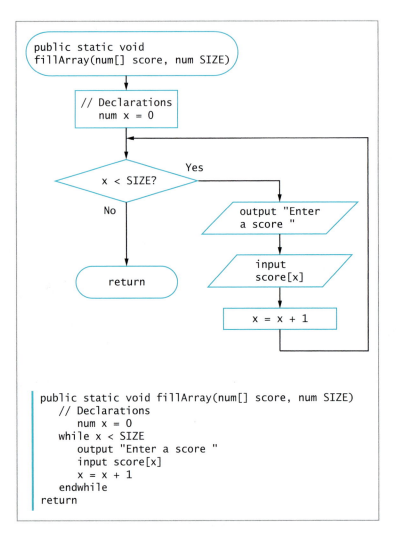

```
public static void fillArray(num[] score, num SIZE)
    // Declarations
       num x = 0
    while x < SIZE
       output "Enter a score "
       input score[x]
       x = x + 1
    endwhile
return
```

Figure 12-3   The `fillArray()` method

In the parameter list for the method in Figure 12-3, the name SIZE is uppercase, which is the convention for named constants. In this example, the intention is that SIZE remains a constant that represents a fixed size for the array. It also would be possible to send a constant to a method where it is accepted as a variable.

The sortArray() method in Figure 12-4 sorts the array elements by making a series of comparisons of adjacent element values and swapping them if they are out of order. To begin sorting this list of scores, you compare the first two scores, score[0] and score[1]. If they are out of order—that is, if score[0] is larger than score[1]—you want to reverse their positions, or swap their values.

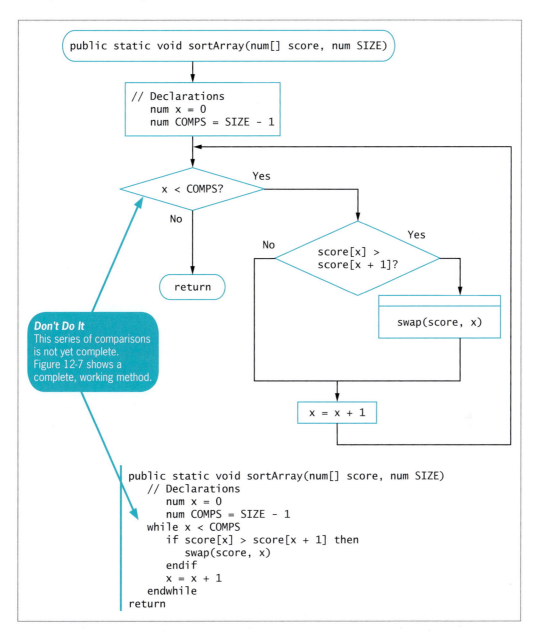

Figure 12-4 The incomplete sortArray() method

For example, assume that the five entered scores are:

```
score[0] = 90
score[1] = 85
score[2] = 65
score[3] = 95
score[4] = 75
```

In this list, `score[0]` is 90 and `score[1]` is 85; you want to exchange the values of the two elements so that the smaller value ends up earlier in the array. You call the `swap()` method, which places the scores in slightly better order than they were originally. Figure 12-5 shows the `swap()` method. This method switches any two adjacent elements in the `score` array. (Notice the similarities between Figures 12-5 and 12-1.)

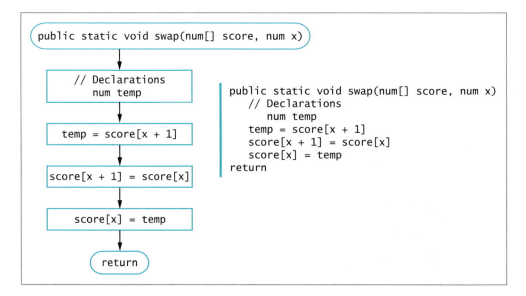

Figure 12-5   The `swap()` method

In Figure 12-4, the number of comparisons made is based on the value of the constant named COMPS, which was initialized to the value of SIZE - 1. That is, for an array of size 5, the COMPS constant will be 4. Therefore, the following comparisons are made:

```
score[0] > score[1]?
score[1] > score[2]?
score[2] > score[3]?
score[3] > score[4]?
```

Each element in the array is compared to the element that follows it. When x becomes COMPS, the `while` loop ends. If the loop continued when x became equal to COMPS, then the next comparison would be `score[4]` > `score[5]`?. This would cause an error because the highest allowed subscript in a five-element array is 4. You must execute the decision score[x] > score[x + 1]? four times—when x is 0, 1, 2, and 3.

For an ascending sort, you need to perform the swap() method whenever any given element of the score array has a value greater than the next element. For any x, if the *x*th element is not greater than the element at position x + 1, the swap should not take place. For example, when score[x] is 90 and score[x + 1] is 85, a swap should occur. On the other hand, when score[x] is 65 and score[x + 1] is 95, then no swap should occur.

For a descending sort in which you want to end up with the highest value first, you would write the decision so that you perform the switch when score[x] is *less than* score[x + 1].

As an example of how this application works using an ascending sort, suppose that you have these original scores:

```
score[0] = 90
score[1] = 85
score[2] = 65
score[3] = 95
score[4] = 75
```

The logic of the sortArray() method proceeds like this:

1. Set x to 0.

2. The value of x is less than 4 (COMPS), so enter the loop.

3. Compare score[x], 90, to score[x + 1], 85. The two scores are out of order, so they are switched.

   The list is now:

   ```
   score[0] = 85
   score[1] = 90
   score[2] = 65
   score[3] = 95
   score[4] = 75
   ```

4. After the swap, add 1 to x, so x is 1.

5. Return to the top of the loop. The value of x is less than 4, so enter the loop a second time.

6. Compare score[x], 90, to score[x + 1], 65. These two values are out of order, so swap them.

   Now the result is:

   ```
   score[0] = 85
   score[1] = 65
   score[2] = 90
   score[3] = 95
   score[4] = 75
   ```

7. Add 1 to x, so x is now 2.

8. Return to the top of the loop. The value of x is less than 4, so enter the loop.

9. Compare score[x], 90, to score[x + 1], 95. These values are in order, so no switch is made.

10. Add 1 to x, making it 3.

11. Return to the top of the loop. The value of x is less than 4, so enter the loop.

12. Compare score[x], 95, to score[x + 1], 75. These two values are out of order, so switch them.

    Now the list is as follows:

    ```
    score[0] = 85
    score[1] = 65
    score[2] = 90
    score[3] = 75
    score[4] = 95
    ```

13. Add 1 to x, making it 4.

14. Return to the top of the loop. The value of x is 4, so do not enter the loop again. Figure 12-6 illustrates the series of steps just completed.

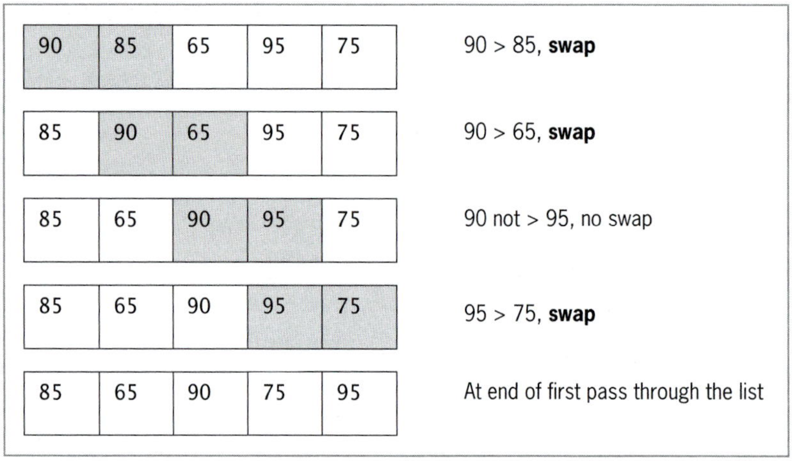

90	85	65	95	75	90 > 85, **swap**
85	90	65	95	75	90 > 65, **swap**
85	65	90	95	75	90 not > 95, no swap
85	65	90	95	75	95 > 75, **swap**
85	65	90	75	95	At end of first pass through the list

Figure 12-6   The steps accomplished in the first loop of the bubble sort

When x reaches 4, every element in the list has been compared with the one adjacent to it. The highest score, 95, has "sunk" to the bottom of the list. However, the scores still are not in order. They are in slightly better ascending order than they were when the process began, because the largest value is at the bottom of the list, but they are still out of order. You need to repeat the entire procedure so that 85 and 65 (the current score[0] and score[1] values) can switch places, and 90 and 75 (the current score[2] and score[3] values) can switch places. Then, the scores will be 65, 85, 75, 90, and 95. You will have to go through the list yet again to swap 85 and 75.

As a matter of fact, if the scores had started in the worst possible order (95, 90, 85, 75, 65), the comparison process would have to take place four times. In other words, you would have to pass through the list of values four times, making appropriate swaps, before the numbers would appear in perfect ascending order. You need to place the loop in Figure 12-4 within another loop that executes four times.

Figure 12-7 shows the complete logic for the sortArray() method. The method uses a loop control variable named y to cycle through the list of scores four times. (The initialization, comparison, and alteration of this loop control variable are shaded in the figure.) With an array of five elements, it takes four comparisons to work through the array once, comparing each pair, and it takes four sets of those comparisons to ensure that every element in the entire array is in sorted order. In the sortArray() method in Figure 12-7, x must be reset to 0 for each new value of y so that the comparisons always start at the top of the list.

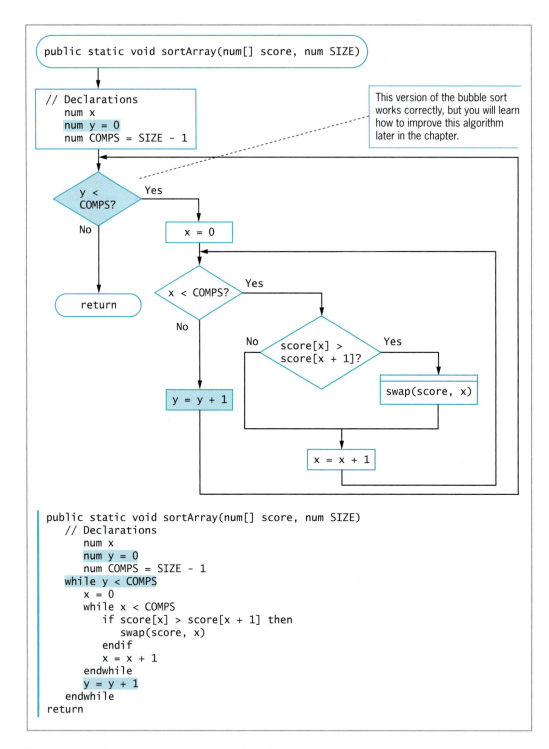

This version of the bubble sort works correctly, but you will learn how to improve this algorithm later in the chapter.

```
public static void sortArray(num[] score, num SIZE)
    // Declarations
        num x
        num y = 0
        num COMPS = SIZE - 1
    while y < COMPS
        x = 0
        while x < COMPS
            if score[x] > score[x + 1] then
                swap(score, x)
            endif
            x = x + 1
        endwhile
        y = y + 1
    endwhile
return
```

Figure 12-7   The completed sortArray() method

When you sort the elements in an array this way, you use nested loops—an inner loop that swaps out-of-order pairs, and an outer loop that goes through the list multiple times. The general rules for making comparisons with the bubble sort are:

- The greatest number of pair comparisons you need to make during each loop is *one less* than the number of elements in the array. You use an inner loop to make the pair comparisons.

- The number of times you need to process the list of values is *one less* than the number of elements in the array. You use an outer loop to control the number of times you walk through the list.

As an example, if you want to sort a 10-element array, you make nine pair comparisons on each of nine rotations through the loop, executing a total of 81 score comparison statements.

The last method called by the score-sorting program in Figure 12-2 is the one that displays the sorted array contents. Figure 12-8 shows this method.

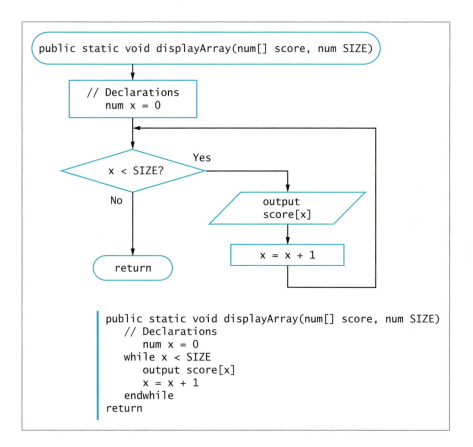

```
public static void displayArray(num[] score, num SIZE)
    // Declarations
        num x = 0
    while x < SIZE
        output score[x]
        x = x + 1
    endwhile
    return
```

Figure 12-8 The displayArray() method

Watch the video *The Bubble Sort*.

Sorting a List of Variable Size

In the score-sorting program in the previous section, a SIZE constant was initialized to the number of elements to be sorted at the start of the program. At times, however, you don't want to create such a value because you might not know how many array elements will hold valid values. For example, on one program run you might want to sort only three or four scores, and on another run you might want to sort 20. In other words, what if the size of the list to be sorted might vary? Rather than sorting a fixed number of array elements, you can count the input scores and then sort just that many.

To keep track of the number of elements stored in an array, you can create the application shown in Figure 12-9. As in the original version of the program, you call the fillArray() method, and when you input each score, you increase x by 1 to place each new score into a successive element of the score array. After you input one score value and place it in the first element of the array, x is 1. After a second score is input and placed in score[1], x is 2, and so on. In the version of the program in Figure 12-9, however, the user can quit before the array is full. When the user quits, x holds the number of scores that have been placed in the array, so x is returned from the fillArray() method and its value is stored in numberOfEls in the main() method. Then, numberOfEls is passed to the other methods where it can be used to limit the number of array elements used in the sort and display processes.

With this approach, it doesn't matter if there are not enough score values to fill the array. The sortArray() and displayArray() methods use just as many array elements as the user entered. For example, if 35 scores are input, the fillArray() method returns 35 to numberOfEls, and 35 is passed to sortArray() as the els parameter. Within the sortArray() method, the constant COMPS will be assigned the value 34, and when the method sorts, it will use 34 as a cutoff point for the number of pair comparisons to make. The sorting method will never make pair comparisons on array elements 36 through 100—those elements will just "sit there," never being involved in a comparison or swap.

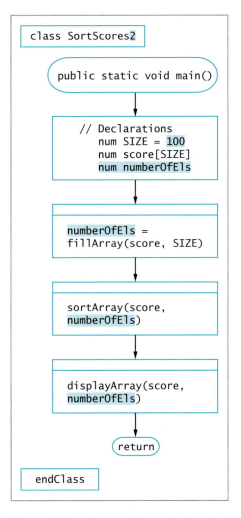

Figure 12-9 Score-sorting application in which number of elements to sort can vary (continued)

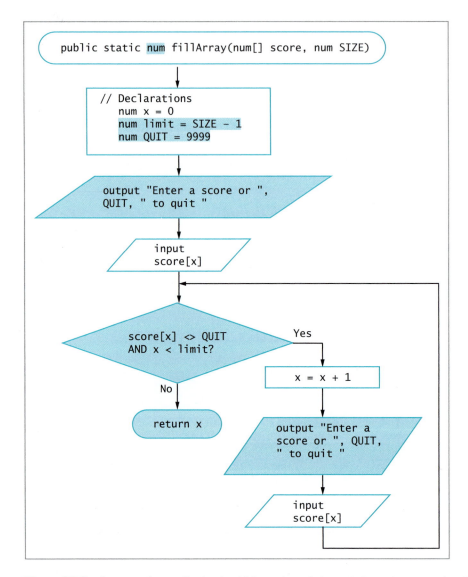

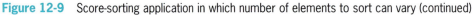

Figure 12-9 Score-sorting application in which number of elements to sort can vary (continued)

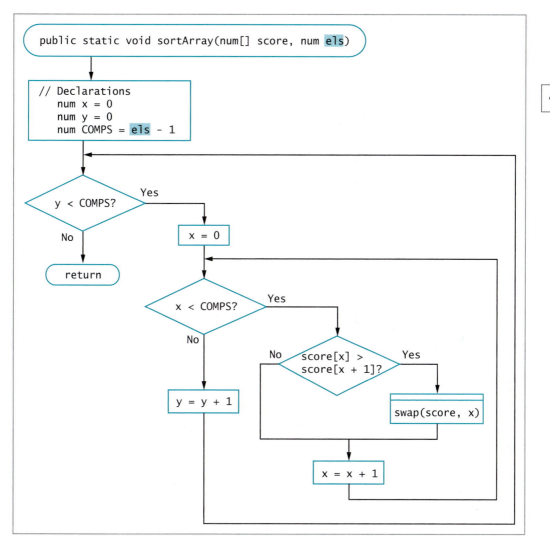

Figure 12-9 Score-sorting application in which number of elements to sort can vary (continued)

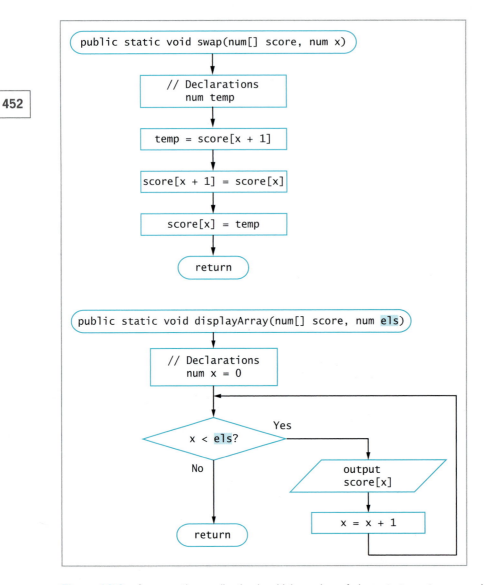

Figure 12-9   Score-sorting application in which number of elements to sort can vary (continued)

```
class SortScores2
   public static void main()
   // Declarations
      num SIZE = 100
      num score[SIZE]
      num numberOfEls
      numberOfEls = fillArray(score, SIZE)
      sortArray(score, numberOfEls)
      displayArray(score, numberOfEls)
   return

   public static num fillArray(num[] score, num SIZE)
      // Declarations
         num x = 0
         num limit = SIZE - 1
         num QUIT = 9999
      output "Enter a score or ", QUIT, " to quit "
      input score[x]
      while score[x] <> QUIT AND x < limit
         x = x + 1
         output "Enter a score or ", QUIT, " to quit "
         input score[x]
      endwhile
   return x

   public static void sortArray(num[] score, num els)
      // Declarations
         num x = 0
         num y = 0
         num COMPS = els - 1
      while y < COMPS
         x = 0
         while x < COMPS
            if score[x] > score[x + 1] then
               swap(score, x)
            endif
            x = x + 1
         endwhile
         y = y + 1
      endwhile
   return

   public static void swap(num[] score, num x)
      // Declarations
         num temp
      temp = score[x + 1]
      score[x + 1] = score[x]
      score[x] = temp
   return

   public static void displayArray(num[] score, num els)
      // Declarations
         num x = 0
      while x < els
         output score[x]
         x = x + 1
      endwhile
   return
endClass
```

Figure 12-9   Score-sorting application in which number of elements to sort can vary

In the `fillArray()` method in Figure 12-9, notice that priming prompt and input statements have been added. If the user enters the `QUIT` value at the first input, then the number of elements to be sorted will be 0.

In the application in Figure 12-9, it does not matter if there are not enough scores to fill the array. However, an error occurs if you attempt to store more values than the array can hold. When you don't know how many elements will be stored in an array, you must overestimate the number of elements you declare.

Refining the Bubble Sort to Reduce Unnecessary Comparisons

You can make additional improvements to the bubble sort created in the previous sections. When you perform a bubble sort, you pass through a list, making comparisons and swapping values if two adjacent values are out of order. If you are performing an ascending sort and you have made one pass through the list, the largest value is guaranteed to be in its correct final position at the bottom of the list. Similarly, the second-largest element is guaranteed to be in its correct second-to-last position after the second pass through the list, and so on. If you continue to compare every element pair on every pass through the list, you are comparing elements that are already guaranteed to be in their final correct position. In other words, after the first pass through the list, you no longer need to check the bottom element; after the second pass, you don't need to check the two bottom elements.

You can avoid comparing values that are already in place by creating a new variable, `pairsToCompare`, and setting it equal to one less than the number of elements to be sorted. On the first pass through the list, every pair of elements is compared, so `pairsToCompare` *should* equal one less than the number of elements. In other words, with five array elements to sort, four pairs are compared, and with 50 elements to sort, 49 pairs are compared. On each subsequent pass through the list, `pairsToCompare` should be reduced by 1; for example, after the first pass is completed, it is not necessary to check the bottom element. See Figure 12-10 to examine the use of the `pairsToCompare` variable.

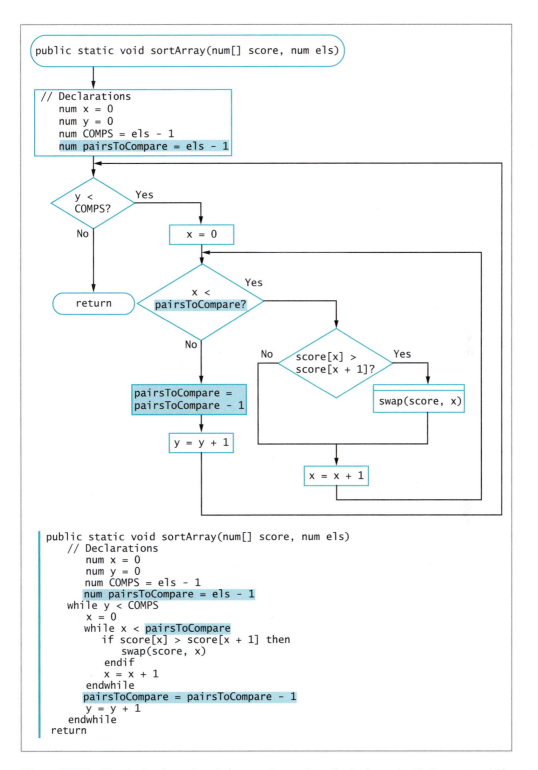

```
public static void sortArray(num[] score, num els)

// Declarations
    num x = 0
    num y = 0
    num COMPS = els - 1
    num pairsToCompare = els - 1

        y < COMPS?          Yes

                            x = 0

        No

    return              x <
                    pairsToCompare?     Yes

                        No          No    score[x] >       Yes
                                          score[x + 1]?

                    pairsToCompare =
                    pairsToCompare - 1              swap(score, x)

                        y = y + 1

                                          x = x + 1
```

```
public static void sortArray(num[] score, num els)
    // Declarations
        num x = 0
        num y = 0
        num COMPS = els - 1
        num pairsToCompare = els - 1
    while y < COMPS
        x = 0
        while x < pairsToCompare
            if score[x] > score[x + 1] then
                swap(score, x)
            endif
            x = x + 1
        endwhile
        pairsToCompare = pairsToCompare - 1
        y = y + 1
    endwhile
    return
```

Figure 12-10   Flowchart and pseudocode for `sortArray()` method using `pairsToCompare` variable

Refining the Bubble Sort to Eliminate Unnecessary Passes

You could also improve the bubble sort method in Figure 12-10 by reducing the number of passes through the array. If array elements are badly out of order or in reverse order, many passes through the list are required to place it in order. However, when the array elements are in order or nearly in order to start, all the elements might be correctly arranged after only a few passes through the list. All subsequent passes result in no swaps. For example, assume that the original scores are as follows:

```
score[0] = 65
score[1] = 75
score[2] = 85
score[3] = 90
score[4] = 95
```

The bubble sort method in Figure 12-10 would pass through the array list four times, making four sets of pair comparisons. It would always find that each score[x] is *not* greater than the corresponding score[x + 1], so no switches would ever be made. The scores would end up in the proper order, but they *were* in the proper order in the first place; therefore, a lot of time would be wasted.

A possible remedy is to add a flag variable set to a "continue" value on any pass through the list in which any pair of elements is swapped (even if just one pair), and which holds a different "finished" value when no swaps are made—that is, when all elements in the list are already in the correct order. For example, you can create a variable named switchOccurred and set it to "No" at the start of each pass through the list. You can change its value to "Yes" each time the swap() method is performed (that is, each time a switch is necessary).

If you make it through the entire list of pairs without making a switch, the switchOccurred flag will *not* have been set to "Yes", meaning that no swap has occurred and that the array elements must already be in the correct order. This situation might occur on the first or second pass through the array list, or it might not occur until a much later pass. Once the array elements are in the correct order, you can stop making passes through the list.

Figure 12-11 illustrates a method that sorts scores and uses a switchOccurred flag. At the beginning of the sortArray() method, initialize switchOccurred to "Yes" before entering the comparison loop the first time. Then, immediately set switchOccurred to "No". When a switch occurs—that is, when the swap() method executes—set switchOccurred to "Yes".

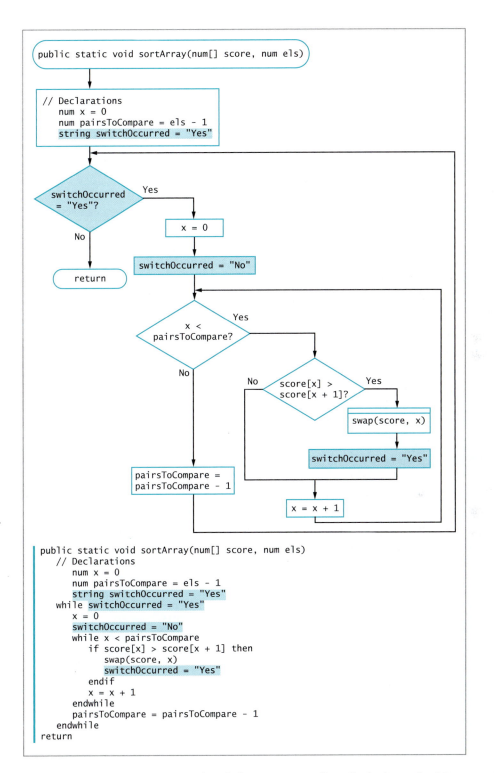

```
public static void sortArray(num[] score, num els)
    // Declarations
        num x = 0
        num pairsToCompare = els - 1
        string switchOccurred = "Yes"
    while switchOccurred = "Yes"
        x = 0
        switchOccurred = "No"
        while x < pairsToCompare
            if score[x] > score[x + 1] then
                swap(score, x)
                switchOccurred = "Yes"
            endif
            x = x + 1
        endwhile
        pairsToCompare = pairsToCompare - 1
    endwhile
return
```

Figure 12-11   Flowchart and pseudocode for `sortArray()` method using `switchOccurred` variable

With the addition of the flag variable in Figure 12-11, you no longer need the variable **y**, which was keeping track of the number of passes through the list. Instead, you keep going through the list until you can make a complete pass without any switches.

458

Sorting Data Stored in Parallel Arrays

Suppose that you have parallel arrays containing student names and test scores, like the arrays shown in Figure 12-12. Each student's name appears in the same relative position in the **name** array as his or her test score appears in the **score** array. Further suppose that you want to sort the student names and their scores in alphabetical order. You can accomplish this by comparing names. Many programming languages define relational operators such as < and > for string variables as well as numeric ones. In languages that do not allow these operators to be used with strings, built-in methods almost always can be used to compare strings.

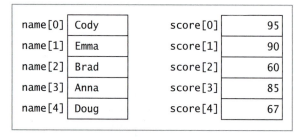

Figure 12-12 Appearance of **name** and **score** arrays in memory

If you use a sort algorithm on the **name** array to place the names in alphabetical order, the name that starts in position 3, *Anna*, should end up in position 0. If you also neglect to rearrange the **score** array, Anna's name will no longer be in the same relative position as her score, which is 85. Notice that you don't want to sort the **score** values. If you did, **score[2]**, 60, would move to position 0, and that is not Anna's score. Instead, when you sort the names, you want to make sure that each corresponding score is moved to the same position as the name to which it belongs.

Figure 12-13 shows the **swap()** module for a program that sorts **name** array values in alphabetical order and moves **score** array values correspondingly. This version of the **swap()** module uses two temporary variables—a **string** named **tempName** and a numeric variable named **tempScore**. The **swap()** method executes whenever two names in positions x and x + 1 are out of order. Besides swapping the names in positions x and x + 1, the module also swaps the scores in the same positions. Therefore, each student's score always moves along with its student's name.

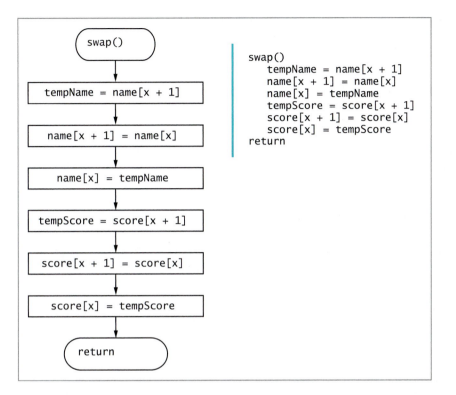

Figure 12-13 The `swap()` method for a program that sorts student names and retains their correct scores

Sorting Objects

So far, this chapter has described sorting simple data items. They are easy to compare because numeric relational operators are built into every programming language, and even if relational operators are not built in for strings, prewritten methods that compare strings are available.

However, when you use object-oriented programming techniques, you also want to be able to sort objects. Suppose that you create a **Student** class like the one shown in Figure 12-14. The class contains data fields that hold a student ID number, last name, and grade point average. You might choose to sort students by their last names or grade point averages, but for this example, assume that you want to sort **Student** objects by their ID numbers.

```
class Student
    // Declarations
        private num idNumber
        private string lastName
        private num gradePointAverage

    num getIdNumber()
        return idNumber

endClass
```

Figure 12-14　Student class

For simplicity, the Student class contains only a single method that returns the ID number. A working class would probably contain one or more constructors and other methods, but the getIdNumber() method is the only one needed to sort Student objects by ID number.

One way to sort student objects is to declare an array of type Student, populate it with objects, and then make comparisons such as the following to determine whether two adjacent elements are out of order:

```
stuArray[x].getIdNumber() > stuArray[x + 1].getIdNumber()
```

A second approach is shown in Figure 12-15. You could add a method to the Student class similar to the isGreater() method shown in the figure. If the Student class contains this method, you can compare two objects in an array by using an expression similar to the following:

```
stuArray[x].isGreater(stuArray[x + 1])
```

```
public boolean isGreater(Student stu)
    // Declarations
        boolean isGreat
    if this.idNumber > stu.getIdNumber() then
        isGreat = true
    else
        isGreat = false
    endif
    return isGreat
```

Figure 12-15　Student class isGreater() method

The method in Figure 12-15 assumes that the language used to code the program supports a Boolean data type named boolean and the keywords true and false. (All modern, object-oriented programming languages support a Boolean type that defines true or false values, but it might have a different name. For example, several languages use the data type bool.)

The comparison expression `stuArray[x].isGreater(stuArray[x + 1])` operates as follows:

1. The `stuArray[x]` object calls its `isGreater()` method, so the `this` reference within the method is the `stuArray[x]` object. The `this` object can use its `idNumber` field directly. In other words, within the method, `idNumber` refers to the object that called the method.

2. The second array element, `stuArray[x + 1]`, is passed to the method and becomes the parameter `stu`. The `stu` object must use the `getIdNumber()` method to access its `idNumber`.

3. Within the `isGreater()` method, a local Boolean variable, `isGreat`, is declared.

4. A comparison is made. The `this` object's `idNumber` (the `idNumber` of `stuArray[x]`) is compared to the `stu` object's `idNumber` (the `idNumber` of `stuArray[x + 1]`), and `isGreat` is set to `true` or `false`.

5. The value of `isGreat` is returned to the location of the original expression in the program, most likely as part of an `if` statement.

After a method for comparing `Student` objects has been established, you can sort them using any sorting algorithm that works with simple numeric values. For example, to sort `Students` using a bubble sort, you simply compare adjacent values in a list and swap them when they are out of order.

Using the Insertion Sort Algorithm

The bubble sort works well and is relatively easy to understand and manipulate, but many other sorting algorithms have been developed. For example, when you use an **insertion sort**, you look at each list element one at a time. If an element is out of order relative to any of the items earlier in the list, you move each earlier item down one position and then insert the tested element. The insertion sort is similar to the technique you would most likely use to sort a group of objects manually. For example, if a list contains the values 2, 3, 1, and 4, and you want to place them in ascending order using an insertion sort, you test the values 2 and 3, but you do not move them because they are in order. However, when you test the third value in the list, 1, you move both 2 and 3 to later positions and insert 1 at the first position.

Figure 12-16 shows the logic that performs an ascending insertion sort using a five-element array named `score`. Assume that a constant named `SIZE` has been set to 5, and that the five scores in the array are as follows:

```
score[0] = 90
score[1] = 85
score[2] = 65
score[3] = 95
score[4] = 75
```

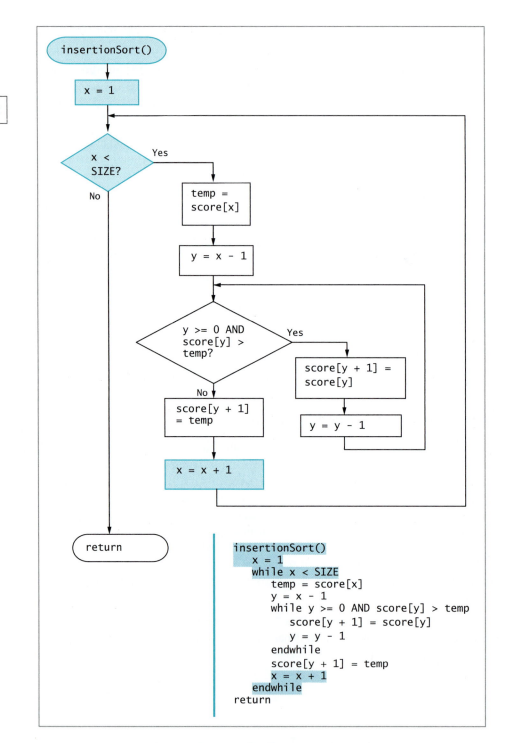

Figure 12-16   Flowchart and pseudocode for the `insertionSort()` method

The shaded outer loop varies a loop control variable x from 1 through one less than the size of the array. The logic proceeds as follows:

First x is set to 1, and then the unshaded section in the center of Figure 12-16 executes.

1. The value of temp is set to score[1], which is 85, and y is set to 0.

2. Because y is greater than or equal to 0 and score[y] (90) is greater than temp, the inner loop is entered. (If you were performing a descending sort, then you would ask whether score[y] was less than temp.)

3. The value of score[1] becomes 90 and y is decremented, making it −1, so y is no longer greater than or equal to 0, and the inner loop ends.

4. Then score[0] is set to temp, which is 85.

After these steps, 90 was moved down one position and 85 was inserted in the first position, so the array values are in slightly better order than they were originally. The values are as follows:

```
score[0] = 85
score[1] = 90
score[2] = 65
score[3] = 95
score[4] = 75
```

Now, in the outer loop, x becomes 2. The logic in the unshaded portion of Figure 12-16 proceeds as follows:

1. The value of temp becomes 65, and y is set to 1.

2. The value of y is greater than or equal to 0, and score[y] (90) is greater than temp, so the inner loop is entered.

3. The value of score[2] becomes 90 and y is decremented, making it 0, so the loop executes again.

4. The value of score[1] becomes 85 and y is decremented, making it −1, so the loop ends.

5. Then score[0] becomes 65.

After these steps, the array values are in better order than they were originally, because 65 and 85 now both come before 90:

```
score[0] = 65
score[1] = 85
score[2] = 90
score[3] = 95
score[4] = 75
```

Now, x becomes 3. The logic in Figure 12-16 proceeds to work on the new list as follows:

1. The value of `temp` becomes 95, and y is set to 2.

2. For the loop to execute, y must be greater than or equal to 0, which it is, and `score[y]` (90) must be greater than `temp`, which it is *not*. So, the inner loop does not execute.

3. Therefore, `score[2]` is set to 90, which it already was. In other words, no changes are made.

Now, x is increased to 4. The logic in Figure 12-16 proceeds as follows:

1. The value of `temp` becomes 75, and y is set to 3.

2. The value of y is greater than or equal to 0, and `score[y]` (95) is greater than `temp`, so the inner loop is entered.

3. The value of `score[4]` becomes 95 and y is decremented, making it 2, so the loop executes again.

4. The value of `score[3]` becomes 90 and y is decremented, making it 1, so the loop executes again.

5. The value of `score[2]` becomes 85 and y is decremented, making it 0; `score[y]` (65) is no longer greater than `temp` (75), so the inner loop ends. In other words, the scores 85, 90, and 95 are each moved down one position, but score 65 is left in place.

6. Then `score[1]` becomes 75.

After these steps, all the array values have been rearranged in ascending order as follows:

```
score[0] = 65
score[1] = 75
score[2] = 85
score[3] = 90
score[4] = 95
```

Figure 12-17 illustrates the steps used in the insertion sort.

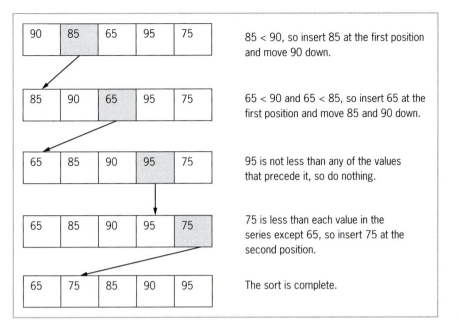

90	85	65	95	75	85 < 90, so insert 85 at the first position and move 90 down.
85	90	65	95	75	65 < 90 and 65 < 85, so insert 65 at the first position and move 85 and 90 down.
65	85	90	95	75	95 is not less than any of the values that precede it, so do nothing.
65	85	90	95	75	75 is less than each value in the series except 65, so insert 75 at the second position.
65	75	85	90	95	The sort is complete.

Figure 12-17   The steps accomplished in the complete insertion sort

Watch the video *The Insertion Sort*.

Many sorting algorithms exist in addition to the bubble sort and insertion sort. You might want to investigate the logic used by the *selection sort*, *cocktail sort*, *gnome sort*, and *quick sort*.

Using Multidimensional Arrays

In Chapter 5, you learned that an array is a series or list of values in computer memory, and all values have the same name and data type but are differentiated with special numbers called subscripts. Usually, all the values in an array have something in common; for example, they might represent a list of employee ID numbers or a list of prices for items sold in a store.

An array whose elements you can access using a single subscript is a **one-dimensional** or **single-dimensional array**. The array has only one dimension because its data can be stored in a table that has just one dimension—height. If you know the vertical position of a one-dimensional array's element, you can find its value.

For example, suppose that you own an apartment building and charge five different rent amounts for apartments on different floors (including floor 0, the basement), as shown in Table 12-1.

Floor	Rent ($)
0	350
1	400
2	475
3	600
4	1000

Table 12-1 Rent schedule based on floor

You could declare the following array to hold the rent values:

`num RENT_BY_FLOOR[5] = 350, 400, 475, 600, 1000`

The location of any rent value in Table 12-1 depends on only a single variable—the floor of the building. So, when you create a single-dimensional array to hold rent values, you need just one subscript to identify the row.

Sometimes, however, locating a value in an array depends on more than one variable. If you must represent values in a table or grid that contains rows and columns instead of a single list, then you might want to use a **two-dimensional array**. A two-dimensional array contains two dimensions: height and width. That is, the location of any element depends on two factors. For example, if an apartment's rent depends on two variables—both the floor of the building and the number of bedrooms—then you want to create a two-dimensional array.

As an example of how useful two-dimensional arrays can be, assume that you own an apartment building with five floors, and that each of the floors has studio apartments (with no bedroom) and one- and two-bedroom apartments. Table 12-2 shows the rental amounts.

Floor	Studio Apartment	1-Bedroom Apartment	2-Bedroom Apartment
0	350	390	435
1	400	440	480
2	475	530	575
3	600	650	700
4	1000	1075	1150

Table 12-2 Rent schedule based on floor and number of bedrooms

To determine a tenant's rent, you need to know two pieces of information: the floor where the tenant lives and the number of bedrooms in the apartment. Each element in a two-dimensional array requires two subscripts to reference it—one subscript to determine the row and a second to determine the column. Thus, the 15 rent values for a two-dimensional array based on Table 12-2 would be arranged in five rows and three columns and defined as follows:

```
num RENT_BY_FLOOR_AND_BDRMS[5][3]= {350, 390, 435},
                                   {400, 440, 480},
                                   {475, 530, 575},
                                   {600, 650, 700},
                                   {1000, 1075, 1150}
```

Figure 12-18 shows how the one- and two-dimensional rent arrays might appear in computer memory.

A One-Dimensional Array

```
num RENT_BY_FLOOR[5] = 350,
400, 475, 600, 1000
```

350
400
475
600
1000

A Two-Dimensional Array

```
num RENT_BY_FLOOR_AND_BDRMS[5][3] =
            {350, 390, 435},
            {400, 440, 480},
            {475, 530, 575},
            {600, 650, 700},
            {1000, 1075, 1150}
```

350	390	435
400	440	480
475	530	575
600	650	700
1000	1075	1150

Figure 12-18 One- and two-dimensional arrays in memory

When you declare a one-dimensional array, you use a set of square brackets after the array type and name. To declare a two-dimensional array, many languages require you to use two sets of brackets after the array type and name. For each element in the array, the first square bracket holds the number of rows and the second one holds the number of columns. In other words, the two dimensions represent the array's height and its width.

Instead of two sets of brackets to indicate a position in a two-dimensional array, some languages use a single set of brackets but separate the subscripts with commas. Therefore, the elements in row 1, column 2 would be RENT_BY_FLOOR_AND_BDRMS[1, 2].

In the RENT_BY_FLOOR_AND_BDRMS array declaration, the values that are assigned to each row are enclosed in braces to help you picture the placement of each number in the array. The first row of the array holds the three rent values 350, 390, and 435 for floor 0; the second row holds 400, 440, and 480 for floor 1; and so on.

You access a two-dimensional array value using two subscripts, in which the first subscript represents the row and the second one represents the column. For example, some of the values in the array are as follows:

- RENT_BY_FLOOR_AND_BDRMS[0][0] is 350

- RENT_BY_FLOOR_AND_BDRMS[0][1] is 390

- RENT_BY_FLOOR_AND_BDRMS[0][2] is 435

- RENT_BY_FLOOR_AND_BDRMS[4][0] is 1000

- RENT_BY_FLOOR_AND_BDRMS[4][1] is 1075

- RENT_BY_FLOOR_AND_BDRMS[4][2] is 1150

If you declare two variables to hold the floor number and bedroom count as num floor and num bedrooms, any tenant's rent is RENT_BY_FLOOR_AND_BDRMS[floor][bedrooms].

When mathematicians use a two-dimensional array, they often call it a **matrix** or a **table**. You may have used a spreadsheet—a two-dimensional array in which you need to know a row number and a column letter to access a specific cell.

Figure 12-19 shows a program that continuously displays rents for apartments based on renter requests for floor location and number of bedrooms. Notice that although significant setup is required to provide all the values for the rents, the basic program is extremely brief and easy to follow. (You could improve the program in Figure 12-19 by making sure the values for floor and bedrooms are within range before using them as array subscripts.)

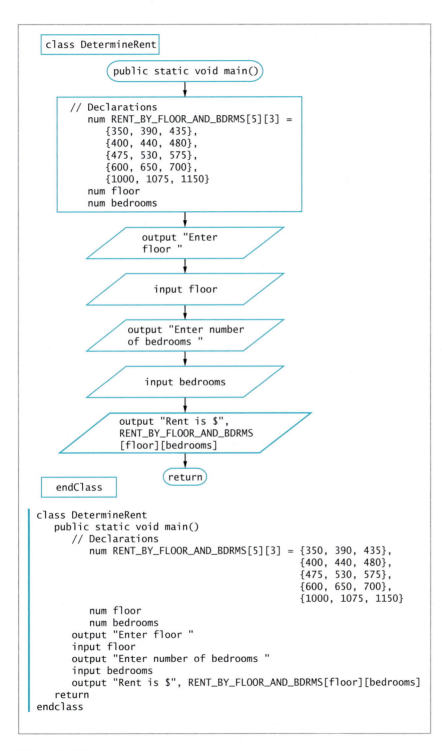

```
class DetermineRent
    public static void main()
        // Declarations
            num RENT_BY_FLOOR_AND_BDRMS[5][3] = {350, 390, 435},
                                                {400, 440, 480},
                                                {475, 530, 575},
                                                {600, 650, 700},
                                                {1000, 1075, 1150}

            num floor
            num bedrooms
        output "Enter floor "
        input floor
        output "Enter number of bedrooms "
        input bedrooms
        output "Rent is $", RENT_BY_FLOOR_AND_BDRMS[floor][bedrooms]
    return
endclass
```

Figure 12-19 A program that determines rents

Watch the video *Two-Dimensional Arrays.*

Two-dimensional arrays are never actually *required* in order to achieve a useful program. The same 15 categories of rent information could be stored in three separate single-dimensional arrays of five elements each, and you could use a decision to determine which array to access. Of course, don't forget that even one-dimensional arrays are never required to solve a problem. You could also declare 15 separate rent variables and make 15 separate decisions to determine the rent.

Besides one- and two-dimensional arrays, many programming languages also support **three-dimensional arrays**. For example, if you own a multistory apartment building with different numbers of bedrooms available in apartments on each floor, you can use a two-dimensional array to store the rental fees, but if you own several apartment buildings, you might want to employ a third dimension to store the building number. For example, if a three-dimensional array is stored on paper, you might need to know an element's row, column, and page to access it, as shown in Figure 12-20.

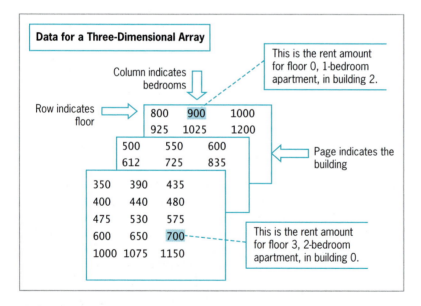

Figure 12-20   Picturing a three-dimensional array

If you declare a three-dimensional array named RENT_BY_3_FACTORS, then you can use an expression such as RENT_BY_3_FACTORS[floor][bedrooms][building], which refers to a specific rent figure for an apartment whose floor and bedroom numbers are stored in the floor and bedrooms variables, and whose building number is stored in the building variable. Specifically, RENT_BY_3_FACTORS[0][1][2] refers to a one-bedroom apartment on floor 0 of building 2.

Both two- and three-dimensional arrays are examples of **multidimensional arrays**, which are arrays that have more than one dimension. Some languages allow many dimensions. For example, in C# and Visual Basic, an array can have 32 dimensions. However, it's usually hard for people to keep track of more than three dimensions.

Using Indexed Files and Linked Lists

Sorting a list of five or even 100 scores does not require significant computer resources. However, many data files contain thousands or millions of records, and each record might contain dozens of data fields. Sorting large numbers of data records requires considerable time and computer memory. When a large data file needs to be processed in ascending or descending order based on a particular field, the most efficient approach usually is to store and access records based on their logical order rather than sorting and accessing them in their physical order. **Physical order** refers to a "real" order for storage; an example would be writing the names of 10 friends, each one on a separate index card. You can arrange the cards alphabetically by the friends' last names, chronologically by age of the friendship, or randomly by throwing the cards in the air and picking them up as you find them. Whichever way you do it, the records still follow each other in *some* order. In addition to their current physical order, you can think of the cards as having a **logical order**; that is, a virtual order, based on any criterion you choose—from the tallest friend to the shortest, from the one who lives farthest away to the closest, and so on. Sorting the cards in a new physical order can take a lot of time; using the cards in their logical order without physically rearranging them is often more efficient.

Using Indexed Files

A common method of accessing records in logical order requires using an index. Using an index involves identifying a key field for each record. A record's **key field** is a field whose contents make the record unique among all records in a file. For example, multiple employees can have the same last name, first name, salary, or street address, but each employee possesses a unique employee identification number, so an ID number field might make a good key field for a personnel file. Similarly, a product number makes a good key field in an inventory file.

As pages in a book have numbers, computer memory and storage locations have **addresses**. In Chapter 1, you learned that every variable has a numeric address in computer memory; likewise, every data record on a disk has a numeric address where it is stored. You can store records in any physical order on the disk, but when you **index** records, you store a list of key fields paired with the storage address for the corresponding data record. You can then use the index to find the records in order based on their addresses.

When you use an index, you can store records on a **random-access storage device**, such as a disk, from which records can be accessed in any order. Each record can be placed in any physical location on the disk, and you can use the index as you would use an index in the back of a book. If you pick up a 600-page American history book because you need some facts about Betsy Ross, you do not want to start on page one and work your way through the book. Instead, you turn to the index, discover that Betsy Ross is mentioned on page 418, and go directly to that page. As a programmer, you do not need to determine a record's exact physical address in order to use it. A computer's operating system locates available storage for your records.

You can picture an index based on ID numbers by looking at the index in Figure 12-21. The index is stored on a portion of the disk. The address in the index refers to other scattered locations on the disk.

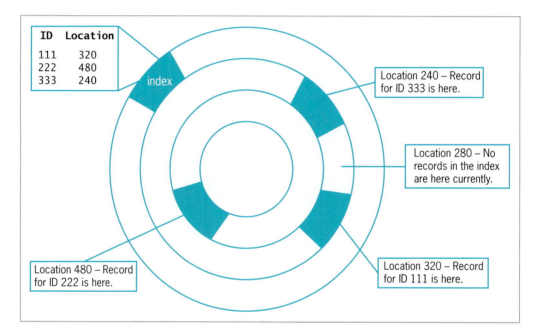

Figure 12-21   An index on a disk that associates ID numbers with disk addresses

When you want to access the data for employee 333, you tell your computer to look through the ID numbers in the index, find a match, and then proceed to the memory location specified. Similarly, when you want to process records in order based on ID number, you tell your system to retrieve records at the locations in the index in sequence. Thus, employee 111 may have been hired last and the record may be stored at the highest physical address on the disk, but if the employee record has the lowest ID number, it will be accessed first during ID-ordered processing.

When a record is removed from an indexed file, it does not have to be physically removed. Its reference can simply be deleted from the index, and then it will not be part of any further processing.

Watch the video *Using an Indexed File*.

Using Linked Lists

Another way to access records in a desired order, even though they might not be physically stored in that order, is to create a linked list. In its simplest form, creating a **linked list** involves creating one extra field in every record of stored data. This extra field holds the physical address of the next logical record. For example, a record that holds a customer's ID, name, and phone number might contain the following fields:

```
idNum
name
phoneNum
nextCustAddress
```

Every time you use a record, you access the next record based on the address held in the `nextCustAddress` field.

Every time you add a new record to a linked list, you search through the list for the correct logical location of the new record. For example, assume that customer records are stored at the addresses shown in Table 12-3 and that they are linked in customer ID order. Notice that the addresses of the records are not shown in sequential order. The records are shown in their logical order by `idNum`.

Address	idNum	name	phoneNum	nextCustAddress of Record
0000	111	Baker	234-5676	7200
7200	222	Vincent	456-2345	4400
4400	333	Silvers	543-0912	6000
6000	444	Donovan	328-8744	eof

Table 12-3 Sample linked customer list

You can see from Table 12-3 that each customer record contains a `nextCustAddress` field, which stores the address of the next customer who follows in customer ID number order (and not necessarily in address order). For any individual customer, the next logical customer's address might be physically distant.

Examine the file shown in Table 12-3, and suppose that a new customer named Newberg is acquired with number 245. Also suppose that the computer operating system finds an available storage location for Newberg's data at address 8400. In this case, the procedure to add Newberg to the list is:

1. Create a variable named `currentAddress` to hold the address of the record in the list you are examining. Store the address of the first record in the list, 0000, in this variable.

2. Compare the new customer Newberg's ID, 245, with the current (first) record's ID, 111 (in other words, the ID at address 0000). The value 245 is higher than 111, so you save the first customer's address, 0000, in a variable you can name `saveAddress`. The `saveAddress` variable always holds the address you just finished examining. The first customer record contains a link to the address of the next logical customer—7200. Store 7200 in the `currentAddress` variable.

3. Examine the second customer record, the one that physically exists at the address 7200, which is currently held in the `currentAddress` variable.

4. Compare Newberg's ID, 245, with the ID stored in the record at `currentAddress`, 222. The value 245 is higher, so save the current address, 7200, in `saveAddress` and store its `nextCustAddress` address field, 4400, in the `currentAddress` variable.

5. Compare Newberg's ID, 245, with 333, which is the ID at `currentAddress` (4400). Up to this point, 245 had been higher than each ID tested, but this time the value 245 is lower, so customer 245 should logically precede customer 333. Set the `nextCustAddress` field in Newberg's record (customer 245) to 4400, which is the address of customer 333 and the address stored in `currentAddress`. In any future processing, Newberg's record will logically be followed by the record containing 333. Also set the `nextCustAddress` field of the record located at `saveAddress` (7200, customer 222, who logically preceded Newberg) to the new customer Newberg's address, 8400. The updated list appears in Table 12-4.

Address	idNum	name	phoneNum	nextCustAddress of Record
0000	111	Baker	234-5676	7200
7200	222	Vincent	456-2345	8400
8400	245	Newberg	222-9876	4400
4400	333	Silvers	543-0912	6000
6000	444	Donovan	328-8744	eof

Table 12-4   Updated customer list

As with indexing, when removing records from a linked list, the records do not need to be physically deleted from the medium on which they are stored. If you need to remove customer 333 from the preceding list, all you need to do is change Newberg's `nextCustAddress` field to the value in Silvers' `nextCustAddress` field, which is Donovan's address: 6000. In other words, the value of 6000 is obtained not by knowing to which record Newberg should point, but by knowing to which record Silvers previously pointed. When

Newberg's record points to Donovan, Silvers' record is then bypassed during any further processing that uses the links to travel from one record to the next.

When you need to access data items in order, using a linked list can offer several advantages over using an array. When you don't know how many elements eventually will be stored in an array, you might have to declare the array to be larger than necessary. If all the elements are not needed, then memory is wasted. Linked lists only occupy as much memory as needed. Additionally, when you insert a new element into an ordered array, you must move every subsequent element to make room for the new one. This process can take time if many elements must be moved. When you use a linked list, no data has to be moved; instead, the relevant links are just updated. However, using a linked list might not be the best approach if data items are small. In that case, adding one or more links to each item might increase its size significantly, and using an array might be the better option.

More sophisticated linked lists store *two* additional fields with each record. One field stores the address of the next record, and the other field stores the address of the *previous* record so that the list can be accessed either forward or backward.

 Watch the video *Using a Linked List*.

Chapter Summary

- Frequently, data items need to be sorted. When you sort data, you can sort either in ascending order, arranging records from lowest to highest value, or in descending order, arranging records from highest to lowest value.

- In a bubble sort, items in a list are compared with each other in pairs. When an item is out of order, it swaps values with the item below it. With an ascending bubble sort, after each adjacent pair of items in a list has been compared once, the largest item in the list will have "sunk" to the bottom; after many passes through the list, the smallest items rise to the top. The bubble sort algorithm can be improved to sort varying numbers of values and to eliminate unnecessary comparisons.

- When you sort records, two possible approaches are to place related data items in parallel arrays and to sort objects as a whole.

- When you use an insertion sort, you look at each list element one at a time. If an element is out of order relative to any of the items earlier in the list, you move each earlier item down one position and then insert the tested element.

- Two-dimensional arrays have both rows and columns of values. You must use two subscripts when you access an element in a two-dimensional array. Many languages support arrays with even more dimensions.

- You can use an index or linked list to access data records in a logical order that differs from their physical order. Using an index involves identifying a physical address and key field for each record. Creating a linked list involves creating an extra field within every record to hold the physical address of the next logical record.

Key Terms

Sequential order describes the arrangement of records when they are stored one after another on the basis of the value in a particular field.

Sorted describes values that are placed in order.

Ascending order describes the arrangement of items in order from lowest to highest.

Descending order describes the arrangement of items in order from highest to lowest.

The **median** value in a list is the value in the middle position when the values are sorted.

The **mean** value in a list is the arithmetic average.

A **bubble sort** is a sort in which you arrange list elements in either ascending or descending order by comparing items in pairs; when an item is out of order, it swaps values with the item below it.

A **sinking sort** is another name for a bubble sort.

An **algorithm** is a list of instructions that accomplishes a task.

To **swap values** is to exchange the values of two variables.

An **insertion sort** is a sort in which you look at each list element one at a time; if an element is out of order relative to any of the items earlier in the list, you move each previous item down one position and then insert the tested element.

A **one-dimensional** or **single-dimensional array** is a list accessed using a single subscript.

Two-dimensional arrays have both rows and columns of values; you must use two subscripts when you access an element in a two-dimensional array.

Matrix and **table** are terms used by mathematicians to describe a two-dimensional array.

Three-dimensional arrays are arrays in which each element is accessed using three subscripts.

Multidimensional arrays are lists with more than one dimension.

Physical order describes the order in which the items in a list are actually stored.

Logical order describes the order in which you use the items in a list, even though they are not necessarily stored in that physical order.

A record's **key field** is a field whose contents make the record unique among all records in a file.

Addresses identify computer memory and storage locations.

When you **index** records, you store a list of key fields paired with the storage address for the corresponding data record.

A **random-access storage device**, such as a disk, is one from which records can be accessed in any order.

A **linked list** contains an extra field in every record of stored data; this extra field holds the physical address of the next logical record.

Review Questions

1. Employee records stored in order from highest-paid to lowest-paid have been sorted in _____ order.

   a. ascending
   b. descending

   c. staggered
   d. recursive

2. Student records stored in alphabetical order by last name have been sorted in _____ order.

   a. ascending
   b. descending

   c. staggered
   d. recursive

3. When computers sort data, they always _____ .

   a. place items in ascending order
   b. use a bubble sort
   c. use numeric values when making comparisons
   d. begin the process by locating the position of the lowest value

4. Which of the following code segments correctly swaps the values of variables named x and y?

   a.
   ```
   x = y
   y = temp
   x = temp
   ```
   b.
   ```
   temp = x
   x = y
   y = temp
   ```

   c.
   ```
   x = y
   temp = x
   y = temp
   ```
   d.
   ```
   temp = x
   y = x
   x = temp
   ```

5. Which type of sort compares list items in pairs, swapping adjacent values that are out of order?

   a. bubble sort
   b. indexed sort

   c. insertion sort
   d. selection sort

6. To sort a list of eight values using a bubble sort, the greatest number of times you would have to pass through the list making comparisons is _____ .

   a. six

   b. seven

   c. eight

   d. nine

7. To completely sort a list of eight values using a bubble sort, the greatest possible number of required pair comparisons is _____ .

   a. seven

   b. eight

   c. 49

   d. 64

8. When you do not know how many items need to be sorted in a program, you can create an array that has _____ .

   a. variable-sized elements

   b. at least as many elements as the number you predict you will need

   c. at least one element less than the number you predict you will need

   d. You cannot sort items if you do not know the number of items when you write the program.

9. In a bubble sort, on each pass through the list that must be sorted, you can stop making pair comparisons _____ .

   a. one comparison sooner

   b. two comparisons sooner

   c. one comparison later

   d. two comparisons later

10. When performing a bubble sort on a list of 10 values, you can stop making passes through the list of values as soon as _____ on a single pass through the list.

   a. no swaps are made

   b. exactly one swap is made

   c. no more than nine swaps are made

   d. no more than 10 swaps are made

11. The bubble sort is _____ .

   a. the most efficient sort

   b. a relatively fast sort compared to others

   c. a relatively easy sort to understand

   d. all of the above

12. Data stored in a table that can be accessed using row and column numbers is stored as a _____ array.

   a. single-dimensional

   b. two-dimensional

   c. three-dimensional

   d. nondimensional

13. A two-dimensional array declared as num myArray[6][7] has —————— columns.

    a. 5   c. 7
    b. 6   d. 8

14. In a two-dimensional array declared as num myArray[6][7], the highest row number is —————— .

    a. 5   c. 7
    b. 6   d. 8

15. If you access a two-dimensional array with the expression output myArray[2][5], the output value will be —————— .

    a. 0
    b. 2
    c. 5
    d. impossible to tell from the information given

16. Three-dimensional arrays —————— .

    a. are supported in many modern programming languages
    b. always contain at least nine elements
    c. are used only in object-oriented languages
    d. all of the above

17. Student records are stored in ID number order, but accessed by grade point average for a report. Grade point average order is a(n) —————— order.

    a. imaginary   c. logical
    b. physical   d. illogical

18. When you store a list of key fields paired with the storage address for the corresponding data record, you are creating —————— .

    a. a directory   c. a linked list
    b. a three-dimensional array   d. an index

19. When a record in an indexed file is not needed for further processing, —————— .

    a. its first character must be replaced with a special character, indicating it is a deleted record
    b. its position must be retained, but its fields must be replaced with blanks
    c. it must be physically removed from the file
    d. the record can stay in place physically, but its reference is removed from the index

20. With a linked list, every record _____ .

   a. is stored in sequential order

   b. contains a field that holds the address of another record

   c. contains a code that indicates the record's position in an imaginary list

   d. is stored in a physical location that corresponds to a key field

Exercises

1. Design an application that accepts 10 numbers and displays them in descending order.

2. Design an application that accepts eight friends' first names and displays them in alphabetical order.

3. a. Professor Zak allows students to drop the two lowest scores on the ten 100-point quizzes she gives during the semester. Design an application that accepts a student name and 10 quiz scores. Output the student's name and total points for the student's eight highest-scoring quizzes.

   b. Modify the application in Exercise 3a so that the student's mean and median scores on the eight best quizzes are displayed.

4. The Keen Knife Company has 12 salespeople. Write a program that a clerk can use to enter each salesperson's monthly sales goal and actual monthly sales in dollars, and determine the mean and median values of each of the two monthly amounts.

5. The village of Marengo conducted a census and collected records that contain household data, including the number of occupants in each household. The exact number of household records has not yet been determined, but you know that Marengo has fewer than 300 households. Develop the logic for a program that allows a user to enter each household size and determine the mean and median household size in Marengo.

6. a. The Palmertown Elementary School has 30 classrooms. The children in the school donate used books to sell at an annual fundraising book fair. Write a program that accepts each teacher's name and the number of books donated by that teacher's classroom. Display the names of the four teachers whose classrooms donated the most books.

   b. Modify the book donation program so that besides the teacher's name and number of books donated, the program also accepts the number of students in each classroom. Display the names of the teachers whose classrooms had the four highest ratios of book donations per pupil.

7. *The Daily Trumpet* newspaper accepts classified advertisements in 15 categories such as *Apartments for Rent* and *Pets for Sale*. Develop the logic for a program that accepts classified advertising data, including category code (an integer 1 through 15) and number of words in the ad. Store these values in parallel arrays. Then sort the arrays so that records are in ascending order by category. The output lists each category, the number of ads in each category, and the total number of words in the ads in each category.

8. The MidAmerica Bus Company charges fares to passengers based on the number of travel zones they cross. Additionally, discounts are provided for multiple passengers traveling together. Ticket fares are shown in Table 12-5.

	Zones Crossed			
Passengers	0	1	2	3
1	7.50	10.00	12.00	12.75
2	14.00	18.50	22.00	23.00
3	20.00	21.00	32.00	33.00
4	25.00	27.50	36.00	37.00

Table 12-5 Bus fares

Develop the logic for a program that accepts the number of passengers and zones crossed as input. The output is the ticket charge.

9. In golf, par represents a standard number of strokes a player needs to complete a hole. Instead of using an absolute score, players can compare their scores on a hole to the par figure. Families can play nine holes of miniature golf at the Family Fun Miniature Golf Park. So that family members can compete fairly, the course provides a different par for each hole based on the player's age. The par figures are shown in Table 12-6.

	Holes								
Age	1	2	3	4	5	6	7	8	9
4 and under	8	8	9	7	5	7	8	5	8
5–7	7	7	8	6	5	6	7	5	6
8–11	6	5	6	5	4	5	5	4	5
12–15	5	4	4	4	3	4	3	3	4
16 and over	4	3	3	3	2	3	2	3	3

Table 12-6 Golf par values

a. Develop the logic for a program that accepts a player's name, age, and nine-hole score as input. Display the player's name and score on each of the nine holes, with one of the phrases *Over par*, *Par*, or *Under par* next to each score.

b. Modify the program in Exercise 9a so that, at the end of the golfer's report, the total score is displayed. Include the player's total score in relation to par for the entire course.

10. Building Block Day Care Center charges varying weekly rates depending on the age of the child and the number of days per week the child attends, as shown in Table 12-7. Develop the logic for a program that continuously accepts child care data and displays the appropriate weekly rate.

	Days per Week				
Age in Years	1	2	3	4	5
0	30.00	60.00	88.00	115.00	140.00
1	26.00	52.00	70.00	96.00	120.00
2	24.00	46.00	67.00	89.00	110.00
3	22.00	40.00	60.00	75.00	88.00
4 or more	20.00	35.00	50.00	66.00	84.00

Table 12-7   Day care rates

11. Executive Training School offers typing classes. Each final exam evaluates a student's typing speed and the number of typing errors made. Develop the logic for a program that produces a summary table of each examination's results. Each row represents the number of students whose typing speed falls within the following ranges of words per minute: 0–19, 20–39, 40–69, and 70 or more. Each column represents the number of students who made different numbers of typing errors— 0 through 6 or more.

12. HappyTunes is an application for downloading music files. Each time a file is purchased, a transaction record is created that includes the music genre and price paid. The available genres are *Classical, Easy Listening, Jazz, Pop, Rock,* and *Other*. Develop an application that accepts input data for each transaction and displays a report that lists each of the music genres, along with a count of the number of downloads in each of the following price categories:

- Over $10.00
- $6.00 through $9.99
- $3.00 through $5.99
- Under $3.00

13. In Chapter 5, you designed the logic for a multiple-choice quiz. Modify the program so it allows the user to retake the quiz up to four additional times or until the user achieves a perfect score, whichever comes first. At the end of all the quiz attempts, display a recap of the user's scores.

14. Design a guessing game that generates a random number and let a player try to guess it. After each guess, display a message indicating whether the player's guess was correct, too high, or too low. When the player eventually guesses the correct number, display a score that represents a count of the number of required guesses. Allow the player to replay the game as many times as he likes, up to 20 times. When the player is done, display the scores from highest to lowest, and display the mean and median scores.

15. a. Create a TicTacToe game. In this game, two players alternate placing Xs and Os into a grid until one player has three matching symbols in a row, either horizontally, vertically, or diagonally. Create a game that displays a three-by-three grid containing the digits 1 through 9, similar to the first window shown in Figure 12-22. When the user chooses a position by typing a number, place an X in the appropriate spot. For example, after the user chooses 3, the screen looks like the second window in Figure 12-22. Generate a random number for the position where the computer will place an O. Do not allow the player or the computer to place a symbol where one has already been placed. When either the player or computer has three symbols in a row, declare a winner. If all positions have been used and no one has three symbols in a row, declare a tie.

Figure 12-22   A TicTacToe game

b. In the TicTacToe game in Exercise 15a, the computer's selection is chosen randomly. Improve the game so that when the computer has two Os in any row, column, or diagonal, it selects the winning position for its next move rather than selecting a position randomly.

483

Case Projects

Case: Cost Is No Object

1. In earlier chapters, you developed classes needed for Cost Is No Object, including Name, Address, Date, Employee, Customer, Automobile, and RentalAgreement. In Chapter 7, you created the Employee class to contain the following fields and get and set methods for each field:

- string idNumber
- Name name
- Address address
- Date hireDate
- num hourlyPayRate

Assume that each employee of Cost Is No Object also has one of the job codes shown in Table 12-8, along with the corresponding title and pay rate.

Job Code	Title	Hourly Pay Rate
10	Desk clerk	15.00
11	Credit checker	15.00
12	Billing clerk	15.00
13	Car cleaner	15.00
14	Chauffeur	19.00
15	Marketer	19.00
16	Accountant	28.00
17	Mechanic	28.00
18	CEO	75.00

Table 12-8   Job titles and pay rates for Cost Is No Object

Complete the following tasks:

- Modify the Employee class to include a job code and title. Include a public method to set the job code. Include a private method to set the job title based on the job code. Modify the existing method that sets the hourly pay rate so that it is private and sets the rate based on the job code. Include public get methods for each field.

- Create an application in which you create an array of 25 Employee objects.

- Prompt a user for data for any number of Employees up to 25. In turn, pass each Employee object to a method that accepts an Employee, prompts the user for necessary data, and returns a "filled" Employee object to the array.

- Pass the Employee array to a method that counts the number of employees in each of the nine job categories and displays a count of each.

- Pass the Employee array to a method that sorts Employees in ascending ID number order and displays a list of Employee first and last names in ID number order.

- Pass the Employee array to a method that displays the last names and pay rates of the employees with the five highest pay rates, including ties. If there are fewer than five employees, display all of them.

Case: Classic Reunions

2. In earlier chapters, you developed classes needed for Classic Reunions, including Name, School, Address, Date, ContactPerson, Employee, Party, and PartyAgreement. In Chapter 7, you created the PartyAgreement class to contain the following fields and get and set methods for each field:

- string partyAgreementNumber
- Party party
- Employee partyCoordinator
- Date agreementDate
- num contractPrice

The Party class contains the following fields:

- string idNumber
- School school
- Date partyDate
- num numberOfGuests
- ContactPerson contactPerson

Assume that the number of guests in the Party class determines the contract price in the PartyAgreement class, as shown in Table 12-9.

Number of Guests	Price per Person
1–12	40.00
13–30	38.00
31–99	36.00
100–199	34.00
200 and up	32.00

Table 12-9   Party prices for Classic Reunions

Complete the following tasks:

- Modify the PartyAgreement class so the method that sets the contract price gets the number of guests from its Party object and determines the contract price by multiplying the number of guests by the price per person.

- Create an application in which you create an array of 10 PartyAgreement objects.

- Prompt a user for data for any number of PartyAgreement objects up to 10. In turn, pass each PartyAgreement object to a method that accepts a PartyAgreement, prompts the user for necessary data, and returns a "filled" PartyAgreement object to the array.

- Pass the PartyAgreement array to a method that counts the number of parties in each of the five categories for number of guests and displays a count of each.

- Pass the PartyAgreement array to a method that sorts PartyAgreement objects in ascending order by party agreement number and displays a list of the dates and contract prices of PartyAgreement objects in party agreement number order.

- Prompt the user for today's date. Pass the PartyAgreement array to a method that displays the party agreement numbers and dates of the parties with the five soonest future dates, including ties. If there are fewer than five party agreements, display all of them.

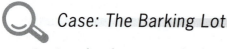

Case: The Barking Lot

3. In earlier chapters, you developed classes needed for The Barking Lot, including Name, Address, Date, Employee, Owner, Dog, and BoardingContract. In Chapter 7, you created the Dog class to contain the following fields and get and set methods for each field:

- `string idNumber`
- `string name`
- `Owner owner`
- `Date birthDate`
- `num weight`

Complete the following tasks:

- Create an application in which you create an array of 15 Dog objects.

- Prompt a user for data for any number of Dogs up to 15. In turn, pass each Dog object to a method that accepts a Dog, prompts the user for necessary data, and returns a "filled" Dog object to the array.

- Pass the Dog array to a method that counts the number of dogs in each of the following weight groups: 0–10 pounds, 11–20 pounds, 21–40 pounds, 41–90 pounds, and 91 pounds and over. Display a count of dogs in each category.

- Pass the Dog array to a method that sorts the Dogs in alphabetical order by name and displays a list of ID numbers and names in alphabetical order.

- Pass the Dog array to a method that displays the names of the dogs with the five highest weights, including ties. If there are fewer than five dogs, display all of them.

Up for Discussion

1. Now that you are becoming comfortable with arrays, you can see that programming is a complex subject. Should all literate people understand how to program? If so, how much programming should they understand?

2. What are language standards? At this point in your study of programming, what do they mean to you?

3. This chapter discusses sorting data. Suppose that a large hospital hires you to write a program that displays lists of potential organ recipients. The hospital's doctors will consult this list if they have an organ that can be transplanted. The hospital administrators instruct you to sort potential recipients by last name and display them sequentially in alphabetical order. If more than 10 patients are waiting for a particular organ, the first 10 patients are displayed; a doctor can either select one or move on to view the next set of 10 patients. You worry that this system gives an unfair advantage to patients with last names that start with A, B, C, and D. Should you write and install the program? If you do not, many transplant opportunities will be missed while the hospital searches for another programmer to write the program. Are there different criteria you would want to use to sort the patients?

Conventions in this Book

Programmers use slightly different conventions when they develop program logic. Logical principles are the same for all programmers, and the syntax used in programming languages is very specific, but flowcharts and pseudocode allow much more flexibility in matters such as punctuation and capitalization. You might see slightly different conventions used by other programmers, but this book uses the following conventions:

- Flowchart logic generally reads from top to bottom and left to right.

- In flowcharts and pseudocode, statements start with a lowercase letter and do not end with a period or other punctuation.

- Identifiers (class, method, and variable names) do not contain any white space.

- Identifiers are case sensitive.

- Class names use upper camel casing, also known as Pascal casing. This means that class names begin with an uppercase letter, and new words within the name also begin with uppercase letters.

- Method names use lower camel casing. This means that method names begin with a lowercase letter and new words within the name begin with uppercase letters.

- Variable names use lower camel casing.

- Named constants use all uppercase letters with inserted underscores for readability.

- All variables and constants are declared together at the beginning of the method that uses them. All declarations are preceded by two front slashes and the word *Declarations*, then all declarations are indented below that header.

- Classes begin with a header that contains the word `class` and end with an `endClass` statement.

- Methods begin with a method header and end with a `return` statement. The method identifier is followed by a set of parentheses.

- Input statements use the verb `input` no matter what hardware device is used as the source of the data.

- Output statements use the verb `output` no matter what hardware device is used as the destination for the information.

- Decision statements start with `if` and end with `endif`.

- Loops start with `while` or `for` and end with `endwhile` or `endfor`.

- A right-slanting parallelogram is used for the input/output flowchart symbol.

- Simple data types are `num` and `string`.

- The flowchart symbol for an internal method is a rectangle with a horizontal stripe across the top.

- The flowchart symbol for an external method call is a rectangle with vertical stripes down the sides.

Flowchart Symbols

This appendix contains the flowchart symbols used in this book.

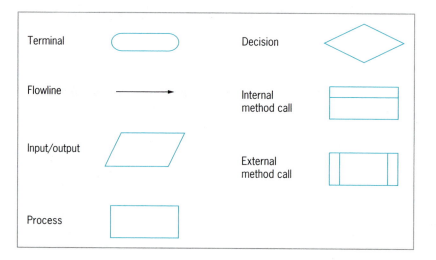

Figure B-1 Flowchart symbols

In other books, you might see the following differences:

- Some programmers use a back-slanting parallelogram to represent input and output.
- Some programmers use the external method call symbol to represent both internal and external method calls.

Understanding Numbering Systems and Computer Codes

The numbering system you know best is the **decimal numbering system**—the system based on 10 digits, 0 through 9. Mathematicians call decimal-system numbers **base 10** numbers. When you use the decimal system, no other symbols are available; if you want to express a value larger than 9, you must use multiple digits from the same pool of 10, placing them in columns.

When you use the decimal system, you analyze a multicolumn number by mentally assigning place values to each column. The value of the far right column is 1, the value of the next column to the left is 10, the next column is 100, and so on; the column values are multiplied by 10 as you move to the left. There is no limit to the number of columns you can use; you simply keep adding columns to the left as you need to express higher values. For example, Figure C-1 shows how the value 305 is represented in the decimal system. You simply sum the value of the digit in each column after it has been multiplied by the value of its column.

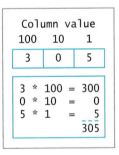

Figure C-1   Representing 305 in the decimal system

The **binary numbering system** works in the same way as the decimal numbering system, except that it uses only two digits, 0 and 1. Mathematicians call these numbers **base 2** numbers. When you use the binary system, you must use multiple columns if you want to express a value greater than 1 because no single symbol is available that represents any value other than 0 or 1. However, instead of each new column to the left being 10 times greater than the previous column, each new column in the binary system is only two times the value of the previous column. For example, Figure C-2 shows how the numbers 9 and 305 are represented in the binary system. Notice that in both the binary system and the decimal system, it is perfectly acceptable—and often necessary—to create numbers with 0 in one or more columns. As with the decimal system, there is no limit to the number of columns used in a binary number—you can use as many as it takes to express a value.

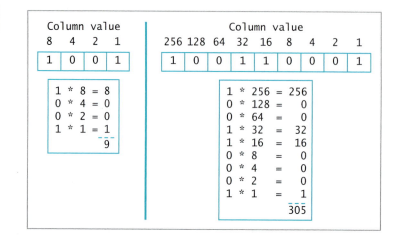

Figure C-2 Representing decimal values 9 and 305 in the binary system

A computer stores every piece of data it uses as a set of 0s and 1s. Each 0 or 1 is known as a **bit**, which is short for *binary digit*. Every computer uses 0s and 1s because all values in a computer are stored as electronic signals that are either on or off. This two-state system is most easily represented using just two digits.

Computers use a set of binary digits to represent stored characters. If computers used only one binary digit to represent characters, then only two different characters could be represented, because the single bit could be only 0 or 1. If computers used only two digits, then only four characters could be represented—the four codes 00, 01, 10, and 11, which in decimal values are 0, 1, 2, and 3, respectively. Many computers use sets of eight binary digits to represent each character they store, because using eight binary digits provides 256 different combinations. A set of eight bits is a **byte**. One byte combination can represent an *A*, another a *B*, still others *a* and *b*, and so on. Two hundred fifty-six combinations are enough so that each capital letter, small letter, digit, and punctuation mark used in English has its own code; even a space has a code. For example, in the system named the **American Standard Code for Information Interchange (ASCII)**, 01000001 represents the character *A*. The binary number 01000001 has a decimal value of 65, but this numeric value is not important to ordinary computer users; it is simply a code that stands for *A*.

The ASCII code is not the only computer code, but it is typical, and it is used in most personal computers. The **Extended Binary Coded Decimal Interchange Code**, or **EBCDIC**, is an eight-bit code that is used in IBM mainframe computers. In these computers, the principle is the same—every character is stored in a byte as a series of binary digits. However, the actual values used are different. For example, in EBCDIC, an *A* is 11000001, or 193. Another code used by languages such as Java and C# is **Unicode**; with this code, 16 bits are used to represent each character. The character *A* in Unicode has the same decimal value as the ASCII *A*, 65, but it is stored as 0000000001000001. Using two bytes provides many more possible combinations than using only eight bits—65,536 to be exact. With Unicode, enough codes are available to represent all English letters and digits, as well as characters from many international alphabets.

Ordinary computer users seldom think about the numeric codes behind the letters, numbers, and punctuation marks they enter from their keyboards or see displayed on a monitor. However, they see the consequence of the values behind letters when they see data sorted in alphabetical order. When you sort a list of names, *Andrea* comes before *Brian*, and *Caroline* comes after *Brian* because the numeric code for *A* is lower than the code for *B*, and the numeric code for *C* is higher than the code for *B*, no matter whether you use ASCII, EBCDIC, or Unicode.

Table C-1 shows the decimal and binary values behind the most commonly used characters in the ASCII character set—the letters, numbers, and punctuation marks you can enter from your keyboard using a single key press. (Other values not shown in Table C-1 also have specific purposes. For example, when you display the character that holds the decimal value 7, nothing appears on the screen, but a bell sounds. Programmers often use this character when they want to alert a user to an error or some other unusual condition.)

Each binary number in Table C-1 is shown containing two sets of four digits; this convention makes the eight-digit numbers easier to read. Four digits, or a half-byte, is a **nibble**.

Decimal Number	Binary Number		ASCII Character
32	0010 0000		Space
33	0010 0001	!	Exclamation point
34	0010 0010	"	Quotation mark, or double quote
35	0010 0011	#	Number sign, also called an octothorpe or a pound sign
36	0010 0100	$	Dollar sign
37	0010 0101	%	Percent
38	0010 0110	&	Ampersand
39	0010 0111	'	Apostrophe, single quote

Table C-1 Decimal and binary values for common ASCII characters (*continues*)

(continued)

Decimal Number	Binary Number	ASCII Character	
40	0010 1000	(	Left parenthesis
41	0010 1001	)	Right parenthesis
42	0010 1010	*	Asterisk
43	0010 1011	+	Plus sign
44	0010 1100	,	Comma
45	0010 1101	-	Hyphen or minus sign
46	0010 1110	.	Period or decimal point
47	0010 1111	/	Slash or front slash
48	0011 0000	0	
49	0011 0001	1	
50	0011 0010	2	
51	0011 0011	3	
52	0011 0100	4	
53	0011 0101	5	
54	0011 0110	6	
55	0011 0111	7	
56	0011 1000	8	
57	0011 1001	9	
58	0011 1010	:	Colon
59	0011 1011	;	Semicolon
60	0011 1100	<	Less-than sign
61	0011 1101	=	Equal sign
62	0011 1110	>	Greater-than sign
63	0011 1111	?	Question mark
64	0100 0000	@	At sign
65	0100 0001	A	
66	0100 0010	B	

Table C-1 Decimal and binary values for common ASCII characters (*continues*)

(continued)

Decimal Number	Binary Number	ASCII Character	
67	0100 0011	C	
68	0100 0100	D	
69	0100 0101	E	
70	0100 0110	F	
71	0100 0111	G	
72	0100 1000	H	
73	0100 1001	I	
74	0100 1010	J	
75	0100 1011	K	
76	0100 1100	L	
77	0100 1101	M	
78	0100 1110	N	
79	0100 1111	O	
80	0101 0000	P	
81	0101 0001	Q	
82	0101 0010	R	
83	0101 0011	S	
84	0101 0100	T	
85	0101 0101	U	
86	0101 0110	V	
87	0101 0111	W	
88	0101 1000	X	
89	0101 1001	Y	
90	0101 1010	Z	
91	0101 1011	[	Opening or left bracket
92	0101 1100	\	Backslash
93	0101 1101	]	Closing or right bracket

Table C-1   Decimal and binary values for common ASCII characters *(continues)*

(*continued*)

Decimal Number	Binary Number	ASCII Character	
94	0101 1110	^	Caret
95	0101 1111	_	Underline or underscore
96	0110 0000	`	Grave accent
97	0110 0001	a	
98	0110 0010	b	
99	0110 0011	c	
100	0110 0100	d	
101	0110 0101	e	
102	0110 0110	f	
103	0110 0111	g	
104	0110 1000	h	
105	0110 1001	i	
106	0110 1010	j	
107	0110 1011	k	
108	0110 1100	l	
109	0110 1101	m	
110	0110 1110	n	
111	0110 1111	o	
112	0111 0000	p	
113	0111 0001	q	
114	0111 0010	r	
115	0111 0011	s	
116	0111 0100	t	
117	0111 0101	u	
118	0111 0110	v	
119	0111 0111	w	
120	0111 1000	x	

Table C-1   Decimal and binary values for common ASCII characters (*continues*)

(continued)

Decimal Number	Binary Number	ASCII Character	
121	0111 1001	y	
122	0111 1010	z	
123	0111 1011	{	Opening or left brace
124	0111 1100	|	Vertical line or pipe
125	0111 1101	}	Closing or right brace
126	0111 1110	~	Tilde

Table C-1   Decimal and binary values for common ASCII characters

The Hexadecimal System

The **hexadecimal numbering system** is the **base 16** system; it uses 16 digits. As shown in Table C-2, the digits are 0 through 9 and A through F. Computer professionals often use the hexadecimal system to express addresses and instructions as they are stored in computer memory because hexadecimal provides convenient shorthand expressions for groups of binary values. In Table C-2, each hexadecimal value represents one of the 16 possible combinations of four-digit binary values. Therefore, instead of referencing memory contents as a 16-digit binary value, for example, programmers can use a 4-digit hexadecimal value.

Decimal Value	Hexadecimal Value	Binary Value (shown using four digits)
0	0	0000
1	1	0001
2	2	0010
3	3	0011
4	4	0100
5	5	0101
6	6	0110
7	7	0111
8	8	1000
9	9	1001
10	A	1010

Table C-2   Values in the decimal and hexadecimal systems (*continues*)

(continued)

Decimal Value	Hexadecimal Value	Binary Value (shown using four digits)
11	B	1011
12	C	1100
13	D	1101
14	E	1110
15	F	1111

Table C-2 Values in the decimal and hexadecimal systems

In the hexadecimal system, each column is 16 times the value of the column to its right. Therefore, column values from right to left are 1, 16, 256, 4096, and so on. Figure C-3 shows how 78, 171, and 305 are expressed in hexadecimal.

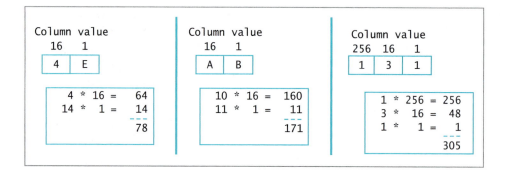

Figure C-3 Representing decimal values 78, 171, and 305 in the hexadecimal system

Measuring Storage

In computer systems, both internal memory and external storage are measured in bits and bytes. Eight bits make a byte, and a byte frequently holds a single character (in ASCII or EBCDIC) or half a character (in Unicode). Because a byte is such a small unit of storage, the size of memory and files is often expressed in thousands or millions of bytes. Table C-3 describes some commonly used terms for storage measurement.

Term	Abbreviation	Number of Bytes Using Binary System	Number of Bytes Using Decimal System	Example
Kilobyte	KB or kB	1024	one thousand	This appendix occupies about 85 kB on a hard disk.
Megabyte	MB	1,048,576 (1024 × 1024 kilobytes)	one million	One megabyte can hold an average book in text format. A 3½ inch diskette you might have used a few years ago held 1.44 megabytes.
Gigabyte	GB	1,073,741,824 (1,024 megabytes)	one billion	The hard drive on a fairly new laptop computer is at least 250 gigabytes. A DVD-R can hold about 5 gigabytes.
Terabyte	TB	1024 gigabytes	one trillion	Some hard drives are 1 terabyte. The entire Library of Congress occupied about 300 terabytes when this book was published.
Petabyte	PB	1024 terabytes	one quadrillion	The Google Web site processes about 24 petabytes per day.
Exabyte	EB	1024 petabytes	one quintillion	A popular expression claims that all words ever spoken by humans could be stored in text form in 5 exabytes.
Zettabyte	ZB	1024 exabytes	one sextillion	A popular expression claims that all words ever spoken by humans could be stored in audio form in 42 zettabytes.
Yottabyte	YB	1024 zettabytes	one septillion (a 1 followed by 24 zeros)	The combined space on all hard drives in the world is less than 1 yottabyte.

Table C-3 Commonly used terms for computer storage

In the metric system, *kilo* means 1000. However, in Table C-3, notice that a kilobyte is 1024 bytes. The discrepancy occurs because everything stored in a computer is based on the binary system, so multiples of two are used in most measurements. If you multiply 2 by itself 10 times, the result is 1024, which is a little over 1000. Similarly, a gigabyte is 1,073,741,824 bytes, which is more than a billion.

Confusion arises because many hard-drive manufacturers use the decimal system instead of the binary system to describe storage. For example, if you buy a hard drive that holds 10 gigabytes, it holds exactly 10 billion bytes. However, in the binary system, 10 GB is 10,737,418,240 bytes, so when you check your hard drive's capacity, your computer will report that you don't quite have 10 GB, but only 9.31 GB.

Key Terms

The **decimal numbering system** is the numbering system based on 10 digits and in which column values are multiples of 10.

Base 10 describes numbers created using the decimal numbering system.

The **binary numbering system** is the numbering system based on two digits and in which column values are multiples of 2.

Base 2 describes numbers created using the binary numbering system.

A **bit** is a binary digit; it is a unit of storage equal to one-eighth of a byte.

A **byte** is a storage measurement equal to eight bits.

American Standard Code for Information Interchange (ASCII) is an eight-bit character coding scheme used on many personal computers.

Extended Binary Coded Decimal Interchange Code (EBCDIC) is an eight-bit character coding scheme used on many larger computers.

Unicode is a 16-bit character coding scheme.

A **nibble** is a storage measurement equal to four bits, or a half-byte.

The **hexadecimal numbering system** is the numbering system based on 16 digits and in which column values are multiples of 16.

Base 16 describes numbers created using the hexadecimal numbering system.

D

Structure

Understanding the Three Basic Structures

In the mid-1960s, mathematicians proved that any program, no matter how complicated, can be constructed using one or more of only three structures. A structure is a basic unit of programming logic; each structure is one of the following:

- Sequence
- Selection
- Loop

With these three structures alone, you can diagram any task, from doubling a number to performing brain surgery. You can diagram each structure with a specific configuration of flowchart symbols.

The first of these three basic structures is a sequence, as shown in Figure D-1. With a sequence structure, you perform an action or task, and then you perform the next action, in order. A sequence can contain any number of tasks, but there is no option to branch off and skip any of the tasks. (In other words, a flowchart that describes a sequence structure never contains a decision symbol, and pseudocode that describes a sequence structure never contains an if or a while.) Once you start a series of actions in a sequence, you must continue step by step until the sequence ends.

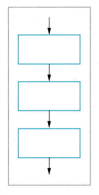

The second of the three structures is a selection structure or decision structure, as shown in Figure D-2. With this structure, you ask a question and, depending on the answer, you take one of two courses of action. Then, no matter which path you follow, you continue with the next task. (In other words, a flowchart that describes a selection structure must begin with a decision symbol, and the branches of the decision must join at the bottom of the structure. Pseudocode that describes a selection structure must start with if and end with endif.)

Figure D-1   Sequence structure

Some people call the selection structure an `if-then-else` structure because it fits the following statement:

```
if someCondition is true then
    do oneProcess
else
    do theOtherProcess
endif
```

The third of the three basic structures, shown in Figure D-3, is a `while` loop. In a `while` loop structure, you continue to repeat actions while a condition remains true. The action or actions that occur within the loop are known as the loop body. In a `while` loop, a condition is evaluated; if the answer is true, you execute the loop body and evaluate the condition again. If the condition is still true, you execute the loop body again and then reevaluate the original condition. This continues until the condition becomes false, and then you exit the structure. (In other words, a flowchart that describes a loop structure always begins with a decision symbol that branches off and then returns to a spot prior to the decision. Pseudocode that describes a `while` loop starts with `while` and ends with `endwhile`.)

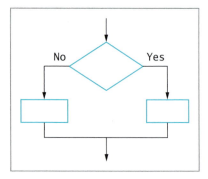

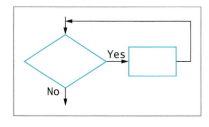

Figure D-2   Selection structure

Figure D-3   Loop structure

Sometimes you must ask a negative question to execute a loop body. The most common example is to repeat a loop while a sentinel condition has *not* been met.

Some programmers call this structure a **while...do structure** because it fits the following statement:

```
while testCondition continues to be true
    do someProcess
endwhile
```

All logic problems can be solved using only these three structures—sequence, selection, and loop. The three structures can be combined in an infinite number of ways. For example, you can have a sequence of tasks followed by a selection, or a loop followed by a sequence. Attaching structures end to end is called stacking structures. For example, Figure D-4 shows a structured flowchart achieved by stacking structures, and shows pseudocode that might follow the flowchart logic.

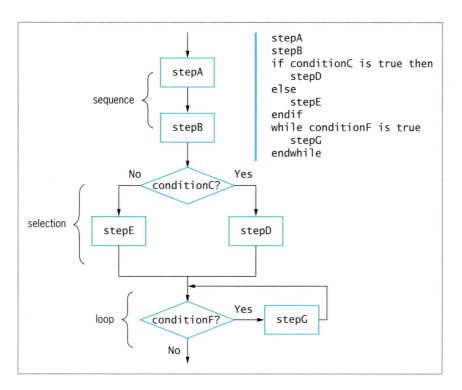

```
stepA
stepB
if conditionC is true then
    stepD
else
    stepE
endif
while conditionF is true
    stepG
endwhile
```

Figure D-4 Structured flowchart and pseudocode with three stacked structures

Whether you are drawing a flowchart or writing pseudocode, you can use either of the following pairs to represent decision outcomes: *Yes* and *No* or *true* and *false*. This book follows the convention of using *Yes* and *No* in flowchart diagrams and *true* and *false* in pseudocode.

Besides stacking structures, you can replace any individual tasks or steps in a structured flowchart diagram or pseudocode segment with additional structures. In other words, any sequence, selection, or loop can contain other sequences, selections, or loops. For example, you can have a sequence of three tasks on one side of a selection, as shown in Figure D-5. Placing a structure within another structure is called nesting structures.

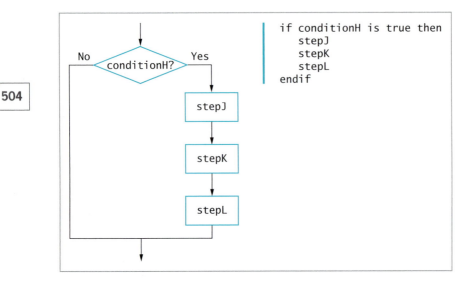

```
if conditionH is true then
    stepJ
    stepK
    stepL
endif
```

Figure D-5   Flowchart and pseudocode showing nested structures—a sequence nested within a selection

In the pseudocode for the logic shown in Figure D-5, the indentation shows that all three statements (stepJ, stepK, and stepL) must execute if conditionH is true. The three statements constitute a block, or a group of statements that executes as a single unit.

  When you nest structures, the statements that start and end a structure are always on the same level and always in pairs. Structures cannot overlap. For example, if you have an if that contains a while, then the endwhile statement will come before the endif. On the other hand, if you have a while that contains an if, then the endif statement will come before the endwhile.

The three structures are shown together in Figure D-6. Notice that each structure has one entry point and one exit point. One structure can attach to another only at one of these points.

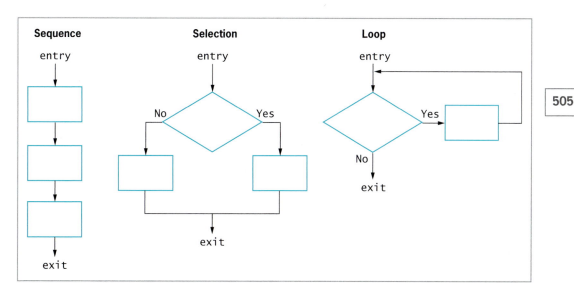

Figure D-6   The three structures

 Try to imagine physically picking up any of the three structures using the entry and exit "handles." These are the spots at which you could connect a structure to any of the others. Similarly, any complete structure, from its entry point to its exit point, can be inserted within the process symbol of any other structure.

In summary, a structured program has the following characteristics:

- A structured program includes only combinations of the three basic structures—sequence, selection, and loop. Any structured program might contain one, two, or all three types of structures.

- Each of the structures has a single entry point and a single exit point.

- Structures can be stacked or connected to one another only at their entry or exit points.

- Any structure can be nested within another structure.

 A structured program is never *required* to contain examples of all three structures. For example, many simple programs contain only a sequence of several tasks that execute from start to finish without selections or loops. As another example, a program might display a series of numbers, looping to do so, but never making decisions about the numbers.

Two Variations on the Basic Structures—case and do-while

You can solve any logic problem you might encounter using only the three structures. However, many programming languages allow two more structures: the case structure and the do-while loop. These structures are never *needed* to solve a problem—you can always use a series of selections instead of the case structure, and you can always use a sequence plus a while loop in place of the do-while loop. However, these additional structures can be convenient at times. Programmers consider them to be acceptable, legal structures.

The case Structure

You can use the **case structure** when there are several possible values for a single variable you are testing and each value requires a different course of action. Suppose that you work at a school at which tuition varies per credit hour depending on whether a student is a freshman, sophomore, junior, or senior. The structured flowchart and pseudocode in Figure D-7 show a series of decisions that assigns different tuition values depending on the value of year.

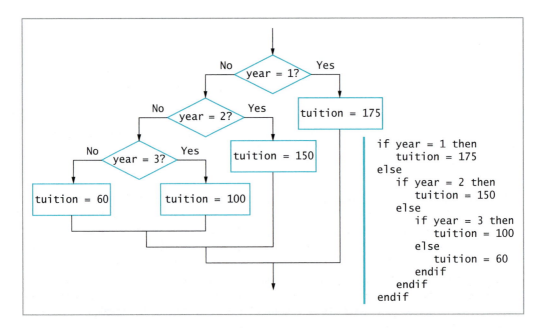

```
if year = 1 then
    tuition = 175
else
    if year = 2 then
        tuition = 150
    else
        if year = 3 then
            tuition = 100
        else
            tuition = 60
        endif
    endif
endif
```

Figure D-7   Flowchart and pseudocode of tuition decisions

The logic shown in Figure D-7 is absolutely correct and completely structured. The year = 3? selection structure is contained within the year = 2? structure, which is contained within the year = 1? structure. (In this example, if year is not 1, 2, or 3, the student receives the senior tuition rate.)

Even though the program segments in Figure D-7 are correct and structured, many programming languages permit using a case structure, as shown in Figure D-8. When using the case structure, you test a variable against a series of values, taking appropriate action based on the variable's value. Many people feel such programs are easier to read, and the case structure is allowed because the same results *could* be achieved with a series of structured selections (thus making the program structured). If the first program is structured and the second one reflects the first one point by point, then the second program must be structured as well.

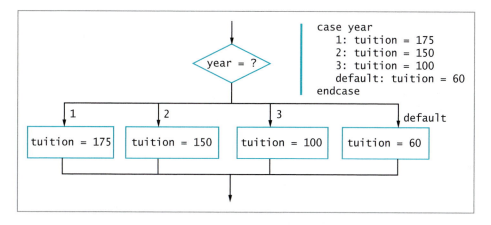

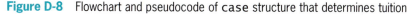

Figure D-8   Flowchart and pseudocode of case structure that determines tuition

The term *default* used in Figure D-8 means "if none of the other cases is true." Various programming languages use different syntaxes for the default case.

Even though a programming language permits you to use the case structure, you should understand that it is just a convenience that might make a flowchart, pseudocode, or actual program code easier to understand at first glance. When you write a series of decisions using the case structure, the computer still makes a series of individual decisions, just as though you had used many if-then-else combinations. In other words, you might prefer looking at the diagram in Figure D-8 to understand the tuition fees charged by a school, but a computer actually makes the decisions as shown in Figure D-7—one at a time. When you write your own programs, it is always acceptable to express a complicated decision-making process as a series of individual selections.

You use the case structure only when a series of decisions is based on different values stored in a single variable. If multiple variables are tested, then you must use a series of decisions.

The do-while Loop

A structured while loop looks like Figure D-9. The **do-while structure** is a special-case loop that looks like Figure D-10.

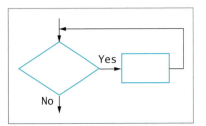

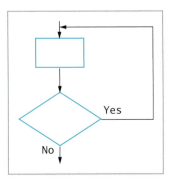

Figure D-9 The while loop, which is a pretest loop

Figure D-10 Structure of a do-while loop, which is a posttest loop

An important difference exists between these two structures. In a while loop, you ask a question and, depending on the answer, you might or might not enter the loop to execute the loop's procedure. Conversely, in do-while loops, you ensure that the procedure executes at least once; then, depending on the answer to the controlling question, the loop may or may not execute additional times.

Notice that the word *do* begins the name of the **do-while** loop. This should remind you that the action you *do* precedes testing the condition.

In a while loop, the question that controls a loop comes at the beginning, or "top," of the loop body. A while loop is a **pretest loop** because a condition is tested before entering the loop even once. In a do-while loop, the question that controls the loop comes at the end, or "bottom," of the loop body. A do-while loop is a **posttest loop** because a condition is tested after the loop body has executed.

You never are required to use a posttest loop. You can duplicate the same series of actions by creating a sequence followed by a standard, pretest while loop. Consider the flowcharts and pseudocode in Figure D-11.

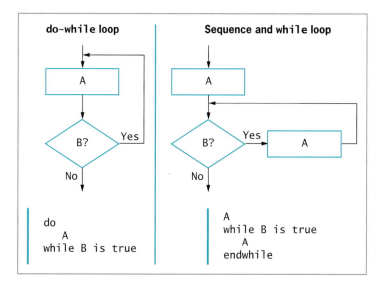

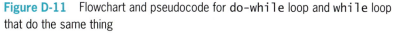

Figure D-11   Flowchart and pseudocode for do-while loop and while loop
that do the same thing

On the left side of Figure D-11, A executes, and then B is asked. If B is yes, then A executes and
B is asked again. On the right side of the figure, A executes, and then B is asked. If B is yes, then
A executes and B is asked again. In other words, both sets of flowchart and pseudocode
segments do exactly the same thing.

Because programmers understand that any posttest loop (do-while) can be expressed with a
sequence followed by a while loop, most languages allow at least one version of a posttest
loop for convenience.

Recognizing the Characteristics Shared by All Structured Loops

As you examine Figures D-9 and D-10, notice that with the while loop, the loop-controlling
question is placed at the beginning of the steps that repeat. With the do-while loop, the loop-
controlling question is placed at the end of the sequence of repeating steps.

All structured loops, both pretest and posttest, share these two characteristics:

- The loop-controlling question must provide either entry to or exit from the repeating
  structure.

- The loop-controlling question provides the *only* entry to or exit from the repeating
  structure.

In other words, there is exactly one loop-controlling value, and it provides either the only entrance to or the only exit from the loop.

 Some languages support a **do-until loop**, which is a posttest loop that iterates until the loop-controlling question is false. The do-until loop follows structured loop rules.

Key Terms

A **while...do structure** is a while loop.

The **case structure** tests a single variable for multiple values when the values each require a different course of action.

A **do-while structure** is a posttest loop that iterates while the loop-controlling question is true.

A **pretest loop** is one in which the loop-controlling condition is tested before entering the loop even once.

A **posttest loop** is one in which the question that controls the loop comes at the end, or bottom, of the loop body.

A **do-until loop** is a posttest loop that iterates until the loop-controlling question is false.

Glossary

A

abstract class A class from which no concrete objects can be created, but which is used as a basis for inheritance.

abstract data type (ADT) A programmer-defined type, such as a class.

abstraction The process of paying attention to important properties while ignoring nonessential details.

access specifier The adjective that defines the type of access outside classes will have to the attribute or method.

accessibility Describes screen design issues that make programs easier to use for people with physical limitations.

accessor methods Instance methods that get values from class fields.

accumulator A variable that gathers or accumulates values.

activity diagram A UML diagram that shows the flow of actions of a system, including branches that occur when decisions affect the outcome.

addresses Numbered storage locations.

aggregation A whole-part relationship in which the part or parts can exist without the whole.

algorithm The sequence of steps necessary to solve a problem or accomplish a task.

alphanumeric values Values that can contain alphabetic characters, numbers, and punctuation.

ambiguous Describes methods that are overloaded in such a way that the compiler cannot determine which version to use.

ancestors The entire list of parent classes from which the subclass is derived.

AND decision A compound expression in which two Boolean expressions must both be true for an action to take place.

AND operator A symbol used to combine decisions so that two or more Boolean expressions must be true for an action to occur.

animation The rapid sequence of still images, each slightly different from the previous one, that produces the illusion of movement.

annotation symbol A flowchart symbol used to hold comments; it is represented by a three-sided box connected with a dashed line to the step it explains.

application A program that users execute to accomplish a task.

application software Programs that users apply to a task, such as payroll, billing, word processing, and game playing.

arguments to a method The data items sent to methods.

array A data structure that consists of a series or list of values in computer memory, all of which have the same name but are differentiated with special numbers called subscripts.

ascending order Describes the arrangement of items in order from lowest to highest.

assignment operator The equal sign; it is used to assign a value to the variable or constant on its left.

assignment statement A statement that assigns a value from the right of an assignment operator to the variable or constant on the left of the assignment operator.

association relationship Describes the connection or link between objects in a UML diagram.

attributes The characteristics or features of entities; the characteristics that define an object as part of a class.

B

base class A class that is used as a basis for inheritance.

batch programs Programs that execute on large quantities of data without human intervention for each record; they accept data from a storage device such as a disk.

behavior diagrams UML diagrams that emphasize what happens in a system.

behaviors of an object The things an object "does."

binary language Machine language.

binary operator An operator that requires two operands—one on each side.

binary search A search algorithm that starts in the middle of a sorted list, and then determines whether it should continue higher or lower to find a target value.

black box tests Software tests in which the tester does not know how the software works internally but only verifies that correct output is derived from various input values.

Boolean expression An expression whose value can be only true or false.

bubble sort A sorting algorithm in which records are arranged in ascending or descending order by comparing items in a list in pairs; when an item is out of order, it swaps values with the item below it.

C

call stack The memory location where the computer stores the list of method locations to which the system must return.

calling a method The act of invoking a method, causing it to execute.

camel casing The format for naming identifiers in which the initial letter is lowercase, multiple-word variable names are run together, and each new word within the variable name begins with an uppercase letter.

cardinality Describes the arithmetic relationship between objects.

cascading if statement A series of nested if statements.

case structure A structure that tests a single variable for multiple values when the values each require a different course of action.

catch block A segment of code written to handle an exception that might be thrown by the `try` block that precedes it.

central processing unit (CPU) The hardware component that processes data.

child class A derived class.

class In object-oriented programming, the definition of the attributes and methods of a category of objects.

class client or **class user** A program or class that instantiates objects of another prewritten class.

class definition A set of program statements that describes the characteristics of the class's objects and the methods that can be applied to its objects.

class diagram A rectangle divided into three sections that show the name, data, and methods of a class.

class header A statement that starts a class; it contains the word `class` and an identifier. In some languages, it contains additional information.

class method A static method; class methods are not instance methods and they do not receive a `this` reference.

coding the program The act of writing program instructions.

command line A location on the computer screen at which a user types text entries to communicate with the computer's operating system.

communication diagram A UML diagram that emphasizes the organization of objects that participate in a system.

compiler Software that translates a high-level language into machine language and issues a message if a programming language statement has been used incorrectly. A compiler translates an entire program at once.

component diagram A UML diagram that emphasizes the files, database tables, documents, and other components used by a system's software.

composition The technique of using a class object within another class object as instance data.

compound condition A condition that contains multiple Boolean expressions.

computer memory A computer's temporary, internal storage.

computer simulations Programs that attempt to mimic real-world activities so that their processes can be improved or so that users can better understand how the real-world processes operate.

computer system A combination of the components required to process and store data using a computer.

conditional AND operator A symbol used to combine decisions so that two or more Boolean expressions must be true for an action to occur.

conditional OR operator A symbol that combines Boolean expressions when any one condition can be true for an action to occur.

constructor An automatically called method that establishes an object.

container A class of objects whose main purpose is to hold other elements—for example, a window.

conventions Standards of format and style that are selected for consistency while acknowledging that other customs might be used by others and be equally as correct.

conversion The entire set of actions an organization must take to switch over to using a new program or set of programs.

counted loop or **counter-controlled loop** A loop whose repetitions are managed by a counter.

counter Any numeric variable used to count the number of times an event has occurred.

D

data dictionary A list of every variable name used in a program, along with its type, size, and description.

data hiding The concept that other classes should not alter an object's attributes—only the methods of an object's own class should have that privilege.

data items All the text, numbers, and other information that are processed by a computer.

data structure A collection of data items that are grouped and organized so they can be used more efficiently.

data type Describes what values can be held by an item, how the item is stored in computer memory, and what operations can be performed on the data item.

dead code Unreachable code.

deadlock A flaw in multithreaded programs in which two or more threads wait for each other to execute.

dead path A logical path that can never be travelled.

decision symbol A flowchart symbol that holds a question that allows program logic to follow divergent paths; it is represented by a diamond.

decrementing The act of decreasing a variable by a constant value, frequently 1.

default constructor A constructor that requires no arguments.

defensive programming A technique in which programmers try to prepare for all possible errors before they occur.

definite loop A loop for which the number of repetitions is a predetermined value.

deployment diagram A UML diagram that focuses on a system's hardware.

derived class A class that inherits from a base class.

descending order Describes the arrangement of items in order from highest to lowest, based on a value within a field.

desk-checking The process of walking through a program's logic on paper without using a computer.

destructor An automatically called method that contains the actions required when an instance of a class is destroyed.

do-until loop A posttest loop that iterates until the loop-controlling question is false.

do-while structure A posttest loop that iterates while the loop-controlling question is true.

DOS prompt The command line in the DOS operating system.

dual-alternative selection A selection structure that includes separate actions when an expression is true and when it is false.

E

echoing input The act of repeating input back to a user either in a subsequent prompt or in output.

element A single data item in an array.

elided Describes the omitted parts of UML diagrams that are edited for clarity.

else clause Part of a decision that holds the statements that execute only when the Boolean expression in the decision is false.

encapsulation The process of combining all of an object's attributes and methods into a single package.

event An occurrence that generates a message sent to an object.

event-driven or **event-based** Describes programs in which actions occur in response to user-initiated events such as clicking a mouse button.

exception An unexpected or error condition that occurs while a program is running.

exception handling An object-oriented technique for managing errors.

exception specification clause A declaration of a method's possible throw types.

execute To run a program; to carry out a program's instructions.

extend variation A UML use case variation that shows functions beyond those found in a base case.

extended class A class that inherits from a base class.

external documentation Documentation that is outside a coded program in separate documents.

F

facilitators Work methods.

fields Object attributes or data held in an object's instance variables.

finally block A block of statements that execute at the end of a try...catch sequence.

flag A variable that indicates whether some event has occurred.

floating-point Describes a number with decimal places.

flowchart A pictorial representation of the logical steps it takes to solve a problem.

flowlines The arrows in a flowchart that show the sequence of steps carried out.

for statement, or **for loop** A statement that can be used to code definite loops. The for statement contains a loop control variable that it automatically initializes, evaluates, and increments.

forcing The act of overriding a data item's value with a specific default value.

fork A feature of a UML activity diagram that defines a logical branch in which all paths are followed simultaneously.

fragile Describes classes that depend on field names from parent classes and are prone to errors.

function A program module.

functional cohesion The extent to which a method's statements contribute to the same task.

functional decomposition The act of reducing a large program into more manageable methods.

G

garbage The unknown values that reside in variables that have not been initialized.

generalization variation A variation used in a UML diagram when a use case is less specific than others and a more specific case should be substituted.

515

get method An instance method that returns a value from a class.

GIGO (garbage in, garbage out) An acronym that means if input is incorrect, output is worthless.

global Describes variables and constants that are known to an entire class.

graphical user interface (GUI) An environment that allows users to interact with a program in a graphical environment.

H

handler body node The UML diagram name for an exception-handling catch block.

hardware The set of physical devices in a computer system.

has-a relationship A whole-part relationship; the phrase describes the association between the whole and one of its parts and the type of relationship that exists when using composition.

help methods Work methods.

high-level Describes programming languages that are English-like.

I

icons Small pictures on the screen that the user can select with a mouse.

identifier The name of a programming object such as a class, method, or variable.

if clause Part of a decision that holds the statements that execute when a Boolean expression in the decision is true.

if-then A single-alternative selection structure.

if-then-else A program structure that is a selection structure.

implementation hiding A principle of object-oriented programming that describes the encapsulation of method details within a class.

implicit conversion A transformation from one type to another that takes place automatically.

in scope Describes the status of items that are visible in a method.

include variation A UML use case variation in which a case can be part of multiple use cases.

incrementing The act of adding a constant value to a variable, frequently 1.

indefinite loop A loop for which the number of executions is not determined when the program is written.

index The process of storing a list of key fields paired with the storage address for the corresponding data record.

indirect relationship Describes the relationship between parallel arrays in which an element in the first array does not directly access its corresponding value in the second array.

infinite loop A loop with no end.

information Data that has been processed and is ready for output.

information hiding The concept that other classes should not alter an object's attributes—only the methods of an object's own class should have that privilege.

inheritance The principle that knowledge of a general category can be applied to more specific objects; the process of acquiring the traits of one's predecessors.

initialize a variable To provide a first value for a variable.

inner loop The contained loop in a pair of nested loops.

inner selection The decision structure nested within one branch of an outer selection in a nested selection.

input The process of entering data into a system using hardware devices such as keyboards and mice.

input symbol A flowchart symbol that contains an input statement and is represented by a parallelogram.

input/output symbol, or I/O symbol A flowchart symbol used to diagram both input and output operations; it is represented by a parallelogram.

insertion sort A sorting algorithm in which each list element is examined one at a time; if an element is out of order relative to any of the items earlier in the list, each earlier item is moved down one position and then the tested element is inserted.

instance An existing object or tangible example of a class.

instance method A method that operates correctly yet differently for each class object; an instance method is nonstatic and receives a this reference.

instance variables The data components that belong to every instantiated object.

instantiate To create an object from a class.

instantiation An instance of a class.

integer A whole number.

integrated development environment (IDE) A software package that provides an editor, compiler, and other programming tools.

interaction diagrams UML diagrams that emphasize the flow of control and data among the system elements being modeled.

interactive programs Programs that execute with frequent intervention from a user with an input device such as a keyboard or mouse.

interactivity diagram A diagram that shows the relationship between screens in an interactive GUI program.

interface to a method A method's return type, name, and required parameters; the part of a method that a client sees and uses.

internal documentation Documentation within a coded program that helps explain the meaning and purpose of program elements.

interpreter Software that translates a high-level language into machine language and issues a message if a programming language has been used incorrectly. An interpreter translates a program one instruction at a time.

invoking a method Calling a method.

iteration Looping.

J

join A feature of a UML activity diagram that reunites the flow of control after a fork.

K

key field The field whose contents make a record unique among all records in a file.

keywords The limited word set that is reserved in a language.

L

left-to-right associativity Describes operators that evaluate the expression to the left first.

libraries Stored collections of classes that serve related purposes.

linear search A search through a list from one end to the other.

linked list A list of records that contains an extra field in every record that holds the physical address of the next logical record.

listener An object that is "interested in" an event to which it should respond.

local Describes data items that are usable only within the method in which they are declared.

logic A sequence of computer instructions in which none is omitted or extraneous.

logical error A programming error that occurs when an incorrect instruction is performed.

logical order The order in which a list of items is used, even though it is not necessarily stored in that physical order.

loop body The statements that execute as long as the loop's controlling Boolean expression remains true.

loop control variable A variable that determines whether a loop will continue.

loop structure A program structure that repeats instructions based on a decision.

lower camel casing The format for naming identifiers in which the initial letter is lowercase, multiple-word names are run together, and each new word within the identifier begins with an uppercase letter.

low-level Describes programming languages that more closely reflect computer circuitry than high-level languages; the lowest-level language is the set of statements made up of 1s and 0s that the computer understands.

lvalue The memory address identifier to the left of an assignment operator.

M

machine language A computer's on-off circuitry language.

magic number An unnamed constant whose purpose is not immediately apparent.

main method An application's primary method.

maintenance The act of making changes to programs that are already finished and in production.

matrix A term used by mathematicians to describe a two-dimensional array.

mean The arithmetic average.

median The value in the middle position of a list when the values are sorted.

method A named set of statements that performs some task or group of tasks within an application; a program module, particularly in object-oriented languages.

method body The set of all the statements in a method.

method client A program or other method that uses a method.

method declaration A statement composed of the method's return type and signature.

method header The first line of a method. It is the entry point to a method, and it provides an identifier, parameter list, and frequently other information.

method return statement A statement that marks the end of the method and identifies the point at which control returns to the calling method.

method type A method's return type.

modeling The process of designing applications before writing code for them.

modularization The process of converting a large program into a set of shorter methods.

modules Small units that are combined to make programs. Programmers also refer to modules as **subroutines, procedures, functions**, or **methods**.

multidimensional arrays Arrays with more than one dimension.

multiple inheritance The ability to inherit from more than one class.

multithreading Using multiple threads of execution.

mutator methods Instance methods that can modify an object's attributes.

N

named constant A named data item that is similar to a variable, except that its value cannot change after the first assignment.

nested decision, or **nested if** A decision "inside of" another decision.

nested loops Describes loop structures when one resides within another.

nonstatic methods Methods that exist to be used with an object created from a class; they are instance methods and they receive a this reference.

NOT operator A symbol that reverses the meaning of a Boolean expression.

numeric constant or **literal numeric constant** A specific numeric value.

numeric variable A variable that can hold digits, have mathematical operations performed on it, and usually can hold a decimal point and a plus or minus sign indicating a positive or negative value.

O

object In object-oriented programming, one tangible example of a class; an instance of a class.

object code Machine language statements that have been translated from source code.

object diagrams UML diagrams that are similar to class diagrams, but that model specific instances of classes.

object dictionary A list of the objects used in a program, including which screens they are used on and whether any code, or script, is associated with them.

object-oriented analysis (OOA) The technique of analyzing a system using an object-oriented approach.

object-oriented approach An approach to problem solving that means defining the objects needed to accomplish a task and developing the objects so that each maintains its own data and carries out tasks when another object requests them.

object-oriented design (OOD) The technique of designing a system using an object-oriented approach.

object-oriented programming (OOP) A style of programming that uses classes to encapsulate objects' data and methods.

one-dimensional array A list accessed using a single subscript.

operand A value that is manipulated by an operator.

operating system The software that runs a computer and manages its resources.

OR decision An expression that contains two or more decisions; if at least one condition is met, the resulting action takes place.

OR operator A symbol that combines Boolean expressions when any one condition can be true for an action to occur.

order of operations Describes the rules of precedence.

out of bounds Describes an array subscript that is not within the range of acceptable subscripts for the array.

out of scope Describes data items that are no longer visible to a method.

outer loop The containing loop in a pair of nested loops.

outer selection The first selection made in a nested decision; the outcome of this selection determines whether a subsequent decision will be made.

output The process of extracting information from a system through hardware such as a monitor or printer so that people can view, interpret, and use the results.

output symbol A flowchart symbol that contains an output statement and is represented by a parallelogram.

overhead Describes the extra resources a task requires.

overload a method To write multiple methods with a shared name but different parameter lists.

overloading The act of supplying diverse meanings for a single identifier.

override a method To create a child class method with the same identifier and parameter list as the parent's version; the parent's version then becomes hidden from the child class.

overrides The action that occurs when a method is used by default in place of another method with the same signature.

P

packages In some languages, libraries.

parallel arrays Multiple arrays for which each element in one array is associated with the element in the same relative position in the other array(s).

parameter list The list of parameters in a method header.

parameters The data items received by methods.

parent class A base class.

Pascal casing The format for naming identifiers in which the initial letter is uppercase, multiple-word names are run together, and each new word within the name begins with an uppercase letter.

passed by reference Describes parameters received by a method as memory addresses.

passed by value Describes parameters received by a method as a copy.

physical order The order in which a list of items is actually stored.

pixel A picture element, or one of the tiny dots of light that form a grid on a screen.

polymorphism The ability of a method to act appropriately depending on the context.

populating an array The act of assigning values to array elements.

portable Describes program features that can more easily be reused in multiple programs.

posttest loop A loop in which the question that controls the loop comes at the end, or bottom, of the loop body.

precedence The quality of an operation that determines the order in which it is evaluated.

pretest loop A loop in which the loop-controlling condition is tested before entering the loop even once.

priming input A first input statement that gets a loop control variable's first value before the loop begins.

primitive data types Simple numbers and characters that are not class types.

private access A privilege of class members in which data or methods cannot be used by any method that is not part of the same class.

procedural programming A technique that focuses on the procedures programmers create to manipulate data.

procedure A program module.

processing The act of manipulating data to turn it into information; processing data items may involve organizing them, checking them for accuracy, or performing mathematical operations on them.

processing symbol A flowchart symbol that contains a processing statement and is represented by a rectangle.

profile diagram A UML diagram used to extend a model for a particular domain or platform.

program A set of executable instructions written by programmers.

program code Written computer instructions.

program comments Nonexecuting statements added to a program for the purpose of documentation.

programmer-defined type A type that is not built into a language, but is created by the programmer.

programming The act of writing software instructions.

programming languages Languages such as Visual Basic, C#, C++, and Java that are used to write programs.

prompt A message that is displayed on a monitor to ask the user for a response and perhaps explain how that response should be formatted.

property A method that gets and sets a field value using simple syntax.

protected access Describes a modifier used when no outside classes should be able to use a data field except classes that are descendents of the original class.

protected node The UML diagram name for an exception-throwing try block.

pseudocode An English-like representation of the logical steps it takes to solve a problem.

public access A privilege of class members in which other programs and methods may use the specified data or methods within a class.

pure polymorphism The situation in which one method implementation can be used with a variety of arguments.

R

random access memory (RAM) Internal computer memory.

random-access storage device A device, such as a disk, from which records can be accessed in any order.

range check The act of comparing a variable to a series of values that mark the limiting ends of ranges.

range of values Any series of contiguous values that fall between specified limits.

real numbers Floating-point numbers.

register To sign up components that will react to events initiated by other components.

relational comparison operators The symbols that express Boolean comparisons. Examples include =, >, <, >=, <=, and <>. These operators are also called **relational operators** or **comparison operators**.

relationships Describes how entities communicate with and react to each other.

reliability The feature of programs and methods that ensures each has been tested and proven to function correctly.

reliable Describes program code that has been tested and is trusted to work correctly.

repetition Looping.

return type The data type for any value a method returns.

reusability The feature of modular programs that allows individual methods to be used in a variety of applications.

reverse engineering The process of creating an improved model of an existing system.

right-associativity and **right-to-left associativity** Terms describing operators that evaluate the expression to the right first.

rules of precedence Rules that dictate the order in which operations in the same statement are carried out.

run To execute a program; to carry out a program's instructions.

rvalue An operand to the right of an assignment operator.

S

scenario A UML variation in the sequence of actions required in a use case.

selection structure A program structure that contains a decision in which the logic can break in one of two paths.

self-documenting Describes programs that contain meaningful and descriptive data, method, and class names.

semantic errors Logical program errors.

sentinel value A value that is tested to determine whether a loop continues or ends.

sequence diagram A UML diagram that shows the timing of events in a single use case.

sequence structure A program structure that contains steps that execute in order with no option of branching to skip or repeat any of the tasks.

sequential order The arrangement of records when they are stored one after another on the basis of the value in a particular field.

sequential search A linear search.

set method An instance method that sets the values of a data field within a class.

short-circuit evaluation A logical feature in which each part of a larger expression is evaluated only as far as necessary to determine the final outcome.

signature A method's name and parameter list.

single-alternative selection A selection structure that includes an action only when an expression is true or when it is false—in other words, when action is required for only one outcome of the question.

single-dimensional array A list accessed using a single subscript.

sinking sort A bubble sort.

size of an array The number of elements an array can hold.

software A set of instructions written by programmers that tell a computer what to do; software is computer programs.

software testers Professionals who test programs for accuracy.

sorted Describes values that have been placed in order.

source code The statements written in a programming language.

source of an event The component from which an event is generated.

stack A location that holds the memory addresses to which method calls should return.

stacked structures Structures that are linked end to end so that one follows the other.

starvation A flaw in multithreaded programs in which a thread is abandoned because other threads occupy all the computer's resources.

state The set of all the values or contents of a class's instance variables.

state machine diagram A UML diagram that shows the different statuses of a class or object at different points in time.

static methods Methods for which no object needs to exist; static methods are not instance methods and they do not receive a this reference.

step value A number used to alter a loop control variable on each pass through a loop.

stereotype A feature that adds to the UML vocabulary of shapes to make them more meaningful for the reader.

storage devices Hardware, such as disks or flash media, on which data is stored.

storyboard A picture or sketch of screens the user will see when running a program.

string constant or **literal string constant** A specific group of characters enclosed within quotation marks.

string variable A variable that can hold text including letters, digits, and special characters such as punctuation marks.

structure A basic unit of programming logic.

structure diagrams UML diagrams that emphasize the "things" in a system.

subclass A derived class.

subroutine A program module.

subscript A number that indicates the position of a particular item within an array.

subtype polymorphism The ability of one method name to work appropriately for different subclass objects of the same parent class.

summary report A report that lists only totals, without individual detail records.

sunny day case A program execution in which no errors occur.

superclass A base class.

swap values To exchange the values of two variables.

syntax The rules of a programming language.

syntax error An error in language or grammar.

system design The detailed specification of how all the parts of a system will be implemented and coordinated.

system software Programs used to manage a computer, including operating systems such as Windows or UNIX and other utility programs not directly used by end users.

T

temporary variable or **work variable** A working variable that holds intermediate results during a program's execution.

terminal symbol A flowchart symbol that marks the beginning or end of a flowchart segment, method, or program; it is represented by a lozenge.

test a program To execute a program on a computer to determine if the output is correct.

text editor A program used to create simple text files; it is similar to a word processor, but without as many features.

this reference An automatically created variable that holds the address of an object and passes it to an instance method whenever the method is called.

thread The flow of execution of one set of program statements.

thread synchronization A set of techniques that coordinates threads of execution to help avoid potential multithreading problems.

three-dimensional arrays Arrays in which each element is accessed using three subscripts.

throw statement A statement that sends an exception out of a method so it can be handled elsewhere.

throwing an exception The process of tossing an exception object to a `catch` block, another method, or the operating system for handling.

time signal A UML diagram symbol that indicates a specific amount of time has passed before an action is started.

trivial expression An expression that always evaluates to the same result.

truth tables Diagrams used in mathematics and logic to help describe the truth of an entire expression based on the truth of its parts.

try block A block of code that attempts to execute while acknowledging that an exception might occur.

two-dimensional array An array with rows and columns of values that is accessed using two subscripts.

type casting The act of converting data from one type to another.

U

Unified Modeling Language (UML) A standard way to specify, construct, and document systems that use object-oriented methods.

unnamed constant A literal numeric or string value.

unreachable code Statements that can never execute under any circumstances.

unreachable path A logical path that can never be traveled.

upper camel casing The format for naming identifiers in which the initial letter is uppercase, multiple-word names are run together, and each new word within the identifier begins with an uppercase letter. Also called *Pascal casing*.

use case diagram A UML diagram that emphasizes how a business works from the perspective of those who actually interact with the business.

users or **end users** The people or entities for whom programs are written and who will benefit from using them.

user-defined type A type that is not built into a language but is created by the programmer.

V

validate data To test data items to ensure their values are meaningful and useful.

variables Named memory locations whose contents can vary or differ over time.

variable declaration A programming statement that provides a data type and identifier for a variable.

visible Describes items that are in scope for a method and superclass members that are not hidden by their derived classes.

visual development environment A programming environment in which programs are created by dragging components such as buttons and labels onto a screen and arranging them visually.

void method A method that returns no value.

W

while loop A structure that tests a Boolean expression; as long as the expression continues to be true, the loop body executes.

while...do structure A `while` loop.

white box tests Software tests in which the tester understands how the software works internally.

white space Describes any character that appears to be empty, such as a space or tab.

whole-part relationship An association in which one or more classes make up the parts of a larger whole class.

work methods Methods that perform tasks within a class as opposed to methods that only get and set data fields.

X

x-axis An imaginary line that indicates horizontal positions in a screen window.

x-coordinate A position value that increases from left to right across a window.

Y

y-axis An imaginary line that indicates vertical positions in a screen window.

y-coordinate A position value that increases from top to bottom across a window.

Index

539